THE BRASS BAND STORY

Trevor Herbert

YALE UNIVERSITY PRESS
NEW HAVEN AND LONDON

For information about this and other Yale University Press publications, please contact:
U.S. Office: sales.press@yale.edu   yalebooks.com
Europe Office: sales@yaleup.co.uk   yalebooks.co.uk

Set in Adobe Garamond Pro by IDSUK (DataConnection) Ltd
Printed and bound in the UK using 100% renewable electricity at CPI Group (UK) Ltd

Library of Congress Control Number: 2026936089

A catalogue record for this book is available from the British Library.
Authorized Representative in the EU: Easy Access System Europe, Mustamäe tee 50, 10621 Tallinn, Estonia, gpsr.requests@easproject.com

ISBN 978-0-300-28257-3

10 9 8 7 6 5 4 3 2 1

For Ieuan Morgan, John Wallace and all band boys and girls

Contents

CONTENTS

Illustrations

I am grateful to the people and agencies cited below for their permission to use illustrations. Unless otherwise acknowledged, items are from the author's collection.

Prologue

Most musicians have a story about how they were introduced to music. Mine is brief: it involved two closely related events, of which the second was the more important. I was born and raised in a village called Cwmparc in the Rhondda Valley in south Wales. The settlement did not exist until the late 1860s, when rich deposits of coal were discovered, and pits were sunk to mine it. My father worked in the colliery, as did every other child's father in the village, except those who were the children of shopkeepers, teachers, preachers, the doctor or the policeman. On Saturday afternoons my parents took me to the cinema. I was ten years old and rarely anticipated these trips with unequivocal pleasure. Cowboy films were great but infrequent; otherwise I found the movies my parents enjoyed tiresome and usually incomprehensible. I had low expectations when I was told that the upcoming film was *The Glenn Miller Story*, in which the eponymous trombonist was played by James Stewart. In fact, it was brilliant. I had heard and seen nothing like that before and was fascinated by the trombone: I could not understand how it worked, but its sound and even its look beguiled me. On the way home I remembered that the colliery band had started a boys' band using surplus instruments and that it was supposed to be good. This, I decided, was where I would learn to play the trombone.

On the evening of its next rehearsal, I went to the band room and told the conductor I wanted to join the band and play the trombone.

He said there was no spare trombone, but I could play the baritone (a new word to me) until a trombone became available. Then he did something entirely unexpected. He showed me how to hold the instrument, pointed to an empty seat in the middle of the band and told me to sit there and pretend to play. 'Don't blow it,' he said, 'just sit there and pretend to blow it, but *always watch me* – I am *the conductor*. Follow my beat but don't make a sound.' I do not know whether this was his usual induction strategy or just an expedient, one-off thing that allowed him to get on with the rehearsal, because the band boys were quickly assembling and warming up. It doesn't matter, because I did what he said, and what happened next shaped the rest of my life. When the band started to play, with me in the middle of it pretending to play, I was hit by successive walls of sound: some quiet, some loud, all coloured differently. It was only a boys' band, hardly expert, but it was more than good enough to do the trick. By the end of the rehearsal, I couldn't have been more firmly captured had I been manacled to the floor. All I wanted was to have more of it and to be a proper part of that sound. My destiny was irrevocably fixed. When I got home, my parents, probably noticing an uncharacteristic spring in my step, asked where I had been. I told them I had been playing in the band.

At the end of the rehearsal, the bandmaster, a young colliery worker who played the euphonium, had explained how to produce a note and how I should practise. He told me that when I played, my lips became my 'embouchure'. The sound was made by my lips vibrating so I had to get them used to this new task. 'Forget about *blowing*,' he said, 'it's about breathing though the embouchure into the instrument. Take deep breaths and play long notes very, very quietly to train your lips to vibrate.' I did this conscientiously until the next rehearsal, and when I got there, I found that a trombone had become available: my bliss was complete. Peculiarly, I have no recollection of what happened next. I have no recall of learning how to read music or of learning to properly play, but it must have been a relatively short process because within a year I was playing with the band in contests, which we usually won.[1] Yet more bliss and episodes of barely containable excitement; I could not imagine being in a better band. I eventually became a professional player and performed with great orchestras and ensembles on many continents, but my memory of the night when the sound of the brass band first hit me is permanent. That's the thing about brass bands: there is nothing quite like them. Their sound is unique and if you play in one you are part of it and the collective output travels to your feelings by the shortest possible route.

Because it was a brass band that gave issue to me as a musician, I claim some credentials for writing a book about its history, but a lot of time has passed since that memorable night, so I retraced some steps. When preparing to write this book I went to contests and concerts of all sorts and mingled discreetly in the modern brass band world. It has changed a lot, particularly since the 1970s, but its core features prevail. The quality of playing is better than it has ever been, and young players seem oblivious to the technical difficulties that confront them in the modern repertoire. The sound of the brass band has changed, but not beyond recognition, because the brass instrument format remains that which was more or less settled by the 1880s. There are more composers writing challenging and exciting original music. There are fewer bands than there once were, but this should not be surprising: there are more competing opportunities for leisure. Contests and concerts still attract large, dedicated audiences.

The most important continuity is the bond players feel to each other both musically and socially, and the contentment and well-being this generates. I have felt a deep envy that I am no longer part of one of those remarkable little music-making collectives. But these are just brass band emotions; writing a book about its history requires a different and more strategic set of tasks.

The British model of the brass band originated in the 1840s, acquired a standard form by the end of the nineteenth century and has since endured as a distinctive part of British musical life. It was taken to Australia, New Zealand and other parts of the former British Empire by colonists, and in the second half of the twentieth century was enthusiastically adopted in many countries in continental Europe, the US and Asia. Brass bands of the Salvation Army require separate attention. For most of its existence, the Salvation Army had a parallel, rather than integrated, relationship with other brass bands, but by the twenty-first century the two were entwined.

While the book is restricted to a history of the brass band and an explanation of the musical, social and cultural factors that have affected it, the story is relevant to wider aspects of British music history. For example, what has been termed the 'English musical renaissance' came at a time when the infrastructure of musical life in Britain had already been transformed and greatly expanded. That growth had several causes, but two important nationwide developments that are seldom given close attention in 'big' histories of British music are dealt with here in some detail: the repurposing and expansion of military music from the late eighteenth century onwards, and the emergence of amateur music-making on a massive scale from the middle of the nineteenth century. Brass bands were beneficiaries of the new military music infrastructure, and the most ubiquitous exemplar of amateur instrumental ensemble music. I hope that the relevance of the brass band story to British music history more generally will be evident throughout the book.

Author's notes

The book was always intended to be accessible to a wide audience. By this I mean that it is not aimed just at brass band people or at any other specific readership – especially an academic audience. Many readers may have only the most general idea of what a brass band is, so I have taken steps aimed at the accommodation of a wide and international readership. The Introduction provides an overview of the narrative content of the entire story and introduces the themes which receive closer attention in subsequent chapters. A brief glossary of musical words and terms is provided at the end of the book, but I have done my best to restrict such technicalities to a minimum.

Discussion of repertoire presents a special challenge. I have commented on repertoire extensively in the text, but only in general terms, and have not included musical notation in any part of the book. Detailed discussion of works of music is meaningless if those works are unknown to readers, and musical notation is similarly meaningless to the majority who can't understand it. This does not suggest that I regard repertoire as subordinate in this story – quite the contrary. To ensure that the sound of music is not absent, I have provided in Appendix 2 an annotated list – a 'Guide to listening' – that directs readers to recorded performances of most of the works mentioned in the text and others that are illustrative of repertoire and performance styles and how they have changed over time. Most are freely available on the internet and are likely to remain so. They are drawn from the entire history of the age of brass band recording and include some of the earliest recordings ever made.

Appendix 1 is aimed at readers who have an interest in early performance history and the place of music-making in Victorian social history. It provides extracts from primary sources about the first two or three decades of the brass band: the instrument formations that were used, and the people – the Victorian working-class men – who made up the first generation of brass band players. It provides their names, locations, the instruments they played and the work they otherwise did in their everyday lives.

I have avoided the academic practice of in-text referencing but have fully acknowledged my many debts to others in notes which are placed at the end of the book. A key to the bibliographical abbreviations I have used for sources is to be found at the start of the Notes section.

Instrument names

In musical terms, 'brass instrument' is not a descriptor of the material from which an instrument is made; it signifies the family of instruments on which musical sounds are generated by the vibration of a player's lips. An alternative, but less-used, descriptor is 'lip-vibrated instrument'. As new brass instrument designs were introduced in the nineteenth century, they acquired different names in different countries. It follows that nomenclatures have been used inconsistently in the period the book covers. Many brass instruments have different names in different languages and there are also variances within individual languages, including English. For example, the euphonium is also referred to as the tenor tuba, and the several individual instruments that made up the original saxhorn family acquired different names by the end of the nineteenth century – tenor horn, baritone and so on. My approach has been pragmatic: I have used the terminologies that are in common use in the English language at the time the book was written, unless quoting a source where a different word is used, in which case I use the original or add an explanatory note in parenthesis.

Geography

Most readers living outside the UK will be less familiar with the geography of the United Kingdom than those who live within it. This is why a map is provided at the start of the book. The Republic of Ireland was part of the UK before 1922 and the organisation of counties underwent changes in the second half of the twentieth century. My map shows county boundaries as they were in 1960 because this is probably the most helpful as far as the content of the book is concerned.

Currencies

In 1971 the UK moved from a monetary system based on pounds, shillings and pence (l, s, d) to a decimalised system in which 100 pennies/pence equated to one pound (£1). The UK did not adopt the Euro currency in the period when it was a member of the Common Market/European Union.

The following is a summary explanation of the UK's pre-decimalisation currency system:

One pound (written as 'l' or £) was equal to 20 shillings
One shilling (written as 's') was equal to 12 pennies or pence
One penny (written as 'd') was equal to two half-pennies or four farthings
A crown was five shillings
A half crown was two shillings and six pence
A guinea was one pound and one shilling (or twenty-one shillings)

Other common vernacular terms used for cash were 'quid' (a pound), 'bob' (a shilling) and 'tanner' (a six-pence piece)

Acknowledgements

I am grateful to those who have allowed me to use illustrative material, and to the libraries, archives and correspondents around the world who have been helpful to me when writing this book. There are other individuals, too many to mention, who caused me to think again or travel in a new direction. I mean those with whom I have had impromptu conversations in bars and tea rooms adjacent to contest and concert venues and whose words have settled my mind or changed it about some fact or opinion. I hope that many who read this book will recognise in it something of their own.

Some have given their time to me particularly generously: they include Stephen Allen, Bill Barlow, Andrew Blyth, Brass Band Trcizc Étoiles, Stephen Cobb, Trevor Cuffull, Géry Dumoulin, Ray Farr, Gavin Holman, John Humphries, Phillip McCann, John Miller, Tim Mutum, Ann-Marie Nilsson, Paul Rabbitts and Howard Snell.

Yale University Press has been helpful and supportive throughout the period of the book's preparation, especially the editorial team – Rachael Lonsdale, Natalie Parker-Burlton and Robert Sargant, Ian Craine who compiled the index, and my commissioning editor Joanna Godfrey. I am also grateful to the reviewers (anonymous to me) who commented helpfully on both the book proposal and the final manuscript.

There is a smaller, closer group who have been especially helpful. I owe a particular debt of gratitude to Iwan Fox of 4barsrest who helped me in many ways. Helen Barlow, who read the entire text and made it better. Also, Arnold Myers and John Wallace who have been my partners in so many writing and performance projects over the years. They have taught me a lot and, like me, have a special place in their hearts for brass bands.

John Wallace, one of the greatest and most influential brass players of his generation, is one of the two named dedicatees of the book. He died as it was being written, as did Ieuan Morgan. It was Ieuan who first put a brass instrument into my hands and explained it to me.

Notwithstanding all this, I emphasise that responsibility for the content of the book, including any shortcomings, rests solely with me.

Trevor Herbert

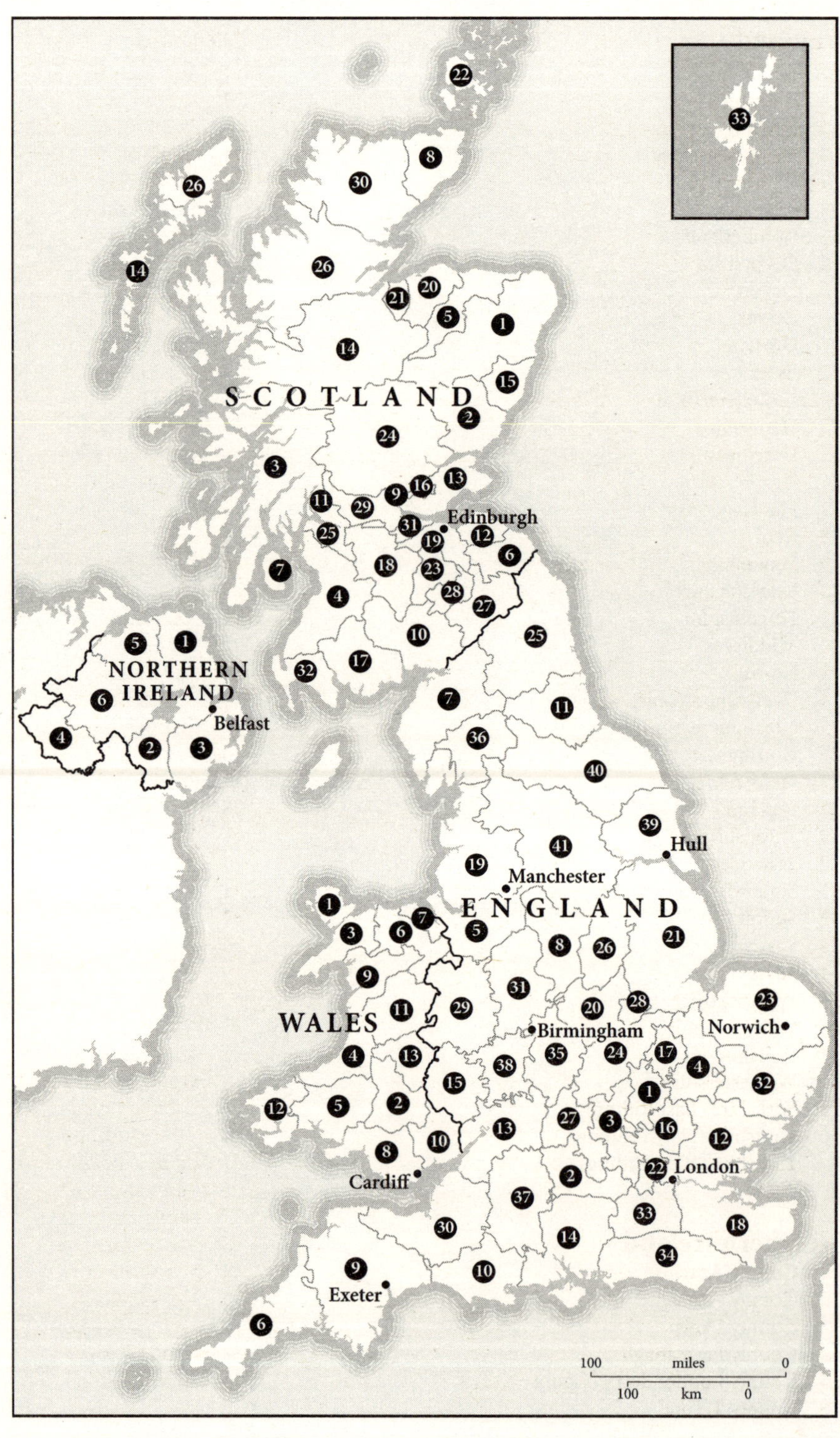

SCOTLAND
NORTHERN IRELAND
Belfast
WALES
ENGLAND
Edinburgh
Manchester
Birmingham
Norwich
London
Cardiff
Exeter
Hull
100 miles 0
100 km 0

England

1 Bedfordshire
2 Berkshire
3 Buckinghamshire
4 Cambridgeshire
5 Cheshire
6 Cornwall
7 Cumberland
8 Derbyshire
9 Devon
10 Dorset
11 Durham
12 Essex
13 Gloucestershire
14 Hampshire
15 Herefordshire
16 Hertfordshire
17 Huntingdonshire
18 Kent
19 Lancashire
20 Leicestershire
21 Lincolnshire
22 Middlesex
23 Norfolk
24 Northamptonshire
25 Northumberland
26 Nottinghamshire
27 Oxfordshire
28 Rutland
29 Shropshire
30 Somerset
31 Staffordshire
32 Suffolk
33 Surrey
34 Sussex
35 Warwickshire
36 Westmorland
37 Wiltshire
38 Worcestershire
39 Yorkshire (East Riding)
40 Yorkshire (North Riding)
41 Yorkshire (West Riding)

Northern Ireland

1 County Antrim
2 County Armagh
3 County Down
4 County Fermanagh
5 County Londonderry (County Derry)
6 County Tyrone

Scotland

1 Aberdeenshire
2 Angus
3 Argyll
4 Ayrshire
5 Banffshire
6 Berwickshire
7 Buteshire
8 Caithness
9 Clackmannanshire
10 Dumfriesshire
11 Dunbartonshire
12 East Lothian
13 Fifeshire
14 Inverness-shire
15 Kincardineshire
16 Kinross-shire
17 Kirkcudbrightshire
18 Lanarkshire
19 Midlothian
20 Moray
21 Nairnshire
22 Orkney
23 Peeblesshire
24 Perthshire
25 Renfrewshire
26 Ross and Cromarty
27 Roxburghshire
28 Selkirkshire
29 Stirlingshire
30 Sutherland
31 West Lothian
32 Wigtownshire
33 Shetland

Wales

1 Anglesey
2 Brecknockshire
3 Caernarfonshire
4 Cardiganshire
5 Carmarthenshire
6 Denbighshire
7 Flintshire
8 Glamorganshire
9 Merionethshire
10 Monmouthshire
11 Montgomeryshire
12 Pembrokeshire
13 Radnorshire

Introduction: Brass bands and history

The British version of the brass band is the only form of literate instrumental music-making that can claim to have originated and matured in Britain and been adopted throughout the world. It is also one of the few sophisticated virtuoso forms to have been developed mainly by amateurs. Its idiom is unique and stands as one of the most distinctive features of British musical life. The purpose of this book is to investigate key questions about how the brass band emerged, why it has endured and to identify the events and trends that created the continuities and changes in its extraordinary existence. I have been especially keen to navigate the many contextual factors that have impacted on brass bands. Context is important, not merely because it provides a background, but because it has often been causal. Factors such as social class, demography, wealth, poverty, economics, education and social attitudes have often acted on the history of brass bands with a greater force than purely musical matters. The ascendancy of British industry and its eventual decline have also impacted on bands at every stage because many of them were embedded in industrial communities. The story is complex and certainly a lot more so than the half-baked clichés through which brass bands are often explained. I have gone further than most other writers in dealing with the musical world that the founding fathers of the present brass band movement entered in the Victorian period. For example, I have sketched the development of concert life in Britain in the mid-nineteenth century, especially the rise and eventual fall of the itinerant virtuoso soloist – many of whom, in Britain and other countries, were cornet players. Those soloists, with their deliberate, self-conscious exhibitionism, were the unwitting expounders of the playing techniques of which brass bands were to take ownership and become strikingly expert. When brass bands entered British musical life, the provinces were already attuned to the relatively new idea of the popular public concert. As the Victorian era ended, the content and manner of those concerts provided a reason why a distinction emerged between highbrow and lowbrow musical tastes. Such distinctions came to shape the way different types of music were categorised. This came to influence the critical reception of brass bands and provide one of the reasons why their musical practices and values became distant from most other forms of music-making.

Chapters in the book are organised thematically; each theme or topic stands individually, but each forms part of the general story. Thematic approaches often lead to repetition across chapters, and such is the case here. I have limited it as much as is practicable but have not tried to eradicate it – a bit of repetition is a small price to pay for the coherence of each chapter. The chapters are not arranged in chronological order because they do not yield a natural chronology. I have organised them in the way I think best, but little is lost if a different order of reading were to be taken.

Myths and anachronisms

In the modern world the brass band sound is routinely appropriated to evoke a particular variety of nostalgia. Usually about time and place, but always about social class. This is because the sound is distinctive, and when deployed for such purposes music does its work swiftly and effectively. In 1973 it provided a homely soundscape for a celebrated UK television advertisement for wholemeal bread.[1] It was a classic of its type: a nostalgic evocation of a Victorian village in the north of England. The distinctively northern, working-class voice-over created part of the effect, which was given added credibility by the background music: a brass band arrangement of the slow movement of Dvořák's

'New World' Symphony. It worked with such effect because the sound and its summoning of place and time was unambiguous. The sound of the British model of the brass band is distinctive because it comes not from a miscellaneous collection of brass instruments, but from a precise formation that has been in place since the late nineteenth century. This standard instrumental format and the way the instruments are played defines the brass band's unique *idiom*. It is this idiom that distinguishes the British brass band model from the many others in the world that choose to call themselves brass bands.

Modern brass bands, in Britain at least, are routinely heard on radio channels devoted to classical music and are integrated into some of the world's great music festivals, such as the BBC's mammoth Proms festival which is held for several weeks over the summer months. But it was not always like this. A good argument can be mustered to suggest that this amateur instrumental genre has not received adequate credit for its contribution to British culture. This is probably true, but there is scope to wonder whether it really matters: whether the lack of genuine and informed empathy that the classical music establishment has often shown to brass bands has had any material effect. Approached from any intelligent angle, the British brass band emerges as one of the most interesting and important phenomena in the world of instrumental music. In the modern world, and despite recurrent views to the contrary, it prevails in good health, with an infinitely expanded range of techniques and possessed of greater musical potential than at any time in its history. Brass bands can no longer be described as 'working class', a label applied to them so liberally in the past that they became synonymous with working-class culture. Bands have been especially strong in northern counties of England such as Yorkshire, Durham and Lancashire. It was in these places that they first emerged, found their footing and produced generations of famous bands. But it has always been a genuinely national activity. For more than the entirety of its first century, brass bands were firmly associated with masculinity. The normalisation of women and girls as brass instrument players came at a rapid speed in the second half of the twentieth century. This was probably the most important development in the brass band story and almost certainly accounts for its survival at that time.

British music history

The place of the brass band in British music history is present throughout this book, at least by implication, but one contextual aspect should be mentioned because it has been overlooked, disregarded or given scant attention in most 'big' histories of British music. The most quoted description of the country's musical life at the start of the twentieth century came from the German critic Oscar Schmitz, who described England (by which he probably meant Britain) as 'Das Land ohne Musik' ('the land without music').[2] It was not an especially intelligent or knowledgeable utterance, but it allowed Schmitz to make a name for himself and it stirred robust challenges from those who had already identified the appearance of an 'English musical renaissance'. This term probably originated in a *Daily Telegraph* review of the Birmingham Music Festival in 1882 which included Charles Villiers Stanford's Serenade in G and Charles Hubert Parry's First Symphony. The reviewer concluded that Parry's symphony 'deserved to rank' with Stanford's work and provided 'capital proof that English music has arrived at a Renaissance period'.[3] This narrative measured 'music' in the currency of the works of classical composers. Missing was the undeniable reality that, by the time Stanford, Parry and the other mainly London-based luminaries (Elgar was still seen as a 'provincial') were gaining credibility, the British music industry, the audience for music and the general state of the music profession had already expanded to an extent unprecedented in its history. It had started with the development of a new species of band sponsored by the British military, and the subsequent rise of amateur music. Both these developments were at a genuinely national level and impacted on every branch of British musical commerce. It prompted the authors of the 1881 United Kingdom *Census Report* to remark on a growth of 37 per cent of 'those who gain their livelihood by music' – a statistic made all the more remarkable because 'the growth of the same group had been 24 per cent, in the preceding intercensal period'.[4]

The growth of the music industry was substantially the product of a need to supply the requirements for the nationwide development of military and amateur music. By the end of the nineteenth century, brass bands were beneficiaries of the former and a shining example of the latter. The English (classical) music renaissance was at least a beneficiary and in some respects a product of those same developments, but the professional classical music sector probably contributed less to the growth of the music industry. This is one of several reasons why the history of the brass band has been important to broader aspects of the country's cultural life. It is a history that has often been difficult to grasp because the brass band 'movement' has, for a large part of its existence, inhabited a relatively private and detached world. Such a contradiction is just one of the reasons why its story is so interesting.

Prehistories, precursors and origins

The evidence points to the 'brass band movement', as it came to be called, emerging in the second half of the 1840s because of several converging circumstances. By that time, new forms of military bands in the regular army and militia had provided part of the infrastructure from which the first amateur brass bands benefited. Most importantly, improvements to the design of brass musical instruments, and the way they were produced, came at the behest of the demands of the military band market which had quantitative dominance in the music industry. But while the military in its various forms provided an important and widely distributed presence for instrumental music making, it did not directly cause the emergence of amateur brass bands as a mass activity. It is therefore important to distinguish the origins of the band movement, by which I mean the origins of modern brass bands, from their prehistory and their immediate precursors. Prehistories provide the distant historic origins of brass instruments; their relevance is that they serve to emphasise how important brass bands were to brass instrument performance and the history of music more generally. They provided the first major interruption by amateurs of a performance tradition that was otherwise, and with just a few exceptions, entirely professional. That profession was relatively small. The ubiquitous modern performances of brass solo parts by baroque composers – the spectacular trumpet parts in works by Bach and

Handel, for example – obscure the fact that performers who could play such music at the time of its composition were rare. But even by the 1870s hundreds of amateur brass band players could exercise unprecedented virtuosity. To see brass bands as a continuation of its prehistory is mistaken: the exact opposite is the case – brass bands fractured the continuity rather than sustained it.

I use the word 'precursors' to include the many and various small village bands, and in some cases private bands, that existed in the first half of the nineteenth century. These, too, should be seen as distinct from the brass band movement even though many of the earliest brass bands were transformations of them. Those early village bands – very few of which claimed to be constituted only of brass instruments – were widely scattered, and seldom had any relationship with each other. Their musical make-up and social functions seem to have been as different as the places in which they existed. Almost without exception, and to the extent we can tell from available evidence, their musical identity and role was firmly established in religious and secular traditions that flourished before the middle of the nineteenth century. They were interesting and important, and are discussed in some detail in Chapter 7, because there is no shadow of doubt that those small village groups created the idea that a band of music benefited a locality – that is why they should be regarded as precursors.

Things suddenly changed from the mid-1840s. At that time – the time when the brass band movement properly started – developments were rapid, acute and, above all, fundamentally modern; they were not fragmented, neither were they organised, but the patterns of activity were so numerous and similar that it is impossible to see it as anything but a new and spreading phenomenon. It is as if a new fashion, a trend, had appeared that was enthusiastically replicated and imitated across localities, then regions, and eventually the nation. The main actors were always ordinary working-class men, but what occurred is a complex story that can't be told without reference to the congregation of social, cultural, demographic and economic factors that gave birth to the brass band as a mass, working-class, amateur activity.

Instruments

The main reason for separating the amateur brass band movement from its precursors is that many of the instruments that make up its core were not invented until the 1840s. The use of these instruments, even though older designs were also embraced, defined brass bands as a modern phenomenon. The species that had the most immediate importance to brass bands were invented in Paris and came to Britain initially through the agency of one man: John Distin. This development coincided with other factors that enabled working-class men to own the instruments, even though they did not have the money to pay for them. New industrial production processes enabled instruments to be manufactured in sufficient quantity for them to be sold relatively cheaply. The instruments that came to make up the standard form were cornets – a family of instruments originally called 'saxhorns', of different sizes but having a similar shape – and trombones. Each of these instruments (other than the trombones) were nineteenth-century inventions. They obtained full melodic capacity through mechanisms that required the manipulation of valves – just three valves – that diverted airways through extra or lesser lengths of tubing (fig. 1). Valve instrument mechanisms were ingenious and revolutionary. They were easy to learn because, once a basic technique of producing notes is acquired, much of the work is then done by the manipulation of valves using the three most dextrous fingers of the right hand.[5]

The instruments were often sold in sets rather than individually and were distributed efficiently because the demographics of the country had changed to create new, denser clusters of population. Most of the new communities had been formed around centres of industrial employment that brought large numbers of the labouring class into proximity; many had migrated from rural areas to industrial employment. Most of the places where brass bands started had passed through the early stages of industrialisation and were already established communities. The reconfiguration of the country's population brought changes to the way lives were led. In a country and at a time when entrepreneurialism was rampant, these new settlements were identified collectively as a new working-class market. It was this market that was

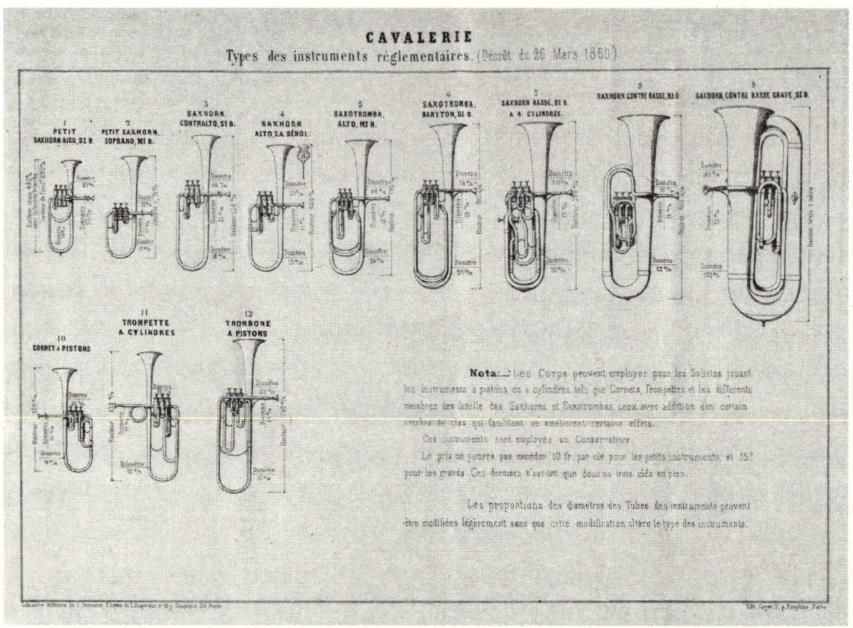

1. The instrumentation devised by Sax for French cavalry bands. The top line shows his family of saxhorns with upward-facing bells.

targeted for the sale of brass band instruments. The important and obvious impediment was that most working-class people lived lives divided unequally between work and rest, with little or no disposable income beyond that required for their necessities. From where, then, did the money come that allowed these very modern musical devices to fall into the hands of people who did not have the money to pay for them – and what motivated those people to play in a band anyway?

Moral values and rational recreation

Attitudes of the upper classes to those they considered their social inferiors played a major part in what was to happen. A rapid growth in the size of the country's population, along with mass migration from rural to urban areas, provided grounds for concern. Communities of a new shape and type had been created where people lived and worked in more densely populated areas, with lives and routines that were different to those of previous generations. Many of the cyclic activities and traditions that had marked out rural existences were lost. These circumstances were untested. Britain had become the world's first great industrial economy, but negative portents loomed for the small percentage of the population that made up the social elite: mainly the aristocracy, the landed gentry (including the clergy) and the industrial and commercial bourgeoisie. The primary concern was that there was an imminent disruption of moral values, and a collapse could threaten social order. Some initiatives emerged from industrialists and philanthropists to counter this. They were systematic, large-scale and holistic, and provided not just places of work but conditions for living: housing, social facilities and open spaces – environments that held the prospect of an ordered, harmonious society. A model had been developed by the Welsh socialist philanthropist Robert Owen at New Lanark in the late eighteenth century. A similar scheme was put in place in Saltaire from 1851, where a model village was created around the textile mills of Sir Titus Salt. Richard and George Cadbury's creation of a Garden Village at Bournville in the countryside south of Birmingham was formed later, but based on similar principles, as were other smaller projects in Copley and Ripley Vale.

Such enterprises required planning and time. Shorter-term and more expedient alternatives appeared because of a shared general attitude that emerged among the upper class. It gathered around a single idea that became known as 'rational recreation'. The underlying principle was that the creation of a responsible and consensual society required the dominant class to do more for working people than to just employ them. They also needed to direct them to activities that would preserve and even enhance moral values. If working people (men in particular) were encouraged to spend their leisure hours in pastimes that were self-improving, docile, respectable and beneficial to the communities in which they lived, it would sustain social cohesion. Support from the dominant class for such projects was often philanthropic, but it can also be seen as an investment in the future of a society they wanted to preserve. Brass bands became a favoured part of those projects, because the right sort of music-making, and attentive listening to it, was seen as a shining example of rational recreation.

The means through which the rational recreationalists supported brass bands were various, but their patronage was consistently important even if, as was often the case, money did not actually change hands between the rich and the poor. Some bands benefited entirely from the generosity of a single sponsor. Such was the case when John Foster, owner of the Black Dyke Mills in Yorkshire, established a brass band in 1855, but that model was neither universal nor even typical. Many bands started by obtaining loans underwritten by guarantees, others depended on the efforts of fund-raising in communities, often with the support of religious or temperance organisations, but even efforts such as these gained strength from the encouragement of people of social substance. Irrespective of what method was used to set up a band, in those early days the rational recreation idea provided the main reason for doing so – and the people who sold musical instruments knew this.

Some of the most successful of the Victorian bands had declined and several had even vanished by the First World War – those that disappeared were either badly organised, just bad, or had stayed too close to the frockcoats of their original patrons. This was a misjudgement to which some bands who enjoyed stellar, but all too brief, success, even in the modern era, were prone: they placed their faith in the longevity of a relationship with little thought of the consequences of it ending. Almost all bands that survived in robust health into the new century and beyond had become self-governing entities. They may have carried the name adopted at the time of their origin, but dependencies weakened. New bands appeared almost continuously. Star bands such as Foden's Motor Works, Fairey Aviation and Grimethorpe Colliery were not formed until the twentieth century, a period in which new models of patronage and sponsorship were to emerge.

Concert life

One of the interesting contradictions about brass bands is that for most of their existence they have resided in a specialist and often very private segment of the musical world but performed in the most conspicuous public spaces. They have been characterised as 'the working man's orchestra'. As with so many clichés, this one became sufficiently exhausted to lose its original meaning – if it ever had one of any utility. It probably referred to the idea that many working-class people were introduced to classical music through versions transcribed for brass bands. This is probably true. Among the favourites were overtures and other derivatives of Italian opera. This came about because until the twentieth century the brass band had very little original music written for it, and much of what was written was mediocre. A more interesting aspect of this part of the brass band's role is that it filled a gap in provincial concert life that was not otherwise filled until the advent of radio. The contribution of brass bands to this stage of British musical life was more important than is usually recognised. Brass bands came into being at a time when new species of commercial provincial concerts were being created. The franchise for musical listening was expanding. Enderby Jackson, the man who laid claim to being the 'inventor' of the brass band contest spent his teenage years helping his father to illuminate the footlights at the Theatre Royal in the northern town of Hull. In his autobiographical memoir he enthusiastically recalled visits from the Jullien orchestra and its exhibitionist virtuoso soloists. He even claimed to have heard Paganini – one of the greatest musical celebrities of the century.

Victorian brass band contests attracted audiences on an unprecedented scale, most being held in the open air. For much of the twentieth century the most common locations for brass bands as concert performers were also in open-air public spaces: in bandstands, the verdant settings of which must have provided great pleasure for the working class. These events, which commenced in the nineteenth century, usually took place on Sundays, the only days when the working class were free to attend. Sabbatarians were quick to predict epic levels of damnation for both musicians and their audiences, but bandstand concerts continued through the twentieth century on a massive national scale. When BBC (British Broadcasting Corporation) broadcasting of bands commenced in the 1920s, it was the varied repertoire and relaxed pleasure generated by bandstand concerts that it tried to capture. It seems to have succeeded, because brass bands became a favourite feature of wireless broadcasting.

By that time, some bands, such as Besses o' th' Barn, Black Dyke, and Brighouse and Rastrick, had gained celebrity status. Celebrity accrued only from success in brass band contests. The epithet 'Champion' was almost as important as the cash prize that accompanied it.

Contests

Contesting holds an interesting and peculiarly strong position in the history of the brass band. It is easy to see why the idea caught on in the Victorian period. It was brilliant entertainment. The new railway system brought tens of thousands together to listen intently to the performances and second-guess the adjudicators. There were also other accompanying attractions at big contests: balloon ascents, flower shows, even athletic races. The first major contest (eventually called the British Open Contest) was held at the Belle Vue Gardens, Manchester, in 1853.[6] It was a spectacular success and has continued in different venues since. A bewildering number of contests were and are held all over the country each year. There is a variety of contest types, each subject to its own regulations and rituals. Bands draw for the order in which they will play. For contests in which the performance of a single 'test piece' is required, the adjudicators are incarcerated in a box: literally, a specially constructed box that lets in the sound but obscures the identity of each band. Prizes come in the form of trophies, cash and sometimes new instruments for top players of the day. In the modern era, global rankings of bands based on contest wins are available online and are regularly viewed and updated.[7]

While it is easy to see the value of contests as a form of public entertainment and a device for standardising and nationalising the brass band movement in the Victorian period, it is more challenging to understand why they have remained central to brass band culture for so long despite the mixed feelings that accompany the idea of musical contests. Through the eras of the Second Viennese School, Stravinsky, Gershwin, the Beatles, and all else that the rest of the musical world has unveiled, the brass band contest has survived unperturbed and fundamentally unaltered. Remarkably, it has also been embraced with unbridled enthusiasm by bands in continental Europe that have adopted the British model.

Comparisons between brass band contests and competitions held in the classical music world are unrealistic. In the world of 'serious' music, competitions are used to attract interest to nascent talent: they provide a way of projecting spectacular new musical careers into the future. There are no contests for established musicians in the world of classical music. Contests exist in other branches of amateur music (for example, in Wales, choral societies and other amateur musicians compete in *eisteddfodau*), but contests prevail nowhere with the importance and frequency that they do in the world of the brass band. The phenomenon can be understood only by reference to the movement's own terms and standards. They do not defy explanation but to the greatest extent they defy comparison, and this is as true in the modern world as it has been in the past. They proffer the opportunity for excellence. Some of the greatest brass band performances have been given at contests before audiences of listeners who are as sophisticated and attentive as any in the world of music. I have experienced these many times as a player and a listener. Contests mark out the calendar of bands, create a continuum and concentrate emotions. Bands win contests by their mastery of musical nuance, an aspect of their collective character that has always eluded intelligent critical comment from the outside world. It is in this very fundamental respect that the rest of the musical world fails to display empathy for what makes brass bands flourish. They neither understand it, nor have they felt the musical intensity that is nurtured by it – and the emotions it stirs.

A parallel world

In 1878 William Booth transformed the Christian Mission he had founded with his wife 13 years earlier. The new Mission had two related objectives: to continue its programme of social care and to extend its evangelism through a widely dispersed network of centres, each united by the same objectives and methods. The name 'Salvation Army' was adopted almost whimsically, but it soon became one the country's most conspicuous organisations. In the same year a convert who had played the cornet with the Salisbury Volunteer Band turned up for an open-air meeting, bringing with him his three brass-playing sons. They played accompaniments to hymns and helped attract a large crowd. This was putatively the first Salvation Army band. Brass bands were not the only musical or even the only instrumental groupings used by the Salvation Army, but they became its most common musical feature. They were suitable for evangelism because they could perform in the open air, they attracted attention to the promise of salvation (Booth's main preoccupation) and they complemented the military metaphor that soon pervaded the entirety of the Salvationist organisation. There were almost as many Salvationist brass bands as there were citadels (Salvationist places of worship) and centres of administration, and they were also transported as part of its global diaspora. From 1893 the Salvation Army met its own demand by manufacturing its own brass instruments; the first full set was made in the following year, and in 1901 it established a new manufacturing plant in St Albans, north of London. It was to be one of the largest such firms in Britain.

There were always many similarities between conventional brass bands and those of the Salvation Army, and this posed a problem for Booth that was not resolved for a century. Three 'General Orders' were in place by 1885 that assured separation of Salvationist bands from those of the brass band movement. The orders could not have been more explicit. They restricted membership of Salvationist bands to attested members of the Army, who were forbidden from playing in any other bands. Only Salvationist instruments were to be used, and their use was restricted to the purpose of the Mission. In 1881 the *War Cry* published a list of measures:

> In order to prevent misunderstandings and to secure the harmonious working of the brass bands . . . No one will be admitted or retained as a member of any Band who is not a Member of the Army [and] . . . In no case are Instruments to be used to play anything but Salvation Music or on any but Salvation Army service.[8]

Further measures were increasingly restrictive and ultimately ill-judged. They originated in Booth's confused perception of the role of music in religious devotion and its effect on its executants. He appropriated many of the tools of popular culture (including 'the devil's choicest tunes') without taking full measure of the reality that popular culture has a life of its own – its capriciousness evades restraint. His response was the usual one: he deployed prohibitive regulation to exact autocratic control.

The relaxation of the Boothian edicts came in the 1990s, not only because a light was suddenly shone to reveal the flaws in this aspect of Salvationist tradition. The business case for its instrument-manufacturing factory had already collapsed and a chain of events had made its independence from the outside world untenable. It did not take long for the Army to integrate itself into the external brass band world with benefits that accrued for both.

Modernisation

A unique feature shared by Salvation Army bands and those of the wider brass band movement was its pitch. Long after it had been abandoned in every other form of music-making, both organisations played instruments tuned to a pitch standard inherited from the Victorian period. This is explained in detail in Chapter 9, but it meant that, from 1939, brass band instruments were tuned almost a semitone higher than those used elsewhere in the musical world. This was an inheritance of measures taken to standardise British military bands in the nineteenth century but, while the British army and navy had shifted to the modern (lower) pitch standard in 1928, brass bands didn't. By the 1960s the only manufacturers making high-pitched instruments were Boosey & Hawkes (which also owned the Besson brand) and the Salvation Army. Both had already started producing instruments to the lower pitch standard and knew there was no long-term future in this niche corner of manufacturing, and an agreement was reached. The Salvation Army's production line stopped completely. Its factory was bought in 1972 by Boosey & Hawkes, which then shifted exclusively to the production of standard-pitch instruments.

These events were momentous because they initiated a series of musical consequences that changed the sound of brass bands and the way composers wrote for them. There were also other changes. From the 1960s the normalisation of women in brass bands, and changes to the way instrumental music teaching in schools and colleges was organised, brought about a major cultural shift. It was developed further by the entry of an influential and iconoclastic generation of band directors who had originated in brass bands before developing their careers in the classical music world. They brought new, radical ideas and encouraged the routine adoption of tuned and untuned percussion for contests as well as concerts. Taken together, these factors created a mode of modernisation that retained the essential character of the British brass band while liberating it from the stultifying and entrenched orthodoxies that had formed by the 1960s. It also portended a new type of internationalisation which took a surprisingly short time to reach maturity.

Another type of history

An important proviso about brass band histories is that they tend, in all but name, to be histories of elite bands and high-level contesting. To an extent, this is understandable, in the same way that it is understandable that so many histories are configured by the actions of monarchs, dictators, politicians and their geopolitical consequences. Such approaches need to be leavened by others that present a more holistic view of the way societies and their cultures develop, and how socio-cultural shifts impact on the day-to-day experiences of ordinary people. I have been conscious when writing this book that, within the broad headline narrative of the history of brass bands, there are a multitude of different stories, many hidden, that reveal the relationships between bands and the places to which they belong. Taken together, those stories might provide a different history than the one I have written, but I am inclined to think it unlikely. Not because they are less consequential than the headline narratives, but because they are inseparably a part of it. One of the most absorbing features of the band story is the way that localities connect with their bands and this feature is as applicable to the most modest and ramshackle of them as it is to the stellar, trophy-laden celebrities. Many communities can, almost literally, claim ownership of their bands (fig. 2). I began the Prologue to this book by mentioning my own entry into the band story. I might at that stage have mentioned another autobiographical corner. Every Friday my mother would ritualistically check my father's wages. She would recite words like 'stoppages', 'superannuation' and 'overtime', and another, equally incomprehensible to me, so much so it reached my childish ears as a single word: 'tuppencefortheband'. This, I was to learn, referred to the agreement that two pence would be deducted, at source, every week, from everyone working in the colliery so that its band could be supported.

This and similar arrangements, and the feelings that lie behind them, explain the many images of bands leading strikers back to their factories

2. *The Llanelly Band, c.1900. A band raised by local subscription; fully formed with one cup won. No uniforms yet, but the caps signal the direction of travel.*

and mines, and their presence in a multitude of other local rituals: there was a debt to repay – not just financial but moral, social and often emotional. As such, it came to pass that localities were given memories by their bands. One of my favourite stories concerns an obscure event that took place in the small Essex town of Braintree on the frosty morning of 1 January 1909. This was the day on which, at the behest of the Liberal government of Herbert Asquith, the British Old Age Pension was introduced. It was to be five shillings a week for a single person and seven shillings and six pence for a married couple. It really was bitterly cold that morning, but half an hour before the village post office was to open at 8.30, an orderly line of pensioners formed outside its doors. Many wondered whether this unprecedented benevolence was real, others worried that the money would run out before some of it entered their mittened hands. There with them, standing side by side, was the Braintree brass band, keeping them company and entertaining them on this momentous day. When the postmaster took his keys out of his waistcoat pocket, he immediately snapped to attention. The band had struck up 'God Save the King'. Then, at its conclusion, as he opened the post office door, it sounded 'Hail Smiling Morn'.

It is a good story and true, and it gains its strength, as is always the case, from the music: it wasn't a speech or a warm mince pie those old people were given – it was music. This is another thing that is sometimes overlooked in band histories: the music. I do not mean the repertoire (that is never overlooked). I refer to the fact that when those Victorians got hold of those saxhorns and formed themselves into bands, they became music-makers. They deployed music for its fundamental purpose – to communicate. This has always been the case. Music is one of the ways humans communicate with each other, and it is a mode of communication that can be more potent than words. Music does its work in its own way. Those same Victorians with their saxhorns may have faltered in spoken words and more certainly in their written literacy but, when joined with others to form a band, they became eloquent. This has never stopped. One need only watch and listen to a band playing to realise that, in the moments of their performance, these people are transformed: they are enlivened and strengthened by their joint endeavour. Banding does this.

Chapter 1

Prehistories and precursors

Bands of the type that can be properly regarded as the originators of the 'brass band movement' did not exist until the mid-1840s. At that time, several musical, social, cultural and economic circumstances coalesced to create the phenomenon that is the subject of this book. Some writers have implied a seamless transition from much earlier wind bands, including the fifteenth-century civic bands that in Britain were called 'waits', in Italy *piffari* and in German-speaking countries *Stadtpfeifer*. It has also been suggested that the roots of the British brass band model can be seen in the sophisticated ensembles that flourished in Europe's major musical centres between the late fifteenth and late seventeenth centuries.[1] Modern transcriptions of repertoire from that period have probably encouraged such thinking, but it is misleading because the circumstances that emerged in the mid-Victorian period were entirely new. Almost all Renaissance brass players were professionals who lived and worked in a world that was strikingly different to the one in which amateur brass bands emerged. The only useful purpose served by such comparisons is that they illustrate the extent to which Victorian working-class amateurs interrupted the historical progress of brass instrument performance.

The British model of the brass band originated and developed rapidly in the late 1840s because of the invention, and large-scale production, of new species of brass instruments – specifically those that were initially known as saxhorns. Many of the first brass bands were called saxhorn bands. At the start of the following century the Salvationist musician Richard Slater, an astute and educated observer of such matters, reflected on the impact of saxhorns:

> There is little doubt but that the possibility of the whole Brass Band world sprang from the invention of valves and the uniform structure of Sax's instruments, so making brass instruments not only comparatively easy to play, but strikingly more complete for musical purposes than the earlier forms of brass instruments.[2]

These inventions appeared when Britain had been transformed from a country that was primarily rural and agricultural to one that was increasingly an assembly of urban industrial settlements. These changes impacted fundamentally on the mass of the people and the way lives were led. Individuals, families and communities experienced their existences differently than their forebears. While the speed of this transition and its possible effect on social order was a cause for concern in some quarters, most alert commercial entrepreneurs saw the growth of urban settlements in more opportunistic terms: they were new and fertile consumer markets. New financial devices were to emerge that made it possible for these sophisticated musical instruments to be owned by thousands of working-class men who did not have the money to pay for them.

Prehistory: The instruments

Despite my rejection of the idea of a continuity between the British model of the brass band and forms that preceded it, the brass band movement had a past, if not a history, that stretched over the centuries before the Victorian era. It is best understood as having two stages – a prehistory and a phase in the first half of the nineteenth century when precursors provided some of the structures, precedents and even ideas from which the launch of the brass band movement benefited.

Just four species of brass instrument were ubiquitous before the eighteenth century. One was not made of brass, but it was a 'lip-vibrated instrument'. 'Lip-vibrated' is the feature that properly defines the 'brass instrument' family – musical notes are generated by the vibration of a player's lips (the embouchure) in an appropriately shaped mouthpiece. This instrument was the *cornett*, an entirely different instrument to the modern cornet. It was made of wood, bound in leather and had holes on its sounding length of a similar pattern to those on a recorder. It was called 'cornett' in England, *cornetto* in Italy, and *Zink* in the German language. It was used in sacred and secular music for playing the treble/soprano lines in ensemble music and supporting the higher parts in vocal music. Surviving music from the very early seventeenth century provides a clue to the agile techniques required by its players: it is often marked *per violino o cornetto* (for violin or cornetto). The cornett was the first instrument of the 'brass' family upon which an elite group of players gained celebrity because of their melodic virtuosity.

The other lip-vibrated instruments used before the nineteenth century were indeed made of brass or a similar alloy; a few are known to have been made of pure silver. These were the trumpet (with no valves, consequently called a 'natural' instrument in modern parlance), the trombone and the horn. The term 'french horn', which appeared in England during the eighteenth century, has never been adequately explained – they were, indeed, used in France, but that country has never had a special claim to them. Before the late sixteenth century, trumpets were used primarily for declamation in public and private spaces and as 'instruments of command' in the military. Horns were commonly used for the hunt before they were adopted as orchestral instruments by the early eighteenth century. The trombone was a development of the trumpet and had most of its modern features by the last quarter of the fifteenth century. Trombones and cornetts were used together in both sacred and secular music in the Renaissance. Because the music for which they were used was complex and there was a lot of it, their players had to be musically literate. Before this time, brass players committed music to memory: the capacity to remember repertoire was a requirement of the job. There is no evidence in contemporary pictures to suggest that trumpeters were musically literate before the late sixteenth century,[3] but for cornetts and trombones such evidence abounds in pictures and documents.

Understanding the consequences of musical literacy is important because it helps us understand how widely repertoire was circulated. The performance of memorised music was usually limited to the localities in which the music was written, unless those local players travelled elsewhere, but written music, printed or handwritten, could be circulated beyond to places distant from where it was first heard. By the early decades of the seventeenth century, most brass players were musically literate. The expectations of military trumpeters were different; they continued to memorise signals, as did horn players who played only for the hunt.

Surviving written music does not fully reveal the way music was performed. Early players almost always improvised musical embellishment to what they saw on the written page. These embellishments were neither random nor capricious; players consistently adhered to prevailing conventions of what was considered good musical taste. We know this because several books and manuscripts of the time explain those practices in detail.[4] Early brass players were almost all professionals, and it was typical for a single family to produce generations of players of the same instrument, with the required skills being passed from fathers to sons. By the late fifteenth century, several of these dynastic groups were internationally itinerant. For example, the accounts of expenditure of the court of Henry VIII of England for April 1532 show that 11 'sagbut' players (sagbut, also written 'sacbut' or 'sackbut', was the old English word for trombone) were in receipt of monthly payments. Not one of them was English, and some surnames were shared by more than one player.[5]

The growth of opera and eventually the symphony orchestra in the seventeenth and eighteenth centuries consolidated the place of brass instruments in classical music, but the cornett fell out of use early in the eighteenth century. No cornett music is known to have been published after 1700.[6] The treble instrument became obsolete, but the bass version, called the 'serpent' (because of its shape), continued to be used in church bands in England and France into the nineteenth century. By about 1840 it, too, was confined to oblivion as new, mechanised brass instruments suitable for playing in the bass range were introduced. One early writer on church bands thought the serpent had a timbre that was more 'mellow and tender' than the brass instruments that eventually replaced it but conceded that it was difficult to play.[7]

Changes to instruments and the way they were used were usually caused by adjustments to musical tastes, preferences and the social requirements they were expected to serve. The trombone was a surprising casualty of such processes. While it continued to be used in some countries in the eighteenth century, especially Austria, it otherwise, and for the best part of a hundred years, fell almost completely out of favour. One of the countries from which it vanished was Britain. When an orchestra was assembled in 1784 to perform a concert dedicated to the commemoration of George Frideric Handel, the organisers, seeing that some of Handel's music required parts for 'tromboni', were at a loss to understand what it meant. Charles Burney, the most important English writer about music at the time, was as confused as most but, as a scholar of music, he at least seems to have linked the 'tromboni' parts with the old English word 'sacbut':

In order to render the band as powerful and complete as possible, it was determined to employ every species of instrument that was capable of producing grand effects in a great orchestra and spacious buildings. Among them the SACBUT, or DOUBLE TRUMPET, was sought, but so many years had elapsed since it had been used in this kingdom, that, neither the instrument, nor a performer upon it could easily be found. It was, however, discovered, after much useless enquiry, not only here, but by letter on the continent that in His Majesty's military band there were six musicians who played the three several species of sacbut.[8]

The three players from 'His Majesty's military band' were Herr Zink, Herr Müller and Herr Niebuhr, all Germans. They were three of the many German musicians who were being recruited through London-based German agencies to play in British regimental bands. Their presence in London was desirable because they brought expertise that did not otherwise exist in sufficient local quantity to meet expanding needs. Military bands and their eventual presence across

Britain provided an essential part of the infrastructure for the eventual emergence of brass bands.

Military music

From the late 1780s a new type of military music developed that was to change the musical life of Europe, the Americas and most of the colonised world. It caused an unprecedented expansion in the music profession and created a route through which people from lower social classes, with no previous connection with music, could become competent and musically literate instrumentalists. This expansion stimulated a growth in the entire music industry, including the part associated with classical music. Most new species of brass instruments were aimed at improving military music, and alongside those developments came more efficient production methods capable of serving a new scale of demand. Military music, as it evolved at this time, contributed to a restructuring of how the music business worked and, in so doing, it laid the basis for the next and most important stage: the mass engagement of amateurs in instrumental music-making.

Developments that occurred in the early nineteenth century are reflected in an interesting change in the way words were used to describe music-makers. The quotation from the writer Charles Burney given above is typical. He did not call the assembled players for the Handel commemoration concert an orchestra, but a 'band'. Larger groups of instrumentalists were always called bands. The first performances of Handel's *Messiah* were accompanied by 'a band'. Then things changed. The word 'orchestra' was introduced for that purpose, and soon others, such as 'ensemble' and terms that defined the number of players for which a piece of music was written – quartet, octet and so on. 'Band' came to be used with a prefix (such as 'military' and eventually 'brass') to define a new and usually more popular form of instrumental ensemble. Early in the nineteenth century, terms such as 'military music' and 'military musical instruments' also emerged in a similar way.[9]

Previously, and leaving aside any solace soldiers resting at camp might have gained from improvised melodies played by pipers, there were just two reasons for musical instruments to be present in the military: the beat of drums (sometimes with fifes or pipes) provided a way of measuring the progress of men on the march; and trumpets or bugles were used to transmit signals to troops from centres of command. Measuring the march meant exactly that. By controlling the speed of drumbeats to each minute (guided by the swing of a simple pendulum, a short length of rope from which a weight was suspended), it was possible to calculate how long it would take to move a body of soldiers from one place to another on foot. Soldiers did not march neatly in step until the late eighteenth century. The introduction of co-ordinated marching to step was deeply controversial because it was thought unmanly and that it resembled dancing: a completely rational view given the style of dancing fashionable at that time. The required skill of the drummer was to keep a regular beat; the role of the soldiers was to shuffle along following the speed he set.[10]

3. An eighteenth-century painting on wood labelled 'Royal Music or Wind Harmony'. Each of the musicians plays attentively from written music, except the trumpeter – loyal to the tradition of memorisation rather than musical literacy, he appears to conscientiously ignore it.

Trumpeters or buglers who played signals did not have a truly *musical* role: their repertoire was usually restricted to those signals which prompted specific actions in and around fields of combat. We know what those melodic fragments were because they were written down, but their commitment to paper was just for the official record. Military trumpeters observed the long tradition of playing from memory (fig. 3). By necessity, they stayed close to centres of command, and this was one of the reasons why they enjoyed a high status. Playing the trumpet was often not their only role. Several, even from the fifteenth century, were conferred with a quasi-diplomatic status and emissarial functions. They carried messages, negotiated for the release of prisoners, and were granted safe passage across enemy lines to do so. Such diplomatic, non-combatant roles for trumpeters were explained as early as 1626 and with emphasis on the way they looked, because they needed to transmit the 'effects' of a gentleman:

> The trumpet is not bound to any arms at all, more than his sword, which in former times was not allowed, but with the point broken: he shall have a faire trumpet, with cordens suitable to the captaines colours, and to his trumpet shall be fast a faire banner, containing the captain's coat of armour: he may wear a scarfe and feather, and all ordinary accoutrements of a horseman; and for his horse, it shall be a good hackney with gentleman-like furniture.[11]

Trumpeters worthy of such description may have been exceptional, but all signalling drummers and trumpeters were critically important in the military, and their role in this respect never disappeared. However, what they did should not be confused with what was required of members of the new type of military band that emerged in the late eighteenth century. From that time a new species of military musician emerged, with a different set of purposes and for which a different set of skills was required. The change was initially caused by the social requirements of the officer class, but it soon encouraged a growth in military ceremony. These new 'bands of music' were assembled from musicians who played wind instruments of the sort that were otherwise used in orchestras and theatres. The players needed to be competent and sufficiently fluent at reading music to engage with large, expanding and increasingly varied repertoires. The repertoires, initially at least, were performed for the entertainment of regimental officers who, almost without exception, were drawn from the aristocracy and landed class.

The evidence for this phase of military music is abundant. It can be seen in surviving officers' mess accounts, correspondence, musical directories, and archives such as that of the Royal Society of Musicians in London. This Society was founded in 1738 to support professional musicians; it was originally titled 'the Fund for Decay'd Musicians'. Members paid subscriptions which accumulated a fund that was used to provide benefits to subscribers and their families if they fell on hard times: it was an early and very specialised form of mutual insurance. Only those who were well established in the profession and posed a minimum immediate risk to the Society's funds were admitted, so applicants were required to explain and evidence the security of their livelihood. The files on individual members exist from 1776. From the end of that century, some wind musicians who had previously cited theatres, pleasure gardens and festivals as their main line of work started mentioning regimental bands. This did not mean that they had joined the army; it meant that their freelance portfolio included work with regimental bands. Regimental officers assembled 'bands of music' to entertain themselves in private and, as appropriate, in public spaces. The open-air events found favour with the public, and this brought unexpected credit to regiments who were always keen to elevate their status. Government funds were not provided for the maintenance of military bands, so each was supported by a 'band fund' to which officers paid regular, mandatory contributions (fig. 4).

The expense attached to such enterprises was not confined to the wages of the players and necessary incidentals: paid intermediaries were involved who provided instruments, players and anything else that a regiment needed. Regular advertisements for their services appeared in London newspapers. George Astor, who operated from a shop in Cornhill, was particularly successful. He was born in Heidelberg in 1752 and emigrated from Germany in 1782. He offered to supply officers of the army and navy with 'complete sets of instruments for

4. A drawing by George Scharf of a band rehearsal at the Royal Marines barracks at Woolwich in 1826.

a band, with good musicians to play the same . . . [and] Several good Masters for teaching a Band'.[12] Most agents were London-based music dealers, most of German origin. The most important appointee was the band leader; he would arrange music, direct its performance and, if the opportunity arose, train local boys or young recruits as musicians. Foreigners were needed because the local supply could not meet the demand. German players were favoured because so many were available: German military bands were numerous and well developed by this time. Also, and perhaps more importantly, it became fashionable for a band to have a German bandmaster.

The voguish regard for German musicians was to continue well into the next century. Another German agent, Heinrich Kohler, on receiving a request for a German bandmaster, found a German musician busking in the street, whom he immediately 'grabbed', cleaned up and 'provided . . . with an outfit' before shipping him off to join a regiment in India.[13] This busker was a man of a completely different set than Kohler normally dealt with. He was a member of what were commonly referred to as 'German bands'. One of the contradictions of the time was that, while German bandmasters and performers were fashionable and respected, 'German bands' were not. The name was used to describe the groups of itinerate, second-rate German musicians who came to Britain expediently in search of work and ended up busking in the streets. The man Kohler sent to India probably couldn't believe his luck.

Agents were necessary because, while regimental officers recognised the need for music, it was not usual for them to know the slightest thing about it. Most seem to have been interested only in what their bands could do rather than how they did it and what was materially necessary for it to be done. It followed that the intermediaries made a good living because their services were also required in the shires and provinces to supply necessaries for bands attached to part-time militia forces and the distributed regiments of the regular army. These units, even the part-time provincial militia, imitated London regiments by forming bands for the same primarily social purposes determined by their officers. Militia officers were also drawn from the aristocracy and gentry. Nineteenth-century novels are replete with references to dashing young military officers and the social circles in which they moved, but there are also original testimonies to the social importance of military music. A young British officer, writing to his mother while stationed in Ireland in 1834, described the importance of the military in the social life of the circles in which he moved. He complained about the quantity of Italian music they performed, but emphasised the value of dances:

> Dancing is most necessary for the man of good education and for the officer. It makes him acceptable or even indispensable at parties when he relaxes in his off-duty hours. It is good for the officer to betake himself to such assemblies, and especially the mixed companies attended by ladies and pretty girls, which are an education for all persons of the male sex.[14]

It followed that in the shires, where the social routines of the elevated classes were more limited than in London, bands of music became an essential asset. In country areas there was an even greater tendency for officers to use an agent to locate a bandmaster who would teach local, usually young, recruits. Local musicians drawn from existing groups, such as church bands, were encouraged or coerced to enlist. Evidence of military bands in the British shires and provinces is as abundant as it is for London, and often sufficiently explicit to reveal the instruments that were used, the music that was played and where it was played. One of the most illustrative sets of records is that of the Shropshire Militia. It shows that in 1806 the band was made up of 28 players (six brass instruments, 17 woodwind plus percussion). Officers paid subscriptions of £7.10.0 or £3.15.10, according to their rank, with the regimental colonel paying £50. These were good levels of funding and ensured that the band was a stable, well-organised and well-led institution: probably much more so than any civilian enterprise within travelling distance. The repertoire was distributed across a set of part-books. A small quantity was designated as 'Military Music' (essentially marches), but the greatest part was dance music, particularly waltzes and quicksteps; there were also arrangements of songs and 'Irish melodies'.[15]

By the late eighteenth century there were militia regiments in all British counties and, while militia bands were formed for the exclusive use of officers, they became increasingly evident in public spaces. Regimental and militia bands provided the first systematic network of instrumental music-making in Britain. While the officers who sponsored these bands were drawn from the landed class, the bandsmen recruits were not. This too was new. Young men from families of modest means learned to play brass instruments and how to read music. An example can be seen in the career of Robert Handel Booth, who successfully applied for membership of the Royal Society of Musicians in 1887, by which time he could cite engagements as a trombone player with all the major London orchestras and provincial music festivals. He had been born in abject poverty in the northern county of Lancashire; his mother signed his birth certificate with a cross because she was illiterate. His father, Amos Booth, was probably also illiterate and worked as a 'night attendant in a lunatic asylum'. At 16, Robert was sent to the navy, where he was taught to play a musical instrument. By the age of 22, he was married and is described in census records as a private in the Royal Marines Light Infantry Regiment. He was a bandsman, not titled as such because playing in a band was a designation of duties rather than a rank. After demobilisation he rose to distinction as a musician.[16] This was not an isolated example. Several men who served in militia battalions or other branches of the military were to work in the music profession; some played an important role in the brass band movement. Among them was John Distin, the man who brought saxhorns to the attention of the British public, who was a member of the band of the South Devon Militia.

Bands as agents for public and foreign relations

The deployment of military bands in public spaces was popular and not just because of their music: military bands in their uniforms were eye-catching and had a positive effect on the public. In 1830 Alexander Alexander, a former soldier with the Royal Artillery, wrote a memoir which he called *The Life of Alexander Alexander: Written by Himself.* In it he recalled how, as a shiftless youth, he encountered his military destiny:

> As I sauntered about the streets of Glasgow, I saw a new guard marching to relieve the old, their band was playing a cheerful air. This being the first military band I had ever heard, I was quite charmed with it, unconsciously taking the step and holding up my head. A military enthusiasm instantly seized me, and I felt as if a soldier's life was the only station for which nature had designed me.[17]

Crowds gathered enthusiastically to watch marching soldiers led by a band because it was a special and colourful occasion: a sonic and visual experience that briefly lifted onlookers from the monochrome of everyday life. Alexander had never heard a band before, and the experience reached him as one of those onlookers; but the impact was not restricted to such casual observers – it acted with similar effect on soldiers, who felt elevated by their ceremonial role, and this gave rise to two additional and important developments. Firstly, because soldiers seemed to bear themselves more impressively when marching to a band of music (by the early nineteenth century they really were marching to step), the army incorporated a role for bands of music into its mandatory drills. In other words, bands became a necessity rather than a decorative element of a regiment. There was no change to the way bands were funded – they continued to be the responsibility of officers; but this appears to have had no detrimental effect. In most cases regimental pride prompted officers to embrace bands as components of regimental regalia.

The second consequence was yet more important. These developments occurred at a time when the way the military looked and sounded in ceremony was becoming increasingly important throughout Europe. Music became part of the way the British military was presented, not just to foreign powers but to the British people. There was a severe need for the reputation of the army to be enhanced. It was not widely liked, not least because, prior to the advent of a properly constituted police force, it was often called on to enforce civil discipline. It also took sons away from families and, when temporarily stationed in shires, soldiers were frequently regarded as disruptive. The government wanted the military to be perceived as a proud representation of the country rather than a disturbance to ordinary life. It also hoped for it to become a statement of nationhood and patriotic sentiment at a time when most people's experience was limited to the narrow confines of their own localities. Uniforms and ceremonial display took on a new importance. In the absence of any obvious alternative, military recruits were often asked to choose the regiment to which they were to be sent by recourse to a series of cards showing regimental uniforms. Officers' uniforms became elaborate and stylised to the extent that they were sometimes so close-fitting that they inhibited free movement.[18] Such ornamentation may, in some instances, have been promoted by vanity, but more profound motivations were also at play. Disciplined ceremonials transmitted messages about stability, order and authority. This idea was not without precedent – elaborate display had been used for this purpose since the Middle Ages; but what happened at this time had a new flavour and was more systematised and exactly targeted.

In France, where the republican government sought social order as well as approval, there was an urgent need to communicate authority and stability in terms that were easily understood by the mass of the people. This was most effectively done through visual and aural impression, because it instantly stirred emotions. It is no coincidence that many of the major developments in military music in the first half of the nineteenth century occurred in Paris. It was deliberate, and measures that signalled the priority given to military music were already under way at the end of the previous century. The Paris Conservatoire, which was to be a model for other institutions that trained professional musicians, was formed of two schools, the École Royale de Chant et de Déclamation, founded in 1783, and, from 1792, a new school created explicitly to train instrumentalists for the band of the National Guard.

Instrument improvements

Most improvements to brass instruments, including those that were to be used in British brass bands, were linked to the military. Joseph Haliday, who patented the keyed bugle, was bandmaster of the Cavan Militia in Ireland; the ophicleide – essentially a bass version of that instrument – was invented by the Parisian maker Halary (Jean Hilaire Asté), who had been commissioned to make keyed bugles for the Russian military, based on Haliday's invention. The tuba was initially the work of Wilhelm Wieprecht, general director of military bands in Prussia.

It was not merely the introduction of more versatile instruments that was important; in a period when so many new instruments were being introduced, judgements had to be made about their quality and how they sounded in combination. There has never been an international standard combination of instruments for the military band in the way that there would be a standard British brass band instrumentation. In some countries – Prussia, for example – there were 'regulation' models that were suitable for different types and sizes of military unit (cavalry, infantry, light infantry and so on), but these regulations were periodically adjusted, and one wonders how frequently they were observed. On the other hand, there was a clear intent for elite military bands to be perceived as representative of their country. In Britain, the bands of the household regiments, such as the Grenadier

Guards and the Coldstream Guards, assumed this mantle, as did the Band of the Royal Marines, the elite band of the Royal Navy.[19] In France, this status was most obviously associated with the band of the National Guard, but in the middle of the century there was concern that its quality fell short of the desired standard. Matters reached a head in 1845. The government established a commission of inquiry under the chairmanship of General Comte de Rumigny; it was charged with determining the future format of French military music. Two models were compared: bands made up of traditional instruments, and those that used modern instruments invented and manufactured by the Belgian, Adolphe Sax, who had lived and worked in Paris since 1842. The commission's decision was resolved publicly at a contest held at the Champ de Mars on 22 April 1845. The band populated by Sax's designs was the winner. It was these same valve instruments, 'saxhorns', that became the basis of British brass bands, and Sax's formulation of brass instruments for cavalry regiments was to be the basis for the amateur 'fanfare' bands that were to become popular elsewhere in western Europe in the later nineteenth and twentieth centuries.

Children's homes and their legacies

The size of the British army varied in the nineteenth century as war and threats of war arose and abated. All regiments that had a public-facing role (rather than supply depots, for example) supported military bands.[20] A precise calculation of the exact number of bandsmen in the British military in the nineteenth century is impossible because they can't be identified since bandsmen were usually listed as 'soldiers'. The only methodical attempt to quantify them came in the period leading up to the establishment, in 1857, of what came to be called the Royal Military School of Music.[21] The project was developed by the Duke of Cambridge, who sought to cover much of the school's ongoing costs through pro-rata contributions from regiments. He wrote to each regiment asking how many soldiers were designated to be bandsmen. The information gathered amounted to a total of four-and-a-half thousand, but this was a serious and deliberate understatement. All military units were required to limit bands to 20 players, but it was an open secret that most exceeded that number – some by multiples. There were times when the Royal Artillery had a band of over 100. It is certain that, by the middle of the century, there were more military musicians than civilian professional instrumentalists in the UK. The expansion was caused by demand. For the first time there was a genuine need to train ordinary working-class recruits to be full-time military musicians.

General recruitment strategies provided some ab initio musicians suitable for training as bandsmen. Young men and boys were best because they were judged to be more receptive and willing learners than older men. A recruit who had a modicum of experience in music, such as one who had played in a village or church band, would have been especially suited, but the greatest need was for recruits with more balanced musical skills. A large proportion who suited this requirement were children who had been deposited in institutions such as workhouses, children's homes, orphanages and industrial schools. Many were orphans, but all were victims of some form of parental destitution.

The army and navy were perfect destinations for such children when they reached working age. Trades such as shoemaking, tailoring and plumbing were always needed by the forces, and performers on band instruments acquired the same status. Children's homes that came under the supervision of local and central governments, along with military regiments, were involved in a system that lasted into the twentieth century. In 1915 a government paper was circulated under the heading *List of Industrial, Workhouse, and Reformatory Schools in the United Kingdom, from which Boys can be obtained, for training as Trumpeters, Drummers, Musicians, Artificers, Tailors, Shoemakers, &c.* It laid out in detail where boys could be obtained for trades, and described processes for their direct transfer to military units:[22]

In the Schools included in these lists there are boys of 14 years of age and upwards, of good character, who have been carefully taught to play brass, reed or other musical instruments, and who are ready to enlist in any regiment where musically-instructed boys are required. As they have not been allowed to enter the bands formed in their respective schools, unless they have shown a natural capacity for music by their possession of a good ear for time and tune, they may be depended upon to form efficient members of military bands.[23]

The lists provided the names and addresses of the schools and the trades in which each specialised. This type of arrangement was replicated for a century under various forms of public and private patronage. The institutions may have been different, but they shared an important and probably unique feature: they systematically brokered a massive and self-refreshing source for the permanent supply of musical recruits. It is impossible to estimate the proportion of military bandsmen who were recruited through this route, but their contribution to the musical infrastructure of Britain was significant. Several individuals and dynasties who were to have an important place in musical life were alumni of the system. They include the Godfrey family, which provided the first British military musician to be given an officer's rank, and the Brain family, whose most famous member was the horn player, Dennis Brain. Perhaps the most celebrated and interesting case is found in the legacy of Tommy Sullivan, the son of a serving soldier who was deposited in the Royal Military Asylum as a child. He was appointed one of the first professors at the Military School of Music when it opened in 1857. Yet more famous was his talented son Arthur, who became Master of the Queen's Music and the musical half of the Gilbert and Sullivan partnership.[24]

The military legacy and earlier amateur bands

The legacy of military music on brass bands was direct and powerful, and it manifested itself in several ways across Europe. Jacob Kappey, a German-born British bandmaster who was commissioned to write the entry on 'Wind Instruments' for the first edition of Grove's *Dictionary of Music and Musicians*, claimed that he had communicated with bandmasters across Europe to determine the number of active military musicians in existence. He omitted certain types of band, including those deployed in the colonies, but concluded that 'at the lowest estimation [there are] over 51,000 military musicians'.[25] The sheer size of the military market had consequences. The instruments that constitute the brass band were introduced for the military band market and many of the first band trainers/conductors were alumni of regimental or militia bands. They also laid down a standard of playing that probably elevated that which was in place for brass players in classical music. That brass bands came to wear military-style uniforms was neither a random choice nor a superficial detail. It was an imitation of the military band because it represented the model to which brass players aspired. This legacy may also explain why attitudes such as discipline and deference to musical leadership were embraced so willingly by amateur brass bands.

The military occupied a position of power and influence in Victorian society and this extended to the rest of the musical world, not least because of its quantitative importance to the British music business. The extent of this influence was made apparent in 1865–6 when the Society of Arts reviewed the quality of musical training in Britain. The existing civilian institutions seemed to be having a limited effect, and the oldest of them, the Royal Academy of Music, was found to be dysfunctional and operating as little more than a finishing school for privileged adolescents. One mother, when asked why her two daughters were students at the Academy even though they had neither an aptitude for, nor interest in, music, replied that her doctor had advised it. Only the military was found to be addressing the needs of the music profession.[26]

In the first half of the nineteenth century numerous amateur bands existed: they were small and usually rural. Some included brass instruments, but few were made up solely of them. Anglican churches formed bands to accompany psalm-singing, most of which were defunct by the second half of the nineteenth century when they were replaced by barrel organs, harmoniums or organs. Many brass bands established from the middle of the century claim distant origins in village bands of one sort or other. The Black Dyke Band traces its origins to a band formed by the publican Peter Wharton in 1816.[27] What Wharton's band was or did is not accurately determined, but it certainly existed. It is tempting to see in such groups the remnants and influence of the first generation of militia bands, because what we know of their instrumentations suggests this, but the evidence is scarce and what evidence there is shows no consistent pattern. In the 1830s and 1840s, bands of various formations were set up on a professional or semi-professional basis and advertised their services as 'quadrille bands' – the quadrille was one of the most popular dances of the day. The one thing of which we can be certain is that in most regions of Britain there was instrumental music-making of some type. Music has always served a social purpose and there is abundant evidence that such purposes were being served. Reports of the local celebrations that marked the coronation of Queen Victoria in 1838, for example, reveal the extent to which small country towns and villages could call on groups of instrumentalists. It has been estimated that in five counties in the southwest of England there may have been five to six thousand instrumental musicians at the start of Victoria's reign.[28] It is unlikely that many played brass instruments because they were not widely circulated by that time. Besses o' th' Barn Band on the outskirts of Manchester claims to have originated as the band of a yeomanry regiment. This makes sense, as do many similar claims.[29] The part-time version of the army was the most likely organisation capable of bringing together coherent ensembles, and there must have been a time when the instruments acquired for militia bands had lost their original purpose and passed to a different use.

More interesting are the scattered claims for the early existence of bands that were constituted exclusively of brass instruments, and particularly why such a characteristic became the subject of boasts. In 1896 Enderby Jackson, an impresario who receives considerable attention later in this book, wrote with typical self-confidence that the first British all-brass band was formed in 1832 in Blaina, Gwent (the old county of Monmouthshire in southeast Wales). More precisely, he claimed it was formed at Brown Brothers' Iron Mill in the village of Pontybederyn.[30] Pontybederyn has left no topographical trace, but Jackson's command of the Welsh language – even in respect of place names – was probably frail. There was, indeed, an iron works in Blaina between 1818 and the 1830s and one of its owners was called Brown, but he had no brothers and there is no evidence that his foundry had a brass band. It is possible that Jackson may have known something that the surviving sources do not tell us, but this seems unlikely.

The most convincing early record of an all-brass band is found in Preston, Lancashire. In 1838 a letter was sent from a Mr Edward Kirkby to a local dignitary, Mr Thomas Clifton of Lytham Hall. Kirkby ran a civilian band that touted for work. The letter, irrespective of its idiosyncratic spellings, tells us much about it and how it conducted its business:

Sir, by the desire of a Fue Respectable Friends of yours in Preston has caused hus to write to you with a petition as a Solisitation for a job of Playing at your Dinnering Day as they told hus is taking place on Tuesday the 10 March Inst. At Lytham which if you are having a Band of Music at Dinner we shall be very glad to be ingadged for you on that Day it is one of the first Bands in the country. Our Band consists of 10 in number it is a Brass Band and the Name of the Band is the United Independent Harmonic Brass Band Preston which our charge is not so much considering the Band the charge or Pay for hus for one Day is 8/6 each man for the number of 10 comes to £4-5-0 and Meat and Drink as soon as we get their and all the time we stay their, if so happen we have to come if you make up your mind for hus to come to Play for dinner on that Day we shall please no doubt.

N.B. if writing for hus you must Direct to our leader Edwd. Kirkby Leader of the United Independent Harmonic Brass Band at No, 31 Alfred St Preston. We can come either in uniform or not according to weather,

From your Humble Servants[31]

Little more is known of Preston's United Independent Harmonic Brass Band or of Edward Kirkby, its conscientious leader (census and other records show the only person of that name in the district was a part-time insurance agent). It would have been interesting to know of what his band was 'independent', but its status as a brass band was regarded as a selling point.

Private brass bands

Most nineteenth-century private brass bands pre-dated the amateur brass band movement and must be regarded as different because their circumstances were always distinctive. The patronage they received was of a very traditional type and often had characteristics similar to those that had been common in the classical music world. Early amateur brass bands often benefited from philanthropic patronage but usually at arm's length and most were soon able to run their own affairs. Private bands were different. They were established to serve purposes determined by their patron. A precedent was set by bands attached to London's royal palaces. For example, the Duke of Cumberland's Band, which pre-dated the accession of Queen Victoria, had a mixed brass and reed instrumentation. Its repertoire, which survives almost intact, reflects the social roles for which it was formed: a mixture of dance music and light music of the type that might have been heard in the background in assemblies of the wealthier classes.[32] Similar bands were established in Britain by members of the aristocracy and successful industrialists. Some became all-brass bands and usually included professionally experienced players. Their purpose was to serve the needs of their patron and the social milieu in which they moved. Repertoires reflected those roles and, unlike amateur working-class bands, they did not develop democratic structures for their governance.

The landowner and parliamentarian Sir Walter Burrell maintained a private brass band which he called the Ockenden Band – Ockenden was the name of his residence in West Grinstead Park, Sussex. The band seems to have been formed around 1860 as a Volunteer band under Burrell's sponsorship. He employed a 'professor' to attend once a week to instruct it.[33] At Christmas the band was required to spend a day 'visiting the principal gentry', delivering a seasonal musical greeting from Burrell.[34] As was the case with other private bands, it was allowed to perform at outside events. Such was the case in 1869, when a harvest festival was 'enlivened during the afternoon by excellent performance of the Ockenden Band, which attended by permission of W. W. Burrell Esq.'.[35]

Terms such as 'attended by permission of' were common when private brass bands played away from home. A similar arrangement pertained for the band of Francis Egerton, who became the first Earl of Ellesmere. It was formed on the Earl's commission by Thomas Lee, an early conductor of the Besses o' th' Barn Band. Little is known about its repertoire, and aspects of its history are unclear. According to W. M. Millington, whose *Sketches of Local Musicians* was published in 1884, the band was mainly made up of woodwind instruments but also included a serpent and two horns.[36] The instrumentation must have changed at some point because several newspaper reports mention public events held at Worsley Hall on the Ellesmere estate at which an unnamed brass band was in attendance. According to Millington, Lee was eventually required to surrender his post because he was not a brass player. The other bandmaster associated with the Earl of Ellesmere was John Ellwood, who appears to have been an important local musician and is cited elsewhere as one of England's few civilian, provincial, professional trumpet players.[37] His status as bandmaster to the Earl earned him an appointment as one of the adjudicators at the first Belle Vue brass band contest in 1853. The other two adjudicators were senior military bandmasters.

Also in Yorkshire was the private band attached to the Marriner textile mills. It was formed in 1845 under the patronage of W. L. Marriner. There is little doubt that Marriner's motives were altruistic and aligned to the rational recreation idea. A surviving minute book states that it was formed 'for mutual amusement and instruction in music, and as peace and harmony are essential to its welfare, it is highly requisite that no dispute or angry feeling should arise among its members'. It went on to enshrine a regulation that imposed a financial penalty 'for every oath or angry expression' issued by members. One can only assume that such a provision was necessary. A second minute book, opened in 1852, states that the band had been 'remodelled' in November that year but remained the 'private band of W. L. Marriner'.[38] The remodelling came about because 'Henry Distin's classification' had been adopted: this meant that the band had adopted Distin's instrumentation based on saxhorns. The band seems to have been run by its players under the strict regulatory control of Marriner.

In Scotland a band was formed in 1804 at Taymouth Castle on the estate of the Marquis of Breadalbane and existed for almost 70 years. The Distin family, which was to have a critical role in the launch of the brass band movement, was connected to this band. John Distin, previously a trumpeter and keyed bugle player in the band of King George IV, was bandmaster and it was here that he trained his four sons to play. They were to become famous as the Distin Family Quintet.[39] The Breadalbane band's musical identity was adjusted as new species of instruments were introduced. At its start, it was made up of 11 apprentice boys and a bass drum player under the direction of a bandmaster. In 1844 it had 21 members, all of whom played brass instruments or percussion. From 1853 the band was using bombardons (see Glossary) and saxhorns. As such, it must have resembled the amateur working-class brass bands that were being formed across the country. Its members received payment for their services, even though most also had other work on the Breadalbane estate.[40]

5. *The Cyfarthfa Band assembled to play at the wedding of the daughter of the band's patron Robert Thompson Crawshay in 1871. Crawshay was almost certainly the photographer, and this is one of the few pictures of brass bands of the period in which the band is not playing but is not posed.*

Probably the most sophisticated private band was the Cyfarthfa Band, which was formed in 1840 at Cyfarthfa Castle in the industrial town of Merthyr Tydfil (fig. 5). At that time, Merthyr was the largest town in Wales and the world's most important centre for the manufacture of iron. The band was formed by Robert Thompson Crawshay soon after he assumed the management of the Cyfarthfa iron works. The Crawshay family was English, but investment in mining in the upper south Wales valleys had produced a wealth sufficient for the building of an entire castle for its accommodation.[41] An invoice from Charles Pace, the London musical instrument dealer, shows that Crawshay bought three keyed bugles in 1840. In the same year a local newspaper announced the band's first appearance 'under the patronage of Mr R. T. Crawshay'. There appears to have been a reset in 1846, the year of Crawshay's marriage, and it is possible that the new mistress of the castle, Rose Mary Crawshay (née Yeates) may have had a hand in this. She was artistically inclined and intellectually gifted, qualities of which her husband could not be accused. A new bandmaster was appointed, along with several experienced players. Most were professionals from itinerant circus and menagerie bands; others had been members of militia or military bands. At least one of the early recruits had been a member of the band of the Vauxhall pleasure gardens in London. The bandmaster was employed full-time for no purpose other than to direct the band and arrange its repertoire. Players were given work that allowed them time to fulfil their musical duties. Those who had defected from travelling-show bands would have found such arrangements a welcome contrast to their previous uncomfortable and unpredictable circumstances.

The Cyfarthfa Band is important because we know so much about it. It is possible to make accurate judgments about *how* it played as well as what was performed and when. No other band of the period, anywhere in the world, has left such a large and vivid collection of sources to reveal its intimate identity. It includes documents, photographs, many of the original instruments and more than a hundred handwritten part-books containing the band's day-to-day repertoire.

It competed in the Crystal Palace contest of 1860 (it won on the second day), but was otherwise exclusively engaged to serve the needs of its founder, and was independent of the wider brass band move-ment. Because its part-books are handwritten with annotations by the players, the repertoire reveals the band's virtuosity and style: it would have been futile for band members to have been presented with music that it could not play. The two major segments of reper-toire are dance music that was played at the elaborate balls that were regularly held by the Crawshay family, and transcriptions of classical music. The latter category includes opera overtures but also complete symphonies – all four movements of works by classical composers. Whoever selected the music for transcription was aware of the latest trends and fashions in European classical music. The music played by the band of Sir Walter Burrell does not survive, but printed programmes show a broad similarity of purpose to that of the Cyfarthfa Band: all intended for the entertainment and edification of a soph-isticated audience.

The Cyfarthfa Band had about 20 players. It used both keyed and valve instruments. Some of its keyed bugle and ophicleide players were among the best in the country. For example, Samuel Hughes, the ophicleide player, was to play with London's major orchestras, and in 1857 became the first professor of the instrument at both the Military School of Music at Kneller Hall and the Guildhall School of Music. When valve instruments were introduced, Crawshay shunned British makers and sent for instruments from the finest makers in Vienna.[42]

In 1850 an article appeared in *Household Words*, a widely circulated magazine edited by Charles Dickens. It was titled 'Music in Humble Life' and described the advent of working-class brass bands and the value of their patronage. It wrongly placed the Cyfarthfa Band in this context:

Another set of harmonious blacksmiths awaken the echoes of the remotest Welsh mountains. The correspondent of a London paper, while visiting Merthyr, was exceedingly puzzled by hearing boys in the Cyfarthfa works whistling airs rarely heard except in the fash-ionable ball-room, or drawing room. He afterwards discovered that the proprietor of the works Mr Robert Crawshay, had established among his men a brass band . . . I had the pleasure of hearing them play, and was astonished by their proficiency. They number sixteen instruments. I heard them perform the overture to *Zampa*, *The Caliph of Bagdad* and *Fra Diavolo*, *Vivi tu*, some concerted music from *Roberto*, *Don Giovanni* and *Lucia* with a quantity of Waltzes, Polkas and dance music . . . The habits and manners of these men appear to have decidedly improved by these softening influences.[43]

The piece was written by the music critic George Hogarth, Dickens's father-in-law. In some respects, it is accurate enough – for example, all the works mentioned were indeed in the band's repertoire and Hogarth was a reliable journalist; but the inference that the band was the product of Crawshay's altruism is open to question. By 1850 people of his social station were keen to be seen as contributing to the 'improvement in manners' of the working class that the article mentioned, but this was never Crawshay's intention: it was an entirely private band founded primarily as an accoutrement of the style of life he had designed for himself. These private bands were important in the history of British music and have been largely overlooked, but their main importance in the formation of the nationwide working-class brass band movement came from the modest inspiration and example they might have provided to others with more genuinely philanthropic motives. Otherwise, they played only a minor role in the Victorian origins of the brass band movement.

Chapter 2

Brass instruments, their technologies and their voices

Of the several circumstances that combined to launch brass bands as a mass activity in Britain, the introduction and wide availability of new species of instrument was the most important. These instruments worked well, whether played individually or together, and had unprecedented musical qualities. They were also elegant, ergonomic and relatively easy to learn. They were invented at a time when commercial structures were sufficiently developed for them to be produced at scale and sold at reasonable prices in new market segments. A newly invigorated sector of the manufacturing and retail business consequently emerged. These three elements – inventions, production and the factors that made their mass distribution and consumption possible – combined to cause the advent of the British amateur brass band.

This was part of one of the great interruptions in the history of musical instruments. The two most important stages through which brass band instruments passed after their initial introduction were the move towards a standard format for contesting bands, and developments in the period following the 1960s that led to modernisations, but the remarkable truth is that the core, distinctive sound of the British brass band was created by the Victorian working class. Subsequent developments to the idiom built on features that were formulated in the first few decades of the brass band movement.

Saxhorns in the age of invention

If a single event can be regarded as the point of ignition of the brass band movement, it is probably the meeting that took place on the morning of 4 February 1844 at the Rue Saint-Georges, Paris, when John Distin and his four sons, who made up the itinerant British brass group known as the Distin Family Quintet, met the Belgian-born instrument maker Adolphe Sax at his workshop (fig. 6). They had seen and heard Sax instruments the previous evening at the Salle Herz. The maker had started to prefix some of his inventions with his name: sax-trumpet and later saxophone, for example. Prominent among them was a complete family of instruments that shared a similar design but were made in several sizes so as to cover the spectrum from the lowest- to the highest-pitched members of the family. He had christened them 'saxhorns'. When the Distins played them at Sax's workshop, the impression gained the previous evening was confirmed and even enhanced: they were the best instruments they had played or heard.

6. The Distin Family Quintet depicted in an 1845 lithograph by Charles Baugniet. The instruments shown are saxhorns with forward-pointing bells. One of those pictured survives in the collection of the Horniman Museum, London.

They immediately adopted them and struck a deal with Sax to be the British agents for his saxhorns. A month later they were back in Paris at the invitation of the composer Hector Berlioz to perform on them at one of his concerts. A letter from John Distin to an Irish correspondent, dated 23 August, captures the sequence of events and the impact they had on him:

> We were on the point of returning to England a long time previous to this, when we were requested to stop and try some newly invented Instruments, which had been tried by several French artists who found them too difficult and complicated to make any effect with them; but we knew immediately we tried them, that they would prove everything wished, and after a little practice we played them with the most unparalleled success. The instruments are of a most peculiarly curious construction, called 'The Sax Horns', and the tone surpassingly beautiful beyond the power of description, – we threw by our own instruments, and have never touched them since – we played at the Grand Annual Concert of the 'Societé Des Beaux Arts' to an audience of above 2,000 persons, where our reception was most brilliant.[1]

The 'Sax Horns' were valve instruments and included what were eventually to be called in Britain tenor horns, baritones, euphoniums and the two sizes of bass instrument (tubas) that were to form the core of the British brass band sound. They were ultra-modern. A band formed in 1850, using saxhorns imported to Britain by Distin, would have been using instruments that did not exist less than a decade previously. In a century when a bewildering number of different brass instrument designs were introduced, there were many that were excellent, but saxhorns stood out and they soon revitalised this segment of the music industry. Some instruments that preceded saxhorns, such as althorns and clavicors, were also excellent, as were the cornets made by Besson and Courtois, but it was saxhorns that ignited interest in the middle of the century. They certainly made an impression on Distin, who regarded their sound as 'beautiful beyond the power of description'. Within a couple of years, other British and European manufacturers were producing instruments that were thinly disguised imitations of Sax's designs. Sax did not invent valve instruments, nor was he the only maker to improve them, but his instruments consistently played in tune and could be learned relatively easily by using just three valves. That there was a family of instruments of similar design meant that instruments of different sizes blended perfectly when played together.

Attempts to improve the design of brass instruments in the nineteenth century were aimed at providing players with more efficient and melodically versatile instruments. The historical progress of these objectives can be broadly understood as they unfolded, by reference to documents submitted by the many makers who registered their designs for a patent aimed at protecting their work from piracy. Patent registrations contain detailed information about the design (including drawings), its inventor (the patentee) and the claims made for its uniqueness. When a patent was registered, it protected the invention for a defined period (usually five years) in a particular country or region. It is difficult to estimate the number of new brass instrument designs or improvements that were introduced because not all were registered for patents, but it is certain that only a small proportion of those developed at that time survived to have common use in the following century. Those not consigned to total obscurity are preserved in museums and other collections. Many were ingenious and practical but encountered neither an immediate market nor a business model that might have created one for them: the two elements that became essential in the new age of music commerce.

Saxhorns were the most successful valve instrument designs of their time. Eventually, but not immediately, valve instruments would replace those such as the keyed bugle and the ophicleide that used older technologies. These older models were not routinely abandoned as new designs were introduced. The keyed bugle and ophicleide, both of which were revolutionary at the time of their introduction, were used alongside valve instruments for at least a generation. Experienced and expert keyed bugle players, for example, will have recognised no urgent need to change from an instrument upon which they had acquired refined skills to another on which they had none. Photographs of early brass bands and other documentary records (such as concert programmes and contest entry forms) show bands to have had a mixture of old and newer instrument types until at least the end of the 1870s. Many mid-nineteenth-century bands also included a clarinet player, who would have been allocated one of the high treble parts. The inclusion of a clarinet player may have just reflected the availability of a skilled player in a particular locality, but in 1861 one band imposed an extra subscription on its members to pay for a new brass clarinet.[2] Understandably, instrument manufacturers did all they could to hasten the transition from keyed to valve instruments. A favoured ploy was to sponsor prizes for the best soloist of the day at brass band contests. Winners were often star ophicleide players – their prize was usually a new euphonium.

The members of the Distin family were entrepreneurial as well as musical; they recognised that Sax's products were special and had a commercial as well as a musical future. They were also able to distinguish between the many alternatives that were in circulation. This was not an easy task because there were so many of them. Among them we might count inventors whose optimism outweighed realism. In this category we can include William Wyatt, a trumpeter at the Royal Italian Opera at Covent Garden and by all accounts a fine player. Even at the end of the nineteenth century he remained resolutely loyal to the chromatic slide trumpet, an instrument that had been abandoned by most players two generations previously. In 1890 he designed a new version in the hope of its resurrection. Several survive in museums, but one wonders how many were originally made and sold.

There were also eccentrics whose grasp on commercial reality was fragile. In this category, Thomas Goulston Ghislin is conspicuous. Ghislin was an insolvent music hall artist and serial correspondent to various newspapers and magazines. Between 1860 and 1864, he registered four separate patents for substances that he believed could be a base ingredient in the manufacture of parts of brass instruments.[3] These substances included dog skin and seaweed. Seaweed was a material in which he appears to have had an obsessive interest. He claimed that after appropriate chemical transformations, it would be a perfect substance for the manufacture of brass instrument mouthpieces. He further claimed that it could also be used for the manufacture of cutlery handles and spectacle frames.

Most nineteenth-century inventors were less inclined to irrational speculation and more strategic. They directed their energies at solving long-standing problems by gaining a careful understanding of them and calculating their scientific solutions. Brass musical instruments were the focus of many fruitful projects through the nineteenth century. New instruments were invented, and improvements were introduced to those that existed. It was the application of inventive brilliance that created brass instruments in the forms in which they became known in the modern world. This led inevitably to adjustments to the way the brass instrument family was understood by composers, performers and the public at large. The pace of change was such that brass musical instruments became a favourite topic for parody by cartoonists (see fig. 7). Some innovations were deeply controversial, especially in the world of classical music, where they were seen as unwelcome interventions to established and cherished continuities. The introduction of the valved french horn as a replacement for valveless 'natural' horns was particularly hotly contested, especially in France. A Paris Conservatoire professor noted in 1865 that the 'prejudice against the *cor à pistons* [valve horn] is so deep rooted that the most skilful artists have disdained this instrument'.[4]

The complaint here was that new technologies were being routinely rejected by the classical music establishment; but it would be wrong to assume that such rejection was the product of reactionary prejudice – it came more often from a heartfelt concern for the demise of the nuanced sound that skilled players of the natural horn had perfected over generations. It was an established musical voice that many held in deep affection. So passionate were the opposing views that the natural horn and the valve horn were taught at the Paris Conservatoire in separate classes by different professors until the start of the twentieth century.[5]

The speed of change caused problems for some in the classical music world because the attendant aesthetic implications were difficult to digest. But the importance of what was happening must have been glaringly apparent to anyone for whom music was important. This is probably why, irrespective of the introduction of instruments such

"A Wind Instrument of the Future!

7. It was not unusual for mechanised brass instruments to be satirised. This drawing, 'A Wind Instrument of the Future', was commissioned by Algernon Rose for his 1895 book Talks with Bandsmen.

as cornets and saxhorns, and leaving aside the introduction of the orchestral tuba, the orchestral brass section remained essentially unchanged at the start of the twentieth century from the configuration of trumpets, horns and trombones that was known to Beethoven. Trumpets and horns gained valves, but their basic shape and much of their musical purpose remained largely unaltered until the second half of the century. But this apparent consistency obscures some important and controversial forces for change. There was a period when cornets posed an existential threat to the trumpet, and the valve trombone posed a danger of equal proportions to the future of the slide instrument.

At the time of their introduction (around 1830), valve trombones were primarily aimed at the bands of cavalry regiments, but they were used extensively in other types of military band of many European countries and soon became the instruments of choice in some orchestras. For example, between 1862 and 1883 valve trombones were used exclusively in the Vienna Philharmonic Orchestra. This means that the first performances by that orchestra of the symphonies of Brahms (often seen as the arch traditionalist) were played on valve rather than slide trombones. Valve trombones were also ubiquitous in bands and orchestras in central Europe and in Italian opera houses. This is why modern trombonists who use slide instruments find some of Verdi's trombone parts tricky – they were originally written for valve trombones. Photographs of early orchestras in the United States usually show valve rather than slide trombones. Many of the instruments used in early jazz bands came from Hispanic South American military bands. According to the testimonies of early players, the slide trombone was unknown in New Orleans until about 1911 – only valved trombones were previously used.[6] Photographs of early jazz bands, including those of the Buddy Bolden band (the earliest known photograph of a jazz band) and Kid Ory, show valve instruments. When slide instruments became available, many players continued using valve instruments for more respectable, 'legitimate' dance music and turned to the slide instrument for 'hotter' jazz in which slide glissando was prominent. It is in this series of events that we find the origin of 'tailgate jazz'.[7] In Britain, valve trombones appear to have had a less sure footing, but many were sold, bought and played. They were sufficiently conspicuous for the organisers of brass band contests, even in the twentieth century, to insist that only slide trombones could be used because it was believed that valve trombone players gained an unfair advantage over slide instrument players.

Newer species such as the euphonium and cornet were introduced in symphony orchestras for dramatic or programmatic effect, but in theatres and opera houses there was greater willingness to admit new colours. For example, the orchestral parts for Bizet's *Carmen* require cornets rather than trumpets and the same was the case in the Savoy operettas of Gilbert and Sullivan. The new families of brass instruments were deployed primarily and liberally in military bands and brass bands. Indeed, the almost universal use of the term 'military musical instruments' in newspaper and magazine advertisements became a signifier of the market at which they were directed. This was an important parting of the ways between orchestras as the agencies of a long-standing sonic tradition, with its own distinctive repertoires and styles, and bands as exponents of sound worlds that were different and essentially new. This distinction was to be permanent, even though brass and military bands were to be the main recruiting ground for orchestral players. It was a matter of idiom, and brass players who have crossed between the two worlds will have experienced its meaning and effect. The one is defined by the legacy of the art music canon and the configuration of the orchestra, the other by a more recent and, in many ways, more radical set of musical rules and experiments. All this converged to change the understandings that had prevailed for brass instruments and their players for centuries.

'Natural instruments' and the chromaticism problem

The matters of greatest impact for brass bands occurred in overlapping stages in the nineteenth century. The chronology is interesting because each new or amended design was usually aimed at resolving a single, long-standing challenge that might be termed the 'chromaticism problem'.[8] The challenge was to design instruments that provided players with unhindered access to a 'chromatic compass'. A chromatic compass can be seen on any piano keyboard: from the lowest to the highest note, each note succeeds the one before in the shortest (semitone) steps across adjacent white and black notes. A basic 'natural' brass instrument – by which is meant an instrument that incorporates no mechanical device such as valves or slides to change notes (a bugle is a good example) – cannot produce all notes in its range because the laws of physics prevent it.

All brass instruments work fundamentally in the same way. Players blow into a 'mouthpiece' which is designed to encourage the lips to vibrate as a passage of air flows through them. A sound wave then travels through a length of tubing (the sounding length) before encountering a terminal horn-shaped flare (called the 'bell') which reflects some of the sound energy back towards the mouthpiece and radiates the rest as audible sound which is heard as a musical note. A fixed length of tubing, with no mechanical apparatus incorporated (which is what a bugle is), can produce a fixed series of notes called a 'harmonic series'. In this series, the notes are not adjacent to each other until very high in the instrument's register, which, for brass players, is more challenging to play than lower notes. The lower notes (easier to play) are separated by significant gaps. This is why bugle calls sound so repetitive of each other and are so easy for composers to imitate: buglers mostly play melodies using just five notes from the lowest part of the series. If an instrument of the same type had a longer length of tubing, it would play a lower series of notes, but the *pattern* of that series of notes would be identical. Several methods have been devised in the history of brass instruments to solve this problem. Trumpeters and horn players used extensions to their tubing (called 'shanks' or 'crooks', according to their size and shape) to lower the overall pitch of their instruments. Elite trumpeters mastered a technique for playing in the high range of the series where notes lie close together (this technique and range is called 'clarino'). Horn players also used a technique known as 'hand-stopping'. But from the start of the nineteenth century, several mechanical solutions emerged in rapid succession. They are best explained by reference to the types of mechanism deployed at different times.[9]

Instruments with slides

Brass instruments can be fully chromatic only if players are able to adjust the length of tubing through which they blow as they are playing and without extraneous effort or interruption. A mechanism that provides an instrument with unhindered access to several different harmonic series would make it chromatic. A vivid example of how this can be done is seen in the design of the trombone – one of the most brilliantly simple and effective of all musical inventions. Early trombones are often called sackbuts, derived from similar words that appear in early English, French and Hispanic manuscripts. However, the word 'sackbut' can be misleading because it might convey an impression that it was a fundamentally different instrument to the one used in modern times. In fact, while the sound of early and more modern instruments is demonstrably different, their mechanism is similar, and in Italian such instruments were always called *tromboni*.

We don't know when or where the trombone was invented, but we can say with certainty that it existed by the final quarter of the fifteenth century. We know this because there is evidence of various types to prove it – most conspicuously, a fresco by Filippino Lippi in the Church of Santa Maria sopra Minerva in Rome, which clearly shows a trombone being played. The fresco was completed between 1488 and 1492, so it is a fair assumption that the instrument was well known and had been in use for several years by that time. It shows all the necessary characteristics of the modern slide trombone.[10] The instrument is also described and illustrated in the earliest printed book on musical instruments, *Musica getutscht* (1511) by the priest and chorister Sebastian Virdung,[11] and in more detail along with other brass instruments in common use about a century later, in *Syntagma Musicum* by the German musician and theorist Michael Praetorius (fig. 8).

Trombone players extend and retract a double, telescopic, 'U'-shaped slide and, in so doing, they extend or shorten the length of tubing that is being blown through. At each position to which the slide is extended, a different, lower-pitched harmonic series is available. It follows that the trombone was fully chromatic from the time it was introduced. It also, and unlike most other wind instruments of the time, had a wide dynamic range: it could be played loudly, softly or at various levels in between. Taking these qualities together, it should be no surprise that the trombone was one of the most important instruments in the Renaissance period. It was made in different sizes, from the bass to the alto ranges, with the tenor instrument being most popular. Attempts to make slide instruments in the higher treble (soprano) range had mixed success until the turn of the eighteenth and nineteenth centuries.

The trombone was obsolete in several countries including Britain for most of the hundred years following the late seventeenth century. This was because of the abandonment of the practice of using them

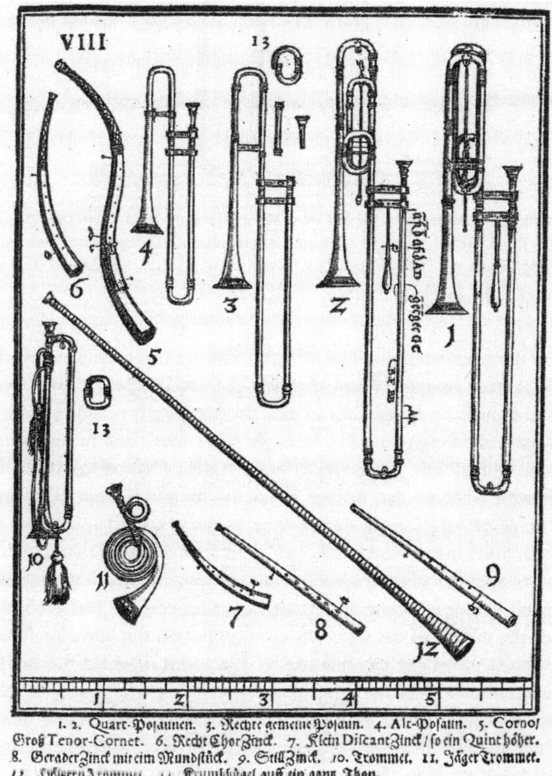

8. *Trombones, a valveless ('natural') trumpet and cornetti/Zinken, illustrated in Michael Praetorius's* Syntagma Musicum, *Vol. II, 1619/20.*

to support vocal lines in sacred music, and a wider tendency to favour matching string and wind sonorities. From the late eighteenth century, it regained favour. Around the same time in London a new instrument of choice for leading professional trumpet players emerged, called the slide or 'chromatic' trumpet. This instrument had the traditional trumpet shape, but it incorporated a short slide with a 'return' device, such as a watch spring or an elasticated strap. The slide was operated by the player's right hand and the return device exerted a light pressure towards the closed position to make its operation easy. It was invented by John Hyde, who described and illustrated it in his *New and Complete Preceptor for the Trumpet . . .* of c. 1799. An important reason for the success of this model was its adoption by Thomas Harper, the greatest British trumpeter of his generation, and his talented son of the same name. The two were professors of the trumpet at the Royal Academy of Music and dominated the trumpet-playing profession in London in the first half of the nineteenth century. Several English chromatic trumpets survive, probably the majority of all that were manufactured because there were not many professional trumpeters in England at this time.

Instruments with finger holes and keys

Other methods for accessing chromaticism were developed before the sixteenth century. The early trombone was routinely partnered with an instrument known in Italian as the *cornetto* (plural *cornetti*), in Britain as 'cornett' and German as *Zink*. This instrument was not related to the nineteenth-century brass cornet, other than that both are lip-vibrated instruments. The cornett was made of wood and bound in leather. It had six finger holes on its upper side and a thumb hole on the underside: in this respect, it closely resembled the design of the recorder. Covering and uncovering the holes had the effect of changing the sounding length, so this instrument too was played using all notes within its range. It was an instrument of immense importance in the Renaissance and some of the greatest virtuosi of the period were cornett players. Modern period-instrument specialists have rediscovered and perfected the techniques originally associated with the instrument to reveal the extraordinary levels of skill and invention that were exercised by its players. The cornett was obsolete by the end of the eighteenth century, but a bass version of the instrument, called the 'serpent' because of its shape, lasted into the nineteenth century.

Instruments such as the 'keyed bugle' and the 'ophicleide', both introduced early in the nineteenth century, also operated on the principle of opening and closing holes on the instrument, but both incorporate key mechanisms like those used on woodwind instruments such as the clarinet and bassoon. The keyed bugle was probably invented by Joseph Haliday, a Yorkshire-born musician serving in Ireland as bandmaster of the Cavan Militia.[12] It received a London patent in May 1810. Some later models were called the 'Kent' or 'Royal Kent' bugle. It was the most successful and popular brass instrument in the treble voice prior to the wide adoption of valve instruments. Its tone colour was distinctive. It was used throughout the world, virtuosi emerged, and it attracted an idiomatic repertoire. The keyed bugle revealed the potential for brass instruments to play the treble/soprano line in both art and popular ensemble music at a time when the clarinet was more usually used for that purpose. It was also the main melodic brass instrument in those brass bands that reportedly and spasmodically existed in Britain before the 1840s, and subsequently, when brass bands used instrumental formats that were a hybrid of older and new designs. The flugelhorn, which gained popularity in brass bands from the 1860s, was introduced as a valved version of the keyed bugle – a sign perhaps that the distinctive sound of the keyed bugle was worthy of preservation. Only one flugelhorn is used in the standard brass band format but at various times there have been advocates for more to be included.[13]

The ophicleide was made in various sizes but was primarily conceived as the baritone/bass member of the keyed bugle family. It was invented in Paris by Jean Hilaire Asté and patented by him in 1821. In his patent submission, Asté mentioned that the instrument's primary purpose was to replace the serpent (the bass version of the cornett) which was, as he put it, 'very unrewarding and of a well-known inadequacy'. This was an interesting comment because at that time the serpent was embedded in both church and military music in France: only a few years previously a *Méthode de serpent* was privileged by its inclusion as one of the 14 instruction books that defined the curriculum of the Paris Conservatoire. The ophicleide preceded the invention of the tuba and was widely distributed. The writer George Bernard Shaw famously castigated it as a 'chromatic bullock', but this was gratuitous and wrong. We know enough about the instrument and the music that its players were required to perform to appreciate how good they were and how versatile the instrument could be. Many British brass bands incorporated ophicleides up to the late 1870s. Ophicleide players, like keyed bugle players, possessed instruments and skills that were sufficiently refined for there to be no reason why they should convert to newer models (fig. 9).

9. *Nineteenth-century instruments of the Cyfarthfa Band showing that different types of brass instruments were used simultaneously. From the top: a (rotary) valve euphonium, a keyed bugle, an ophicleide and a piston valve cornet.*

Valve instruments

The introduction of valved brass instruments is correctly regarded as a moment of immense importance in music history. When depressed, a valve diverts the airway to make the passage of notes longer, thus the pitch descends.[14] Several different valve designs have been patented, but each serves this same purpose. The most frequently encountered designs are piston valves, which are used in British brass bands, and rotary valves, which are favoured in the orchestras of many countries in continental Europe. Three valves, used individually and in combination, are sufficient to make an instrument fully chromatic. A fundamental feature of saxhorns, and the reason why they are referred to as a *family* of instruments, is that a similar pattern and shape was applied to instruments irrespective of the size – from high soprano to the low bass range – in which each was voiced.

The history of the development of the valve is lengthy and at times complex.[15] There were very early attempts at applying mechanisms to achieve the purpose that valves eventually fulfilled. For example, as early as 1766, Ferdinand Kölbel, a musician of the Bohemian court, developed a horn which combined six integrated crooks that were operated by push-buttons. The design generally recognised as the first modern valve system was also applied to the horn. It was developed no later than 1814 in Prussia by Heinrich Stölzel, himself a horn player, and Friedrich Blühmel, an oboist in a miners' band. The first petition for protection for a new chromatic horn was in Stölzel's name, but a patent registered in 1818 was in the names of both men. Early valve models were neither perfect nor widely distributed, and many contesting patents were registered. There have always been challenges for designers. Among these is the requirement for notes to be consistently in tune, irrespective of the valve combinations that are depressed; and similarly, the depression of valves should not impact negatively on the colour of the sound – the instrument's *timbre*. Other imperatives were also important for instruments to gain commercial success; for example, they needed to be ergonomic and light enough to be played comfortably by performers. The experience of playing the instrument needed to be uncomplicated and satisfying. Yet another consideration in the nineteenth century was for instruments to be free of complexities that might impact on their potential to be manufactured at scale. In general, these qualities were easier to achieve on brass instruments because, while there was always a need for detailed accuracy in their manufacture, the instruments were less delicate than members of the string and woodwind families (fig. 10).

Production and distribution

Nineteenth-century brass instrument designers and manufacturers vied for ascendancy in an environment that was unyieldingly competitive and often rancorous. Adolphe Sax was not immune: he was the subject of many litigations that could have ended in his ruin. Being Belgian, he was always regarded as a foreign interventionist by the French and was often the target of allegations of plagiarism. None

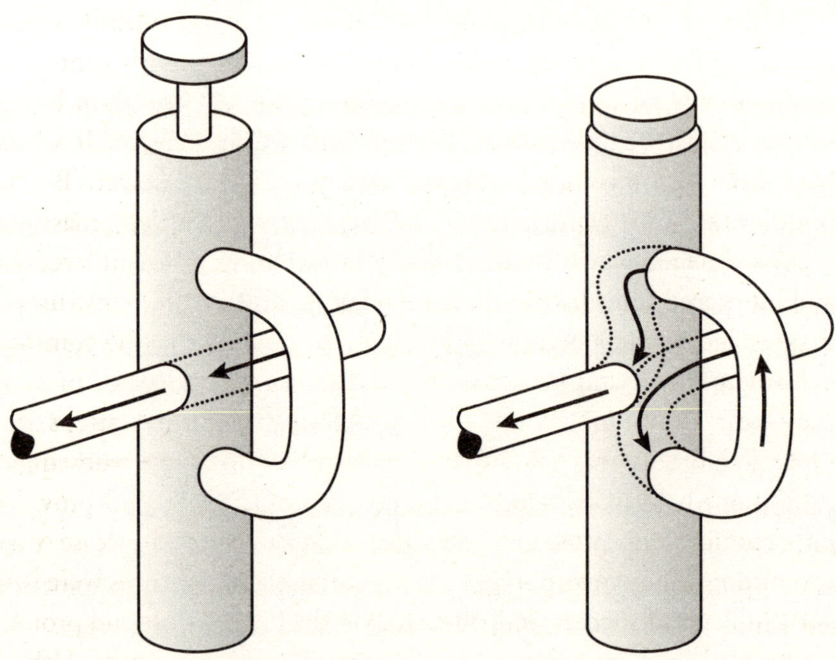

10. *Diagram showing how a valve when it is depressed causes the overall length of tubing to be longer. Other valve designs achieve the same results in different ways.*

of these charges have been fully substantiated by modern scholars. Plagiarism charges were not unusual in the nineteenth century, and it is often difficult to decipher whether instruments that had shared features were copies or were independent and coincidentally similar to each other. For example, the keyed trumpet (*Klappentrompete*), a chromatic instrument for which both Joseph Haydn (in 1796) and Johann Hummel (in 1803) wrote their trumpet concertos, was designed in Vienna by Anton Weidinger, probably based on a German model produced a few years previously. The keyed trumpet had a much more modest distribution than did the keyed bugle but, while both instruments employ very similar mechanisms, there is no evidence that Haliday knew of the Austro-German developments when he patented his keyed bugle in 1810.

Modes of manufacture and distribution changed quickly in the second half of the nineteenth century. In the eighteenth century, a trumpet or horn would have been made in a small workshop by the labour of just one craftsman, perhaps with an apprentice. It would have been commissioned directly by a professional player. By the middle of the nineteenth century, military bands had fuelled a massively increased demand, which was met by faster modes of manufacturing and more accessible distribution and retail systems. Musical instrument makers and retailers became increasingly conspicuous in the commercial environment and proactive in the markets they targeted. In 1851 the Great Exhibition of the Works of Industry of All Nations (the Great Exhibition) was held in Hyde Park in London. It and subsequent exhibitions held in Britain, continental Europe and the US provided opportunities for musical instrument developers to showcase their inventions. Many incorporated a competitive element; prizes were won and emblems of success were engraved on the instruments and proudly proclaimed in manufacturers' catalogues and advertisements. Urbanisation had made communications easier and more effective. The circulation of newspapers increased, as did the number of different newspapers and magazines that were in circulation. The literate working class tended to do their reading on Sundays, and newspapers such as *Reynolds's News* and the *News of the World* came into being to serve that market, but they were primarily political, devoid of 'human interest' stories and with stolid, unattractive formats. Most advertisements for brass band instruments were placed in regional newspapers, which also carried announcements relevant to band contests, and eventually in magazines aimed at bands. Magazines comprised a substantial part of the Victorian reading matter and probably had the greatest influence on the class of people who were influential in the funding of amateur brass bands. These magazines included *Household Words*, which ran from 1850 to 1859, and *All the Year Around* (1859–70), both of which were subtitled 'Conducted by Charles Dickens'. Dickens was the editor of both, with W. H. Wills his subeditor and co-owner. Each cost nine pence a month and were aimed at a wide readership that included the middle class and other influential sectors of society. There were no illustrations or advertisements, but the few substantial articles devoted to brass bands – such as 'Music in Humble Life', which focused on the Cyfarthfa Band under the patronage of Robert Thompson Crawshay – were probably influential.[16] 'Music in Humble Life' was well written, engaging, convincing and largely true. It was widely circulated and espoused the value of the patronage of this type of working-class music-making. As such, it verified the cultural value accrued from the patronage of amateur brass bands. These two ideas – that playing in a brass band was an inherently virtuous and rational activity, and that the working class could be easily diverted to such activity if the necessary facilities were available to them – were the main story in the article.

Such articles were known to manufacturers and distributors of brass instruments. Larger British firms, such as Pace, Besson, Boosey, Distin, Hawkes and Rudall Carte, were based in London. The main centre for manufacture in the nineteenth century was London, relatively distant from the north of England which was, initially at least, to be their primary market. While few amateur brass bands were set up in London, the most influential military bands, such as those of the household regiments and the Royal Artillery, were London-based. The skills of instrument making were traditionally centred in London and the necessary expansion was met to a significant degree by London-based foreign craftsmen. A further reason for setting up or expanding businesses in London was that it was the main source for credit through banks and other finance houses. But it did not take long for enterprising makers and retailers to establish businesses in the provinces. In Birmingham, Gisborne and Son opened in 1839, and in Manchester Joseph Higham opened three years later. It was Higham that supplied the instruments for the foundation of the Black Dyke Band:

John Foster & Son, having lately become acquainted with the depressed state of the [Queenshead village] band determined to make an effort themselves to raise it up again. Accordingly they have purchased from the eminent maker, Mr Joseph Higham, Victoria Bridge, Manchester, a new set of instruments which have this week been delivered to the band, that in future is to be denominated the 'Black Dike Mills Band'.[17]

Provincial businesses benefited from their proximity to a local market, but they never matched the production capacities of the London firms. By 1880 Higham employed a workforce of over 70 at its Manchester works and retail outlet.[18] In 1871–2 it claimed to produce around 750 brass band instruments a year. In the same period, Boosey, just one of the London-based firms, produced 1,600 instruments annually. Besson, a well-established French company, recognising that British people preferred to buy British rather than foreign instruments, set up a manufacturing plant in London in the 1850s. For much of the nineteenth century the internal stock books of the company's London plant were written entirely in French. By 1890 it employed 131 workers and was producing 100 instruments a week. It claimed to have produced a total of 52,000 instruments and had some 10,000 bands on its books. These figures have never been fully verified and are probably exaggerated, but there is little doubt that it was a thriving business that served a mass market.[19] The Distin family had the British agency for Sax and other Paris manufacturers but held them for only about six years before establishing its own business in London in 1850; it also published sheet music. In 1851, after giving up the Sax agency, it started designing and manufacturing its own instruments. By 1862 the company was employing 50 workers, most of whom were foreigners. Distin's instruments resembled those of Sax, but the 'sax' prefix was dropped in favour of other names, some of which are used in modern times. In 1868 the company was sold to Boosey.

The purchase of Distin by Boosey was one of the first of many such absorptions. Probably the largest was the merger of Boosey & Co. and Hawkes & Son in 1930. William Henry Hawkes had been a state trumpeter to Queen Victoria. He set up a repair shop in partnership with Jules Rivière in 1876 and developed a music-publishing company. In 1924 the company had a reported workforce of over 200 in a factory that had a floorspace of over an acre.[20] Other companies were established to serve the steadily expanding market. Brass instruments were not the only instruments made and sold by these companies, and the brass band market was not the only one to which brass instruments were sold, but it was a major segment and there are grounds for believing that the rapid appearance of brass bands from the mid-nineteenth century onwards contributed significantly to a more general and unprecedented growth of the music business at that time – a growth that has been termed by the leading economic historian of British music as 'the flood' because of its size, scope and the speed of its expansion.[21]

An important collection of the business records of brass band manufacturers and retailers survives under the custodianship of the Horniman Museum, London. It provides a valuable profile of the way businesses were run.[22] The archival documents of Distin & Co., including those for the period when the firm was operated by Boosey & Co., show that individual instruments or batches of instruments, whether made in response to particular orders or just to replenish stocks, were allocated to individual workmen, perhaps with assistants and/or apprentices, rather than to a less personalised production line. But the quantity of instruments produced each month suggests that basic components such as tubing, bells and valve sets were the product of specialist parts of the factory, while the final fabrication and assembly was in the hands of individual craftsmen. This practice, a hybrid of mass production and hand-finishing, may have been at the behest of the Boosey manager David Blaikley who, as an inventor and the leading British brass instrument acoustician of his day, would have been aware of the precision needed in brass instrument production. The system may have supplied a mass market, but it fell some way short of 'mass production' in the modern sense.

Most of the makers seem to have supplied bands rather than individual purchasers. Stock books show that each type of instrument was graded by quality. In the nineteenth century, instruments were often advertised and sold as sets rather than individually. This is one of the reasons why several manufacturers – Distin, Boosey, and Besson, for example – moved into music publishing. They published simple arrangements sold by subscription that could be easily adapted for the instruments at hand but were ideal for the set of instruments they recommended and sold. (More detail of this process and examples of the instrumentation of journal music is given in Appendix 1.)

The manufacturers' stock books also record despatches to military officers, indicating that the funding of military bands by officers' contributions to band funds continued well into the twentieth century. This was especially true of Rudall Carte & Co., which retailed instruments made by several manufacturers, sometimes rebranded with the Rudall Carte name. It had many British clients but also supplied Australia, New Zealand and South Africa. Some sales went directly to bands while others were directed to retailers, such as Whitehouse & Marlor in Brisbane, Marshall and Sons in Auckland, Hargreaves in Ontario and H. J. Bentley in Hong Kong.

'Silver bands' and other later developments

By 1900 British brass band instrumentation was almost entirely standardised for contesting. Manufacturers used as many advertising techniques as they could conjure to persuade bands to enhance their sound by buying a complete new set of instruments. Brass band periodicals, which were read avidly across the movement, were never free of trade interests; most were owned by, or were connected to, instrument manufacturers or music publishers. One of the most successful ways that manufacturers promoted sales from the 1880s was by advertising the prospect of a transformation from a brass to a 'silver band'. This meant that a new set of silver-plated instruments would be supplied. The acoustical impact of the process was entirely neutral, but many bands were seduced: they became 'silver bands' and adjusted their titles accordingly. It was not long before electro silver plating became a standard stage in manufacture.

New bands that were established after the Victorian period contributed to the buoyancy of the market. Among the bands that appeared in the first few decades of the new century were Foden's Motor Works Band (1902), Grimethorpe Colliery Band (1917) and Tullis Russell Mills (1919). The Munn and Felton Band (originally a shoe factory band but later operating under different names) was established in 1933, and the Fairey Aviation Band was formed in 1937.

While minor improvements were made to instruments at the turn of the century, particularly to euphoniums and basses, there were no major changes or adjustments to brass band instruments between the start of the century and the 1960s. A band that changed its instruments in the 1920s or 1930s may have been influenced by the commercial hype to which they were routinely subjected, but the only rational reason to have done so would have been a perception that the existing set had reached the end of its primary life and it was time to pass it on to its juvenile band. Throughout this period the suppliers of instruments to British brass bands were British, with three firms dominating the market – Besson, Boosey & Hawkes, and the Salvation Army, which supplied its bands through its own manufacturing plant north of London. The suppliers used similar instrument designs and, irrespective of claims to the contrary, it is difficult to discern a fundamental distinction between any of them. In this very basic sense, the brass band idiom became at least consolidated and more probably entrenched. They all used the same instrumentation and effectively the same or very similar instrument designs. Different bands dominated contests from time to time and several performers achieved stunning levels of virtuosity, but the main pillars of the idiom – the instruments and the way they were played – became settled and orthodox. Bands that rose above others – and many did so majestically – exercised the same orthodoxies with greater levels of accuracy and musical intelligence than others, but the most visible factor that generated contest success was the person who was conducting.

This, of course, was the period when original brass band repertoire made its major entrance. The composers who wrote those pieces did so with a clear idiom in mind and few did much to extend or challenge it. When a pitch change occurred in the 1960s it had various effects, but a key consequence was the eventual (temporary) decline of British-manufactured instruments in favour of American and Japanese. American trombones replaced older British models, but newer models of valved instruments were incremental developments of traditional British designs. Since the nineteenth century, American makers had been sensitive to the different musical markets that were developing and the types of instrument that each required. There were many more American than British manufacturers. Many of the finest were clustered in the small town of Elkhart, Indiana. Prominent among them was the company founded by Charles Gerard Conn in 1876.[23] The company records for the Conn corporation survive to reveal the various objectives for Conn instruments and the markets at which they were aimed. In the first half of the twentieth century it recognised three primary market segments: orchestras, which tended to use instruments suitable for the increasingly large halls and opera houses that were being built across the US; dance band and jazz players, who favoured smaller instruments (with narrower tubing); and probably its largest single market, the burgeoning college/high-school marching bands. The rise of the latter was substantially due to a collaboration between Conn and America's most celebrated band leader, John Philip Sousa. Sousa was seen as a musical emblem of America and Conn exploited sentiments that were not distant from the rational recreation idea used in Britain in the Victorian period (he visited Britain in 1876) to sell the moral and patriotic value of marching bands.

By the 1960s American brass instruments were ubiquitous in British orchestras, and lower-priced but good-quality instruments were also available as Japanese imports. The pitch change occasioned a switch to instruments that were often identical in design to those used in orchestras. This marked a major adjustment to a brass band sound world that had otherwise been uninterrupted for the greatest part of a century. It provided the material circumstances for a new era of creativity and performance excellence. This, in turn, led to further developments that saw the emergence of highly successful brands from new British and continental brass instrument manufacturers.

Chapter 3

The Victorian origins of the brass band movement

Brass bands originated as a mass working-class leisure activity when several events, trends and attitudes coalesced in the mid-1840s. The most important was the invention in about 1843 of saxhorns, a new family of brass instruments that became a central component of the British model of the brass band. This coincided with the introduction of new methods of production and distribution that made them available to an amateur working-class clientele. A further critical factor was the transformation that had occurred in the demography of Britain. From the start of the century there was an exponential increase in the size of the population, accompanied by major adjustments to its distribution. Much of the labour force shifted from rural work and habitation to occupations and settlements in more densely populated communities clustered around centres of industrial employment, such as mines, textile mills, foundries and factories. The speed and scope of these changes was a source of concern to more elevated classes, who saw in its pace and scope a threat to the maintenance of moral values and potentially to the preservation of social order. Several potential panaceas were exercised to counter these concerns. Prominent among them was the encouragement of 'rational recreation'. Rational recreation became a catch-all term for the idea that a collateral effect of urbanisation was the loss of traditions that had contributed to community cohesion, and that this unwelcome trend could be countered by the promotion of working-class leisure activities which, if they had a docile and improving nature, were likely to promote attitudes conducive to the building of a stable and morally healthy society. Working-class people, particularly men, were encouraged to spend their available time in activities compatible with this ideal. Allied to this was a belief that harmless communal activities that encouraged co-operation among groups of working-class men were especially welcome because they necessitated harmonisation. This would provide a basis from which mutually responsible social interchanges could flow. Music-making was seen as an especially potent form of rational recreation. 'The tendency of music is to soften the mind [and for the working man it is] a relaxation from toil more attractive than the haunts of intemperance', wrote one advocate in 1846.[1] Ideas about rational recreation quickly gained currency among the upper classes. For evidence of their weight, and the scope of their circulation, we need look no further than the *Girl's Own Paper*, a magazine for schoolgirls who were assumed to be destined for good middle- and upper-class marriages and their attendant social responsibilities:

A village band should not be, and must not, be a mere decorative and aesthetic appendage to rural life: it should be made of some real, substantial use in a parish. It must be a strong influence in the cause of temperance, both in giving rational, healthy amusement to performers and listeners, and in making the working man feel that intellectual pleasures are better than mere animal enjoyment.[2]

'Animal enjoyment' was clearly a bad thing but, as the girls were instructed, there were several ways of distracting the 'working man' from such attractions. The same sentiment lay behind the encouragement of choral societies and eventually organisations such as mechanics' institutes with their libraries, reading groups and other self-improving activities. They gained approval and were willingly supported, not just as acts of altruism, but because they were perceived as an investment in the sustenance of social structures that the higher social classes were keen to preserve. It is unlikely that the brass band movement would have had such a promising start had these factors not been present in the middle of the nineteenth century, because the working classes, irrespective of their implicit acceptance of the rational recreation ethos, lacked the funds needed for the setting up of such projects. It followed that the earliest bands were groups of men that, through some means or other, had access to resources that allowed these new, sophisticated musical instruments to reach their hands, even though the immediate means to pay for them were absent.

Demographics

The growth of urban communities provided a primary context for the origin of the brass band movement. This does not mean that all early brass bands were in industrial areas; in fact, many were founded in rural villages. However, industrialised regions were important because they were centres of population and, as such, were identified by instrument makers and retailers as a new working-class market. A farmer might have employed a couple of dozen men to work on a large expanse of land. The owner of a textile mill would have employed several hundred to work in a much smaller space, which was adjacent to their housing. The new demographics also made it possible for sellers to communicate with buyers with unprecedented ease. Rural areas benefited from this effect but played a lesser part in causing it.

Many communities experienced stunning population changes. No datasets on population of the nineteenth century are perfect, but the most reliable come from British decennial census records. The first census was held in 1801. In that year the total population of England, Wales, Scotland and the island of Ireland was 9,061,000. By 1851, about the time that the first wave of saxhorn bands was formed, the population had tripled to 27,393,000. In 1891 it had risen further to 38,522,000. The expansion can also be seen in more local terms. The northern counties of Lancashire and Yorkshire, where brass banding had its first major impact, provide a good example. In 1801 the population of Lancashire was 673,000; in the same year in Yorkshire, it was 860,000. By 1851 the two counties had grown to 2,031,000 and 1,798,000, respectively. Across Britain there were variations in the patterns of growth. For example, urban expansion and rural contraction in Wales was similar in its scale and effect to that in other parts of Britain, but it occurred significantly later because the discovery and exploitation of coal in the southern valleys was not fully under way until the 1860s. However, during the century the general trend was the same: Britain had an increasingly large population and there was a move from the countryside to urban communities.[3]

A caveat should accompany an explanation of how these factors impacted on the formation of brass bands. Words such as 'industrial' and 'urban' are often applied to the Victorian era in a way that summons images of large, congested and increasingly expanding towns and cities. While some early brass bands appeared in such places, most were not formed in the densest centres of population. They seem to have been raised in small towns, villages even, that had grown to serve the needs of one or two centres of industrial employment. One historian has accurately pointed out that, while industrialisation may have changed the balance between the rural and the urban, the 'urban' culture of the time was often more rural than might be imagined: 'most of the new industrial towns did not so much displace the countryside as grow *over* it'.[4] The Black Dyke Band, the Mossley Temperance Band, the Linthwaite Band and Meltham Mills Band – all major stars of Victorian band contests – emerged in such places. These small settlements became larger, and their character may have been modified, but they retained a discernible sense of community and a shared sense of belonging, precisely because they had not been digested by a larger metropolitan conglomerate.

In these smaller industrial settlements, the members of brass bands were often drawn from a single place of employment and were almost always working-class. We can be sure of this, not just because so many bands carried the name of a particular mill, mine or factory, but because surviving written records identify individual band members in detail. Membership of a Victorian brass band required assiduous paperwork for two reasons: firstly, irrespective of how the money was raised to buy instruments, in most cases each player was personally involved in the arrangements, so written records were essential to identify who they were and the obligations to which they were committed; and secondly, contesting brass bands were restricted to amateur instrumentalists, so evidence of their amateur status was made explicit in their contest entrance forms by requiring them to state the work that each player did to earn a living (fig. 11).

CRYSTAL PALACE, SYDENHAM.

TABLE OF PARTICULARS to be Filled-up by each Band intending to compete in the Brass Band Contests to be held at the above Palace on Tuesday and Wednesday, July 10th and 11th, 1860.

Name of Band .... *Flush Mills Heckmondwike*

Name of Contests entered for .... ~~Cloth Blankets & Carpets Twin Portadown~~ *Sydenham only*

Title of Music, Composer's name, &c., selected to play on ~~Tuesday~~ *Wednesday*, July 10th, 1860 .... *Grand operatic selection from "Maritana," Wallace / Young England Quadrille, E. Jackson*

~~Title of Music, Composer's name, &c., selected to play on Wednesday, July 11th, 1860~~ ....

Name of Companies' Railway, also the Railway Station you wish to start from, and the distance from nearest large Town .... *The Lancashire & Yorkshire Rail Compy from Heckmondwike about the same distance from Halifax, Bradford, Huddersfield, Leeds & Wakefield, 2 miles from Dewsbury*

Particulars of Prizes won during the years 1858 and 1859 .... *this is our first contest*

Have you portable Music Stand you can bring to Sydenham if required? If so, please describe it; also please state if you can appear in Uniform .... *we have 20 portable music stands, the bottoms are tapp'd for the uprights to screw into, the tops have A black with Holes to fit on the uprights, we have leather cases to pack them in — one for bottoms, 1 for uprights and two for the tops, we have uniforms making and put them on for the first time on July 7th*

Names of Performers.	Profession or Trade.	Instruments played upon.	Key the Instruments stand in.
J. M. Sykes	+ Cloth Percher	Conductor	
Peter Mortimer	Assistant do	Cornett	Db
Saml Schofield	"	"	Ab
John Crowther	"	"	Ab
Ben Moore	overlooker	"	Ab
W. H. Fearnley	office clerk	"	Ab
G. F. Mortimer	Spinner	"	Ab
Benjn Firth	office clerk	Tenore Sax	Eb
Wm Townend	Loom Tuner	"	Eb
Abm Fawthrop	Warehouse man	Euphonian	Ab
John Fearnley	"	"	Ab
Sutcliffe Greenwood ~~Baritone~~	"	Baritone	Ab
George Charlesworth	Machine Tenter	Bombardone	Eb
Jonn Collett	Spinner	"	Eb
John Mortimer	"	"	Eb
Jas Whiteley	Overlooker	Trombone	C
Geo Crabtley	Washer	"	Bb
Wm Rouse	Machine Fettler	"	G

Baritone & C Trombone players are to fill up A sick mans place and A vacancy

Bands necessitated by sickness or other causes to make any alteration from the particulars here given must obtain the Referee's sanction before any deviation can be granted.

N.B.—Any Band not returning this Form properly filled-up to the Managing Secretary, Mr. Enderby Jackson, 21, Prospect-Street, Hull, on or before Thursday, the 21st day of June, 1860, will be considered as declining to compete, and their Entrance-Fee, or Fees, in consequence, be forfeited.

John Howe, Printer and Bookbinder, Old Corn Exchange Printing Rooms, 50, Market-Place, Hull.

11. *The entry form completed by the Flush Mills Band, Heckmondwike, for the 1860 Crystal Palace contest. Each band was required to provide extensive details about its players, instrumentation and the railway transport it would use.*

The entry forms for the Crystal Palace contests held between 1860 and 1863 required such detail. The Flush Mills Band from Heckmondwike in Yorkshire was constituted almost entirely of workers on the production line of that one mill, together with a couple of its office clerks. Bands that did not carry the name of a place of employment often show more varied occupations. Ripponden Band, also in the Yorkshire textile area, appears not to have been sponsored by, or connected to, a single place of employment. In 1861 its members included cotton twisters, cotton spinners and wool sorters, but there was also a blacksmith, a tailor and a stone quarrier. The most southerly band to win at the Crystal Palace contests in the 1860s was from Blandford Forum in rural Dorsetshire. In 1860 it was a band of ten players, made up of an innkeeper (the leader and keyed bugle player), two cabinet makers, two cordwainers, a schoolboy, a tailor, a gun maker, a baker and a painter. They won the 1863 contest, having enlarged the band by six players, three of whom were shoemakers.[5]

Economics

Brass bands were not the only musical manifestations of rational recreation, but no other form of instrumental ensemble music grew so rapidly on the back of its sentiment, and few needed a similar level of capital investment at its start. Why did brass bands gain popular approval so quickly and how did the players afford the instruments? It is obvious that the people who played in saxhorn brass bands had little disposable income: we know their circumstances because it is possible to identify so many of them individually. The striking feature of the development of brass bands among the working class was its speed and scope. Only slightly later in the century was there an equally marked increased in the sale of domestic pianos, but the conditions that drove that phenomenon were different.[6] As was the case with brass instruments, the increased consumption came about because of the introduction of new designs, efficient methods of production and distribution, and the identification of a new consumer market. There was also a similarity in the motivating sentiment – playing in a brass band was rational and self-improving, a domestic piano signified refinement and respectability.

But the market segment at which the piano was directed was the middle class and those who aspired to it, and most purchasers had an employment status that allowed them to borrow. Early brass band players were not middle-class and there is little evidence that such aspirations were prominent in their thinking. They were working-class, relatively poor and seldom creditworthy. They and their families may have been housed, clothed and fed, and may have led happy and contented lives, but they were unlikely to have had money to spend beyond what was required for the sustenance of those basic needs. This is why two critical questions about the Victorian origins of the brass band movement are so compelling. Firstly, how did these new musical instruments find their way into the hands of groups of men who could not afford them; and secondly, why, anyway, did they regard the idea of playing in a brass band as an attractive proposition? It certainly happened, and at scale: hundreds, possibly thousands, of bands had been formed across the country by the mid-1870s.

Brass instruments were advertised, sold and bought, but the details of how sales were transacted is not always clear. It is certain that more than one model was used, each of which involved some form of patronage, or credit, or more frequently both. However, almost all bands that lasted into the twentieth century (not all did so) developed into self-supporting and largely democratic institutions within a decade or two of their founding. Direct, philanthropic patronage played a part in the origin of several brass bands, but the contribution of generous industrialists is often overstated and sometimes misinterpreted. The most quoted case of direct patronage is that of the Black Dyke Mills Band, which was assembled in 1855 by the mill owner John Foster, who paid for instruments, uniforms and a bandmaster. The instruments were bought from Higham of Manchester, and Foster's generosity was duly and fully reported in northern newspapers. A more detailed chronology of patronage survives for a band that was to have a less celebrated and considerably shorter life than Black Dyke. It, too, was formed in Yorkshire, in the town of Keighley, also under the patronage of a textile manufacturer, W. L. Marriner. Marriner's was an important company, known in the Victorian period for its adoption of modern manufacturing methods. The band was supported as a central part of W. L. Marriner's intent to provide facilities for the entertainment of the mill workers, perhaps as a response to industrial unrest that had affected neighbouring districts in recent years. An account book shows that the band was formed as a private band:

> This band was first commenced about 12th of May 1844. It originated with Mr W L Mariner [sic] who, having heard some time previous the celebrated musicians Williams and his three sons perform on brass instruments in the Mechanics Institute Keighley, felt a strong desire to form a band.[7]

It goes on to describe how 'bugles', a trombone and a 'copper cornopean' (see Glossary) were bought. In 1852 control of the band passed to Lister Marriner, who reformed it as a saxhorn band; unusually, he also acted as a putative agent for the band's external engagements. By this time, the band was known as Marriner's Caminando Band.[8] A surviving band account book covers the 30-year period following the band's re-formation as a brass band in November 1852. It shows that the instruments were bought by Lister Marriner from Henry Distin. Each instrument was allocated to a named individual in the band, but Marriner retained ownership of them. The initial purchase was for 11 instruments, including two drums. By 1865 the number of instruments had risen to 15 but, by this time, some players were using instruments they personally owned: probably those originally purchased by Marriner but now bought from him by individual players. The funds for such purchases were earned from engagements: the account book makes it clear that all moneys earned from engagements were to be divided equally between the players. The financial health of the band was aways good because of Marriner's financial backing, but it came as a series of loans rather than as unconditional patronage. Debts could be settled on time from engagement income which was buoyant because of Lister Marriner's negotiating skills when hiring the band out.

Borrowing from employers was not unusual. It was common for company accounts to record the issue and settlement of loans to company employees well into the twentieth century. Musical instrument manufacturers themselves issued loans to their workers.[9] W. L. Marriner's band could eventually pay £20 a year to a professional conductor. The band was run consistently by the workmen as an efficient enterprise even though they had the benefit of Lister Marriner's interest and remained under his sponsorship. By 1865 it was even able to deploy older instruments to good purpose by establishing a 'juvenile band'.

The story of Marriner's band is distinctive but not entirely unusual. It is certainly illustrative of how the patronage model was often blended with a form of entrepreneurialism, and there are other instances to show that money did not always flow in one direction. In 1840 Robert Thompson Crawshay, owner of the Cyfarthfa iron works in Merthyr Tydfil, bought the first tranche of instruments to form his private band from the London dealer Charles Pace, but surviving documents show that by 1867 the band's members were making regular weekly payments to Crawshay to pay for the instruments they were playing.[10]

Some early bands are referred to as 'subscription bands'; this model, too, had several variations. It was based on members, and sometimes others, paying weekly subscriptions to cover initial costs, followed by continued subscriptions from players once the initial costs had been met. The Irwell Springs Band, another success story of the Victorian period, appears to have adopted this model after a group from the Bacup Old Band (a longer-established reed band) visited a Belle Vue contest and decided to re-form itself into a brass band. The players funded the enterprise by paying the hefty subscription of £1 each, or 6d a week for those who could not afford the £1 as a single payment.[11]

The account books of instrument makers and retailers do not survive in quantity or detail until later in the century, but consistencies emerge from other surviving evidence about selling and buying. While individual instruments were available for purchase, most sales to amateur bands were as a set appropriate for the formation of a band of a particular size – a band of eight players, or 12, and so on. The client was always the band rather than its individual members; when an individual is cited in an instrument company's account books, it denotes the name of the nominated correspondent rather than the owner of the purchased instruments, unless it was a patron. To put it differently, it was always the band as a collective rather than its individual members that was the client: the band members were jointly committed to a debt. Subscriptions were paid weekly, but this, of course, did not cover the initial costs. To meet them, bands often embraced communities and their institutions or agencies, such as a church or one of the many organisations (such as temperance societies) that opposed alcohol consumption. When the Llanelly Band set up in 1886, having paid 'the lowest trade price' (£75.13.3) for its instruments, it was able to raise almost the entire amount from public subscriptions and from the proceeds of events such as 'a concert' and an 'Athletic Sports day', together with £14 from the band's players, who would also pay ongoing subscriptions for maintenance and other expenses.[12] These were substantial sums, but they were not untypical. The St George's Works Band of Lancaster operated a monthly balance of £4, made up of members' subscriptions, but it quickly realised that a concert could raise more than that in an evening. Some offered imaginative schemes to manufacturers.[13] In 1896 a meeting of the directors of the Besson company approved a request from a band which asked for the loan of a set of second hand instruments so it could use them to raise sufficient funds to buy a complete new set.[14] There was no shortage of money-making opportunities. It did not take long for brass bands to be a standard requirement for community and celebratory events. Some were engaged for rallies, including those linked to radical causes; for example, in 1840 a band formed part of the procession that followed the release of Chartist leaders from Warwick prison.[15] However, while bands were usually symbolically aligned to left-wing organisations, one gains the impression from the variety of events at which they appeared that sentiments were negotiable if the price was right. A further economic model (if it can be graced with that title) for the initiation and sustenance of early bands came from the 1859 Volunteer movement, which is dealt with in detail below (see p. 88).

12. The elaborately liveried Leeds Forge Brass Band as it appeared at the opening of the new permanent building of the Royal College of Music, London, in 1882. The band was assembled under the patronage of Samson Fox, owner of the Leeds Forge and a major sponsor of the College. The presence of a brass band emphasised the College's intention to attract students from a wide social range.

All early brass bands benefited from the prevailing idea that rational working-class recreations were an investment in community coherence and social stability. By the late 1850s this strategy appears to have been yielding the required results. Many were providing a focus for community leisure and the building of local identities, and band members seem to have bought in to the idea of self-improvement. One of the ways that the collective identity and coherence of a band was expressed was through the wearing of uniforms. Band uniforms were designed, made and sold by companies that existed for no other purpose. After the purchase of instruments, uniforms were the greatest capital cost. This was sometimes moderated by the acquisition and adaptation of uniforms made for some other purpose. Even in the 1960s the Pegswood Colliery Prize Band was wearing redecorated former police uniforms.[16] That they were always military-style uniforms should not surprise: they carried messages about discipline and order as well as a sense of ceremonial splendour. The fact that some were more Ruritanian than realistic was hardly important (fig. 12). Bands were invariably keen to be captured in photographs. Some, in the early stages of their existence, show their players proudly standing with instruments in their hands wearing their Sunday best suits supplemented by a specially commissioned quasi-military hat, or even just a white belt that signified the organisational direction in which they were travelling. This was especially the case in rural communities, where many bands were initiated by posters calling for community consultations on the basic idea of raising a band. In some rural areas, patronage was boosted by a collective of appropriately placed persons or agencies. This model was used for the formation and sustenance of the Blandford band. It was led and probably formed by Robert Eyers, its keyed bugle and cornet player, who was otherwise an innkeeper, an occupation of choice for many successful amateur bandleaders and conductors of the time. Eyers was the organiser of the band: it was his name and address that appeared on the application forms for the Crystal Palace contests. A report of a banquet held by local dignitaries to celebrate the band's success at the 1863 contest shows that among the prizes was a set of new instruments. Members of the band were also presented with 'envelopes' containing (cash) 'tokens of esteem' for the fame and credit the band had brought to this small market town. Gratitude was expressed to the Mayor and Corporation of Blandford who 'had done a good deal for music as well as agriculture'.[17] The impression gained is of a financial structure that involved players, a local government authority and a set of dignitaries. The local dignitaries and the civic authorities were likely to have been the same set, but reports of the band's activities reinforce the view that people of influence were easily persuaded to support a band if it was coherently organised and serving a discernibly beneficial community role. The Blandford band was the only band in southern England to have gained such celebrity in the nineteenth century. Much of this achievement might be laid at the door of the multitalented and energetic Robert Eyers, who was to become the town mayor and the owner of the largest tavern in the town as well as a wine business; he was also the local railway agent and ran the Blandford inland revenue office.[18]

By about 1860 a momentum had been created, and bands were conspicuous on the British landscape. Start-up bands could be assembled by groups of working men who were able to secure a loan through what was essentially a hire-purchase agreement, even though they were not individually creditworthy. They did this by persuading someone, or some agency, to guarantee the loan. This system, which was probably very common from the mid-nineteenth century, is explained vividly by Algernon Rose, who wrote one of the few important books about the brass band to be published in the nineteenth century.

In 1893 the proprietors of the Broadwood piano factory decided to convert its string band to a brass band and engaged Rose to give a series of lectures on brass instruments to members of the putative band. Rose subsequently added material to form a book which he called *Talks with Bandsmen*. One of his chapters is devoted to 'How to form a brass band'. He described in practical terms the steps that a group of like-minded men should take. His advice included a sample letter that could be adapted and sent to a prospective guarantor:

To the proprietors of the 'Universal Soap Works, Trincomalee'

Dear Sirs, – We the undersigned, being desirous of employing our leisure time in practising music, request your permission to form a brass band in connection with this factory. We shall feel honoured if Mr So-and-so (naming one of the partners likely to support the project) will consent to become President of the Band. Unfortunately, we are unable at the beginning to defray the entire cost of the purchase of the instruments. Messrs Red, White and Blue, musical instrument manufacturers, of London are, however, prepared to sell us the brass instruments required, provided that the firm, whose name we should take, will act as surety for the deferred payments.

We are dear sirs,

Yours respectfully

(Here should follow the signatures of everyone in the mill or the factory in favour of the scheme, whether desirous of becoming performers, or merely honorary members.)[19]

Rose was describing a system that might be called a deferred-payment scheme underwritten by a guarantor. The guarantors were employers or local dignitaries who would have been happy to support such a scheme, especially as it was likely to cost them nothing. The payment obligations were satisfied by individual subscriptions from band members along with income from engagements and perhaps cash prizes won at contests. The model also suited retailers and manufacturers.

The idea that bands were based on credit is also confirmed in the minute books of instrument companies. For example, the Boosey company regularly reported on the progress of bands that had trouble in meeting their debts, but it was a tiny proportion of the schemes that were in place, and few were unable to extricate themselves from problems.

Media and communications

A major and lasting influence on the brass band movement, and the commercial enterprises with which it engaged, came from the establishment of specialist brass band periodical magazines. The first was *Brass Band News* (1881–1958), then came the *British Bandsman* (1887–2022),[20] *The Cornet* (1893–1940) and the *Brass Band Annual* (1894–1910). More followed in the twentieth century. In 1890 *Brass Band News* claimed a circulation of 25,000, which must have been an exaggeration. In 1891 the *British Bandsman* claimed to have doubled its circulation in the previous year to 5,000, which was probably also exaggerated but closer to the truth. However, it should be emphasised that the readership was multiples more than the number of copies sold. Britain's most successful mainstream music periodical, the *Musical Times* (which claimed to sell 15,000 copies monthly), acknowledged that brass band publications had a 'mission to fulfil in stimulating amateurs and professionals to attain that degree of excellence which may make them in their turn patterns for imitation or centres of musical civilization'.[21]

Most brass band periodicals grew out of an existing enterprise, such as a music publishing house which founded a magazine to promote its own interests. This was common across the publishing industry. Following its purchase from Joseph Mainzer in 1844, the London-based *Musical Times* was effectively the house journal of the Novello publishing house.[22] For the duration of their existence, brass band magazines were the major vehicles for advertising instruments, uniforms, music and other commodities: all promoted in unashamedly hyperbolic terms. Editorial content varied over time, but some general features were consistent. News of bands and contests at both local and national level was a major feature. A large proportion of articles were essentially didactic. It was as if the prevailing view was that its readership needed to be taught how to play, how to organise themselves, win contests – and, with surprising regularity and condescension, how to behave. It is easy to detect a sententious tone in many articles, a sense that everyone needed to be regularly reminded of their moral responsibility to the collective whole. This may have been a worthy approach, and in the nineteenth century it may have had the desired effect; it certainly galvanised the most important role that these publications were to assume. They were the central agency for communicating with and connecting the entire brass band movement. Contests also served this role, but the network of contests would have been significantly weaker without the periodicals that persistently kept them in the consciousness of the entire brass band community. Copies of band magazines were sold in shops, railway stations and anywhere else where such items were purveyed. They went beyond the industrial regions, into the shires and their rural villages where so many small brass bands were scattered and would have otherwise been isolated. In so doing, they created common attitudes and even a vocabulary that was to become exclusive to the brass band world.

Repertoires and instrumentation

The most performed printed music of the nineteenth century was 'journal music'. Journal music was supplied once a month on subscription. Each issue contained five or six pieces that were entertaining but technically undemanding and arranged with sufficient flexibility to be adaptable for whatever instruments were at hand. They provided a basic repertoire, but for many instrumentalists they also provided a first encounter with musical notation. Basic guides to musical notation were published and parts were arranged simply, avoiding many of the complications that pervade musical notation; for example, most parts were written in the treble clef, irrespective of whether they were for a treble or bass instrument.[23]

Some simple one-off publications preceded both journal music and the introduction of saxhorn bands, but they appear to have had a very limited circulation. They included *Eight Popular Airs for Brass Band* (1836) by McFarlane, and D'Almaine's *The Brass Band*, which was made up of arrangements by John Parry, a former militia bandmaster. 'Parry's Brass Band', as it became known, was a staple of W. L. Marriner's band. *Wessel's Journal*, which was published from the early 1840s, provided parts for cornets, trumpets, keyed bugles and french horns. Wessel's was an important London-based classical music publisher. Set up by a German immigrant in 1824, it held the English publishing rights for the music of Chopin. It is doubtful whether its eyes were on the amateur brass band market. Trumpets and french horns were relatively rare as amateur instruments in England at this time and were not regular components of the new species of brass band which used a more homogenous group of instruments, which were produced in much greater quantities. Some publications, notably some of *Distin's Brass Band Scores* published in the mid-1850s, incorporate brass band instruments with trumpets, horns and woodwind in what, at first sight, appears to be an imaginative military band format, but the arrangement is such that it could be performed effectively using only brass band instruments.[24] However, Smith's *Champion Brass Band Journal*, published in Hull from 1857, was aimed specifically at the new market. From the 1850s, several instrument manufacturers set up a publishing arm to support their strategies for selling instruments in sets for bands of various sizes. Probably the most widely circulated was *Distin's Brass Band Journal*, which was published from about 1857 and was taken over by Boosey from 1869. It cost 10s. 6d. per annum for a band of ten instruments made up of cornets, tenor horns, euphoniums, baritones, bombardons and percussion. But, as each issue made clear, the band could be expanded to a wider, more ambitious, instrumentation:

> This Journal is arranged to suit a Band of any size, and extra Parts may be had for the following instruments: Repiano Cornet in B flat; Cornets, 3rd and 4th, in B flat. Solo Tenor in E flat, 2nd Baritone in B flat and 1st and 2nd Trombones in B flat (either in the Treble or Bass clef); Bass Trombone; and Contra-bass in B flat. Price of extra or duplicate Parts Two Pence Each, or to Subscribers Three Halfpence.[25]

The interesting thing here is that, if one combines the instrumentation provided in the regular subscription with all the additional parts, it comes close to the format that was to become the standard instrumentation a decade or two later, but it is likely that Boosey was imitating current trends rather than creating them. (More information on the instrumentation of journal music is given in Appendix 1.)

Brass bands played an important part in popularising certain forms of classical music and opera. Only a tiny proportion of the British population heard opera in an opera house, but favourite opera overtures and arias, which were released independently of the complete works, were hummed by people across the country because they had heard them played by brass bands. Many opera derivatives circulated as brass band versions long before they were otherwise heard in Britain. For example, Verdi's *La forza del destino* (The Force of Destiny) was first performed in St Petersburg late in 1862, but its overture was in circulation in Britain as a brass band arrangement early the following year. The full opera did not have a UK performance until 1867.[26]

The driving force for both repertoire and the standard brass band instrumentation quickly shifted to what was performed and heard at major contests. Bands played arrangements of existing works, and opera selections were highly favoured. Elite bands played bespoke arrangements made by their own bandmasters, and it was the most successful of them that influenced the eventual adoption of the standard format. John Gladney, Alexander Owen and Edwin Swift were the most successful contest conductors of the century and the architects of the standard brass band formulation, even though this was unlikely to have been their intention.

There appears to have been no single moment when a decision to use a standard format was consolidated, but photographs of bands taken in the 1870s hint very strongly that a broad consensus was forming. John Gladney, often referred to as 'the father of the brass band movement', and probably the most influential force, seemed to confirm this in a letter written three decades later:

In 1871, when I conducted Burnley, the band had no fixed instrumentation – the average band numbered fifteen or sixteen. Ophicleides had been in use right up to then. Keyed bugles and clarinets were in use up to the 1860s, but none were used in the 1871 [Open] contest. When I took up Meltham [Mills Brass Band] in 1873 I at once remodelled the instrumentation on to lines thought out and discussed, i.e. to a band of twenty-four, with three slide trombones, in fact the same as are now in use. The great success of Meltham [Mills Band] soon made all the other bands fall in line.[27]

Gladney's formation, as he described it here, shows only three deviances from what was to be the standard instrumentation: he used seven B flat cornets rather than nine, two flugelhorns rather than one, and just one each of the two bass instruments rather than two of both sizes. However, a photograph of the band, dated 1876–8, shows four or possibly five bass instruments. All of Meltham Mills' instruments were supplied by Besson, who boasted of it at every opportunity. By the last decade of the century, there was a common understanding that a contesting brass band was usually made up of 25 players with a broadly common line-up of instruments.[28]

By the 1870s the brass band had acquired most of the features that define its modern form. Estimates of the number of bands in existence at the end of the century are various and unverified. The publishers Wright and Round claimed there were 40,000 bands in 1889, but later in the same year gave it as 30,000.[29] There has never been an accurate method for counting them. The *Brass Band Annual* of 1893 listed contesting bands which had won a prize of any sort in the previous year – there were about 350 of them – but this seems to have been based on an arbitrary and limited selection of contests. There is a strong possibility that the number of bands which regularly contested was less than those that didn't. If this were not the case, there would be a significant disparity between the number of contesting bands and what we know of the output of instrument manufacturers. Besson claimed that it had 10,000 bands on its books by 1890.[30] It is likely that this was just one of its calculated exaggerations but claims of there being thousands of active brass bands by the end of the century were probably realistic, if one takes into account all non-contesting bands. It is certainly true that, by that time, brass bands were ubiquitous and established as an important part of the country's musical landscape. From 1859 many of them had been provided with a surprising new line of encouragement, and even nourishment.

The 1859 Volunteers

Entrants for brass band contests from the 1860s onwards included a significant number of bands that carried a military title. This was because several had aligned themselves with a nationwide scheme aimed at bolstering the security of the country. These apparently public-spirited endeavours may have drawn admiration at the time, but patriotism often played a subsidiary role to self-interest. The relationship between brass bands and the nationwide movement that became known as the 1859 Volunteers is one of the most interesting developments in brass band history, and its importance is often overlooked.

Throughout the nineteenth century the size of the British regular army expanded and contracted as foreign combats arose and were resolved. Britain always had a formidable army and navy, but a large proportion of it was usually deployed in the expanding Empire. In the middle of the century there were deep-rooted concerns that the island nation was insufficiently protected. Worries centred on France and its adventurous leader Napoleon III. Early in the century French troops had landed in west Wales with malevolent intent and, while that incursion was easily dealt with, it sharpened awareness of the country's vulnerability. A part-time militia had been established in the eighteenth century in the form of local units under the leadership of provincial dignitaries who held the title 'County Lieutenant', but by the middle of the nineteenth century that initiative had lost much of its effectiveness. Parliament passed a new Militia Act in 1852 which enabled the government to enlist men compulsorily by ballot,[31] but by 1859 Francophobic concerns had accelerated to the extent that more urgent steps needed to be implemented. The Secretary of State for War instructed all County Lieutenants to form a volunteer force that would be 'called out in case of actual invasion', the members of which, when activated, would be 'bound by military law'.[32] These words may have been accurate, but they were not conducive to the encouragement of volunteering among the country's young men. Combative soldiering was not an attractive leisure proposition, and many will have been alarmed by an utterance from politician Benjamin Disraeli proclaiming that war was 'not a matter of weeks or days [away] but of hours'.[33] Probably with this in mind, and just 13 days later, the Secretary of State issued a further statement in a more palatable tone:

> The conditions of service should be such, while securing and enforcing the above necessary discipline, to induce those classes to come forward for service who do not . . . enter the regular army or militia . . . Drill and instruction for bodies of volunteers should not be such as to render the service unnecessarily irksome.[34]

In effect, the government really was attempting to sell volunteering as a leisure activity, with the additional and seductive incentive that, while volunteers would be required to attend 24 drills a year, they would be exempted from the mandatory militia ballot, which was generally regarded as a particularly grim prospect. These measures, together with the promise that recruits would be able to spend a lot of time firing real guns with actual bullets in their training, seem to have done the trick. By the end of November 1859, the number of men volunteering had reached 1,328 a day.[35] The pattern of enrolment fluctuated, but the trajectory was generally upwards: in 1861 the force stood at 161,239; in 1878 it had risen to 203,213; by the end of the century it had reached 277,628.[36] The establishment of this part-time soldiery was not universally welcomed. Some senior military men worried that the government was assembling an undisciplined amateur rabble, but others regarded it positively: apart from all else, it was seen as character-building. The resonances of loyalty, patriotism and good intent, associated with volunteering, were closely reminiscent of those that underpinned the rational recreation ethos. As one commentator put it, 'a dissipated man rarely makes a good shot'.[37] It was a genuinely voluntary organisation. Thousands of young men were seen to be sacrificing their leisure hours in a collective and disciplined endeavour aimed at protecting the country from the reckless and unpredictable French. A misty-eyed correspondent of *The Times*, reflecting on a Volunteer review he attended in June 1860, saw it as a date 'to be remembered in the annals of the nation', and 'a revival of the military spirit of the British people':

> Something – an impulse, an influence, an instinct perhaps – it is difficult to define it – has passed over the land, entering into the heart and life of our manhood. In a few short months of preparation the soil of this commercial and industrial England echoes to the tread of legions of soldiers and the rarely-accorded gleams of this summer's sun have glanced back from a thousand bayonets. Hosts of men trained to occupations of peace, to whom war and military life a year ago appeared so foreign that a conviction of a national unfitness for them had gone abroad in the world, have turned from the beaten paths of their ordinary pursuits, and – almost as by the wave of an enchanter's wand – appeared ranked side by side with the 'men of war from their youth', and in no essential quality inferior to them.[38]

The involvement of brass bands in all this was uneasy and very peculiar from the start. The problem was twofold. Volunteers enjoyed firing guns but their interest in drills and marching was much more limited. This was problematic: drills were essential because their primary purpose was to instil military discipline. Commanding officers noticed that drills and marching became significantly more palatable if a band of music was in attendance to invest those occasions with authenticity and even glamour. Unfortunately, the terms drawn up for the funding of Volunteer units made provision for neither the recruitment nor the maintenance of bands of music; in fact, the implication was that they were proscribed. A 'capitation grant' was distributed to all corps from 1863 but no provision was included specifically for bands until almost 30 years later.[39] Commanding officers needed bands because experience had shown them to be essential. Some were raised using a variant of the patronage system that had been implemented for the funding of civilian bands. Charles E. Murray, a captain responsible for the 16th Middlesex Rifles, explained in a letter to *The Times* that he had formed a band from 'tradesmen of the respectable artisan class', because 'marching without a band would be a dismal business':

Out of some 30 applicants . . . I have formed a band of 17 performers . . . from separate subscription I have furnished them with instruments and clothes and given them paid instruction. The terms on which they serve are

1. They are attested members of the corps.

2. On leaving they are bound to resign their instruments, etc.

3. They agree (beside meetings for practice) to play once a week at 6pm at HQ.

4. If wanted for a whole day, for instance for a great review, then and only then to be paid for loss of time.[40]

Captain Murray's endeavours were undoubtedly laudable but even this modest initiative required an element of improvisation with the War Office funding ration. Fund-raising events of the sort that had been used by civilian bands were also implemented. Several units raised money by recourse to band funds through mandatory contributions from officers. In 1860 the London Rifle Brigade, which was famously wealthy, extravagant and effectively representative of the City of London, expected contributions from each officer according to rank: 12 guineas for a lieutenant colonel, reducing to 3 guineas for an ensign. Few Volunteer officers in this part-time army could afford such expenditure, especially in the provinces. The Preston Volunteers determined that:

> Each officer do pay the sum of one shilling, and each private three pence, weekly on every Monday morning, in to the hands of such person, as a majority of the officers shall direct as a Fund for the payment of the wages of the Band of Music belonging to the corps.[41]

The corps also allocated a total of £28 for uniforms for the band. This was an example of the more expedient and riskier route taken by many corps of buying in an existing band. The benefit was that an established band could operate immediately and competently. But by this time, brass bands in the civilian world had acquired guile: they were well experienced in running their own affairs and capable of driving a hard bargain. Such was the case with the band formed at Higham's instrument factory and retail outlet in Manchester which, from 1859, operated as the band of the 1st Manchester Volunteers. It clearly had the shrewd and relentless hand of Joseph Higham behind it. When approached by the corps, the band seemed to be delivering the orders rather than receiving them. It laid down five conditions under which it would serve:

1. That the uniforms of the band be supplied by the above Reg[t] and the Instruments and music by Mr J Higham.
2. That the band shall consist of about thirty performers and are to play every Saturday afternoon if required from the date thereof.
3. That all extra times the band may be required to play except Saturday afternoon each man to receive the sum of eight shillings for such attendance.
4. That in order to have an efficient band it is requisite the members attend practice two nights per week, and that each man be allowed 3 shillings and 6 pence per week for practice as allowed to other bands, Yeomanry etc.
5. That all drum heads that are broken whilst on duty, to be paid for by the above Reg[t]. [42]

13. The Fraserburgh Volunteer Rifles Band (Aberdeen), c.1880s. Volunteer bands always had smart uniforms and Scots bands usually incorporated the tartan. The band members were probably as alert to the prospect of an invasion as was their dog.

More was to come to light about the way bands were used and funded. The 1859 Volunteers was a genuinely national movement, but individual corps were organised locally and concerns developed about the consistency of their operation (fig. 13). The government established two inquiries to clarify what was going on: in 1862 a Royal Commission on the Condition of the Volunteer Force under Viscount Eversley, and in 1878–9 a Departmental Report chaired by Lord Bury, the Under Secretary of State for War. These were supplemented in 1887 by a Volunteer Capitation Inquiry that focused on funding. Evidence was provided in writing and in person. None of the inquiries had a specific brief to assess the place of bands in the volunteering project, but it emerged as a noticeable topic. Viscount Enfield, giving evidence to the Royal Commission as an honorary colonel of the Volunteers, admitted that the cost of bands (his corps had two) was the main item of expense. Asked whether a drum and fife band might be an adequate substitution, he recounted with some embarrassment an incident that had occurred the previous Whit Monday:

> We were to march out into the country for battalion drill. The drum and fife band attended, but the full band did not attend, and several of the men fell out and said they would not go out unless they had two bands to accompany them. I remonstrated with them, but it was to no avail, and the men left me.[43]

The Commission also interviewed Lord Lyttleton, who testified that the cost of a band was the primary burden on his corps:

> 'Do you think that these companies would go on prosperously without a band?'
> 'Yes, they could certainly, but the band is a very popular thing, I would never for a moment advocate any public fund for the purpose of defraying such expense as that which is purely for pleasure.'
> 'You do not think that you could get rid of that expense?'
> 'I do not think they [his Worcestershire corps] would have it unless you actually prohibit it . . . I do not think they would like it . . . I am confident that nothing would stop it but actual prohibition.' [44]

Everyone knew, even if they did not voice it, that the prohibition of bands was not a viable option. Captain Flood Page of the London Scottish Corps said what most people thought:

> 'Could you get on without a band?'
> 'Certainly not.'
> 'Do you think you could get on with fifes and drums?'
> 'Certainly not . . . I think it would be impossible to keep the corps together without a band.'[45]

As late as 1886, Parliament was debating the funding of bands in volunteer units. Howard Vincent, MP for Leeds Central, pointed out that 'a band has always been found necessary, at all times, in every military body'.[46] That was all very well, but there was also the question of military discipline. Volunteers trained for combat were termed 'effectives'. Members of bands seldom qualified as such and those that had been bought in en bloc were usually lamentably unfit for that status. Officers were confronted with a dilemma. On the one hand, bands were necessary because they encouraged recruitment and ensured the smooth running of corps but, on the other, they had no appetite for doing anything that they did not particularly want to do. Some were directly and even wilfully insubordinate. A commissioned officer writing to the *Volunteer Service Gazette* saw them as 'one of the main causes of disgrace which has recently fallen on the Volunteer force'. He spoke of some who were 'too drunk to stand' and another who, while on a railway train, had 'challenged a fellow passenger to a fight'. He concluded that:

> it is from the bandsmen of some corps that the volunteers get into disrepute. They are notorious for straggling away from the corps and feeling themselves under no sort of constraint and acknowledging no authority whatever.[47]

This example is probably unusual, but the fundamental problem was that Volunteer corps, by co-opting ready-made bands, had enlisted self-contained groups of men who were emboldened to ignore military orders as they saw fit. Bands also caused a severe drain on finances. The Dobcross Band from Yorkshire charged the 34th West Yorkshire Volunteers £60 a year for doing little more than carrying its name: all other duties were up for negotiation.[48] The Whitehaven Band was costing its local force £54 a year, and in 1874 the Penrith Band was getting £74 a year.[49] This was at a time when a set of new instruments for an entire band could be obtained for less than £100 before discount.[50]

Adjutant Bull of the Middlesex Engineer Voluntary Corps openly admitted to the Bury Departmental Inquiry that the average expenditure on the band of his corps was £280. His testimony had echoes of how regular army officers funded bands at the start of the century:

That expenditure will be lower in the future. We have a new system. We pay the bandmaster £12 a year and he provides instruments, clothing and everything for the band. We enrol any men that he likes and we give him the capitation grant for those men. If he has 30 men he can draw the capitation allowance [for that number].[51]

Some units spent yet larger amounts on their musicians. The London Rifle Brigade was probably the most extravagant. It carried a band of 23 members who played a new set of instruments supplied by Henry Distin. A letter to *The Times* in August 1860 from a correspondent signing himself 'A Lieutenant Colonel' quoted a summary of the unit's audited expenditure at the time the corps was founded in the previous May. It showed that a set of special uniforms was made for the band and its officers and the sergeant. Additional costs of the band, including its instruments and 'salaries', amounted to £620. 9. 0. There was an additional monthly expenditure of £35. 5. 0. Such arrangements may have been exceptional in scale, but this band, which was obviously packed with professionals, must have made a mark, especially at public events.[52] One of the main activities of Volunteer corps was to assemble for 'sham fights' and public reviews. Bands such as that of the London Rifle Brigade would have made a striking impression.

Reviews became a conspicuous feature of Volunteer activity. Rank-and-file Volunteers enjoyed them (each man was issued with 20 rounds of blank ammunition for sham fights), and thousands of spectators assembled. It is easy to imagine that their grandeur was intended to impress people on both sides of the English Channel. A Grand Review held at Dover, the closest English town to France, involved the participation of 16,000 volunteers. Even more modest events, such as one at Salisbury in 1867, saw more than 5,000 volunteers in action. Here, as was the case for brass band contests, the railway companies were enlisted for the transport of volunteers and their supporters. Records of this review survive in sufficient detail to reveal the size of bands and the proportion of their entire corps they occupied. The 13th Wiltshire Corps, which had just 42 rank-and-file volunteers, included a band of 12 as well as two buglers. Taking each of the Wiltshire corps together, the 604 officers and rank-and-file volunteers included 73 bandsmen.[53] A smaller review at Exeter, also in 1867, had just 700 volunteers, of whom 127 were bandsmen. This review probably included the Torquay corps, which had just 55 men, 22 of whom were members of its band. In Exeter in 1861, a contest was held exclusively for bands of Volunteer corps. It attracted 14 bands from Devonshire; the prizes (presented by the High Sheriff) amounted to £80.

Volunteering continued in Britain for the rest of the century. The bands that joined en bloc had taken advantage of an opportunity to settle or even swell their funds. Such opportunism should obscure neither the contribution they made to the Volunteer movement nor the value that these 'engagements' provided for their sustenance. Bands that negotiated such attachments may have done so for pecuniary reasons but, at this time, funding had become increasingly necessary as more bands competed for paid work, and contest prizes became dominated by an elite set. The sense that volunteering was easily aligned to rational recreation was valuable because it may have revived and even extended the burst of philanthropy that emerged earlier in the 1850s, even though it came in a different form.

Entirely new bands formed by Volunteer corps became part of the brass band movement, and many appeared in localities distant from the places where most had been founded a decade earlier. The Volunteer movement was genuinely national, and it caused brass bands to have a similar spread. Without this intervention, brass bands might have remained tightly restricted to the few industrialised localities in which they gained their initial foothold; as such, it extended the popularity of the brass band to many new audiences.

There were other positive outcomes. Developments in the late 1840s and 1850s might have lost their momentum in the late 1850s. This would have impacted negatively on the music industry and its infrastructure. The 1859 Volunteers revitalised and sustained manufacturing and retailing of brass instruments for much of what was left of the century. There were also longer-lasting aesthetic and cultural advantages. The activities with which bands engaged as part of the Volunteer movement resurrected and consolidated their role in public spaces, and especially in secular public ritual. This, of course, had been initiated by military bands more than half a century earlier, but the events that followed 1859 shone a light on one of the key purposes for which brass bands were to be appreciated and needed in the future. The core reason why bands were integrated in Volunteer corps, with all the expense and fuss and elements of comedy this entailed, was that Volunteers would not march in silence. The silence needed to be broken by sounds that inspired. The breaking of silences was to be an important feature in future stages of the brass band story.

Chapter 4

The brass band contest

Nothing separates the brass band more clearly from other parts of the musical world than the resilient centrality of contesting in its culture. Brass band contests originated as a form of working-class mass entertainment, but to bands they acquired greater meaning and significance. They provided the first generation of bands with immediate benefits, not the least of which was public exposure and connectiveness to each other. Cash prizes became an income stream, and the status conferred on winners stimulated ambition. Besses o' th' Barn Band claimed that, in the first 30 years of contesting, it had won prizes to a total value of £3,359 17s. Such precision suggests accuracy but, as with most Victorian boasts, it deserves a measure of scepticism: it undoubtedly includes the value of instruments won by individual players.[1] The histories of elite bands are usually replete with chronologies of winnings because victories came to be regarded as the most unambiguous verification of a band's worth. There have always been other ways of making money and gaining status, but the contest and the magnetism that draws bands to it has never lost its potency. To appreciate the weight of contests in brass band culture, one must understand not just where they came from, but how they make contestants feel: the momentum they stimulate, and the emotions they generate. This is the thing: the brass band contest is about feelings, and it is unrealistic to assume that it can be explained by recourse to other forms of reasoning.

Charles Dickens characterised the brass band contest as a 'Musical Prize Fight'.[2] This may have been a harmless parody, but it provides a neat illustration of how contesting came to be seen from the outside. It appears to be at odds with the values to which music-making should naturally subscribe. Opponents and cynics usually emphasise the obvious aesthetic paradox, that music is an expressive art in which the weighing up of performances to generate scores has no discernible artistic purpose: performance should be focused on artistic expression rather than the idea of victory – how is it possible to compare and judge between two performances that might be equally expressive in different ways? This logic seems undeniable and provides a dilemma that adjudicators have probably confronted many times, but it does not follow that contesting routinely strips musical performance of its expressive worth. An alternative argument can easily be mustered to show that contests do not deny musical expression; they encourage it. They are won by great and often memorable performances. The other factor missed in the aesthetic argument is that contests are emotional: they engage players and audiences in events that are calculated to promote pleasure and excitement. For the bands, they have also served other pragmatic purposes. They have raised and sustained standards, encouraged the creation of repertoire and, perhaps most important, brought assemblies of bands and their people together to listen to each other play. Such congregations have clarified and unified the musical idiom and created a nationwide community of common musical understandings. Within this community, supporters and audiences should be counted. Band contests have elevated the musical sensitivities of players and those who listen to them. There are few audiences possessed of a more educated and nuanced way of listening. Furthermore, brass bands and the individual performers in them deploy extremely sophisticated musical sensitivities and techniques; those who deny this do so through ignorance or prejudice.

History

The musical cultures of the ancient world were radically competitive. The public musical contests (*agôn mousikoi*) took place before audiences that were well attuned to them. Contests could make or destroy musical careers. Images on material objects, such as ancient Greek jugs, show what has become known as 'schoolroom contests', in which children took part in various forms of musical competition.[3] The history of music is littered with evidence of contesting in classical and popular music, but public contests did not gain popularity until the nineteenth century. The brass band contest was one of the first to gain maturity as a species and it may have been influential on the musical contest more generally. For example, the jazz band contests held in Belgium between 1932 and 1939 seem to have been inspired by the British model.[4]

The oldest form of musical competition in Britain, of which we have a reasonably sound knowledge, are probably those that formed part of the Welsh cultural festivals known as *eisteddfodau* (literally 'sittings'). The *eisteddfod* can legitimately claim medieval ancestry, but it was in its modern, nineteenth-century form that it became a competitive music event for amateurs; its more ancient manifestation was restricted to the harpists, singers and poets who were permanently attached to aristocratic courts.[5] There are also precedents for contesting in more recent and elite quarters. The *concours* (contests) of the Paris Conservatoire have been one of its most famous features since its foundation in the late eighteenth century. At the end of their studies, students were matched against each other for the institution's *première prix*, in which candidates performed a designated solo work and public sight-reading tests. The *première prix* conferred advantages on the winners and, because the works set for the competitions were carefully selected or specially commissioned each year, they incrementally created much of the foreground repertoire for each instrument and contributed to the way their idioms are understood. This latter feature can be compared with brass band contest test pieces, which have also contributed definitively to the development of repertoire and shaped the brass band's musical identity, but there the comparison ends.[6] In almost all respects, meaningful comparisons between brass band contests and other musical competitions serve only a limited purpose.

The difference between brass band contesting and other forms of musical competition is best defined by its scope, its significance and its history. In the classical music world, competitions such as the International Tchaikovsky Competition and the BBC Cardiff Singer of the World are commercially organised events aimed at projecting brilliant young performers into stellar careers. Brass band contesting has never been restricted to such a limited constituency. Its primacy has been permanent: contests directly or indirectly provide the structure and content for much of the entire brass band endeavour. Without contests, bands would not have obtained a standard format, and their identity as a distinctive musical species would be less obvious. In the nineteenth century, cash prizes were an important source of income for bands with debts to settle for the instruments they had bought. In the modern world, similar circumstances prevail but at a different level. The prizes are bigger and for some bands they make an important contribution to their financial health, but the cultural capital gained by winners is more important: winning attracts sponsors, creates status and nourishes a band's emotional state.

Positive views on contesting have not been consistently universal even within the modern brass band community. In its purest form, a contest requires an audience to sit through as many performances of the same piece of music as there are bands competing. It takes a certain sort of listener to enjoy this, but there appear to be plenty of them, and the format tends to promote interest in a work rather than the opposite. Many of the professional conductors who came to brass bands from the classical music world in the latter decades of the twentieth century – the trumpeters Elgar Howarth and James Watson, for example – felt that traditional contests restricted the brass band's development in the modern world. Howarth identified the introduction of the 'entertainment contest', in which bands perform a freely selected group of pieces, as a means through which contesting might extend repertoire, minimise some of its idiosyncratic rituals and engage a wider audience.[7]

Not all brass bands compete, but most draw benefits from the competitive network because of the structure it provides. Systems that allow bands of similar experience and competence to compete against each other have been in place since the nineteenth century: bands perform music that has technical demands appropriate for each level.

Modern British bands compete in one of five different 'sections' (equivalent to leagues): a championship section and four lower sections (section 1 to section 4). Bands can compete for national prizes and reach the finals through regional qualifying rounds: each band plays the predetermined test piece for its section. There are many more locally sponsored contests. Some use an *own choice* model, in which each band plays a piece of its own choosing. In an *entertainment contest*, bands play a selection of works, also of their choosing, within a prescribed time limit. *March contests*, in which bands are judged by their musical and more general deportment when marching, are less popular nationally but are a special feature of banding in some parts of the country where they are linked to local traditions. Most contests also offer cash prizes and awards for the best individual players. There are separate contests for youth bands and those attached to universities and conservatoires.

Perhaps the most important development since the later twentieth century has been the systematic expansion of contests beyond Great Britain, especially to continental Europe. National and 'open' contests are held in several European countries, and the best British and European bands share the same standards at the elite level. It is interesting that European bands, who might well have adopted the British instrumentation and its repertoire, have also adopted contesting with great enthusiasm. Contests have been important in Oceania since the nineteenth century. Some of the best Australian and New Zealand bands and their soloists have been influential on banding in Britain.

Origins

The most cited early brass band contest of consequence took place in 1845 at Burton Constable in the East Riding of Yorkshire, about 10 miles from the northern fishing port of Hull. It was held on the estate of Sir Clifford Constable as part of the entertainments at the annual July Magdalen Day fête. Five bands competed for a cash prize. Each had a different instrumentation, and the standard of performance was said to be inconsistent, but at least one of the bands included two saxhorns, suggesting that it was ambitious, well organised and modern. Among the spectators on that day was Enderby Jackson, an 18-year-old flautist. Jackson was the son of a Hull tallow candle-maker. He was inspired to take up music when assisting his father with the footlights at the town's Theatre Royal. Hull is more than 200 miles north of London, but its theatre was a venue on the touring route of major itinerant entertainers. Paganini and Jullien were among the many stars who performed there and inspired Jackson. He was a talented musician – he also played the horn and had taken lessons on the chromatic trumpet – but on Magdalen Day 1845 he was not at Burton Constable as a brass band competitor; he was there to play the flute in a quadrille band that had been engaged for the costume ball at Constable's stately home that evening.[8] What we know of that event comes largely from Jackson's account of it.[9]

Jackson had a significant influence on the early history of the brass band and was probably the most important impresario of the brass band contest in its formative years. At the time of his death, he was widely cited as the inventor of the brass band contest, a claim largely promoted by Jackson himself but broadly accurate.[10] He is one of the few characters from the Victorian period who wrote about brass bands often and descriptively as a direct observer. He was not a modest man – much of what he wrote is rich in the first person, with a good measure of elaboration thrown in – but his talents were various. He published newspaper articles and wrote an important semi-autobiographical memoir on the origin of contests; he organised contests, dabbled in civil engineering, was the clerk of the course for Hull's horse-race course and agent for foreign musical tourists including the British tour of Patrick Gilmore's band from New York in 1878. He travelled internationally, attending the 1885 International Music Congress in Vienna.[11] He said that the Burton Constable event had provided him with the idea that brass band contests could be an elaborate form of popular entertainment, but his imagination was further fired by the behaviour of people who flocked to his other enterprises, especially horse races and agricultural shows.[12] He accurately predicted that the pleasure people gained from second-guessing judges about which was the best cow, chicken or pig in a show would be greatly enhanced in contests that focused on musical entertainment. He also identified the importance and energising power of rivalry as the driving force for any form of competition. It was rivalry and its capacity to be contagious that made his horse-racing enterprises successful:

> I saw the excitement produced, was it entirely to see the horses run the people cared for? No, I thought it is the rivalry: and if this rivalry could be instituted amongst Workmen with music instead of horses, my work would be inaugurated.[13]

Jackson was acutely aware of the potential for brass bands to become a major feature of an entertainment industry that was changing to accommodate patterns of popular leisure in the new mass working-class market. In 1853 he was indirectly involved in the first major contest at the Belle Vue Gardens, Manchester. Though he was persistent in his claim that he invented the idea of the commercial band contest and that the Belle Vue event was based entirely on his ideas, he appears to have had no direct role in the 1853 event other than as an observer and perhaps unwittingly an adviser. The primary organiser was John Jennison, the Belle Vue owner, who, having come close to bankruptcy a few years previously, had cautiously laid on a contest for drum and fife bands in 1852 to test whether a brass band event had pecuniary potential. It was a modest success, so he proceeded and enlisted the support of one of Jackson's associates, the Manchester musician James Melling, who had close connections with Lancashire and Yorkshire brass bands. Jackson claimed that 'the suggestion of attending' was 'anything but attractive' but was persuaded to go.[14]

The first Belle Vue brass band contest had few rules: all bands paid £1 to compete and, while no standard instrumentation was required, bands had to be no less than ten in number and include no professionals other than their conductor. Prizes of £16, £8, £4 and £2 were awarded to the first four winners. The adjudicators were two military bandmasters and the bandmaster to the Earl of Ellesmere, who were stationed in a box screened to ensure that the bands' identity was shielded from them: a practice that was to last. Eight bands competed; each played an arrangement of an orchestral work or an operatic selection of their own choice. The *Manchester Guardian* reported that the skill of these amateur players was only a little short of professional, and the crowd, which comfortably 'exceeded ten thousand', delighted in them. The winning bands, in order, were Mossley, Dewsbury, Bramley and Bury Borough.

All this must have been gratifying for the organisers and Jackson, who was 'astounded' by the event, but better was to come. Within a week of the contest a letter was published in the *Leeds Mercury*:

> I find, in looking over the Leeds Mercury of Saturday last, an account of the prizes awarded to those bands which took part in the musical contest at Belle-Vue, Manchester. The prizes in my opinion, were unfairly awarded, and it is generally believed, both in Lancashire and Yorkshire; by those who were present, that the judges showed the grossest partiality.
>
> According to your report of the 'contest' the Mossley sax horn band received the first prize of £16; and that the Bramley temperance band received £4; thus showing that the Mossley and the Dewsbury bands were more talented than the Bramley band. The fact however is just the very reverse, as the twelve thousand persons present on the day of the trial would, I have no doubt be ready to fully corroborate. The Bramley band, after performing their pieces of music, were most enthusiastically applauded, and the general opinion was that they deserved the first prize, but instead of their receiving it, it was given to a very inferior band, as was admitted on all hands. It was also said that the Mossley players were the worst performers, and that, had they not been very much connected with those who were judges they would have come off without a prize at all.[15]

It went on to imply the enactment of a shadowy scheme designed to prevent the Bramley band from winning and declared that it would remain 'ready to enter the lists with any country band in

England for £100, providing those who may think proper to engage with them will allow disinterested and impartial musicians to act as judges'.[16]

A response was immediately issued by Jennison, rebutting the charges and emphasising that the judges, because they were screened, did not know which band was playing anyway. But both he and Jackson will have dwelt little on such tittle-tattle. They were astute enough to recognise a much larger and more promising picture. The controversy, which was to spread across the towns and communities in the north of England, had stirred a measure of publicity and interest, of which they could have only dreamed. Jackson would have seen that it had 'rivalry' written all over it. They must have known, even at this early stage of their enterprises, that they had invented a popular-culture product that was replete with commercial potential. The Belle Vue contest was to be named the British Open Brass Band Championship and (leaving aside three interruptions) remains the oldest continuous brass band contest.[17]

Railways

The Belle Vue event was due to start at 1 p.m. but was delayed until 2 p.m. because a train bringing one of the bands and its supporters was delayed. This was not a major problem, but the arrival of a great swarm of spectators from the late train served to illustrate the importance of rail travel to the promoters. A single train had carried a band, but it also carried many hundreds of supporters from a distance that would otherwise have been impractical for them to travel. It was abundantly clear that the future of the band contest would be assured only if it could be integrated with facilities newly afforded by the developing railway network (fig. 14).

It is difficult to overstate the cultural importance of the Victorian railway system. The main expansion coincided with the time that brass band contesting was developing. There can be little doubt that contests would have had less of an effect on bands and the entertainment industry more generally had railways expanded at a slower pace or been more restricted in their reach and accessibility. In some countries,

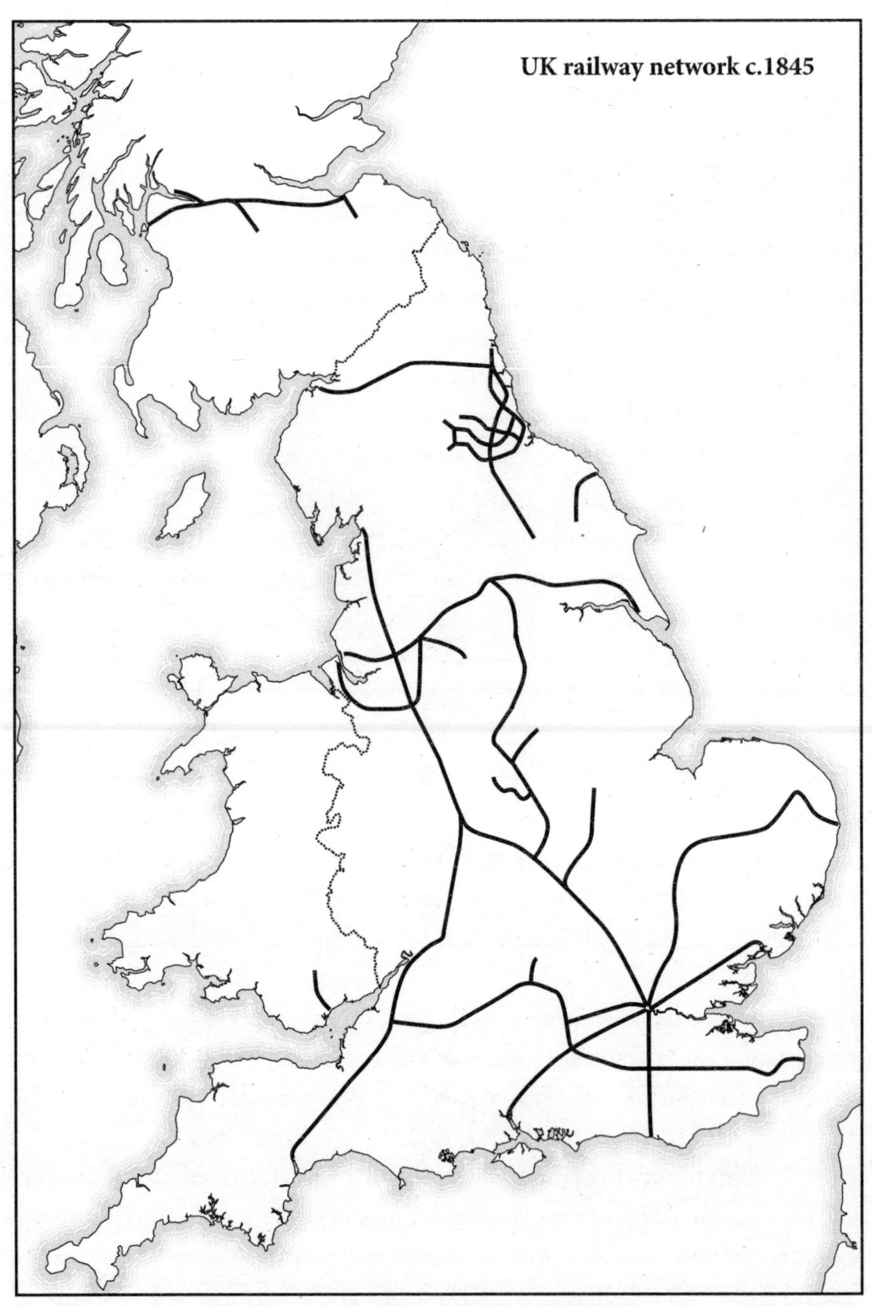

14. *Maps illustrating the growth of the UK railway network between c.1845 and c.1870.*

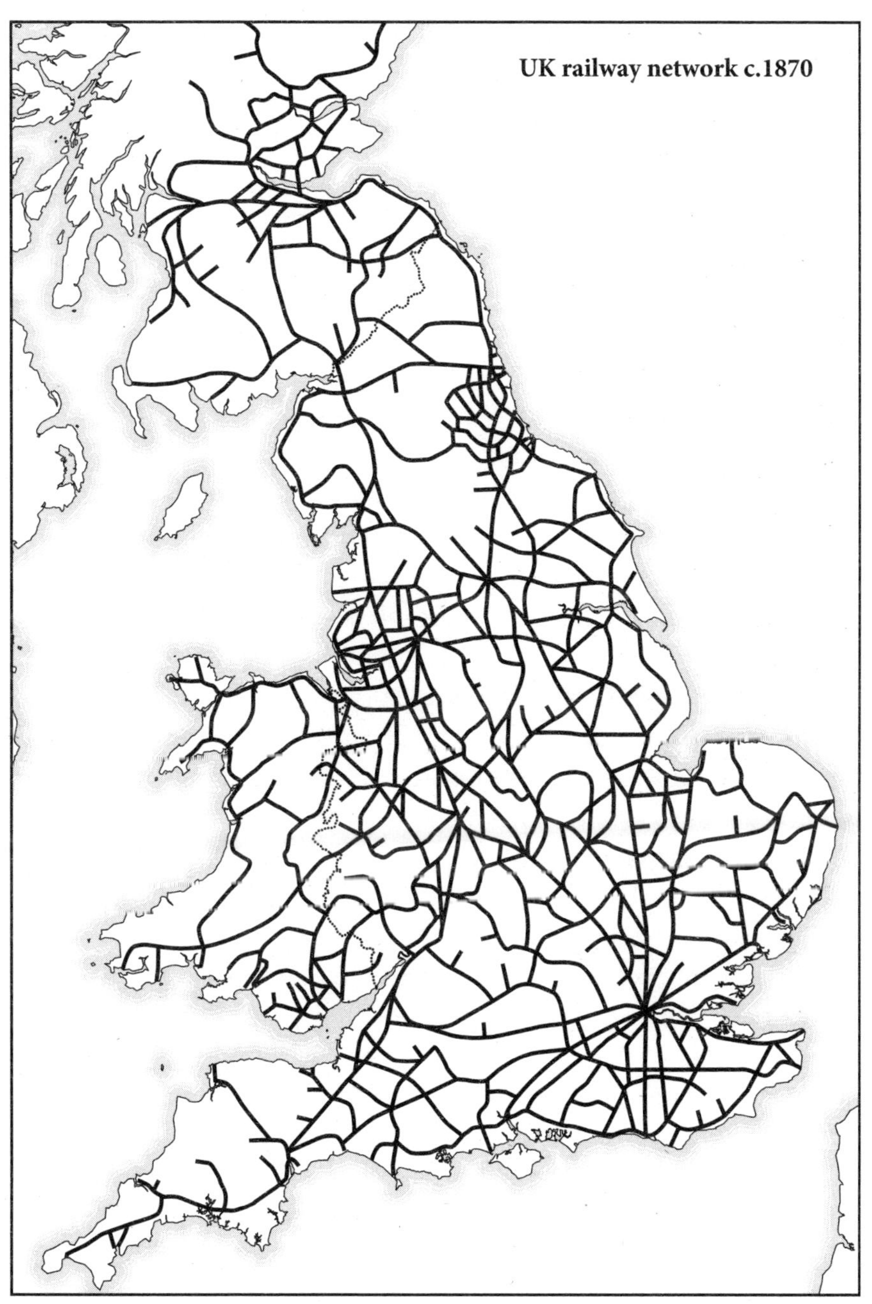

UK railway network c.1870

railways were government projects, but the railway network in Britain was developed by private, independent companies. By 1840 the country had 1,497 miles of rail track; ten years later there were 6,084 miles and a decade later it had increased to 9,060 miles. By the end of the century the British rail system had 18,680 miles of track stretching across the country, with stops at all large towns and a vast number of much smaller settlements. Even in 1850 there were 67 million rail journeys, a figure which doubled in the next decade and increased to 322 million by 1870. At the end of the century, when the population of the country stood at about 41 million, there were well over a billion journeys a year on the British railway system.[18]

Few other aspects of British enterprise in the period had a comparable impact on so many walks of life. Railways carried all manner of goods to make them commonly accessible across the country, including musical instruments, published music and the various other accoutrements necessary for banding. But they also carried people and, in so doing, they carried ideas, attitudes, news, opinions and information about how lives were led across the breadth of the nation. It followed that, whatever band contests offered in terms of musical engagement and entertainment, they also caused thousands of working-class brass players to assemble, and to listen attentively to each other play. This may not have caused bands to sound the same immediately, but differences between them must have become increasingly blunter, and a tendency must have emerged for the best of them to be imitated.

It soon became clear that railway travel made large and even smaller brass band contests more viable commercially. As well as the facility for transporting large groups of people from one place to another, it provided added value: people anticipated each journey as a new and exciting pleasure. Enderby Jackson visited the offices of each railway company to persuade them to create special fares for contest days: he argued that there should be 'cheap day excursions'. They were reluctant, but he persisted and enlisted the support of mayors and other dignitaries to his cause, emphasising the inherent *educational* value of his endeavours and the enlightenment his events provided to the working class. His efforts reached fruition when the railway companies finally realised what they should have known from the start: there was money to be made from working-class travellers if the prices were set at an affordable level. The eventual deal with railway companies was based on mutual benefits: contest organisers would incorporate train travel into their business model, and the rail companies would create a discounted price for the journeys which were generally set at 50 per cent of the normal fare. By 1860 railway travel was so integrated into the organisation of contests that bands were required to state the name of the railway company with which they and their supporters would travel, and the station of departure and return, on their entry application forms. At the start of his project Jackson had identified three challenges: solving the difficulties in forming bands, identifying enough of them to make contests viable, and 'the cost of bringing them together when found'. He knew that the deal with the railway companies was critical to his mission: the greatest obstacle was overcome, 'the workman and his family could now visit towns before *entirely debarred* from them by excessive costs'.[19]

Enderby Jackson and the Crystal Palace

Jackson ran several successful band contests, including one at Hull's Zoological Gardens from 1856. He also staged events as far south as Exeter, but in 1860 he faced the formidable task of organising a contest on the outskirts of London. The Crystal Palace had been built in Hyde Park in central London for the Great Exhibition of 1851. It was designed by Joseph Paxton and manufactured in prefabricated sections. The Exhibition lasted from May to November and was an enormous success: it attracted an estimated six million visitors. The building was never intended to be a permanent fixture in Hyde Park, which was one of the reasons for the prefabricated design. In 1852 it started to be dismantled and reconstructed on Sydenham Hill, more than eight miles south of London. The building was opened on its new site in June 1854. The Crystal Palace directors were keen to ensure that it would maintain the original objective of the Queen and her husband Prince Albert, that the project should be perceived as a facility for the nation rather than just for Londoners. To further this principle, 'national festivals' were organised. A brass band contest was included because, apart from its proven success as a popular event, the genre was, even at this early stage, being perceived as quintessentially British: the country, as one newspaper put it, was 'apt to associate something national with brass bands'.[20] Railway travel would be essential to the scheme; several of the Crystal Palace directors had interests in the railway companies so would have been aware of Jackson's previous enterprises in this regard. The business model, as with others at the Crystal Palace, ensured that a share of the combined income from entry and railway tickets would accrue to the Palace. However, leaving aside the logistical challenges, there were other concerns. The Crystal Palace directors were committed to establishing a reputation for musical excellence. Would brass bands contribute to that ideal? Would such a contest attract an audience unfamiliar with brass bands, and what of the relatively inferior social standing they had among some? In 1859 Jackson organised a trial event to test the viability of the proposition – not with brass bands but with hand-bell ringers. His main aim was to impress the directors with his organisational skills. He promised a dozen Yorkshire bell-ringing teams. In fact, it turned out to be a concert for just two, but it was sufficiently successful for him to be given permission to proceed the following year.[21]

The brass band contest was a much more ambitious enterprise. Jackson planned it in fine detail. It was to run over two consecutive days, with six preliminary rounds on each day, played on eight different open-air platforms.[22] Each day culminated with a final in which 12 bands played. There were 18 adjudicators, most of whom were bandmasters from the regular army. Jackson personally adjudicated the final – it is not entirely clear why. The first day was called the National Contest and the second the Sydenham Amateur Contest, which was confined to bands that had not won a prize of more than £20 in the previous year – an early example of the ranking of bands. The first day's contest was won by the Black Dyke Mills Band from Yorkshire, the second day by the Cyfarthfa Band from Merthyr Tydfil, south Wales. Cyfarthfa also came third on the first day but qualified for the second day because, in the 20 years of its existence, it had otherwise not entered a contest.

The cost of admission for the first day was a half crown (two shillings and six pence), and one shilling for the second day. Forty-three bands entered for the first day; 47 entered the second. Both days concluded with a concert played by all bands en masse, which Jackson conducted himself.[23] One wonders how much he enjoyed that experience. Over a thousand instrumentalists played together; the extent to which their instruments were tuned to the same pitch standard – and to that of the great Crystal Palace organ – is not known but, given the number of players involved, it probably didn't matter. *The Times* described it as 'tremendous', the *Era* called it 'a torrent of sound', the *Leeds Mercury* said that the organ, which was normally 'apt to drown everything, was scarcely audible'.

The event was advertised by individual railway companies, with special trains timetabled to transport bands and their supporters from appropriate stations using information that had been provided to Jackson in the entrance application forms. Prices were heavily discounted, and children could travel free or at a yet more discounted price. Travellers were encouraged to spend three or four days in London before returning (fig. 15). Attendance for the first day was in the order of 7,000, the second day attracted more. *The Times* reckoned it to have been 'considerably over 22,000', while the *Era*, which probably had access to box-office data, was able to express it more precisely as 22,304. Critical assessment by the press, which reported the two days separately, was good and often excellent. *The Times* made an interesting comparison between the brass bands and the *Orphéoniste* choirs of the French provinces, which had performed at the Crystal Palace the previous month, and between Jackson and their distinguished director Eugène Delaporte. The *Daily Telegraph* praised the techniques of the band players and noted how the competitive spirit had contributed to an elevation of standards:

It is interesting to observe that these stalwart workmen are daunted by no difficulties and have no hesitation in attacking the difficulties of 'Preciosa' and 'William Tell'. The Saltaire Band is composed entirely of men in the employment of Mr Titus Salt . . . It is rumoured that Mr Salt promised a considerable sum of money to his band in the event of their winning the first prize. The band affords an example of the rivalry which has resulted in these gigantic

Midland Railway.

GREAT NATIONAL
Brass Band Contest

AT THE
CRYSTAL PALACE, SYDENHAM.

ON MONDAY, JULY 22ND, 1861,
A CHEAP EXCURSION TRAIN WILL LEAVE

SKIPTON, BRADFORD, LEEDS, SHEFFIELD

And other Stations on the Midland Railway, for

LONDON,

AS UNDER.

Fares there and back and Times of Starting:

STATIONS		a.m.	First Class	Cov. Carr.	STATIONS		a.m.	First Class	Cov. Carr.
Skipton	dep.	7.45			Wakefield By Omnibus to Oakenshaw		9.40		
Kildwick	„	7.55			Oakenshaw - -		10.10		
Steeton	„	8. 0			Barnsley By Omnibus to Cudworth	„	8.50		
Keighley	„	8.12			Cudworth By Ordinary Train to Masboro'	„	9.11		
Bingley	„	8.20			Wath	„ „	9.27		
Bradford	„	8.30			Swinton	„ „	9 32		
Shipley	„	8.40	20s.	10s.	Sheffield Special Train	„	10.35	20s.	10s.
Apperley	„	8.50			Masboro'	„ „	10 55		
Calverley	„	8.55			Eckington By Ordinary Train to Derby		10.12		
Kirkstall	„	9. 2			Chesterfield Special Train	„	11.25		
Leeds (Wellington Sta.)	„	9.30			Wingfield By Ordinary Train to Derby		10.56		
Woodlesford By Ordinary Train to Masboro'		8.30			Ambergate	„ „	11. 8		
Normanton Special Train	„	10. 0			Belper	„ „	11.18		

London arrive about 4.30 p.m.

Children under Three Years of Age, Free; above Three & under Twelve, Half-Fares. Tickets and Bills may be obtained at all the above-mentioned Stations, at Mr. Bennett's Omnibus Office, Wakefield, and at the Royal Hotel, Barnsley.

The Return Train will leave the Euston Square Station, London, on Friday, July 26th, at 12.35 noon. Tickets are not Transferable, and will be available for returning by this Train only. Luggage must be conveyed under the Passengers' own care, as the Company will not be responsible.

TEN MINUTES WILL BE ALLOWED AT DERBY FOR REFRESHMENTS BOTH IN
GOING AND RETURNING.

JAMES ALLPORT,
General Manager.

Derby, June, 1861.

W. Bemrose & Sons, Printers by Steam Power, Derby.

15. One of the posters produced and deployed locally by railway companies to promote travel to brass band contests — in this case the Crystal Palace contest of 1861.

performances. The natural rivalry between factory and factory gradually extends to towns and cities until at length entire districts are roused to emulation.[24]

Unfortunately, the Saltaire band did not win the first prize – they came second; but the words were well chosen because the quantity of supporters from distant places who attended suggests that the bands had taken on a representative role. A remarkable feature was the number of bands who travelled to the contest having never previously won a prize. This was an indicator of the status that bands were achieving in their localities, but for contest promoters (and railway companies) it portended profits.

The Enderby Jackson version of the Crystal Palace contests lasted just four years. The ticket sales, even though they always numbered in the thousands, decreased after the first year, fewer bands competed, and the events drew less attention. There was also some discontent expressed in the northern press about the prominence given to the London event; this may have been reflected in the number and quality of bands that entered in subsequent years. Just 21 bands entered the 1863 contest, which was reduced from two successive days to just one.[25] The two days on which the contest was held in 1860 attracted almost 30,000 visitors. The 1863 one-day event attracted 13,366, which can hardly be regarded as a failure.[26] It was won by the Blandford Forum band from rural Dorset. Conveniently and possibly coincidentally, Blandford Forum railway station, at which the band and its supporters boarded and to which they returned, had opened a new extension just two weeks before when the Somerset and Dorset Railway company was formed. The leader of the Blandford band was its agent.

In 1863 the Crystal Palace company judged that the event 'had failed to realise considerable results'.[27] The idea of staging a contest that would involve bands from France and other parts of the continent was considered but never materialised. Jackson probably recognised the downward path of the London project and turned his attentions once more to the north. He was also nearing a period when his entrepreneurial skills were starting to be applied to the organisation of tours for foreign bands and artistes. The annual contests at Belle

Vue, Manchester, and at Hull had become settled and anticipated annual events and new alternative opportunities were presenting themselves. Jackson's claims for the success of the Crystal Palace contest, and especially the evidence he provided for those claims, has been questioned.[28] There is no doubt that he routinely exaggerated the impact of his projects, but this should not detract from the importance of his Crystal Palace contests and his influence on the brass band movement more generally. Several of his boasts have stood up to scrutiny. Apart from all else, he had shown that using the Crystal Palace as a venue for a national contest was a tenable prospect. Its size and grandeur were unmatched and the logistics, if handled properly, could be easily resolved. This was recognised almost four decades later by an equally large personality with enthusiasm and energy to match that of Jackson.

John Henry Iles

By the end of the nineteenth century most brass bands were self-governing and free of the debts incurred during their formation. Several local associations were formed to promote their interests and organise local contests, but there was no body capable of co-ordinating the entire movement at a national level. The first National Bands Federation was not established until 1930 and received a mixed reception. Consequently, entertainment entrepreneurs functioned as surrogates for national leadership, a situation which was benign and has, in various subsequent manifestations, remained in place. Enderby Jackson was the most prominent impresario in the first 40 years of contesting. John Henry Iles succeeded to that role in the late 1890s. The successive influence of these two men on British brass bands spanned almost a century. Jackson's ideas led to the first major brass band contests in the mid-1850s; Iles became involved in about 1898 and remained influential until after the Second World War.

Like Jackson, Iles was a gifted musician – an organist, conductor and singer; but his greatest talent was as an entrepreneur. By all accounts he was a gregarious, larger-than-life character and a minor celebrity as a cricketer: he was an occasional member of the Gloucestershire side in the period when it also included England's greatest batsman, W. G. Grace. His career started in his father's timber business, but his sights were always set on other enterprises. He soon moved into publishing, the development of amusement resorts and other ventures in the entertainment industry. He was a brilliant and opportunist businessman, but not brilliant enough to avoid bankruptcy in July 1938 because of reckless speculations in UK and foreign entertainment projects. Brass bands benefited from his considerable gifts and personal connections when he was in his prime. He claimed his interest in brass bands was ignited at the 1897 Belle Vue contest, which he visited on a whim while on a business trip to Manchester. He may, even at that early stage, have identified a profitable line of business, but he also seems to have been genuinely impressed by the musical quality of brass bands and the disparity between their value and their critical reception in the wider musical world. He will also have been aware of the consistent popularity of brass band contests and their potential for further development. In 1895 the *Brass Band Annual* published a retrospective article on contesting in the previous year:

> On every hand 'Progress' is written in large characters – a very desirable state of affairs. Band Music – the Music of the Masses, is becoming a power in the land, and bands are coming to be recognised at large . . . Without doubt the main factor in this all-round advancement is the contesting movement. Contesting has revolutionised the whole world of brass music.[29]

It must have been starkly obvious to a businessman like Iles that brass banding was more than a minor esoteric activity: it was a market segment that directly engaged more than 100,000 practitioners, and a further, incalculable number of devotees. In 1899 he bought the main publishing house for brass band music, that of Richard Smith & Co., along with its monthly magazine, the *British Bandsman*, which he transformed into the only weekly publication for the brass band movement. At a stroke, he gained control of a major source for the supply of printed music to brass bands and what was already being regarded as their main vehicle for communication.

16. *A band performing in the 1902 Crystal Palace (Open) contest. The players stand in square formation, which was the usual practice until the 1920s, when it gave way to the modern seated format. Square formation was a legacy of military practice.*

In 1900 he staged the first of his National contests at the Crystal Palace (fig. 16). By this time, Enderby Jackson's events of the 1860s were a distant memory. Unlike Jackson, Iles was attuned to the entertainment business in London and the tastes of its audiences because all his enterprises were run from offices in the Strand in the centre of the capital. For a new Crystal Palace contest to be successful, it needed more than the co-operation of bands and deft organisation: it needed a strategy that would attract the attention of Londoners to a form of entertainment of which most knew next to nothing. The audience needed to be well primed before the contest was announced. Iles used an acquaintance with Britain's most celebrated musician – Sir Arthur Sullivan. He persuaded Sullivan to conduct an arrangement for massed brass bands of his setting of Kipling's patriotic song, 'The Absent-minded Beggar', in a benefit concert for charities associated with the South African wars.[30] The Kipling/ Sullivan collaboration was a main component of a nationwide charitable appeal organised by the recently launched newspaper, the *Daily Mail*. Iles cleverly attached the brass band world to this widely popular sentiment by labelling the event as the *British Bandsman*'s contribution to this outstanding charitable cause. The concert was given to a packed Royal Albert Hall on 20 January 1900. The reviewer from the *Morning Post*, mindful of London audiences' detachment from brass bands, deployed a necessarily didactic approach:

The Patriotic Band Festival at the Albert Hall on Saturday evening attracted a huge audience. The concert was organised by Mr Henry Iles of the *British Bandsman*, on behalf of the *Daily Mail* Kipling Poem Fund, and the proceeds are to be given to the wives or children of men called to the Colours and to the relief of sick and wounded soldiers and sailors. The occasion was in many respects unique owing to the presence of several champion brass bands . . . As their name implies, these bands are composed of brass instruments and do not contain any members of the woodwind family, such as flutes, clarinets, oboes, and bassoons which figure in our military bands. This naturally produces an unavoidable uniformity of colour. To the cornets are allotted passages that in an orchestra would be played by strings, and the greatest task is necessarily put on the capabilities of the executants. The performance of the bands merits high praise. The Besses o' th' Barn Band realised really wonderful effects of lights on shade.[31]

This success emboldened Iles to proceed with the first of his National contests at the Crystal Palace in the following July, and again he enlisted the support of Sullivan. To draw the largest possible audience, and following the pattern established by Jackson decades earlier, other attractions were arranged for the day, targeted at different interest groups: 'a hundred miles bicycle race for the Carwardine Cup', a fireworks display and a 'Great Flower show in Celebration of the Bicentenary of the Sweet Pea'. The following day the London correspondent of the *Leeds Mercury* reported:

Of late years Brass Band festivals have been becoming more and more popular in London, but none of them have yet come up to the big contests in the Midlands so far as enthusiasm and creditable performances are concerned. One of the best competitions in London was held yesterday at the Crystal Palace at which there were 48 bands, numbering some 1,200 instrumentalists . . . Later in the day the combined bands gave a successful concert, made up of Mendelssohn's 'Cornelius' and the Tannhauser [sic] marches, both conducted by Mr Augustus Mann [the music director of the Crystal Palace] and the Absent-minded Beggar March, Rule Britannia and the National Anthem conducted by Sir Arthur Sullivan.[32]

Iles had created a genuinely national band contest. It was to be a permanent annual fixture until 1936, when the Crystal Palace was destroyed by fire. It then moved to Alexandra Palace in north London for the two years before the Second World War, continuing from 1945 at the Royal Albert Hall as its new venue.

Magazines, journals and the contest ethos

When Iles bought the *British Bandsman* in 1898, print was the only effective method of mass communication. Magazines were targeted at categories of readership stratified by gender, class and interests. He had been in the publishing business for more than a decade; his first major business venture was his acquisition of the *Organist and Choirmaster* magazine. The first generation of brass band magazines was published to further the interests of an existing line of business, usually a publishing firm, but the centrality of contesting was apparent in the banner titles of most of them from the start. The *Brass Band News* carried the extension title '*and Musical Contest Advertiser*'. The *British Bandsman* adopted the extension '*and Contest Field*'. Contests were also the primary theme of their relentlessly didactic content: the assumption was that all readers really wanted was to be taught how to win contests. Top of the list was the musical orthodoxies that needed to be respected and mastered for successful contesting. Thus, in its first years of publication, the *Brass Band World* carried articles on 'Contest Judges', 'Articulation', 'Quality of Tone' and 'Flexibility of Tone'. These articles were of no great merit and cast little light on their subjects, but for bandsmen they were probably seen as authoritative sources of information. In style and content, they managed to convey a moral and, at times, piously superior tone which was presumably part of an intention to elevate the cultural status of the brass band movement. A persistently prominent subject was the condemnation of unruly behaviour at band contests, a topic about which the *British Bandsman* took an especially sanctimonious view. In 1897 it carried an editorial suggesting that 'the contest field is dying because of the riotous assemblies. The military bandmasters [a reference to the adjudicator class] are looking at us with utter contempt.'[33] There can be little doubt that some brass band contest results stirred passions that led to punch-ups, usually under the influence of drink, but such reports need to be read with an element of scepticism. There was, after all, a lot at stake, especially in times of financial hardship. Local rivalries were raw, and it could be argued that the *British Bandsman* and the *Brass Band World* had encouraged them. There was also a general mistrust of the military bandmasters who were enlisted to adjudicate and – for no obvious reason – were treated with heightened deference by contest organisers. Bandsmen often took a different view. Even in the late nineteenth century, military adjudicators were seen as outsiders who engaged with brass bands only for the fat fees attached to such appointments. Reports of minor disturbances may also have been prompted by more mundane and self-interested factors. Band periodicals competed for readership and were seldom oblivious of circulation figures. It is easy to detect the shadow of hypocrisy lurking in the self-righteous tone with which skirmishes were reported. Scandal sold copies – probably more than mind-numbing articles such as 'Cleanliness in the band room', which was the main editorial item in one issue.[34]

Test pieces

A prerequisite for the meaningful development of a distinctive brass band repertoire was the adoption of a standard instrumentation

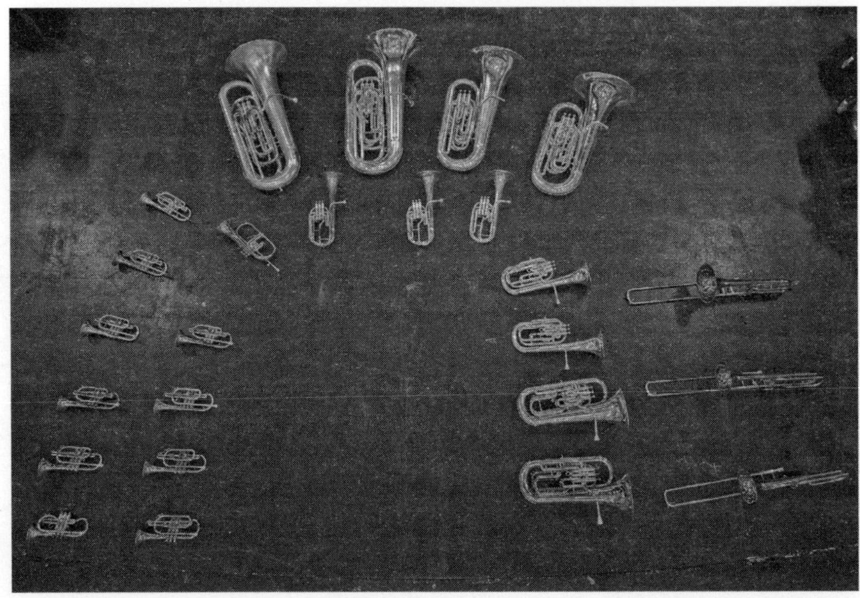

17. *The brass instruments in a standard brass band arranged in one of the common seating formats. Tuned and untuned percussion are added according to the requirements of the work that is to be performed.*

format (fig. 17). A consensus emerged by the late 1870s but it took longer to be consolidated. Variances and suggestions for adjustments prevailed into the twentieth century. Some bands experimented with the inclusion of saxophones and, decades after the standard was established, Denis Wright, the BBC's organiser of band music, was regularly lamenting the absence of additional flugelhorns. Standardisation was important for two principal reasons: a common format allowed competing bands to be adjudicated with greater ease and accuracy, and it would encourage original idiomatic compositions to replace the prevailing system in which bandmasters were responsible for arranging existing works for their preferred line-up of instruments – or more expediently, for the instruments that were available. The move to a standard format is not easily untangled because surviving musical scores and parts from the period are few and inconsistent, but there is little doubt that, for most bands, expediency and local preferences played a major part in musical decision-making. The entry forms for the Crystal Palace contests of the 1860s provide the largest sample from the Victorian period. It reveals the extent to which the instrumentation of bands differed, but this was to change as the best bands became increasingly sophisticated and provided a model that others followed. A sample of the data from the 1860 contest forms is given in Appendix 1.

In 1882 Wright and Round's *Brass Band News* published an article under the confusing heading 'Classification', which was a survey of the different models of instrumental format that were regularly in use at that time.[35] Wright and Round was also a publisher, so it is difficult to judge whether the article was a genuine observation of current practice or an outright advocacy of its own interests. It suggested that the instruments comprising a brass band 'shouldn't be less than 14, and if possible 20'. It went on to name all the instruments, often equating them with orchestral parts: 'the second and third cornets act as the second violins', 'the solo euphonium is the violoncello of the brass band' and so on. It also emphasised the need for three slide trombones, one of which should be a 'bass trombone pitched in G'.[36] It stopped short of prescribing the number of cornets that were needed, and quoted Berlioz's orchestration manual of 1844/1856,[37] before concluding with a broad recommendation of how bands of 14 or 24 players should be constituted.[38]

There is little doubt that the main influence on standardisation came primarily from the three conductor-arrangers who had the most success in contests up to the turn of the century: John Gladney, Alexander Owen and Edwin Swift. They dominated brass band contesting in the closing decades of the nineteenth century. Gladney, a clarinettist with the Hallé Orchestra, was the son of a military bandmaster. Owen was raised in an institution for pauper children. He joined the Stalybridge Old Band and established himself as a brilliant soprano cornet player before becoming a brass band trainer and conductor. Swift had a similarly modest background and, like Owen, received his musical training in a brass band. He, too, was a virtuoso cornet player, but his talent was as precocious as it was brilliant. He was arranging music for his band when he was little more than a child and was appointed bandmaster of Linthwaite Band before his 14th birthday. Gladney had received both a training and a broad musical experience in his itinerant childhood. The three were brilliant trainers at a time when contest test pieces were often circulated as 'short' (abbreviated) scores which bandmasters were expected to arrange for the available instruments. Owen was particularly ambitious as an arranger, transcribing lengthy modern works by major classical composers, including those of Richard Wagner, for performance by the Besses o' th' Barn Band. Between 1873 and the end of the century, with only one exception, the British Open Contest was won by a band conducted by Gladney, Owen or Swift. Each could live comfortably on his income from brass band conducting. At one stage in his career, Owen was training 25 bands and, in 1898, he conducted ten different bands at the Belle Vue contest. What is written about the three of them testifies to their resolute personalities but primarily to their prodigious musical talents. Because much of their work involved the transcription of music for the brass band medium, it followed that their choice of instrumentation yielded the most refined and satisfactory formats.[39]

Prior to his first Hull contest in 1857, Enderby Jackson wrote his 'Yorkshire Waltzes' which he circulated as a piano score for bandmasters to arrange, but it did not take long for 'selections' from operas or other large works to be the favoured test pieces. These potpourris of melodies and other musical episodes demonstrated the musical skills of individual players and a band as whole. Between 1872 and 1916 the selections for the Belle Vue contest were usually the work of the Charles Godfreys: a father and son of the same name, both military bandmasters. Whether this peculiar and suspiciously nepotistic arrangement was simply a matter of inertia on the part of Jennison, who was still running the contests, or a feeling that the Godfreys really had no equals as independent expert judges, is unclear, but it came to be deeply resented by many, including Alexander Owen, who was probably a more intelligent musician than either and certainly a better brass band expert. While bands determined their own instrumentation, the 'arrangements' – here meaning the outline content of any given selection – were determined by one of the Godfreys.[40] Eventually, Owen, avoiding mention of either Godfrey by name, wrote a strident letter for publication in the *Brass Band News*, drawing attention to 'the many unpleasant features' of the Belle Vue contest, which included the 'injustice' of having the same judge every year and the fact that the 'arrangement of the test piece seems permanently confined to one musician'.[41]

Owen also complained about the lack of ventilation in the performance hall and that the views of adjudicators were never made public. His feelings gathered such strength that he boycotted the 1886 contest, leaving Gladney to conduct five of the 20 bands who competed and Swift to conduct seven. Such was his popularity that appeals were made for Owen to resume his association for the 1887 contest, which he did, but the source of his displeasure would last until the next century when the Belle Vue contest was forced to share its lustre with that of the Iles project at the Crystal Palace.

By the end of the nineteenth century, contest organisers were faced with two key problems: the need to find a rational way of limiting the number of bands that entered each contest, because so many regularly applied, and the question of repertoire – it was time to consider the commissioning of original works that would consolidate the standard instrumentation. Both problems were to be resolved by entrepreneurs and publishers rather than by the bands themselves. In 1886 a July contest was introduced at Belle Vue that was restricted to bands that had not won a prize in their previous four contest attempts. This effectively disqualified the elite bands, but not their conductors, who could temporarily divert their attention to the development of lesser bands. In 1910 this was formalised into a two-section system that portended the four-section and eventually the five-section systems that were to follow. Contests were then usually restricted to 20 bands in each division.

The first original published work written specifically as a test piece for a brass band contest, and using the standard instrumentation, was the tone poem *Labour and Love* by the 34-year-old Percy Fletcher. It had a mixed reception. Some bands regarded the standard format as an unwelcome intrusion into their current and more flexible practices. Fletcher was a minor composer and a less than minor theatre conductor who, in 1916, became well known in London as the conductor of the long-running musical comedy *Chu Chin Chow*. *Labour and Love* is often cited as the first original work for brass band, but this is not true. Several other earlier works legitimately challenge that claim. Iles was keen to promote the idea of original works as test pieces and was to directly or indirectly issue several commissions, but *Labour and Love* was not one of them. It was sent speculatively by Fletcher to Smith & Co., where it was judged to fit the bill.[42] It was moderately effective but musically unremarkable. Structurally, it resembles the episodic format that bands were so used to tackling in operatic selections. This may have been deliberate on Fletcher's part. He called the work a tone poem and was doubtless inspired to do so by the format used by Liszt, Berlioz and Richard Strauss to much greater effect. The genre requires the evocation of an extramusical topic such as a poem, story or picture in music. The story of *Labour and Love* was of Fletcher's making and is carefully spelled out in a prefatory synopsis to the score. It portrays a working-class parable about a 'downtrodden' working man who gains redemption from lethargy through the love of a virtuous woman who inspires him to 'improve his position by continued devotion to his employer's interests'. There is scope to wonder whether this celebration of deference was received in the intended spirit in 1913, and this may have contributed to its limp reception by bandsmen. It was the first of many original works commissioned or used as test pieces for National contests that used the tone-poem idea; fortunately, some used it to better effect. Many minor composers were attracted to write test pieces, but the commissioning process seems to have been haphazard. The Welsh composer Cyril Jenkins probably gained his first two test piece commissions, *Coriolanus* (1920) and *Life Divine* (1921), on the strength of his influential position as director of music for London's parks; it is less easy to understand why he was engaged to write a further two, other than that he was an outrageous self-publicist. Another parks director was Hubert Bath, whose first work for brass band was *Freedom* (1922). Bath was to become one of the first great British film music composers. Denis Wright, who was to be an important figure in banding, was a total outsider. The son of a London surgeon and educated under Stanford at the Royal College of Music, he wrote his *Joan of Arc* for the 1925 National contest in response to an advertisement placed in the *Musical Times*. He was working as a schoolteacher and was understandably attracted by the 100-guinea commission fee, which he said was equal to three months of his salary as a teacher. He admitted to having been unaware that 'there existed a Brass Band World', but when he saw the advertisement he 'became suddenly very vividly conscious of the fact'.[43] He had never written for a brass band previously and had not knowingly heard one play. Among the many others who became specialist brass band test piece composers before the 1960s, and perhaps the most skilful, was the Salvationist Eric Ball. Ball was deft at writing effective pieces for bands of high as well as much lower technical competence. His test pieces, more so than any others of the period, have endured to modern times.

An important direction of travel by composers of original test pieces was their abandonment of the idea that instruments of the brass band needed to imitate the sound of orchestral instruments. This practice gained strength when, under the influence of military adjudicators such as the Godfreys, transcribed orchestral works were mandatory as test pieces. The skill of imitating an orchestral sound was prominent in the training schedule at Kneller Hall since the middle of the nineteenth century when its most eminent professor of music theory, Charles Florian Mandel, produced his treatise on the subject.[44] The advent of original works should be regarded as the point at which the musical idiom gained independence from this practice, but finding composers to write them was not easy.

Works by composers such as Ball and Wright served their purpose, but the real challenge for Iles was to attract the attention of well-established classical music composers. He was aided in this endeavour by Herbert Whiteley, a Yorkshire-born musician who served as editor of the *British Bandsman* between 1906 and 1930. Compared to Iles, Whiteley was a reclusive figure, but he was a discriminating musician. The first major composer he attracted was Gustav Holst, who had been a professional trombonist. His *A Moorside Suite* was written for the National contest of 1928. In 1930 Granville Bantock's *Oriental Rhapsody* was written for the Open contest, and in the same year Britain's greatest composer Sir Edward Elgar wrote *Severn Suite* for the National. Other works came from Herbert Howells, John Ireland, Arthur Bliss and Ralph Vaughan Williams. There were also two commissions from the concert pianist Helen Perkin. While each drew attention because of the celebrity of their composers, it is questionable whether they advanced the idiom to any significant degree. For most of these composers, it was a brief flirtation with the genre. The criticism they often received illustrated how isolated some sectors of the brass band movement had become. One band commented that Holst's *Moorside Suite* was not a good test piece because 'there wasn't a single semiquaver in the whole work'.

It was Herbert Whiteley who persuaded Elgar to write *Severn Suite* for brass band. It took him a long time to build up to it, and he was clearly star-struck when he communicated with the composer:

The Minuet is just lovely, & the muted cornets and trombones will be most effective. This movement will make a big appeal owing to its simplicity. I ought to have said before that you have shown the youngsters 'how to do it' in the double fugue.[45]

Denis Wright, a rounded and dispassionate observer, took a different view. He pondered on the value of these celebrity commissions, but from a different perspective than the more conservative voices within the brass band movement:

The Severn Suite, for all its brilliant Toccata and quiet organ-like Fugue, was not really good Elgar. But it was good brass music even though the minuet was over-long and repetitive and the muting of more than half the band was not altogether a successful innovation from a tonal point of view . . . [On the other hand] *A Downland Suite* [by John Ireland] was good music, good brass music and good Ireland. I have a fancy it will outlast all the others if bands will only make the effort to keep it alive.[46]

On balance, there is no doubt that the group of works by major composers served the dual intentions of adding good works to the repertoire and elevating the status of the brass band, but the most frequently performed pieces were those written by composers who were continuously associated with brass bands. Selections were not used as test pieces after the mid-1920s, but arrangements of overtures had intermittent comebacks after the Second World War. Frank Wright's arrangements were popular, and in 1960 the British Open test piece was a Mozart *Fantasia* arranged by the celebrated orchestral conductor Malcolm Sargent; but in the 1960s the main excitement was attracted by the music of Gilbert Vinter, who wrote a series of works that portended a new and acceptable manifestation of modernism in brass band writing.

Many have seen Vinter's compositions as something of a watershed in brass band test piece writing because he tested performers in new ways and extended the palette of sounds of which the brass band was capable. In many respects, he anticipated a much greater level of experimentation from a later group of yet more gifted composers. He achieved this through the precision and cleverness of his scoring. He deployed mutes, which were seldom used in brass band contests at that time, and integrated percussion instruments. He was not the first composer to incorporate percussion – for example, Eric Ball scored percussion in his *Journey into Freedom* (1967); but those parts were written for concert performances and were dispensed with for contests. In 1969 the Open contest admitted percussion instruments for the first time because they were scored in Vinter's *Spectrum*.

Chapter 5

Concerts, virtuosos, 'cornet mania' and the emergence of highbrow and lowbrow

The expansion of brass bands as a mass activity benefited from changes to the way people congregated to listen to music. The public concert, in its modern sense, was a nineteenth-century development. Indeed, words such as 'concert', 'audience' and 'conductor' did not gain their modern meanings until that time. This does not mean that people did not previously gather to listen to musical performances: rather, it is that the way such events were organised and publicised became different, and the franchise for listening to music embraced a much wider constituency, in terms of both social class and geographical distribution. A further development was the emergence of new protocols for attentive listening. Concertgoers in the eighteenth century experienced no embarrassment if they arrived late for performances and seldom hesitated to chat with each other throughout. The novelist Fanny Burney described a musical event in her novel *Cecilia* (1782), which was probably more realistic than fictional:

They entered the Great room during the second act of the Concert, to which no one of the party but herself had any desire to listen, no sort of attention was paid; the ladies entertaining themselves as if no Orchestra was in the room and gentlemen with equal regard to it, struggling for a place by the fire.[1]

Such behaviour lingered well into the nineteenth century in some quarters. The diarist Captain R. H. Gronow of the 1st Foot Guards was often a guest of Lady Flint, who held musical soirees at her house in Birdcage Walk near Buckingham Palace:

Among those of the fashionable world in London who patronised music . . . no one was more conspicuous than Lady Flint . . . Lady Flint's desire to gratify her friends, however, was often frustrated by the annoying conduct of those who had no taste for music, who disturbed the enjoyment of some of the most beautiful pieces by the rattling of their cups and saucers, and the tone in which their conversation was carried on. Jarnowickz, the violin player, having upon one occasion commenced a concerto by Beethoven, accompanied by his little orchestra, consisting of Cramer, Spagnoletti, Lindley, and Dragonetti, suddenly ceased playing, and apologised for so doing by stating, that the discord caused by the tea-drinkers was such as to mar the effect of the immortal composer's music. He added, that those who thus showed that they did not understand music, would perhaps appreciate better the piece which he was about to play,—viz., 'God save the King', to which they would listen at least with respect. The reproof had a good effect, for always afterwards a complete silence reigned during the performance.[2]

This event occurred around 1820 and the fact that the violinist felt emboldened to complain about his audience's behaviour suggests that he was starting to get used to more civilised attention.

The social elite were probably the first to notice behavioural changes that were to take place because, to the greatest extent, it was to their world (fig. 18). Their exclusive access to refined music diminished and was eventually lost as it spread to a newly emerging middle class and then to what came to be called a 'popular audience'. Shifts in the consumption of live music are important to the brass band story because the introduction and routine appearance of popular, public concerts reconfigured the infrastructure of the country's musical life. Brass bands were to become an increasingly visible part of that infrastructure and one of the agents of its change.

ADVERTISEMENTS FOR MAY, 1826.

NEW ARGYLL ROOMS.
MORNING CONCERT.

PIO CIANCHETTINI has the honour to inform the Nobility, Gentry, and his Friends, that his

ANNUAL CONCERT

Will take place this Year, on Tuesday Morning, the 9th of May; on which occasion several New Instrumental and Vocal Pieces of his Composition, will be performed.

Vocal Performers.—Signora Bonini, Signora Marinoni, Signora F. Marinoni, Miss Cianchettini, and Miss Paton. Signor Curioni, Signor Torri, Mr. Pearman, Signor Sola, Mr. Sapio, Signor Pellegrini, and Signor De Begnis.

Instrumental Performers.—*Violin*, Mr. Mori; *French Horn*, Signor Puzzi; *Flute*, Signor Sola.

I. Signori Gambati will perform a Duet on two Trumpets with the newly invented Keys.

Piano-forte and Conductor, Pio Cianchettini.

The Concert will begin at One o'Clock precisely.

Tickets *Half-a-Guinea each*, to be had at Messrs. Clementi and Co., Cheapside; Messrs. Chappell and Co.; Messrs. Birchall and Co.; and Messrs. Latour and Co., New Bond Street; Messrs. Willis and Co.; St. James's Street; Royal Harmonic Institution, 246, Regent Street; Messrs. Cramer, Addison and Beale, Regent Street; and of Pio Cianchettini, 183, Regent Street.

18. Concert advertisement in La Belle Assemblée, or, Bell's Court and Fashionable Magazine, *1 May 1826. The cost, venue, start time and the fact that the advertisement was placed in this publication define the social class of the audience. Interestingly, the programme included a duet for the keyed trumpet performed by the Gambati brothers.*

From the middle of the nineteenth century, concerts were purposefully crafted and performed for popular audiences. As was so often the case in the Victorian period, cultural change was promoted by commercial rather than purely artistic interests. Charles Dickens wrote of how high and low culture was mediated by 'those little screws of existence – pounds, shillings and pence'.[3] He was right, and such factors acted as strongly in amateur music as in the profession. Brass bands were just one of many forms of music that were under the influence of new forms of commercialism: the mass production and sale of pianos to middle-class homes was another. Later came the rise of music hall, a genre that was directed unashamedly at popular audiences seeking uninhibited pleasure. Popular concerts became available to anyone who could afford the price of a ticket. The price of entry was an important determinant: it cost a shilling to hear the

Hallé Orchestra in 1860, but other events may have cost less than half that. Concerts became *occasions* in which people of like mind came together for no other purpose than to be entertained. Audiences started to include people of more various social strata, and advertisements in daily newspapers reveal the range of musical tastes that were accommodated. People flocked to see and hear musical celebrities whose reputations preceded them. They were especially thrilled by virtuosity and, as the century progressed, brass band soloists were among the brightest stars. Many in the working class were introduced to classical music and opera through arrangements of it performed by brass and military bands. Then came a paradox. Despite the democratisation of listening – to which brass bands were such an important contributor – a new and divisive trend emerged. By the beginning of the twentieth century, the distinction between popular and classical music became more pronounced. This was not an especially British phenomenon. In other countries, including the US, new edifices and agencies such as opera houses and symphony halls were built that emphasised a separation between popular and classical music cultures. Terms such as highbrow and lowbrow became widely understood. By the twentieth century, such developments had critically influenced the way that brass bands were to be categorised in the musical world.

Expansion

The popularity of classical music in the nineteenth century was accelerated by the rise of amateurism, and this encouraged working-class people to engage with a wide spectrum of repertoire. For much of the nineteenth century, brass bands favoured derivatives of Italian operas for contests and concerts, and the many choral societies that emerged across the country were attracted to works by both contemporary composers and those of the past. Large-scale performances of sacred oratorios, such as Handel's *Messiah* and Mendelssohn's *Elijah* (which had its first performance in Birmingham in 1846), became greatly anticipated events, but they were also major community projects that involved months of preparation. The intensity of those experiences on choristers was important because it caused and even required them – ordinary men and women – to gain an intimate understanding of large-scale musical works.

The expansion of amateurism was both a cause and a beneficiary of the growth of the music industry. In 1841 there were 6,600 professional musicians (including music teachers) in England and Wales. This number had almost tripled by 1871. By 1901 it had grown to more than 39,000 and the trend was to continue.[4] These figures come from decennial census returns, but they do not include the thousands of serving military bandsmen in the British army and navy. They might properly have been regarded as full-time musicians but were identified in census returns only as soldiers or sailors. In 1871 the government office responsible for the census noticed a remarkable increase in the number of people working in the creative arts. Its report of the 1881 census showed a further upward trend of sufficient significance to have merited comment:

> Among artists and other persons who minister to our amusement, by far the most numerous were the Musicians. Of these, including all grades down to the street-organ player, 25,546 were enumerated, showing an increase of 38 per cent, upon the corrected total in 1871. The appliances of music were provided by 9,249 Musical Instrument Makers, who also had increased by 28 per cent in the course of the decade, and by 1,440 Printers and Sellers of Musical Publications. Taking them all together, the persons who gain their livelihood by music amounted to 36,235, and had increased since 1871 by 37 per cent. This increase was the more remarkable, inasmuch as the growth of the same group had been 24 per cent, in the preceding intercensal period.[5]

Britain was clearly a musical nation, but the signs were apparent much earlier. In the 1840s amateur choral singing had benefited from the introduction of tonic sol-fa notation and the singing classes associated with it. Tonic sol-fa is often attributed to the English Congregationalist minister John Curwen but, while he was a central proponent of its use, he played only a part in its invention.[6] It was introduced to improve congregational hymn and psalm singing but was soon adopted for secular use among the working classes. Public sol-fa meetings were held across the country; some attracted as many as 30,000 participants. The ambition, initially at least, was not to impart refined singing techniques, but just to encourage the population to engage in choral singing. Joseph Mainzer, author of *Singing for the Million*, was one of the most influential pioneers of choral singing for the masses. He started his singing classes shortly after arriving in Britain from Germany in 1841. At the end of the century an observer who had attended his 1842 classes reflected on the experience:

> Through all the years between then and now I have retained consciousness of the physical effect made upon me by more voices than I ever heard singing together. It mattered not that they were rough and uncultivated, or that they were kept monotoning on *sol*, with plenty of creep down to *la*, or down to *fa*, as a first step towards compassing the entire scale, The effect, anyhow, was a revelation to my youthful mind, and one which memory brings back, when I wish it with most pristine impressiveness.[7]

Mainzer was a major advocate for widening the franchise of music-making in Britain and achieved much in the ten years between his arrival in the country and his untimely death a decade later. One of his other enterprises was the establishment of the magazine *Mainzer's Musical Times*. This was the basis for the *Musical Times* which, under different names, was published continuously until 2024.[8] Such magazines, devoted mainly to classical music, played an important part in establishing a thriving musical life in Britain and supporting the idea of music as a valuable social enterprise. They were published in London but circulated nationally and contributed to the country's reputation as a place to which the greatest European performers could be attracted: not just to London but also to the large and expanding provincial centres. Public fascination was especially stirred by the brilliance of visiting itinerant virtuosos. In 1831 one of the greatest and most charismatic arrived in London. The editor of the music periodical, *The Harmonicon*, attended his first concert and was impressed:

His powers of execution are little less than marvellous, and such as we could only have believed on the evidence of our own senses; they imply a strong natural propensity for music, with an industry, a perseverance, a devotedness and also a skill in inventing means, without any parallel in the history of the instrument.[9]

This was the Italian violinist Nicolò Paganini, the son of a Genoese docks worker, who combined fabulous technical and expressive musicianship with a magnetism that charmed and captivated audiences. He was a fine composer, but it was his brilliance as a performer that made him famous, even among people who had never heard him play. The performance technique with which Paganini engaged was used in both vocal and instrumental music and had become popular with more elite audiences late in the previous century. The Italian word *bravura* (literally 'bravery') had been adopted to describe it. It signalled the obvious implication that such levels of virtuosity were synonymous with risk, and this explains why performers such as Paganini generated such excitement. He travelled widely and tirelessly. In 1831, at a time when travel in the British Isles was arduous, he toured the country for almost a year performing a staggering 131 concerts. He was a brilliant player and knew how to work an audience. In Birmingham, an orchestral overture preceded his appearance on the platform:

A breathless silence then ensued, and every eye was watching the action of this extraordinary violinist, and as he glided from the side scenes to the front of the stage, an involuntary cheering burst from every part of the house, many rising from their seats to view the spectre during the thunder of this unprecedented cheering – his gaunt and extraordinary appearance being more like that of a devotee about to suffer martyrdom, than one to delight you with his art. With the tip of his bow he set off the orchestra in a grand military movement with a force and vivacity as surprising as it was new. At the termination of this introduction, he commenced with a soft streamy note of celestial quality; and with three or four whips of his bow elicited *points of sound* that mounted to the third heaven, and as bright as the stars. A scream of astonishment and delight burst from the audience at the novelty of this effect. Immediately an execution followed that was equally indescribable, in which were intermingled tones more than human, which seems to be wrung from the deepest anguish of a broken heart.[10]

Paganini was immensely influential on British concert life because he set extraordinary precedents. He was one of the first to *thrill* popular audiences through virtuosity and charisma. He had a very special product to sell but, in so doing, he demonstrated a particular model of entertainment – and did so across the country, including the towns around which brass bands were to thrive. No subsequent violinist successfully imitated him. In the second half of the century, it was the cornet that was often the popular vehicle for virtuosity in British popular concerts. The best players unashamedly labelled themselves 'the Paganini of the cornet', and the most anticipated piece in their programmes was a version of the great man's signature encore, his variations on *The Carnival of Venice*.

The public concert

Prior to the nineteenth century, the performance of music was private, exclusive – or both. Private because it often took place behind the closed doors of the magnificent edifices that patrons of composers and performers inhabited; exclusive because attendance was restricted to those who subscribed, at significant cost, to a performance, or a series of them, which had to be paid for in advance. This business model defined the class of people who could attend. We know the identity of many of the attendees because they were often named as subscribers in the printed programmes. In 1848 almost 60 per cent of the 284 subscribers to the Philharmonic Society concerts came from the gentry, the professions and different branches of commerce.[11] Even by this time, social status of its audiences had 'fallen rapidly' and subscriptions and tickets for individual concerts could be bought in music shops.[12] Despite the growing import-ance of the British provinces, the centre of concert life was always London. In the first half of the nineteenth century, a season of refined entertain-ment was available in the form of theatre and concert performances. The season was extended in provincial festivals held annually across the country to which London musicians travelled to perform. Provincial festivals were also aimed primarily at the elevated classes. The extent to which audiences universally engaged with the music is debatable. Concerts were widely, probably even primarily, perceived as social occasions, which – along with other events in the social calendar, such as horse races and assizes – caused the landed classes to congregate but, irrespective of such provisos, the provincial music festivals provided the structural basis for the more popular developments that were to follow.

The same period saw the gradual development of public concerts that resembled those of modern times. London theatres had orchestras and theoretically it was possible for anyone to attend, but there were no permanent British orchestras analogous to modern symphony orchestras. The Philharmonic Society, which was formed in 1813, was an important but private concert society that commissioned new works and organised an orchestra to play a limited number of performances each year using freelance players.[13] Eventually, orchestras were established that performed more regular and accessible concerts, such as that formed in the late 1850s when the Crystal Palace moved to south London, and Charles Hallé's orchestra founded in Manchester in 1858.

A further development was the building of venues capable of accommodating public concerts. Some were established in London, but an important expansion accrued from the desire of Victorian metropolitan authorities to exhibit civic pride through the construction of elaborate civic buildings. These buildings served their primary purposes as administrative centres, but they were also public statements: expressions of ordered grandeur. Many included assembly halls that were designed as performance spaces. They became stages for concerts by local organisations, such as choirs and brass bands, and eventually were part of a network of venues for international touring celebrities. Attention to local and visiting artists was heightened by popular interest in the buildings themselves, and tickets for concerts often fell short of demand. When Leeds Town Hall was opened in 1858, the loyal speech to the Queen (who presided over the opening ceremony) expressed the hope that she would approve of such a grand building in this 'thriving seat of English industry' and emphasised that:

> For the mere purpose of municipal government, a less spacious and costly building might have sufficed [but] . . . we are also desirous to provide a place where large assemblies might meet in comfort to exercise their constitutional right of discussing public questions . . . or to enjoy innocent amusements.[14]

At the lighter end of commercial entertainment were the 'song and supper evenings' that provided the origins of music hall, which developed at a greater pace in the later nineteenth century. Their ornate buildings were soon seen in British towns of any size. Most were licensed to sell alcoholic drinks; consequently some developed a doubtful moral status at a time when respectability had a high currency across most social classes. The expansion of respectable musical entertainment to a broader social spectrum grew fastest when species of concerts were introduced that were reputable but unambiguously intended to entertain audiences rather than educate them. Three elements seem to have been especially effective: music that was melodically lyrical, such as dance music and arrangements of popular operatic arias; music that was spectacular because of the elaborate resources needed for its presentation; and performances that exhibited stunning displays of virtuosity. All were found in the concerts of one remarkable, if eccentric, musician, who arrived in Britain in 1840 in flight from various Parisian creditors.

The Jullien phenomenon

A hint of the eccentricity in Louis-Antoine Jullien's family is found in his given names. In total, he had 36 of them because his parents conferred on him the names of each of his godparents. The most entertaining, if far-fetched, biographical account of Jullien's origins, is found in a series of articles by his friend, the celebrated journalist James William Davison, published in the *Musical World* in 1853. If the story is to be believed, his father Antonio was 'band-master to the *Cent Suisse* – a regiment celebrated, at the time, for its bravery, its loyalty, and its admirable discipline', when the regiment 'was massacred in the palace of the Louvre. Not one of the gallant fellows escaped – Antonio Jullien excepted.'[15] Antonio then went to Rome where he befriended the Pope, who made him music director of the papal bodyguard. He eventually returned to France on foot across the Alps with his two daughters and pregnant wife. On 23 April 1812, near the little French town of Sisteron, they spent the night in a hunters' cabin where Louis-Antoine Jullien was born. The article goes on to describe Jullien's childhood, which was punctuated by a series of remarkable and highly improbable near-death events. In his late teens, and following military service, he entered the Paris Conservatoire.[16] This was followed by work in Paris conducting orchestras and bands. He was successful enough to challenge the acclaim of France's leading conductor of popular orchestral music, Philippe Musard. Musard had directed a series of open-air concerts at the Champs-Elysées that became known as the *Concerts-Musard*. They were famously popular, so much so that in 1840 he was invited to stage similar presentations at the Drury Lane Theatre in London. Musard's success may have prompted Jullien to choose London as his destination when he left Paris in the same year. He formed an orchestra of carefully selected and expert players, who performed in the pleasure gardens that had been providing recreation and amusement in the city since the eighteenth century. He was a gifted composer of light music, charismatic and exuding Parisian *panache*. His flamboyant style appealed to audiences, who often gazed at his antics with disbelief. He named his performances 'promenade concerts' because audiences were at liberty to stroll during the performance rather than sit stoically throughout. This was a direct imitation of the *Concerts-Musard*, but its form was elaborated and consolidated in London by Jullien. Audiences were admitted for prices as low as a shilling, and what they saw and heard was colourful, relaxed, entertaining, often exciting and free of any burdensome expectation that they were there to be educated in the traditional way. His intention was, he said, 'To ensure amusement as well as attempting instruction, by blending in the programme the most sublime works with those of the lighter school.'[17] His early provincial concerts drew criticism for their modest resources, but he soon put this right. It was probably inevitable that Jullien's popularity drew criticism, especially when he overcame a faltering start and became a national celebrity.

In 1849 he organised a Beethoven Festival at the Drury Lane Theatre. A reviewer from the *Illustrated London News* could hardly restrain his displeasure at the way works of 'the immortal composer' were presented by him:

Unpardonable liberties were taken with the inspirations of the mighty master-mind, and the interpretation, in many instances was marked with coarseness and boisterousness. Will M. Jullien explain whether he found in the score of the C minor [symphony] the parts for four ophicleides and a Saxophone, besides those of his favourite regiment of side drums?[18]

It should come as no surprise that Jullien was dismissed as a degenerate charlatan and an outrageous showman. He was certainly a showman, something of a charlatan and probably degenerate, but he was also brilliant. Through his London series and many provincial tours, he revolutionised concert life in Britain, and later had the same effect in the US.

He combined operatic selections and classical music with dances (especially quadrilles) and works designed to display the skills of individual performers. One of his most appreciated items was the *British Army Quadrilles*, for which his orchestra was joined by at least two, usually three, full military bands (fig. 19). Claims in advertisements that there would be 400 instrumentalists on stage were not far from the truth. Prominent among his soloists was the German cornetist Herman Koenig, who performed his famous *Post Horn Galop* as a finale. This he played on a German post-horn after completing some spectacular solos on the *cornet à pistons*. Concerts were invariably sold out. In Bradford, where brass bands were already well established, Koenig was described as 'the perfect master of his instrument and the favourite of the public',[19] but one feels that it was the instrument as much as the man that drew the plaudits. It was a new sound, with an idiom of unprecedented versatility, and many of the best players were exercising a mode of performance that was equally unprecedented. Koenig became so important to Jullien's operation that advertisements eventually carried the banner headline 'Conductor M. Jullien. Principal

19. *Jullien and his orchestra performing the* British Army Quadrilles *at Covent Garden in 1846, replete with military bands and 'monster percussion'. Massive audiences attended these spectacles.*

Cornet à Pistons Herr Koenig'. Jullien took the wise step of contracting him exclusively on an annual basis. Members of brass bands in the north of England travelled distances to hear Jullien's concerts.[20]

Jullien's career was spectacular and his effect on the concert life of Britain and America emphatic. His personal life was less successful, and he frequently appeared in bankruptcy courts. He died in a Parisian lunatic asylum in 1860.

Jules Levy, Jean-Baptiste Arban and cornet mania

Koenig was neither the first nor the most accomplished of the cornet soloists of the nineteenth century, but his association with Jullien was important in the popularising of the cornet.[21] He was, by all accounts, more than a mere showman; he had a fabulous technique and a gift for phrasing melodies. Other brilliant cornet players were to emerge from the brass band movement, but initially the popularising of the cornet came from the music profession: it was the professional showmen and the music they played that provided the model for the first brass band soloists. They also defined many aspects of the performance techniques that were to create the virtuosic idiom of the brass band – the techniques known as double and triple tonguing, for example. These virtuosi came thick and fast, and few were burdened by modesty. Not the least among them was Jules Levy, who was born in London in 1824. His introduction to the cornet is obscure: a story of his impoverished family buying him a cornet in a pawn shop, and of him being self-taught, may be true, but there is no evidence of it and it seems a little crafted. By 1856 he was a cornet soloist with the band of the Grenadier Guards, where he would have had a disciplined musical training. It was probably with the Grenadiers that he started performing his own composition and signature piece, *The Whirlwind Polka*, which he claimed to have performed at Buckingham Palace. When he left the army, he became a concert soloist at the Crystal Palace and the Promenade Concerts and was widely and consistently advertised as 'the world's greatest cornet player' – a description of which he was probably the author. This, too, may have been true, but there were competitors who adopted the same descriptor, and by this time there was scope to wonder what, in any useful sense, the term was intended to mean. He was certainly one of the first British players to achieve celebrity on both sides of the Atlantic and that marks him as significant. Showmanship came naturally to Levy: he was persistently vain and egotistical. In America he refused to wear the military-style uniforms routinely worn by the US bands with which he was engaged to perform, instead appearing resplendent in evening dress decorated with medals of obscure provenance, and for no apparent reason wearing a monocle. But like other great cornet soloists of his time, he legitimised an instrument that was still very new to musical audiences: an instrument that became so popular that some, with good reason, saw it as presenting an existential threat to the future of the trumpet.

The origins of the cornet are uncertain, but there is broad agreement that its design was based on the idea that valves could be applied to the circular post-horn, and that it was probably developed in France around 1830, where it was called the *cornet à pistons*. Its first known and verified use in a public performance was in 1833. There is no record of it being registered for a patent but, at the end of that same year, a Parisian maker, Joseph Isidore Pertus, registered a patent for a new type of square section valve for the cornet. In doing so, he made no claim that he was the inventor of the cornet: his application was for an improvement to an existing design. The earliest cornets had just two valves, but a third was soon added, and a new type of piston valve, designed by François Périnet, was incorporated. Périnet valves were subsequently used in the design of many brass instruments. Early instruments are sometimes referred to as 'cornopeans' but, though very similar, cornets and cornopeans were developed separately and had distinctive characteristics. The cornopean also has obscure origins: it, too, was never patented, but it is believed to have originated in Britain, where it was especially popular in the 1840s.[22]

The cornet gained popularity and common use at remarkable speed. From the 1840s, cornets were being produced in quantity for military and brass bands as well as the greatly expanding music profession. One writer has estimated that only about 50 civilian trumpeters made a living in Britain between the last quarter of the eighteenth century and the end of the nineteenth.[23] Sufficient sources are available to make such an estimate, and this one seems realistic. According to the 1871 edition of the London-based *Musical Directory, Annual and Almanack*, which listed the names and addresses of musicians available for work across the country, there were 31 trumpeters. More than five times that number were advertising themselves as cornet players, and all but one of the registered trumpeters also listed themselves as cornet players.[24] Even Thomas Harper (the younger), one of the most revered English trumpeters in the mid-nineteenth century, was appearing as a cornet soloist. There are grounds for believing that most theatre players and many in orchestras opted for the cornet rather than the trumpet on a day-to-day basis, irrespective of what was designated in the score. Some composers deliberately scored for the cornet rather than the trumpet. These included Arthur Sullivan in his Savoy operas and Georges Bizet in his opera *Carmen*. At an assembly of London's

Musical Association in 1894, Walter Morrow, the Professor of Trumpet at the Royal College of Music, said that 'the cornet has crushed the trumpet out of the orchestra all together. One rarely hears the sound of the real trumpet now.'[25] By 'the real trumpet', Morrow was referring to the type of trumpet he played: the large trumpet (pitched in six-foot F), which was significantly bigger than modern B-flat trumpets, but his comment remains an important and probably accurate description of how traditions were being challenged.

By this time, the cornet-playing world was subject to the global influence of Jean-Baptiste Arban, yet another who was routinely described as 'the world's greatest cornet player'. This might also have been true, but more certain is the claim that his instruction book on the instrument was the most influential force throughout the world that sought to explain how valved brass instruments were to be understood and played. Arban was born in Lyon in 1825 into a family that appears not to have been musical. His father had a successful business manufacturing fireworks and arranging pyrotechnic displays. Jean-Baptiste studied trumpet at the Paris Conservatoire, where he demonstrated exceptional talent and gained first prize in the Conservatoire's *concours*, the annual prize competitions. In the mid-1840s he collaborated with Adolphe Sax to promote his saxhorns and became Professor of Saxhorn in the military wing of the Conservatoire. The association with Sax probably prompted Arban to direct his talents from the trumpet to the cornet. Reports of Arban's playing occasionally mention his virtuosity, but its beauty was spoken of with equal frequency. One writer has described him as 'the first complete technician on the cornet'.[26] His version of the variations on *The Carnival of Venice* became a standard brass band cornet solo.

In 1869 he became Professor of the Cornet at the Conservatoire, but only after failing to persuade the then director, the composer Daniel Auber, that the cornet and trumpet should be taught together in a single class. A letter from Arban to Auber, dated 2 November 1868, shows that concerns in Paris about the relative status of the two instruments matched those in London, but it is interesting that Arban, the most sophisticated advocate of the cornet, was equally resolved to protect the future of the trumpet, which he believed to be on the point of extinction:

Dear Director and Master,

I hasten to give you the detailed information you kindly asked for during the interview you recently condescended to grant me.

It is a fact that to-day hardly anybody plays the trumpet anymore and that the provincial theatres – and even those in Paris – no longer have artists playing this instrument.

Almost everywhere the trumpet has been replaced by the cornet à pistons. I well realise that the latter is the younger brother of the trumpet, but its timbre is nevertheless quite different. There is also no doubt that most operas contain important cornet parts and you, yourself, dear Master, were the first to make use of the instrument, because you immediately understood all of its possibilities.

The trumpet class at the Conservatoire has not been able to stave off this complete change, for it is generally known that one can be an excellent trumpeter yet starve to death, whilst everybody can live comfortably by playing the cornet à pistons.

Here, dear Master, is the remedy which I submit to your judgment. If you want artists to play the trumpet, I am convinced that the best thing to do is to create ONE class for both trumpets and cornets à pistons. That is to say, no pupil should be allowed to join the class if he is not willing to play the two instruments alternatively . . .

This dear Master, is the truth about the question of the decline of the trumpet. The time has come to apply an effective remedy in order to prevent the complete disappearance of this instrument from the orchestras, if one wishes to hear it still in the performance of masterpieces of the past – not to speak of the services it may render in the future.

Accept dear Master, my most affectionate compliments.

J. B. Arban[27]

The most important legacy and influence of Arban is found in his instruction book, *Grande méthode complète de cornet à pistons et de saxhorn*, which was first published around 1859,[28] but subsequently put out in numerous editions and languages throughout the world. It may have been the most published and distributed didactic treatise for any instrument up to that time. Its popularity is evidenced by the scope of its distribution and the extent to which it was imitated by others, but its primary historic significance accrues from what it did. It was the first publication that, in its overall scheme and content, directly addressed the stark reality that valve instruments were a permanent feature of the musical landscape, and that their idiom needed to be defined by a set of distinctive techniques and musical features. The book sets out a systematic method for learning those techniques and, in so doing, Arban did more than anyone to clarify, for composers as well as players, what valved brass instruments could do in the hands of competent performers. Several subsequent players and writers have made adaptations and amendments to the Arban *Méthode,* but its content has remained fundamentally intact, and versions of it have been published for every valved instrument.

The activities of nineteenth-century virtuoso cornetists such as Arban may seem distant from the brass band movement, but they had a formidable influence on the development of its idiom. In general terms, these soloists exploited three aspects of brass instrument technique in a modern way: the long-line lyrical melody; rapid florid passages that could be played effectively only on valve instruments; and a range of articulations. 'Articulations' – the way that notes are initiated by the tongue behind the embouchure – can create expressive effects, from nuances in slow melodies to displays of spectacular virtuosity. The techniques known as single, double and triple tonguing may not have been nineteenth-century inventions (though Arban claimed to be a pioneer of soloistic double and triple tonguing),[29] but it was the itinerant virtuosi who, through their concerts and particularly the instruction books they wrote, introduced them directly or indirectly to brass bands.

Sousa and the idea of America

In Europe and the US between about 1860 and 1920, popular audiences, which constituted the majority of concertgoers, were more likely to be entertained by bands than orchestras. Events were staged in pleasure gardens and other places that could accommodate a large audience. America had experienced its own brass band revolution. One estimate suggests that in 1861, on the eve of the American Civil War, there were 3,000 brass bands in the US with about 60,000 participants, but it is difficult to see how such an estimate could have been obtained.[30] We can be certain that many of the players in US bands in the second half of the nineteenth century were recent European immigrants. There were many successful concert bands, but the most influential professional US bandmaster in the second half of the century was Patrick Sarsfield Gilmore, who had emigrated from Ireland to America in 1848. He became famous for his 'gigantic concerts', in which up to 500 performers participated. Gilmore was influenced by Jullien, in whose orchestra he had played. Like Jullien, he recognised that large audiences could be drawn to see and hear spectacular entertainment.

Gilmore died suddenly in St Louis in September 1892. His funeral in New York had a grandeur of the type normally reserved for major statesmen. Present in the city at that time was David Blakely, a journalist who had recently and opportunistically turned impresario. Recognising that Gilmore's passing created a void in the entertainment market, he approached John Philip Sousa, who had established his reputation directing the US Marines Band in Washington, DC. Blakely invited him to form a New York-based civilian band under his management. Sousa had most of Gilmore's musical gifts and the additional advantage of being a talented composer with a special flare for marches. The Sousa band was quickly assembled from the best of Gilmore's players and others who were attracting attention. Correspondence and other documents concerning the formation of the new Sousa band survive to show the enthusiasm that players had for the Blakely/Sousa enterprise.[31] The quality of the band was unprecedented and was soon able to perform in major US cities on tours that followed the developing railroad system from the eastern conurbations. In 1900 it undertook its first tour of Britain. The model used by Sousa was like that of other touring bands: great hand-picked players, impressive and disciplined visual appearance, eclectic programming and stunning brass soloists. Sousa's own compositions were well known, so the concerts were hotly anticipated. His larger-than-life and carefully manicured persona was a major part of the offering, as was the central theme to which Sousa was unerringly committed – the idea of America as a new, culturally distinct and artistically developed nation. European audiences were bombarded with the message that the band represented a manifestation of the US at its most efficient, disciplined and colourful. The London *Standard* noted that 'in Mr Sousa and his band we have the musical epitome of all that is bright and sparkling in the characteristic personality of our American cousins across the water'.[32] Those puzzled by the absence of his marches in the programme needed only to wait for the encores. They came in abundance and, at the climax of 'The Star-Spangled Banner', American flags were unfurled across the stage. Programmes also included what Sousa sometimes and peculiarly called 'native American music'. In the US, this music was already being called 'ragtime'.

The 1900 tour was restricted to England. It was a mixed reed and brass band with percussion – a harp was also included in the regular instrumentation.[33] There were 55 in the band as well as soloists. The soloists usually included female singers, a violinist and brass soloists. The most frequently used brass soloists were the cornetist Herbert Clarke and Arthur Pryor, 'the greatest trombone player of all time'. In 1901 the band performed on 70 consecutive days in venues between Southampton in the south and Newcastle in the north; there were usually two shows a day. Four years later, it was back for a tour of England, Wales, Scotland and Ireland that lasted five months, with usually two concerts on each consecutive day. The schedule was unrelenting: there were no free days, irrespective of the distance between one venue and the next.[34] This was typical. In 1911 the band undertook a further world tour that again included Britain. One of the saxophonists, Albert A. Knecht, kept a diary of that tour, which reveals what life was like for touring musicians at that time. He wrote of the many adversities the band endured: trudging through mud to get to Dublin station; inadequate accommodation; extremes of temperature in many venues; in Merthyr Tydfil, part of the stage collapsed during the performance; in Plymouth, the two lady vocal soloists were found unconscious in their dressing room, having been overcome by escaping gas.

Knecht was diligent in recording the number of miles travelled and the accrued takings:

March 3 [1911]
Left London (Paddington Station) at 11 o'clock. Played to a fair house at the Coliseum. This was our last concert in England, and every one in the band appeared well pleased. Train left at 6:33 arriving at Bristol 10.20. Stopping at the Waverley Hotel.
Mileage Bristol to Plymouth 128. London to Bristol 117½. Total 245½.
Total Mileage of the British tour 4,360.
Total Receipts of the British Tour $87,000.[35]

The Sousa band was probably the most famous ensemble in the world at this time, and consistently popular in the US until the late 1920s. It is historically important because, while there were other American musical exports in the period, Sousa and his band were the most globally conspicuous. Its repeated visits to Britain were an indicator of the interest it received. Also, and counter-intuitively, it stands as an example of cultural decline. At the start of the century, it was new and exciting, but after the First World War it lost some of its attraction. The decline was also an indicator of a more general trend, in which the difference between popular and classical (or 'art') music was becoming clearer.

Sousa's concerts were almost invariably sold out. Newspapers carried few direct comparisons with British brass bands but, while the critical reception was consistently positive, there was sometimes a sense of reserve. The *Shrewsbury Chronicle* said, 'it can hardly be disputed that the immense popularity of the band lies chiefly with the personality of its conductor'.[36] The *Manchester Guardian* commented, 'You may not like it, but it is certain to have an effect on you', and continued:

One is forced to borrow from the language of sport because the most lasting impression produced on listeners by the band is one of physical fitness. It is probably the finest team of musical athletes that has ever been got together; they are strong men, delighted to run a race in which they know they can outlast the most powerful listener . . . It is annoying to feel that one has seen a record broken and have nothing to prove it.[37]

The sacralisation of culture

For much of the period between the time that the popular concert took root and the start of the First World War, bands rather than orchestras were at the forefront of musical entertainment in many countries. But even in the later nineteenth century, a process was under way that came to define and eventually create the infrastructure of what was to be termed 'the classical music establishment'. A critical consensus had emerged earlier that identified what was referred to as 'the canon': a body of musical works possessing a level of aesthetic excellence that defined music as an art rather than merely an entertainment. The music of composers such as Bach, Handel, Mozart, Haydn and Beethoven exemplified the best. Despite the role that bands and other modes of performance played in the popularising of classical music, it became acknowledged that 'great works' by 'great composers' could be properly realised only in their complete and 'authentic' state. This led to a disaggregation of music that was created or used for popular entertainment from the *classical canon* that was believed to be a timeless expressive treasure. This transition was not confined just to ideas and attitudes: it gave cause for the setting up of institutions such as permanent symphony orchestras and music colleges, and the consolidation of fields of study in universities that would be devoted to cataloguing and understanding 'great music'.

In this process, brass and military bands, along with musicians who offered virtuosity for its own sake, came to occupy a lesser position in music culture. It was a slow process, but the suppression of the showmen virtuosi was warmly welcomed in some quarters where they were judged to have become tiresome and unrelenting. This was especially obvious in the US. Theodore Thomas, one of the most important American orchestral conductors of the nineteenth century, known for his series of concerts in New York's Central Park, breathed a sigh of relief when cornet soloists were dropped from his concerts. 'At last,' he wrote in his diary, 'the summer programs show a respectable character, and we are rid of the cornet! Occasionally a whole symphony is given.'[38] Thomas was writing at a time when a transition was gaining momentum in American music that would define a more elevated aesthetic than was offered by bands. It was more obvious in the US than in Britain because America was a new nation and free of the weight of Britain's cultural legacy. The process has been described by one writer as 'the sacralization of culture'.[39]

It was no longer relevant that it was bands that had taken the first steps to popularise classical music. When Sousa heard of the death of Gilmore, he was quick to the remark that he had 'gone into the highways and byways of the land, playing Wagner and Liszt and other great composers in places where their music was absolutely unknown, and their names scarcely more than a twice-repeated sound'. When Sousa took over the US Marines Band, he found 'not a sheet of Wagner, Berlioz, Grieg or Tchaikovsky' in its library and quickly went about rectifying it.[40] But by the turn of the century, classical transpositions were less widely accepted than they once were: the format and character of band concerts was contrasting vividly with what was being presented by the developing classical music institutions. Jullien was criticised for his crassness and audacious juxtaposition of works by Beethoven with the 'Katy-did Polka', and Gilmore's 'jumbo' or 'monster' concerts were remembered as the stunts that they undoubtedly were. At the National Peace Jubilee in Boston in 1869, he had hired a hundred Boston firemen to strike anvils in a performance of the 'Anvil Chorus' from Verdi's opera *Il trovatore*.[41] In New York, a different stunt had been arranged: Levy was matched against Matthew Arbuckle, another British-born cornet player. Both were members of Gilmore's band, but it was well known that they shared no collegial fondness. Gilmore managed the rivalry by arranging a musical duel at New York's Madison Square Garden. It was immensely popular, but it also contributed to the downward categorisation of band music in the US. In 1880 the *New York Times* ran editorials attacking the 'horrible thirst for brass', besides which 'the prevalence of drunkenness becomes insignificant and opium eating hardly deserves notice'. 'Brass bands,' it went on, 'have the musical character of a machine shop in busy operation.'[42] While it is easy to see these words as representative of journalistic licence, it probably reflects the reality that audiences and the critical reception of music were changing. One performer advertised the claim that he had 'broken the world record' for the highest note ever played on a cornet.

The same trend occurred in Britain, with only a slightly lesser force. By the end of the nineteenth century, there was a clear demarcation between music that was designed to be popular and entertaining and music that was intended as *art*. Such stratification was hastened by the emergence of new forms of commercial music, especially those from America. In more modern parlance, these categories became known as 'highbrow' and 'lowbrow'. A little later there was 'middlebrow', but this descriptor was never intended to have an elasticity sufficient to accommodate the fringes of 'high' and 'low'; it referred to a specific group of works that were widely popular in the first half of the twentieth century. It included some of the more popular and tuneful 'cross-over' classics, but also the music of composers such as Eric Coates, Ronald Binge and Albert Ketèlby, whose vastly popular compositions were otherwise condescendingly described as 'light'. It is a pity that the brass band movement did not engage more meaningfully and extensively with those composers. It did so only slightly. The Devonshire composer Hubert Bath, who wrote two test pieces, can be placed in this category. He was otherwise known for his *Cornish Rhapsody*, written for the 1944 film *Love Story*, and *Out of the Blue* which, for decades, was the theme music for BBC sports report programmes. Yet more talented was Ronald Binge, whose best-known work for brass band was the short, but tuneful and idiomatic, concert piece, *Cornet Carillon*.[43]

Terms such as 'highbrow', 'lowbrow' and 'middlebrow' were important because they were used liberally in the music industry to define discrete markets. Concerts, magazines, recordings and eventually broadcasting channels were configured to the imagined preferences of categories of listener. Fitting brass bands into this picture was difficult. The problem, if it can be referred to as such, has been that, for much of their history, certainly until late in the twentieth century, brass bands fitted no category other than the one they constructed for themselves. This changed in the twenty-first century, but previously — and for reasons that are explained elsewhere in this book — 'the movement' was culturally separate from most other forms of music.

Chapter 6

'The devil's choicest tunes': Brass bands and the Salvation Army

The most popular and emblematic form of Salvation Army music has always been the brass band. They have always been strong and well organised, and many of the world's greatest classical and jazz brass players were introduced to music in them. Like other British brass bands, they originated in the Victorian period, their members were almost entirely working-class amateurs and they used a similar combination of instruments. Salvationism soon developed into a worldwide movement and made an important contribution to the internationalisation of British brass bands. At the start of the twenty-first century, after more than a decade of incremental decline, it could still claim to have almost 45,000 band members, active in 109 countries.[1] Like other brass bands, but for entirely different reasons, Salvation Army bands have always worn military-style uniforms. They have their own repertoire, and their musical idiom overlaps with that of the standard British brass band model. In the twenty-first century, Salvationists make an important contribution to the non-Salvationist brass band world as conductors, adjudicators and composers, and play a central part in its media structure, but these are relatively recent developments. For over a century, barriers were erected between these two groups of working-class, amateur music-makers for the sole purpose of keeping them apart. The reasons for this peculiarity are interesting and reveal much about the place of music in Salvationist doctrine, but even more about the organisation's 'Founder', William Booth. Others were complicit, but it was he who was primarily responsible for creating a schism between Salvationist and other brass bands that lasted for a century.

The Founder and his Mission

William Booth was born in 1829 in Sneinton, a suburb of Nottingham. His father died when he was 13 years old, leaving the family impoverished – he later referred to his childhood as 'blighted'. He was not a gifted scholar and gained neither value nor direction from formal education. As a teenager he was apprenticed to a pawnbroker, and the many encounters with the poor entailed in that work seems to have left a lasting impression and turned him to religion. He experimented with a variety of denominations and was enthused by itinerant preachers and radical left-wing political orators whose meetings he regularly attended. This probably caused him to develop his own brand of fiery preaching. In 1849, by which time he had aligned himself to Wesleyan Methodism, he moved to London in search of work. There he met Catherine Mumford, the daughter of a cabinet-maker. They married in 1855. Catherine shared Booth's faith but was gifted with an intellectual depth that eluded her husband. Her measured manners and views contrasted strongly with his rough, instinctive and fundamentally simple preaching rhetoric. She refined many of his ideas and made a definitive contribution to the success of the movement they jointly founded; she was also the inspiration for Booth's subsequent and consistent views on gender equality. In 1865 the couple established a Christian Mission in Whitechapel, an impoverished area in east London. Booth broke all ties with the established church and became an independent revivalist. The Mission was both a place of worship and a refuge for the poor. Its welfare work attracted volunteers who became so numerous that they were spoken of as a 'volunteer army'. The name 'Salvation Army' transpired from this casual title: it was formalised and used for the first time in print in the *Christian Mission Magazine* in September 1878.

Booth has been described as 'a brash, Bible-based, open-air' Christian, whose robust, often controversial but persistently forthright preaching style suited 'the realities of slum life'.[2] His beliefs were genuine, simple and consistent. He had little time for philosophy, science and most things intellectual. He believed in the potential for everyone to be reclaimed from sin, the cleansing power of conversion and the prospect of damnation for those who purposefully evaded redemption. He saw the work of the devil in all forms of human or societal malevolence, and this convinced him that no task was more urgent than the conquering of it. Throughout his life, he was personally punctilious, self-confident, an autocrat and a disciplinarian. Allied to these complex, single-minded features was an unusual, instinctive and profoundly felt compassion for the poor. The sight of poverty-stricken children frequently moved him to tears. He championed society's lost people and abandoned the liturgical rituals of other churches, including the celebration of the Eucharist, in favour of a direct, easily comprehensible and practical form of Christianity. Quasi-militarism suited these objectives because it contrasted so fundamentally with the ecclesiastical rituals about which he and Catherine were so deeply equivocal. Salvationism was doctrinally simple but also colourful, and it communicated directly with masses of ordinary people at a time when congregations of the established church were in decline. It also served another purpose that Booth had favoured since his early days as a Wesleyan: it ensured that the Army would grow not merely as a loose association of local organisations but as a co-ordinated national and international body connected through a shared set of beliefs and processes. This connectiveness required discipline and the means to regulate it. Many converts became 'soldiers', so it took little time for the Army to grow. Booth was a complex and, in many respects, difficult individual, but his influence and inspiration were to be a permanent anchor for the fundamental beliefs of his movement, and traces of his influence were visible even in the period of its eventual modernisation.

William Booth's eldest son Bramwell Booth is credited with having persuaded his father to adopt the military metaphor and the ancillary structures and narratives it entailed. It soon pervaded every aspect of the Mission's work. Uniforms were worn, ranks were established, churches became 'citadels', religious leaders were 'officers', Booth was 'the General'. There were flags and marching, 'crusades' were conducted in 'territories': Salvationists were fighting a war against the devil and his works. Discipline was essential, so 'Orders and Regulations for Soldiers' were quickly established. The reward for Salvationists at the end of life was 'promotion to glory'.

William Booth was initially ambivalent about the quasi-military idea but soon embraced it. For him the idea that it was a metaphor was soon dismissed: this was literally a war, and it took courageous men and women to fight it. By 1880 the name 'Salvation Army' was formally registered by deed poll and the British Parliament had recognised it as a legally constituted Protestant denomination. It also became part of the social as well as religious landscape of Britain. Outdoor meetings were the most conspicuous forms of worship. Many were disrupted by disorderly 'roughs'. Some attacks on Salvationists and other temperance rallies were organised and premeditated by violent groups styling themselves the 'Skeleton Army'. Brewery owners, who feared that the message of abstinence was gaining a positive response, sometimes encouraged disruption. The Salvation Army became what was probably the most successful social-welfare project of the nineteenth century: a century in which social welfare was sorely needed. Booth, utterly charismatic as an orator and always an ardent publicist for his organisation, became a reluctant celebrity; he was consulted by bishops, prime ministers, presidents and royalty. He once persuaded Cecil Rhodes, the mining magnate and politician, to kneel in prayer with him in a crowded railway carriage.[3]

Bands attract crowds

The first performance by a brass band at a Salvationist meeting occurred in March 1878 in Salisbury. Charles William Fry, a carpenter and builder, along with his three sons, accompanied hymns at an open-air gathering. Fry was a convert who had played the cornet with a Rifle Volunteer Band. The Founder approved because the band attracted attention, drew crowds and served a practical purpose by leading hymn-singing. Booth was a famously enthusiastic appropriator of some aspects of popular culture while ignoring others. For example, he had little to say about football and other sports. Music, on the other hand, was a gift of God and hymn-singing raised spirits: it should be turned to the service of salvation, irrespective of where it originated. Popular song invested with the sentiments and words of the scripture became tools for conversion and devotion. In his famous and often misquoted phrase:

I don't care much whether you call it secular or sacred. I rather enjoy robbing the devil of his choicest tunes, and, after his subjects themselves, music is about the best commodity he possesses. It is like taking the enemy's guns and turning them against him.[4]

A corps band, formed at Consett in County Durham late in 1879, is usually regarded as the first citadel band,[5] but others were soon formed across the country. In 1883 the *War Cry*, the Salvationist publication used for communication to the wider movement, was reporting that there were hundreds of brass bands and over 5,000 instruments in the service of the nationwide evangelical mission. Booth proudly declared:

The playing of these bands has been made a great ground for complaint against us everywhere but far from there being any sign of them being objectionable, this is one of the surest evidences for their virtues.[6]

At first, bands played hymns from existing hymn books, but in 1882, at the Founder's request, Fred Fry, one of Charles Fry's sons, produced a set of cards costing sixpence with seven popular hymn tunes that could be easily adapted for any set of brass instruments. This was the first music produced by, and aimed directly at, Salvationists. A year later, a further set was issued containing original material. This was to be called the *Salvation Army General Band Journal* and was probably an imitation of similar publications produced for non-Salvationist bands: a collection of easy pieces delivered monthly on subscription and adaptable for whatever instruments were at hand.

Bandmaster's and Band Member's Bond.

To WILLIAM BOOTH,
Of 101, Queen Victoria Street,
In the City of London,
General of The Salvation Army.

In Consideration of your appointing or considering the proposal to appoint me _______________________

of _______________________

in the County of _______________ to be a _______________

of The Salvation Army _______________ Band, attached to the _______________ Corps of The Salvation Army, situate at _______________ in the County of _______________ and numbered _______________ or to any Band attached to any other Corps of The Salvation Army in Great Britain or Ireland, I do hereby solemnly promise and engage and pledge my faith and loyalty, and agree and undertake with and to you or other the General for the time being of The Salvation Army, and declare as in the sight of God as follows :—

1. To carry out the Orders and Regulations of The Salvation Army now in force or at any time hereafter to be issued.

2. To use any Instrument or other property which may be entrusted to me, or which may in any way come into my hands, for the purposes of The Salvation Army only, as set forth from time to time in General Orders or in Orders directed to me in particular.

3. To deliver up, in the event of your cancelling my appointment or proposed appointment, to the Divisional Officer, the Commanding Officer of the Corps, or any other person whom you may appoint in that behalf, any and all Moneys, Musical Instruments, Cases, Boxes, Stands, Books, Papers, or any other property of which I may have become possessed by virtue or in consequence of my said appointment or proposed appointment.

In Witness my hand with solemn and serious purpose, this _______ day of _______ One Thousand Nine Hundred and

Proposed Bands-}
man's Signature \| _______________ | 6d. Stamp to be affixed here. | _______________ *(Age)* _______

WITNESS :—
(Name) _______________
Address) _______________
(Occupation) _______________

WRITE SIGNATURE ACROSS THE STAMP, THUS CANCELLING THE SAME.

N.B.—It is not necessary for Members of Timbrel and Drum and Fife Bands or Songsters' Brigades to affix the Stamp.

20. *The Bandsman's Bond. All Salvation Army band members were required to agree to its terms. A signature over a stamp of the Royal Mail implied a legal obligation.*

Under Booth's leadership, the Salvation Army quickly developed an obsession for regulations, and bands were especially targeted (fig. 20). In 1881 came a 'General Order' signed by Bramwell Booth and published in the *War Cry*. It was intended to 'prevent misunderstanding, and to secure the harmonious working of the Brass Bands with the various Corps to which they are attached'. But unwittingly, it signalled a problem that the Army leadership had already identified – there was a need to isolate its bands within the Salvationist cause. It was made clear that 'the following regulations [were] to be strictly observed':

1. No one will be admitted or retained a Member of any Band who is not a Member of The Army.

2. All instruments in every Band are to be the property of The Salvation Army, no matter by whom they may be purchased, or through whom they may be presented. The words 'Salvation Army Brass Band' followed by the number of the Corps, must be marked on every Instrument. In no case are Instruments to be used to play anything but Salvation Music, or on any but Salvation service.

3. In the event of any Member of the Band resigning his position as such, he will leave his instrument behind him.

4. In no case will any Committee be allowed in connection with any Band.

5. In every case the Captain of the Corps to which the Band is attached shall direct the movements of the Band, and shall appoint a Bandmaster.

6. In no case will any Band, or Member of any Band, be allowed to go into debt, whether for Instruments, or for anything else connected with the Band.

7. In no case is the practising of the Band, or any Members of it, to interfere with the meetings of the Corps.

8. It is strongly recommended that in cases where a Treasurer or Secretary is required by a Band, the Treasurer or Secretary of the Corps to which it is attached shall act in that capacity.

9. Any Band that may have been, or may be formed, which does not carry out the Order will not be recognised as a Salvation

Army Band, and must not in future be allowed to take any part in the operations of The Army.

10. Any Band failing to carry out this Order will at once be disbanded.[7]

More was to come. In 1882 a Trade Department was established to negotiate favourable bulk-rate purchase prices for commodities needed by Salvationists. This included printed music and eventually instruments. It aimed to make the Salvation Army self-supporting and independent of external capitalist interests, but there were other considerations. An attitude was being formed under Booth's persuasion that was to create a division between his movement and the outside world, and especially between Salvationist and non-Salvationist musicians. Things moved swiftly. In 1885 a further 'General Order' was issued in the *War Cry*:

From this date no Band will be allowed to play from any music excepting *The Salvation Army General Band Journal*, the Journal published by us from time to time, and other music issued by HQ. Quicksteps and Introductions are strictly prohibited.[8]

The band instruments originally acquired by the Army for sale to corps through the Trades Department had been imported from France and were of inferior quality. Manufacturing of brass instruments by the Army started in 1889 on a modest scale, but it grew to make the Army one of the major producers. Six years later, the *War Cry* published a reflective article on what had, by then, become one of the Army's major retailing projects:

The main object in establishing this department was that we should be able to meet the needs of our bandsmen and be in a position to supply them with extra-superior instruments as well as those of the cheaper class. We started with two men in a room about twelve feet by six feet, under great difficulties, but praise God the way is now much brighter. We have at present a staff of sixteen skilled workmen, some of whom have worked at the best houses in London. These men have left the workshops of prominent makers who are seeking worldly interests, and have come to us, not so much to benefit themselves as to be engaged in a shop where work is being turned out and used only for the extension of God's Kingdom.[9]

This Trade Department was consolidated as the Salvationist Publishing and Supplies Ltd (SP&S) in 1917.[10] Each development was accompanied by edicts emphasising that Salvationists alone could buy and use products sold by the Salvation Army and repeating the other restrictions that had been spelled out in the 1881 regulations. The regulations had intentionally created a monopoly and, along with other prohibitions, ensured absolute isolation of the Salvation Army from the rest of the musical world – particularly from secular brass bands. Why was this and how did the Salvation Army rationalise its inherent contradiction? Salvationism – an evangelical organisation dedicated to penetrating all branches of society – was deliberately distancing itself from part of the secular world for no conspicuous reason. The monopoly was to cause complex and lasting difficulties, not least when the British Broadcasting Corporation (BBC) was established. The BBC was prohibited from advertising and the exercise of favouritism. In 1936, as the Corporation was selecting bands that were fit for broadcasting, it recognised that some Salvation Army bands were perfectly comparable with others it was already employing, but there were concerns about its limited repertoire and the cause of the limitations:

The available repertoire [is] . . . somewhat limited, owing to the fact that these particular bands are only allowed by their headquarters to include items published by the Salvation Army Publishing and Supply Stores. D.E.S. raised the question as to whether this was accepted policy by the Corporation, inasmuch as if Reginald King and his Orchestra – merely for the sake of example – submitted programmes of items published exclusively by one firm such programmes would not be accepted.[11]

Popular culture and its perils

The Salvation Army's isolation from other forms of music was primarily a product of Booth's way of thinking. He had seen how 'civilian' brass bands had developed by the 1880s. Many were preoccupied with contesting and its monetary prizes. Some had become clandestinely semi-professional, and more were dependent on financial loans. Then there was the sizeable group that originated in the temperance movement but had loosened their connection to that cause. The more profound concern lay in the belief that, when unrestrained, the performance of instrumental music held dark powers. Booth had a dilemma. He had appropriated an element of popular culture for a purpose for which it was not intended, and it was returning to haunt him. Brass bands in the secular world were not assembled to save souls: they were motivated by the exhilarating power of music-making. The idea that Salvationists could suppress the pleasures that made brass bands so popular had limited prospects, but Booth did not grasp this. Popular culture is inherently seductive: that's why it is popular. It resists intervention because it has a life of its own which is organic and capricious. Furthermore, most Salvationist band players were ordinary people who were innocently doing all they could to serve their corps. It followed that some Salvation Army brass bands were showing signs of musical excellence, and its players were experiencing the pure enjoyment of music-making. This was never intended. Booth had approved of bands for a much more limited set of purposes.

Events appear to have reached a crisis point in William Booth's mind by the end of the century. It was not until late in his preaching career that he allowed band music in his own services, because he suspected their potential to divert attention from the mission. He always insisted that the purpose of Salvationist bands was limited to attracting attention to the evangelical cause, but things were out of control. The delight in performing music for its own sake that was so evident in non-Salvationist bands appeared to be reaching his soldiers – and it frightened him:

You must be careful not to over-estimate its importance or come into bondage to it. Music, in itself, has neither a moral nor a religious character, this can only be imparted to it by the thoughts of feelings of the soul when under its power. That is to say, if music is to have any holy, any Divine influence on the hearts of those who listen, it must be associated with holy feelings and with Divine thoughts.[12]

Here, as in so much of what Booth wrote and said about music, one senses a struggle to be understood. He knew next to nothing about it, and what he did know confused him: he was never an intellectual, but his shortcomings were usually and easily overridden by a faith strong enough to provide him with a bank of simple, self-evident truths on which he could unerringly rely; however, when it came to music he was challenged. Two issues concerned him. Firstly, he could not conceive of a way that music could project spirituality without direct scriptural reference through the deployment of the words of ordinary language, as was the case in hymns; and secondly, he observed (probably accurately) that musical performance held a covert power capable of diverting and even 'corrupting' its executants. His nagging worry that music-making would have the contrary effect to what he intended led him to entrust his third son, Herbert Booth, to supervise this part of the operation when a 'Music Department' was inaugurated. In an article published in 1897 under the heading 'Self-Denial of Bandsmen's Wives', William Booth drew attention to the hidden dangers to which he believed bandsmen were vulnerable. He might also have witnessed with heightened concern that some were acquiring virtuosity, which he saw as proximate to vanity. This is why he believed the wives of bandsmen had 'important work':

A bandsman has special temptations that do not cross the path of an ordinary soldier . . . they are often in spiritual danger . . . There is likewise a possibility of musical interests and activity usurping the Salvationist ideal . . . what a chance a wife has of watching the rise of these various kinds of danger.[13]

One wonders what those wives made of this, or how the educated musicians who made up the staff of the Salvation Army's Music Department felt they should respond. Herbert Booth himself, unlike his autocratic brother Bramwell, appears to have adopted a relatively relaxed position before enthusiastically accepting a foreign posting and eventually resigning from the Army.

The Slater effect

The Music Department's main responsibility was to expand the repertoire for its 'songsters' (choirs) and bands. It was set up experimentally in 1881 and consolidated two years later. Its three members were Fred Fry, Harry Hill and Richard Slater. Slater was the most talented and important of the three and came to be regarded as 'the father of Salvationist music'.[14] His relationships with William and Bramwell Booth were not consistently easy because he had a much more open and educated musical mind than either. Within three years of the Salvation Army being founded, its music was being regarded as both a blessing and a problem. The steps taken to control it were remarkable. No other religious organisation of its size and eventual global scope had attempted to exercise such autocratic and regulated control. There were, however, pockets of thought that believed it necessary: some held the view that Salvation Army brass band players were indulging their musical interests as a form of recreation which distracted from the core evangelical purpose that was intended to unite the entire movement. The idea that appears to have evaded open consideration was that musical expression and deft musical skills were not axiomatically incompatible with unhindered faith and spiritual devotion. Johann Sebastian Bach had demonstrated this on a daily basis, as had many other previous performers and composers. It was this lingering dilemma that the Salvation Army inherited when the Founder died in 1912 and Bramwell Booth became the Army's leader. Bramwell had inherited his father's legacy and autocratic style. This did not subdue or clarify the ambiguity surrounding the spiritual role that bands were to serve. Richard Slater was to play a major, if uncomfortable, part in defining the future of Salvationist music.

Slater was born in London in 1854. His father was an accomplished musician, but his death at the age of 28 meant that Richard's childhood, like that of the Founder, was impoverished – his mother supported the family by taking in washing. He was intellectually brilliant and largely self-taught. His abiding interest was in phrenology, and this could have provided the direction for his career had not Salvationism and his prodigious musical gifts intervened. He received some lessons from Sidney Jones, the distinguished military bandmaster, and was also advised in his studies by George MacFarren, editor of the *Musical World*. He became a successful professional violinist and encountered a wide range of classical repertoire and was especially interested in and inspired by the works of Richard Wagner (he named his daughter Brünnhilde), seeing in Wagner's music a capacity to stimulate and exalt religious sentiments. Like William Booth, he had experimented with various denominations, but was converted to Salvationism in September 1882 at a meeting at the Regent Hall citadel in London. Booth recognised Slater's talent and appointed him to serve in the Army's 'Grecian Corps'. The name came from the Grecian Theatre which was attached to 'The Eagle' public house, 'one of the most notorious, devilish dancing places and theatres in London'.[15] Booth had 'captured' it (through purchase) in 1882 and turned it into a theatre of Salvation.

Slater was more talented than the other members of the Music Department and by 1893 was putatively its director. The *Musical Salvationist* provided most of the department's work. It was referred to as a musical monthly magazine. First published in July 1886, it had circulated about 3,000 pieces by 1908 and was to form the core repertoire for Salvationist songsters and bands.[16] Slater was unambiguously a Salvationist, but he was also an instinctive musician who recognised the power of music to touch the human spirit. Inevitably, this brought him into conflict with senior officers who saw the role and function of music in more monochromatic terms, insisting that:

> [you] should go back to the early style regardless of the consequences; there should be no note but was connected with a word, and the side and bass drums with 6 or 8 instruments were all that were needed in a Band . . . the General never allows modern Band music in his meetings.[17]

This must have been difficult for Slater, who recognised that he was 'the source and main strength of all this so-called musical liberalism in the Army'.[18] In many ways, he was perfect for his role: a competent and pragmatic administrator, a talented, educated and experienced musician, and a committed Salvationist who had been well regarded by the Founder. He eventually led developments that provided brass bands with roles in Salvation meetings that satisfied religious imperatives without dampening the instinctive musical enthusiasms of players. This, at least, was his intention, but maintaining an acceptable balance between both objectives was a permanent challenge.

Slater was a tireless worker. In 1908 he composed 139 hymn settings and marches for the Army's repertoire. He also transcribed several classical works, including the march from Wagner's *Lohengrin*. A year later came his first programmatic work for band – a set of six *Bible Pictures*. Also in 1908–9 came a clear indication of his reluctance to ignore the external musical world. He single-handedly wrote *The Salvation Army Dictionary of Music*: a short pocket-book dictionary but one of the most impressively concise and wide-ranging music reference books of the time. It contained entries on music theory and much about the elements that contribute to musical expression. It was available only to attested Salvationists, so Slater could have had no intention other than to provide its captive readership with a worldly education in music. It is not known whether William or Bramwell Booth approved or even knew of the book's contents. Either way, it was a force for a growing liberalism that must have become worryingly obvious at the International Congress of 1908, which included a festival of Salvation Army music at the Crystal Palace.[19] Hundreds of bands were assembled and, despite objections to the introduction of new music at the expense of old favourites, all music performed had been written in the previous 12 months. The blame – and it came in industrial proportions – fell primarily on the hapless Commissioner Howard who had organised the event, but Slater's influence was obvious. Entries in his diary show that he knew the extent of displeasure felt by both the Booths. Bramwell had been sufficiently upset 'as to leave the platform on more than one occasion'.[20]

The 1908 Congress might also have been inspired by events that occurred at the 1904 Congress in London, which included a 'Gigantic Bands Festival' in which 'about 200 bands' took part (fig. 21). Such

21. *Detail from a photograph of the mass bands' performance at the Salvation Army International Congress at the Crystal Palace in 1904. William Booth appears (white hair and beard) at the foot of the picture.*

an excess of musical exhibitionism would certainly have excited Booth's displeasure. The *British Bandsman* devoted a major article to the event, which would have annoyed Booth. It concluded that the Salvation Army had modelled the event on the Crystal Palace contests and Concerts devised by John Henry Iles a few years earlier.[21] Bands had been assembled from several of the territories in which the Army operated by that time, including the United States, Canada, Bermuda and more than a dozen European countries. The *British Bandsman* was struck by the decorative uniforms worn by some foreign bands and that many used the latest foreign rotary-valve instruments. Their standard of playing was reported as being not as high as in Britain, except for the New York Staff Band, which was a reed band (brass and woodwind) and decidedly 'Yankee' in its style – a phrase which, at the time, referred to emerging popular forms such as ragtime.

Four years after William Booth's death and Bramwell's appointment as his successor as General, a 'Commission of Inquiry' was established aimed at guiding the future direction of Salvationist music. The commission was to take account of 'the salvation of the people, and the building up of a simple and zealous soldiery'. It took evidence from many Army personnel, including musicians and music leaders. The interview transcripts survive to provide evidence of the rigour and scope of the process – and the conflict it was intended to resolve.[22]

The outcome, expressed in broad terms, was that the recent developments in Salvationist music, both vocal and instrumental, had been of advantage to the Army. Music had attracted crowds to outdoor meetings as well as to some indoor meetings. The hymn book needed updating, but the role of bands in accompanying singing remained important. On the difficult matter of music speaking to the hearts of the people, feelings were uncomfortably mixed. There was no difficulty with songster brigades because words literally enunciated the message of Salvation, but:

> In instrumental music, there is, undoubtedly, a greater difficulty –
> the evidence indicates that the music has not fulfilled expectations
> in reaching the hearts of the unsaved to the extent hoped for and
> earnestly desired.[23]

Two factors were culpable, but neither excluded the possibility that instrumental music had the potential to act effectively in the cause of Salvationism. Firstly, there was an insufficient supply of music for bands 'both in character and length' (whatever that was intended to mean). The music needed to be good but devotional, with no 'fireworks finale' (also ambiguous but probably a comment on some prevailing exhibitionist practices).[24] Secondly, and this is also abundantly evident in the interview transcripts, there was a near-total absence of meaningful and cordial communications between leaders of Salvationist meetings and their bandmasters. A further and critically important observation was that there was little appreciation of bands and the sense of community that had developed naturally within each of them. This latter idea was especially interesting because the proscription of the setting up of band committees in the 1881 regulations was deliberately aimed at preventing bands from forming a discrete sense of community within corps. It was believed at that time that the establishment of a coherent sub-group within a citadel would potentially undermine discipline.

Other outcomes included a need to restate the purpose of music in worship, and a 'rearrangement' of published band music that would take account of the 'various grades' of bands operating at that time. This, too, was interesting because, while it benefited less efficient bands, it tacitly acknowledged that others had developed to a much higher level. In 1923 a 'Festival' series of band works was launched for the benefit of more elite bands. But even at this stage it came with the proviso that all works to be included would be 'censored by the Music Board'.[25] The first publication in the series was Frederick G. Hawkes's 'Gems from the Messiah No. 1'.[26] There was also a reaffirmation of the three primary purposes of Salvationist bands: to draw attention to Salvationist meetings; to accompany hymns; and to perform music which, by its character, held the prospect of promoting spirituality. These objectives showed little change from those that had been articulated since the Army's foundation. The objective for 'music to promote spirituality' continued a tradition of ambiguity that was to prevail, with only a few minor adjustments, through the twentieth century. The 1977 regulations said more or less the same thing about the purpose of instrumental music: it needed to convey 'by association of ideas, salvation messages [that would go] direct to the hearts of the hearers. This is likely to take place when tunes or selections are wisely chosen.'[27]

It was the enshrinement of this idea as *a regulation* that had always been at the heart of the problem: its openness to interpretation had blighted Salvation Army music for a hundred years. The words may have made perfect sense to the person (or committee) who wrote them, but the extent to which they were understood by the thousands who were required to read and act on them was always more open to question. This was not a trivial matter. It signified something that was real and manifest in the beliefs and practices of each Salvationist soldier. Throughout the inter-war period, many worried about the extent to which bands and songsters were using worship as little more than an opportunity to perform music. In 1922 Alfred Braine, the National Director for Bands and Songster Brigades, complained:

It is no uncommon criticism of Bands and Songster Brigades that they monopolise too much time on Sunday evenings, playing and singing pieces that are not only too long but unsuitable to the character of the Meeting.[28]

In the next decade a similar criticism came from General Edward Higgins, implying that bands, and possibly songsters too, were usurping the participation of congregations:

Our indoor meetings in some places are becoming much less alive in their character than once was the case. I have been in some, and heard of others, in which the congregation has taken part only once in the whole service, and that was the opening song![29]

A revision: 'Save the sinner and bless the saint'

Higgins had been promoted to the leadership of the Salvation Army in 1929, following one of the greatest shocks in its history. The Salvation Army's High Council met on 8 January to debate a single proposal and concluded that Bramwell Booth was no longer fit to act as the organisation's head. The explanation put forward by the Council was Booth's failing health (he was already seriously ill in January and died in June that year, but he did not resign), and that a formal adjudication was necessary which was supported by the organisation's most senior figures, including his sister Evangeline, points to the level of concern. Bramwell Booth's autocratic style had been a source of anxiety since the organisation was founded. This was an important moment for the Army and, while it seems to have had no immediate or direct effect on its musical activities, it is probably from that time that bands were able to develop repertoires and styles of playing without fear of such close censorship, and perhaps even adopt a more pragmatic position in their relationship with the outside world.[30]

For much of the twentieth century, bands were used in five types of meeting.[31] Outdoor Meetings were aimed explicitly at the unconverted, with the intention of advertising the gift of salvation and raising funds through collections. Holiness Meetings and Praise Meetings both emphasised prayer and spirituality, with Praise Meetings being more celebratory of the gift of salvation. Gospel (or Salvation) Meetings were aimed at conversion. There were also special assemblies such as international congresses and other events that fell into the Festival category and which Slater described as:

A meeting in which music has the chief place, and which in quantity and quality is beyond that used for ordinary meetings. Thus, Festival implies a meeting which is exceptional for the amount and character of the musical effort put into it. To make a Festival a success the end of all army meetings must be kept in view, which is to save the sinner and to bless the saint.[32]

The most distinctive form of devotional music designed specifically for brass band performance was the Meditation, which, as the name suggests, was aimed at inspiring prayer and reflection. The prototype of the Meditation is believed to have been introduced by Slater in 1902, but surprisingly it is not mentioned in his *Dictionary*. The form originated as a straightforward instrumental version of a hymn.

It then developed so that each verse was given a contrasting harmonic or textural treatment and joined together by short decorative sections termed 'episodes'. The hymns chosen for Meditations will have been known to the assembled Salvationists, so their spiritual message always underpinned the instrumental performance. In 1965 Ray Steadman-Allen, Head of the Army's Music Editorial Department, devised what he called a 'recipe' for the Meditation: this was a framework for colouring each verse and assigning obbligato solo passages to the episodes.

By the 1960s the isolationism still existed, but its enactment was more subdued, and one wonders how conscientiously it was observed. Some bands, including one that eventually became the basis for the Callender's Cableworks Band, found the regulatory restrictions stifling and left the movement en bloc, but most settled into their local routines. The Salvation Army was a worldwide organisation, still committed to its mission of evangelism and social welfare. Soul-searching about its adherence to a Victorian doctrine that lacked a coherent theological basis was hardly a priority. The New Zealand Salvationist Dean Goffin had supplied the test piece for the 1949 Open contest and other Salvationists were becoming involved in the wider brass band world – including contesting.

Elites

Later instrumental forms used and published by the Salvation Army have been all but identical in format and content to the same species in secular bands. These include the *air varié* solo (a melody with incrementally virtuosic variations), the *selection* (a potpourri of arrangements borrowed from existing works), *arrangements* of existing (usually classical) works, and free-standing pieces that are defined less by their form and content than by the simple expediency that they were approved for publication in the Festival series. The Festival series also included 'tone poems': single movement works that are 'programmatic' in the sense that they are meant to convey or evoke an extramusical narrative or sentiment. Most secular brass band test pieces were abbreviated versions of the tone-poem form and gained increasing sophistication in the twenty-first century. Some of the most celebrated examples were written by composers who originated as Salvation Army musicians.

One of the most important artistic influences between the two world wars was the composer-conductor Eric Ball, a Salvation Army officer who worked in its Music Editorial Department. He also became a major figure in the brass band movement. Frank Wright, an Australian cornet virtuoso who also became a leading personality in the secular brass band movement, reviewing a concert given by the Salvationist Publishing and Supplies (SP&S) Band – which Ball had established in 1928 – referred to Ball's scoring of his composition *The Triumph of Peace* as a 'masterpiece'. Wright believed the band was comparable to secular contesting bands and commented that 'everything he [Ball] does shows taste and musicianship'. In 1942 Ball became bandmaster of the elite International Staff Band of the Salvation Army and was promoted to the rank of major. Two years later, he abruptly resigned from the Salvation Army. This was prompted by his involvement with spiritualism, but it was also suggested that his expansionist attitude to Salvationist music was unpopular with his superiors. There was an eventual reconciliation, but the remainder of Ball's career was spent as a conductor and composer outside the Army and he was editor of the *British Bandsman* magazine for two periods, between 1951 and 1967.

That the Army had elite bands at all is an indicator of how its bands had developed a life of their own. Most of the best Salvationist performers were in the Army because of their faith. If such were not the case, there would have been nothing to prevent them from shifting to musical environments where their talents would have been more comfortably accommodated. One suspects that this may have happened in many cases. The International Staff Band was formed in 1891 literally as a staff band: a band for the staff of the Army's headquarters. Fred Fry was its bandmaster. It had been preceded in 1887 by a band that had only a six-year existence but provided a prototype for the fundamental idea that elite music-making could have a place in Salvationism. This was the Household Troops Band. Slater described it in his *Dictionary*: 'It was organised for continuous musical work, so that its members volunteered for this kind of labour as the ordinary candidate does for Field Operations.'[33] In fact, it was the closest thing the Army ever had to a full-time professional band. It was formed through an advertisement placed in the *War Cry* inviting volunteers for a band that would remain in continuous service.[34] It was part of a scheme that included religious study, physical exercise and musical performance. The students were given lessons, allocated practice time, and there were rehearsals each day. It undertook tours of Britain and a tour of Canada and the US – the first Salvationist band to do so. During the brief period when it flourished, the band attracted 126 players. Many became leaders of bands in corps in Britain and abroad. Why it was wound up in 1893 is not entirely clear, but it evidently overstepped the limits imposed by the Founder. In a meeting in London's Regent Hall in 1924, almost 30 years distant from the band's existence, Richard Slater afforded it an unusual level of praise:

> The band acted as a pioneer for Army bands, at least to a great extent, in the favour of the musical people, the critics, the musically trained part of society proving that the Army band music could arrest, impress and give satisfaction to the musically cultured as well as gain the attention of the average man and woman.[35]

A clue to its dissolution may be found in an utterance of Catherine Booth shortly before her death. She had heard the band and praised it, but added:

> the moment you (or any other bandsmen) begin to glory in the excellency of the music alone, apart from spiritual results, you will begin at that moment to lose your power.[36]

Realignment with the civilian world

Composers such as Eric Ball, Wilfred Heaton and, later, Peter Graham moved seamlessly between the Salvation Army and secular brass bands, composing test pieces for major contests. The test piece for the 1988 National contest was written by Ray Steadman-Allen. Robert Redhead, his successor as Head of the Army's Music Editorial Department, wrote the 1996 test piece. By the middle of the twentieth century, the differences between the two sectors had become narrow as well as glaringly artificial, and were probably routinely disregarded by many. Eventually, the difficulty was dissolved. Formal change came in two stages, both of which were prompted by commercial imperatives rather than doctrinal resolutions.

The establishment of the Trade Department, followed by the Salvationist Publishing and Supplies (SP&S) company, created successful production and distribution operations that were, in effect, monopolies within the constituency of the Army's vast international organisation. The instrument-manufacturing company, which had started as a small operation in east London, moved to a large factory in St Albans in 1901, but even by 1894 it had produced more than 1,500 instruments. Several of the workmen were Salvationist converts who had worked with other instrument manufacturers. As with secular bands, a large part of the business model was concentrated on the sale of sets of instruments rather than individual items, but there were secondary sales as new instrument models were introduced. In the late Victorian period, there were public appeals for the donation of instruments, but soon the Army was itself the sole source of supply. In the 80-year period in which it traded, the brass-instrument factory produced 34,283 instruments.[37] In 1922 there were an estimated 1,926 brass bands, 963 of which were in Britain, the others in Europe, Asia, Oceania, North America and beyond.[38] One of the more remarkable indicators of the Salvation Army's success was the rapidity of its global spread. Even in 1907, less than 30 years after it was founded, the Army was present in 53 countries. Between 1918 and 1939, the number of territories in which it was active increased from 63 to 97. After the Second World War, most of the SP&S instruments were despatched to foreign campaigns.

In the decade following 1956, there was a decline in sales and the company recorded repeated losses. By 1964 Boosey & Hawkes Besson, (which had relocated to the Boosey & Hawkes factory in 1948) and the Salvation Army were the only large-scale manufacturers of high-pitched brass band instruments.[39] In February 1964 a meeting was held between the two manufacturers that signalled the end of the production of high-pitched brass instruments. It was also the beginning of the end of instrument production by the Salvation Army more generally. An orderly transition was eventually agreed that saw SP&S workers shift their employment to Boosey & Hawkes, which took over the lease of the St Albans factory. The process was completed in 1972.

The doctrinal and practical measures that created an isolation that had prevailed for almost a century were finally and formally dismantled in 1992, when the Salvation Army issued a press announcement:

The Salvation Army, after more than a hundred years, is scrapping the regulation, which prevented its instrumental music from being sold to, or performed by, non-Salvation Army musicians. For too long The Salvation Army has had a ghetto mentality when it comes to its music. The Lord has lavished on it a unique measure of the gift of music, and for too long we have kept it to ourselves.[40]

This followed the deliberations of a working party set up to 'determine the future direction of Salvation Army Music'. In August of the same year, a further measure was put in place that rescinded 'the regulation which debars Salvationist musicians from participating in non-Salvation Army music', with the proviso that individual territories could ultimately decide on its implementation. A further regulation came into force in March 2003 which allowed Salvationist bandsmen to play in non-Salvationist bands, 'provided it did not interfere with their Salvation Army service'. Stephen Cobb, a life-long and highly respected Salvationist musician, was part of that working party. He commented, 'Having felt stifled for so many years, the privilege of being part of the group that made these significant decisions was immense.'[41]

What followed was in stark contradiction to what had passed in the previous century. Robert Redhead, one of the Army's most respected musicians, returned to Britain from service abroad. He was appointed Territorial Music Director and had an important influence on the transition to greater openness. Not only did the Salvation Army accept close involvement with non-Salvationist brass bands but, over time, it became the provider of most of their commercial and media services. Paradoxically, it was well placed to do so: it had an overall administrative and business infrastructure that the brass band movement lacked, and there was no shortage of energy and well-placed ambition among Salvationists to make integration work. By 2025 the Salvationist Publishing and Supplies (SP&S) company provided the necessities for its soldiers throughout the world, but it also embraced entirely secular products and services. This included major online retail operations for printed music and other materials. Its *World of Brass* operation retailed recordings of Salvationist and non-Salvationist brass bands. It also introduced *Wobplay*, a brass music streaming service that provides real-time and retrospective access to UK and European band contests as well as other events. It established the *World of Sound* audio and production company and *Just Music*, which publishes brass band music. For a brief period, the Salvation Army owned the *British Bandsman*, and it also acquired the distribution rights for the Richard Smith & Co. music publishing house founded in Hull in 1857 to serve the first generation of brass bands. Each of these commercial companies generated profits for the Salvation Army's various missions.[42]

The association with the brass band movement benefited the Army's mission but, while commercial imperatives provided an opportunity, they were not the principal motivation for abolishing the schism between Salvationist and non-Salvationist bands. The decision was taken on the basis that separation contradicted the fundamental principle that Salvationism existed to join people together rather than keep them apart, and that greater openness advanced the Army's primary purpose: to integrate itself with all aspects of ordinary life. This, of course, was in direct contravention to the separatist attitude that had dominated Salvation Army music for so long, but the change was demonstrably successful.

Chapter 7

'Village life': Brass bands and their localities

Winston Churchill's statement that 'history is written by the victors' was an observation about how political histories have been formed, but the principle has a wider utility: it holds true of any historical narrative that stands in danger of allowing dominant actors to obscure a wider perspective. Such thoughts prompted the inclusion of this chapter. 'Village life' is used both literally and metaphorically to capture two aspects of the brass band story that might otherwise be overlooked. Firstly, those bands that thrived in parts of the country, particularly rural areas, where brass bands have not traditionally been prominent and evaded notice because they are absent from lists of contest winners. Their number is incalculable, but evidence of them is abundant in other source categories. The area surrounding the Buckinghamshire town of Milton Keynes provides an example: in the early 1980s, and not including youth bands and the Salvation Army, there were as many as eight fully operational bands in the group of villages that surround the town. Each had 15 to 30 players. They seldom contested but were keenly aware of their history and traditions and felt part of the brass band movement. One of them also met as a madrigal choir led by one of the horn players.[1] Secondly, and this may seem contradictory, the term 'village life' refers to contesting bands that gained national celebrity as winners, but whose immediate day-to-day lives were embedded in local communities where they acted out other roles and responsibilities. Put differently, even the most prolific winners were also local bands and their communities nourished them. Three characteristics have always been common to both categories. All were, or became, *brass* bands; all felt part of a national network; and all were 'entrepreneurial' amateurs who were collectively dependent on their localities for the means and incentives that ensured their existence and contentment.

For at least the first hundred years of their history, brass bands were made up of amateurs who played for the love of it. It was a hobby – often an all-consuming one – but relatively few players aspired further. Playing in a brass band was part of everyday lives and often stood in sharp contrast to what they otherwise did for a living. Phineas Bower, the Black Dyke Mills trombone and euphonium player and one of its greatest early stars, was a 'warp dresser'; the cornet player and conductor Thomas Rimmer (father of the more famous William Rimmer) was an 'engine fitter's labourer'. Occupations often reflected the main source of employment in a locality but sometimes not: a Derby band had three 'painter and gilders' as well as two 'watch makers'; Heckmondwike Albion band was full of carpet makers; a band from the wealthy town of Chester included a 'reporter', a 'solicitors clerk' and a 'photographist'; and among the 'confectioners' and 'grocers' in a band from the southern town of Sittingbourne, Kent, was the soprano cornet player George Young who was a 'naturalist'.[2] This wide and variegated pattern changed very little until the second half of the twentieth century when myriad societal changes caused bands to be peopled by computer scientists, doctors, teachers, housewives and all manner of other occupations. Some of the best brass players became national celebrities but many more were local heroes. Locality has always been fundamental to banding; this is evidenced by the number of travelling supporters who sat with their bands on those Victorian railway trains that carried them to distant contests. The business model that made the entire brass band enterprise viable depended on the activation of localities, the events that occurred within them and the feelings stirred by contesting.

A local historian of the Bacup band in Yorkshire described the excitement and anticipation that swept through the valleys and dales when contesting was introduced:

The excitement in the neighbourhood was intense and for days before the contest the fate of the band at Belle Vue was almost the sole topic of conversation. The practices of the band in the yard of the Mill at Broadclough on the Sunday previous to the fateful day was attended by thousands of persons. On the morning of the contest, the Belle Vue excursions from Bacup were packed with people, and most of the mills were obliged to stop. Two special trains were run, the local bookings being as follows: Bacup 1093 [passengers], Stacksteads 200, Newchurch 519, and Rawtenstall 323.[3]

Bands became representative of the spaces in which their members lived and worked. Local people took ownership of them and bestowed on them an emotional investment. The measure of this, and the validity of the local hero idea, is neatly and movingly illustrated in the way localities marked the passing of Edwin Swift in 1904. Swift had no formal education in music but showed precocious talent as a cornet player when he was a child. He became leader of the Linthwaite Band when he was 14 years old. In adulthood he became famous as a band teacher and leader of several bands in neighbouring Yorkshire villages. On the cold February day of his funeral, hundreds from those villages formed his cortège. They were led by 80 uniformed bandsmen from the bands he had trained; they carried their instruments but did not sound them. The engines in the local mills and factories fell silent. All that was heard was the beat of drums that had been muffled by black drapery from the Linthwaite mill in which he had worked as a boy. The day was heavily charged with sadness and symbolism, but the story is not apocryphal: it happened. The people who formed that cortège did so because Swift was theirs.

Almost all bands had responsibilities in their localities that were broadly of the same scale, if different in type. Many became components of long-standing cyclical local rituals and of others that were newly invented.[4] Bands in rural areas usually transformed into brass bands less quickly than those in industrialised areas and stayed loyal to inherited practices and traditions. They were also less driven by contesting and the implications associated with it. Most seem to have responded to what their localities expected of them; it was as if they had conceded to a limited set of purposes predetermined by their communities.

Rural bands

Traditions lasted longer in rural communities because they were usually more distant from the primary influences of modernity than industrial regions. When migration occurred from rural to industrialised areas, it was usually younger generations that moved, but country villages did not become culturally moribund. As William Cobbett, the nineteenth-century parliamentarian and inveterate observer of rural life, said, 'It is a great error to suppose that people are rendered stupid by remaining always in the same place.'[5] Most country village bands in the first half of the nineteenth century were the product of one of two earlier musical formations. Some were reformations of bands that had been attached to county militia units that had been formed in the late eighteenth century. Militia bands were established across the country and there is plenty of evidence to show that fragments of them continued long after that early version of the militia had outlived its military purpose.[6] More numerous and enduring were bands connected to Anglican parish churches where makeshift and miscellaneous assemblies of instrumentalists were formed to accompany singing. Congregational singing did not become common until later in the nineteenth century, but the singing of metrical psalms by church choirs has a longer ancestry. Church bands played in galleries constructed at the western end of churches. Traditionally, and unless circumstances intervened, the altar in an Anglican church is placed at its eastern end so that congregations and priests face the rising sun in morning services – musicians' galleries were usually behind the congregation. Many such galleries survive and, where they have been removed, architectural traces reveal their previous presence. It is the ecclesiastical orientation of those galleries that provide the name by which such bands are usually known: 'west gallery bands' (fig. 22). There was no set instrumentation, but they often numbered about five players, some fewer, some more: a band in Chedworth, Gloucestershire, had

12 players in 1838, but this was exceptional.[7] Given the extensive distribution of rural Anglican churches, it is easy to imagine that there were many west gallery band players. They were made up of string and woodwind instruments (sometimes home-made), but bass parts were often played on serpents. There is also scattered evidence of the adoption of other brass instruments during the nineteenth century, particularly keyed bugles, cornets, trombones and ophicleides.[8] West gallery bands gradually declined during the nineteenth century, but a few survived until the 1890s. They were made redundant when barrel organs, harmoniums and organs were introduced.[9] Published writings about west gallery bands can convey the idea that they were a phenomenon restricted to southern and eastern counties of England, but this is a reflection of the places where scholarly interest has been applied to the subject rather than the scope of the activity itself: they existed across the country.[10] An interesting literary account of the transition away from west gallery bands is given in Thomas Hardy's 1871 novel *Under the Greenwood Tree*. Hardy had been a witness to such a process, so his story provides a sympathetic and probably realistic portrayal of an important stage in rural music-making.

22. Nineteenth-century engraving after a painting by Thomas Webster of a west gallery band.

Church band instrumentalists also undertook secular roles. As such, they established an important principle from which all rural brass bands would benefit: the idea that in villages, or clusters of them, a band was a social necessity. The collapse of a traditional band usually created a void accompanied by a widely acknowledged need for it to be filled. Accounts of the musical quality of west gallery bands are seldom complimentary, but their secular manifestation was greatly appreciated. Some players struggled with the switch from the sacred to the raucously secular. James Nye, a Sussex gardener who experienced a religious conversion in 1852, loved playing in his church band but sensed spiritual peril when his skills were deployed for secular purposes:

> I joined a band and this was like a snare to me . . . I have been in ungodly company playing music for them to dance to . . . I cannot help being carried away with the sound rather than the substance.[11]

By the time Nye was writing, brass instrument makers were beginning to deploy the marketing techniques that had proved successful in industrial districts in rural areas (fig. 23). The wide introduction of saxhorns and cornets coincided with the demise of west gallery bands but did not cause it and there was some overlap; euphoniums were sometimes introduced to replace ophicleides, and in the 1850s the village church at Chiddingstone in Kent had a band made up of two cornets, a baritone and a euphonium.[12] The use of brass instruments in rural areas accelerated when the Volunteer movement swept the country from 1859.[13] This marked an important change in rural musical life. The association of Volunteering with patriotism provided a new reason for local gentry to support the creation of bands. It was not an inexpensive enterprise, but it was generally deemed necessary as well as worthwhile, not least because there were many who believed that volunteering projected 'military values into the public at large'.[14] This sentiment applied to rural areas as much as it did elsewhere, and with equal effect. The manipulative behaviour of those brass bands that struck a financial deal with the Volunteers was largely absent in Volunteer bands that were formed ab initio; and because they were assembled specifically for a quasi-military role rather than contesting, there was scope to limit

LYNN WORKING MEN'S
SAX-HORN BAND.

The Public are respectfully informed that the above Band having secured the services of MR. BARTLE to conduct and arrange, and MESSRS. FARMER and COE as Leaders, they are now practising a different style of Music, which they hope shortly to introduce to the Inhabitants of the Town, by playing as heretofore on the New Walks.

Lynn, July, 1855.

J. M. MATSELL, PRINTER, LYNN.

23. *A mid-nineteenth-century poster distributed by the band of the small town of Lynn in Norfolk. It suggests a recent transition to saxhorn instruments from an older formation.*

their cost to what was essential, but the brass band format was the overwhelmingly popular choice for Volunteer units, and this contributed importantly to transformations in the character of rural music-making, especially in larger centres of rural population.

Such a transformation is illustrated in the way old and newly developing instrumental music cultures coexisted in the Sussex town of Horsham. A public fund was set up in the town around 1910 to finance the publication of the memoir of Henry Burstow (1826–1916). Burstow was a local shoemaker, but also a celebrated bell-ringer and singer of traditional songs. It was said that he had memorised 400 songs, which he sang cyclically each evening to his wife – presumably with her agreement. His book provides a profile of the many roles music played in the town's social life in the nineteenth century. In the 1860s the town band was made up of 12 players: four woodwinds, seven brass and a drum. Seven of its players had the same surname

(Potter) and lived at the same Horsham address, obviously members of a single family.[15] Wherever repertoire was mentioned in newspaper reports, the music played was of the same type: not Italian opera derivatives but arrangements of traditional ballads such as 'The Roast Beef of Old England'. Burstow's book conveys a picture of Horsham as a growing village that had acquired the status of a thriving rural town (its population doubled to about 10,000 in the second half of the century). He did not mention other developments of which he must have been aware. William Albery, a local saddler and associate of Burstow, had been in contact with 'some of the magnificent bands of the North and Midlands' and was determined to emulate them 'in instrumentation, numbers (minimum twenty-four members) and style of performance':

In the North and Midlands these bands have led the way to a musical atmosphere and tradition, they have been playing, flourishing and competing for over a century, and it must be admitted Sussex had not the necessary will or means, or both to follow them. In Yorkshire and Lancashire particularly band competitions of great frequency and musical severity during this period under professional brass band teachers and judges cultivated and stimulated talent there to perfection.[16]

The Horsham brass band was indeed formed. Three-quarters of its musicians were trained within the band. It was independent of a church or any other agency and was in place for no other purpose than to provide pleasure for its players; this was reflected in its original title: the 'Horsham Recreational Band'. At the turn of the century, it was even gaining a measure of success in contests. The First World War reduced its numbers from 28 to nine, but it was this group of music-makers that survived as the town's band.

Getting up a country band

Village bands were often the product of endeavours in which local people provided funds or credit guarantees, but the presence of moneyed support always helped; as one writer put it, 'The kindness of rich inhabitants and neighbours in the parish [often] provides the funds for the purchase of the instruments.'[17] Bands that were formed or became consolidated as part of the 1859 Volunteer movement benefited from the intention that volunteering should be a genuinely national initiative. Others may have adopted ideas advocated by Algernon Rose:

> Three or four enthusiasts who have made up their mind to constitute a band, which shall, by and bye, be spoken of as a credit to all connected with it, will achieve that success 'if they are Britons', because the more one gets about in the world the more does one realise that, despite a tendency to run down his kith and kin, John Bull still possesses remarkable tenacity of purpose.[18]

Such a sentiment was not rare, and it is easy to detect in it a veiled version of the rational recreation theme, but the practical steps necessary to form a band were less straightforward in places with no prospect of industrial sponsorship. In rural areas, the moral value of music-making among the plebeian class was supplemented by a practical requirement for the services of a band of music in localities where traditional forms of music-making were disappearing:

> On the one side there is a devout and sincere love for music [in the countryside], and on the other the most meagre of opportunities for learning or guidance in it. Country people need a brightening of their lives, just as much as the inhabitants of the over-crowded quarters of cities, and it seems a pity that they should not have better chances of making progress in that innocent and delightful art which happens to be the only one of which they have an inkling.[19]

It was a combination of benevolence and subscription that allowed village bands to be formed, but sometimes it was necessary for a band to be attached to an existing agency. In inner cities, this may have included temperance societies or churches of any denomination. The instigation of a new parish band always gained approbation from the rural press:

Parochial Band – We are happy to congratulate our fellow parish-ioners on the prospect of having a band in this place. A few respectable young men of the parish have come forward, and articles etc. are drawn up, each of them entering into a weekly subscription to defray the expenses of purchasing music, books, etc, and meet for the purpose of practice every Tuesday and Saturday. We wish them success and hope they will meet with encouragement from the Clergy and Gentry of the parish.[20]

This report was of developments in Rotherfield, Sussex, in 1839, too early for it to be an all-brass band, but it implies the emergence of a form of patronage that was to become common. The 1872 memoir of William Smith, an orphan who, in adult life, established himself in Oxfordshire as a major manufacturer of blankets, also suggests that finances were found locally for the establishment of a band:

After joining the teetotal Society it was considered desirable to form a band for society purposes, and religious festivals. No sooner was this suggested than it was adopted and the money was at once raised for the purchase of twelve instruments . . . [We were] under the tuition of Mark Talboys, [a local glover] who had for years taken part in a select band . . . After receiving our instruments, progress was very rapid, and within the first week we ventured our first tune beneath the town hall. The air was 'We lived and loved together'.[21]

A primary reason why some local bands did not take part in contests was that they were too small, an issue that became increasingly intract-able as contest regulations imposed a minimum size and consistent instrumental format. James Ord Hume, who was to play a major part in the development of bands in Australia, believed that the absence of contesting deprived village bands of the main device for elevating standards. He advocated a system in which groups of small rural bands would contest against each other and eventually combine their best players to form a full contesting band. He claimed to have experimented with such a system.

Now is just the time to think out your neighbouring bands, meet one and other and talk this matter over. Lose no time, because your programme will require a good deal of consideration, and a good deal of working up, if you intend to do the thing tip top ... try the experiment no matter how small your little bands may be. Unity is strength![22]

Contesting had less purchase in rural areas than in industrial communities but, when contests were held in southern English counties, they attracted several competitors and large audiences. As early as 1861, a contest was organised by Enderby Jackson in Exeter's Northernhay Gardens, which were 'literally covered by a multitude of persons amongst whom we observed was a goodly sprinkling of the *elite* of the community'.[23] The winner was the Blandford band, which was gaining brief but national celebrity through its appearances at Jackson's Crystal Palace contests. The runners-up in Exeter were from Torquay, Teignmouth, Gloucester and Dawlish.

Towns and cities

Bands in the boroughs of large conurbations did not consistently focus on contesting. Manchester was typical of the larger provincial cities in having bands that were supported by charitable organisations. Parts of the large repertoire of the Openshaw Lads Club survive. It contains a quantity of journal music but also several operatic selections.[24] The Bridgewater Methodist Church also supported a juvenile band between 1930 and 1940. Funds came from public donations and engagement income. Money was also provided for band boys and children from 'ragged society' homes to be taken on various excursions. One of the donors was another (unnamed) brass band.[25]

Temperance bands came in various shapes, sizes and denominations across the country. Several seem to have had an ambiguous and inconsistent relationship with abstinence – many were expelled because of their drunkenness. The problem seems to have been particularly acute in south Wales, where the word 'temperance' seems to have been totally misunderstood in some quarters; in 1908 the William Sutherland

Total Abstinence Band was taken to court and required by a magistrate to return its instruments because its players could not be genuinely described as teetotal.[26]

London bands must be seen differently to those in other parts of the country. In the Victorian period, and for some time after, bands were numerous but they seldom contested, and this impacted on both their standard and coherence. There were modest exceptions. Sam Cope, the editor of the *British Bandsman*, conducted the London Temperence Band which, at the start of the twentieth century, won some lower-section prizes, and the Fulham Borough Band was sufficiently organised to be the subject of a profile in the *British Bandsman* in 1896, even though it had been in existence for little more than six months.[27] The absence of high standards among London bands was still apparent in the 1930s, when the BBC was keen to broadcast bands of appropriate quality from the London area and could find none closer than the county of Kent. Bands that were not attached to churches or one of the temperance societies were usually entrepreneurial. Football clubs assembled bands and paid them to play at their home matches. The Arsenal Football Club Band was formed for that purpose in 1914, a large part of it made up of recusant members of the Highgate Salvation Army Band. It became a popular part of the match-day experience. Churches supported juvenile bands in Sunday schools and adjunct organisations such as the Church Lads Brigade, which was founded in Fulham in 1891.[28]

Many Victorian and Edwardian bands in London seem to have been assembled randomly, possibly from retired military bandsmen. The social framework of the city did not yield the type of coherence present in industrial and rural settlements elsewhere. Bandstand concerts, especially those in London's major parks, such as Hyde Park, Green Park and the Embankment Gardens, were popular and well organised. They were mainly served by bands of the regular army and in summer months by some top civilian contesting bands. Local bands – often taking the name of their boroughs – also played in their local parks but not always as part of the formal programmes. Several seem to have done whatever they saw fit if it held the prospect of pecuniary gain. In many cases, their activities were little more than a thinly veiled form of busking, and this drew unwanted attention. The Mile End Assembly Hall Band played regularly in the borough's Victoria Park on Sundays. Assembling on a day for which it was apparently not formally booked, the band was apprehended by 'a London County Council inspector, accompanied by a police sergeant and about eight constables':

> [They] appraised the musicians that they were transgressing the park regulations, and that intimation had been received from the London County Council that proceedings were to be taken against them if they refused to desist. The conductor vehemently protested against such interference and arbitrary action on the part of the council. 'Abide with me' was then played very impressively, whereupon the police officers demanded the names and addresses of the players – a demand which, at the instigation of the spectators, the players refused to concede. The inspector then said he would have to arrest the whole of them. He, however, refrained from adopting that extreme step on their undertaking to walk down in a body to the police-station, which they did, accompanied by some five or six thousand people, with police officers at their head. Arrived at the Wick Road station, the instr[u]mentalists filed in, and jocularly enquired if tea was ready. Their names and addresses were taken, and they were informed that summonses would be issued against them.[29]

There the story stops: we don't know whether the summonses were issued, and we can't be sure whether the size of the spectating party was journalistically exaggerated. We can be certain, however, that while brass bands in inner-city boroughs were often more popular than the police and officers of the local authority, they were treated with less respect than their counterparts in other parts of the country.

An impediment to the formation of good contesting bands in London was the street environment in which Londoners lived and its perpetual noise. This was often caused by the tiresome 'German brass bands' that were a ubiquitous and irritating feature of London streets for much of the nineteenth century. But there were other perpetrators of the continuous 'musical' activity that Londoners encountered on a day-to-day basis. Henry Mayhew, in his 1851 survey of *London Street Life*, estimated there to be in excess of a thousand people who made their living from performing in the streets as musicians every day, and this included bands of one sort or another.[30] Late in the century, Salvation Army bands added to the soundscape, and players were regularly arrested and prosecuted for not 'moving on' or, to put it differently, holding their ground when ordered to move by the police. They must have gained some solace from the fact that the police were keener to make arrests than magistrates were to prosecute. For example, in 1900 the magistrates found no case to answer when the Lavender Hill Temperance Band appeared under the charge of 'not moving on', but others were not so lucky. The circumstances in which many of London's local bands existed were grim and offered a marked contrast to the appreciative reception received by those in other regions. In 1896 the *British Musician* published a copy of a letter originally sent to its local authority by the secretary of the Fulham Borough Brass Band concerning disturbances at the band's concerts at the Lillie Road Recreation Ground. This really was a brass band with prospects. It had been formed from an amalgamation of the band of the Chelsea branch of the Operative Bricklayers (trades union) and had attracted other competent players through newspaper advertisements.[31] Within a year, it was good enough to win contests and gain approval to perform in parks, but it threatened to withdraw this service:

> Unless something is done to prevent the children throwing stones and otherwise disturbing the band, and also the bigger ones from indulging in shouting and fighting. We do not object to them joining in the comic airs with the band, but we do to noise, as it prevents the respectable listeners from hearing the band ... Three of the instruments were damaged by stones last night, although I will admit that the stones thrown were not aimed at the band-stand but were missiles thrown by the boys at one another.[32]

Rituals

Almost all brass bands acquired a role in local ritual, even if it was no more than an annual appearance to play Christmas carols. Many did a lot more. In many parts of the country, specific traditions focused on brass bands or absorbed them to the extent that they became essential components. The Saddleworth brass band festival, which centres on five West Yorkshire villages, is an example. From about 1870, brass bands were incorporated into an older Whitsun tradition. On Whit Friday (the first Friday after Pentecost), children would walk in procession to their church, giving rise to the term 'Whit Walks'. The tradition eventually embraced adults and then bands as part of a more elaborate procession. As with so many traditions that originated in religious ritual, there was a gradual transition to the secular. A contest was added, initially for local bands, and this too expanded. In the twenty-first century, the event embraced more localities, and between 50 and 70 brass bands compete in multiple marching contests held on a single day.[33] One report claimed that the 2015 event 'attracted 126 bands from all round the UK'.[34] It is just one of other similar events in which local bands play a prominent part. Many held in the summer months include 'March' and 'Hymn Tune' contests. The Northumberland Miners' Picnic, held since 1864, is one of many that continued long after coal mining stopped in the county. An episode of *Monitor*, a BBC flagship documentary television programme, was devoted to the 1960 event. In a single day, 25 bands took part, accompanied by their supporters and local beauty queens. The bands marching through the streets were judged for deportment by a sergeant major from the Grenadier Guards, and a Manchester adjudicator assessed their musical quality from an open window above a shop in the main street. This was followed by eating, drinking and a series of left-wing political speeches.[35]

A similar, and yet larger, gathering is the Durham Miners' Gala, which was inaugurated in 1871 as a celebration of coal mining and its communities in County Durham. It grew to be an explicitly left-wing festival in which trades unionism was celebrated with marches and the parading of banners. Its modern manifestation is held in July of each year in Durham city and advertised as 'the world's greatest celebration of community, international solidarity, and working-class life' (fig. 24). In 2024 approximately 50 bands took part in the parade, which attracted more than 200,000 participants and spectators.[36] There

24. A parade led by a brass band at the Durham Miners' Gala.

are few rituals on such a scale that link brass bands so closely and conspicuously with their working-class origins and the organised trades union movement. The event was destined for oblivion before it was rescued by sponsorship. Between 1913 and 1923, there were 170,000 working coal miners in Durham's 304 collieries.[37] The last working pit closed in 1994. In that year the number of people attending the Gala dropped to 10,000, but by 2016 a popular feeling that the traditions of coal-mining communities should be retained caused attendances to increase twentyfold. This was not all. More bands engaged with their communities in preparation for the event, and new banners were designed and made for ceremonial display in villages where mining had disappeared many decades previously. This raises the question of whether the Durham Gala and events like it can be understood as important festivals of community history, or just modern nostalgic rituals that have gained popular purchase because of their annual repetition. It is probably both, but their potency remains evident. Whatever has been lost through the closing of mines and other industries, the bands have retained a capacity to summon feelings of locality and identity. One former miner and trades unionist expressed a sentiment that may have been felt by many:

> The Gala. It's almost like an icon for people who are looking for something . . . The Gala's there, it's the only one left and it's getting bigger every year. I don't want to sound too romantic but it's something, you can go there and charge your batteries. You see people, I see people there, I see them once a year, right?[38]

Deindustrialisation as it affected coal-mining communities featured in the 1996 movie *Brassed Off*, a fictionalised account of the impact of a colliery closure on its brass band.[39] The full weight of the film's portrayal of the social and cultural consequences of the pit's closure and the threat to its band (the fictional name is Grimley Colliery, but it is based on real-life events using the Grimethorpe Colliery Band) may have been lost on audiences outside the UK. In the US, the film was marketed as a 'romantic comedy', but British audiences saw it in different terms and, if only briefly, the social roles and musical identity of brass bands entered popular consciousness.

In Wales, *eisteddfodau* provided the earliest band contests. While *eisteddfodau* have a more distant origin, it was their nineteenth-century version that placed musical contest at its centre. The National Eisteddfod (*Eisteddfod Genedlaethol*) is held annually, at a different location each year. By the time brass bands were introduced, local rivalries were already deeply embedded, even in industrial communities of the southern valleys that had hardly entered the second decade of their existence. The first brass band contest at the national event appears to have been held at Wrexham in 1876. Seven bands entered the contest, which was won by the Tredegar Band. Brass banding developed rapidly in Wales after the 1860s when the southern valleys were transformed by a new wave of industrialisation. Places that a decade previously had no settlements became chains of terraced houses clustered around coal mines. In the densely populated valleys of Glamorganshire and Monmouthshire, mines and their bands were often separated by less than a mile, but this did not prevent localities from developing heated rivalries. This was partly a product of the physical geography of the valleys, but also of the way that individual pits and their contiguous communities organised themselves, with their shops, chapels, pubs and miners' institutes. Miners' institutes owed their origins to patronage, but their development was in the hands of the miners themselves and a great enthusiasm for committees developed. These committees, the sheer numbers of which are evidenced by surviving minute books, were not just agencies for democratic governance on a small and local scale: they were, for their participants, a leisure activity.[40] Workers' clubs and institutes had developed in English rural areas under the patronage of landlords and clergymen as a means of attracting working men away from beer houses. To the greatest extent they failed:

> The prohibition of beer which prevailed in most of these pioneer establishments was much disliked, but the greater offence of the first club supporters in the eyes of members was their intrusive supervision of club affairs, a particular failing of the clergy. These problems bulked large in the history of the developing club movement.[41]

These observations by a leading historian of British leisure touch a theme that runs through the history of brass bands and the localities and working-class agencies that supported them. They were resentful of the idea that their free time should be the subject of hierarchical control. This is why bands became independent of patronage at the earliest opportunity. Most Welsh colliery brass bands were indirectly created, and often directly sustained, by the committees of institutes and clubs: it was they who had the organisational savvy to join people together and trades unions were soon established to back them up. Their ubiquity provides some explanation of why and how these new micro-communities formed with such indecent speed and in such crude and deprived circumstances were nevertheless socially coherent and capable of generating well-being. An adult education bulletin, published in 1929, summed up a typical profile of mining communities with a good degree of accuracy:

The miner and his wife may pay a visit to Cardiff once or twice a year or spend a Bank Holiday on Barry Island, but it is quite likely that he has never been into the next valley, while the one beyond may be entirely *terra incognita* to him. Communications are bad and the geographical isolation has led to a corresponding mental isolation. This is aggravated by the fact that the whole population of the valley is dependent on the coal industry. There is no variety in industrial life, and there is almost no differentiation into social grades such as may be found in an ordinary town. This makes for an extraordinarily friendly spirit; there is little shyness and much hospitality.[42]

In several respects this provides a neat summary of 'village life' as the term is used in this chapter. At one level, it emphasises isolation, but at another it explains the importance and happiness of local life and the contentment it provided. In localities that had great bands, such quiet continuities were happily broken when heroes returned victorious. Such was the case in 1913 when the Irwell Springs Band returned to the Yorkshire village of Bacup having won the 1913 Crystal Palace contest playing Fletcher's *Labour and Love*:

Preparations at Bacup for the home-coming of Irwell Springs Band resembled those connected with a royal visit. Shops and warehouses were closed, flags, bunting and festoons were to be seen all over town. Thousands met the band at the station.[43]

It was acclamation such as this that bands worked and hoped for, but they also knew that survival required a succession strategy. This is why juvenile or junior bands became important centres for community music education at a time when alternative facilities were in short supply.

Phillip McCann, who was principal cornet player with the Black Dyke Band from 1973 to 1989, and one of the finest players of his generation, testifies to this. He was born in Bo'ness, Scotland, and started playing with the local Kinneil Colliery band before he was ten years old:

I started with my little town band which is the happiest banding of my life. People look at me sometimes in amazement when I say that, but as regards the happiest banding it truly was; and I was seven years old, eight years old, all I can remember is standing on the pavement in the town of Bo'ness and the band was walking past, marching past and I was just standing with my grandfather and it sticks with me so vividly and I just pulled and [said] I want to play, I want to play. I went to the Kinneil band room the Sunday morning and joined the junior band and went every Sunday morning and paid a shilling a week or whatever it was to play in the junior band.[44]

Phillip McCann's story is interesting and points to a critical feature of the brass band that could easily be overlooked. Elite bands may have basked in their celebrity and enjoyed the musical pressures that accompanied their status, but all bands generated happiness for their members. Players love playing in a band, and to find themselves in the company of others of the same persuasion twice a week was comforting. Without the positive social dynamics conjured by the sheer joy of playing, the brass band movement may not have survived beyond its first few decades. The ingenious invention of 'sections' – the leagues that allow bands of the same quality to compete nationally – enables them to share levels of competitive excitement that are no less intense than those experienced by the elite.

Chapter 8

'The movement', 1900–60

In the mid-1960s the British government, as a part of a national regeneration strategy, decided to build a new city 55 miles north of London. It would be a dormitory town for London commuters and eventually develop its own identity as a centre for industry and commerce. The city centre would be built on an area of unused land and expand outwards and circularly to embrace existing villages. These villages would provide a chain of suburban settlements with ready-made identities to counter it being seen as a shapeless urban mass. The new town was named after one of the villages: Milton Keynes. As well as a shopping and business centre and a new railway station, it was to have a theatre, a library, a cathedral and a new university – the Open University. The university was built on a former manorial estate surrounded by villages. During the long period of transition that lasted into the 1980s, when much of the area was a building site, a young Open University anthropologist investigated the musical life of the villages that were soon to be obscured by the new unitary conglomerate. She discovered a vibrant but hidden musical landscape with amateur choral groups, orchestras, brass bands, children's music clubs, pubs in which folk singers and jazz bands were a regular feature, nascent pop groups, string quartets, bell-ringers and a lot more. She looked at what they did, how they organised themselves, how they communicated with each other and how their music-making impacted on everyday lives. She had identified an important moment in the musical history of a region that was about to experience irrevocable social change: she captured an image of a music culture at a moment of transition. When she came to brass bands, she was struck by how different they were to any other musical activity she had encountered, and particularly by the extent to which this very public form of music-making was otherwise exclusive, with discrete and unique practices, all of which were subject to shared instincts and values held within what seemed like a private environment:

> Brass band players were exceptionally articulate about their traditions; 'it's a world on its own', I was constantly told, 'a whole world'. Among all the musical spheres in Milton Keynes it was the brass band and their players that most emphatically made up a self-conscious 'world with its own specific and separate traditions'.[1]

The findings of the project were not published until 1989 but the profile of the brass band it unveiled might have been observed at most times in the previous 60 years. Despite all that had happened in that period, the dominant characteristic was constancy: a proud faith in tradition, and a consensual embrace of its rules and values. Brass bands, irrespective of whether they were distinguished, undistinguished, geographically central or remote, were groups of (usually) men confident in their beliefs and feeling part of a national community of shared interests.[2] Those interests, and the means through which they were executed, were solidly and, so it seemed, irrevocably fixed.

The new century

By the start of the twentieth century, brass band instrumentation was, to the greatest extent, standardised and key aspects of the infrastructure that shaped its style and idiom were firmly in place. By 1914 more than 70 local associations had been formed, which provided the fundamentals for a connective framework that supported an annual cycle of local and national contests. There were robust commercial agencies that led the organisation of large national contests. Contests attracted congregations of like minds. Bands may not have talked to each other very much, but they certainly listened to each other play. Perhaps the most uniting element was subscription to the idea that every band and every player in it was part of a brass band *movement*. The word 'movement' was deployed by various organisations from the nineteenth century onwards to signify a collective mission aimed at a particular end: the labour movement, the suffrage movement, the temperance movement, and so on. It is impossible to identify its first association with brass bands, but it was widely articulated and tacitly accepted by the start of the new century: tacitly, because while 'the movement' was, and to the greatest extent still is, one of the most frequently deployed phrases in brass band narratives (I use it liberally in this book), no one appears to have asked what it was supposed to mean. On what journey was this movement, at what destination was it intended to arrive, and how would it know when it got there? In 1930 the *British Bandsman* published one of its many pious responses to reports of the rowdy behaviour that occasionally accompanied the conclusion of contests:

> Remember gentlemen, that you are but part of a wider movement, and your conduct in public may go a long way towards lowering us in the eyes of the public. See to it that you do nothing that may let the brass band movement down.[3]

This probably suggests at what 'the movement' was aiming: it was something do with respectability – or perhaps a little more. At one level, 'the brass band movement' became a handy phrase, deployed readily in band magazines when addressing its readership, but it also signalled an aspiration for this working-class endeavour to attain cultural legitimacy. In a period when the distinction between highbrow and lowbrow was becoming categorised with increasing clarity, brass bands fitted neatly into neither. Magazines such as the *British Bandsman* and *Brass Band World* became the central communication media, and one does not have to examine them long to find that, as well as providing news and consolidating the language of brass banding, they assumed a custodial mantle of moral leadership. That it was an entirely working-class 'movement' did not clarify the issue: it complicated it. The brass band was not just working class – it had become a symbol of it and, as such, implied that its location was both fixed and distinct from the highbrow. Statements such as 'One of the most vital expressions of working-class culture was the brass band movement'[4] emerged and remained as standard descriptors in cultural histories of Britain.

Recourse to this type of class symbolism was neither new nor unusual; it had become natural. On the day the Royal College of Music opened the doors of its new permanent building in London in 1882, the Prince of Wales emphasised its mission to attract talented students from across the country, irrespective of social class. He was pleased to report that among its foundation scholars were 'a mill girl, the daughter of a bricklayer, the son of a blacksmith and the son of a farm labourer'.[5] To add emphasis to these worthy intentions, the Leeds Forge Brass Band – the works band set up by Samson Fox, the College's major sponsor – resplendent in Ruritanian uniforms, was booked to play on the College steps as the ribbon was cut (fig. 12, p. 80).

When the *British Bandsman* was first published in 1887, its talented co-editor Sam Cope claimed that he chose the magazine's title to define brass bands as *British* and to distinguish them from the urban buskers known as 'German bands' that were especially prevalent in London and the largest provincial towns. Almost two decades later, he reflected more broadly on the magazine's mission:

> First, I wanted to raise the status of bandsmen and to see the merits of this deserving class duly recognised; and secondly because I wanted to effect an improvement in the instrumentation of brass bands, so that there would be more variety of one colour. No doubt I am still premature in the last desire, but I prophesy the time will come when our best brass bands possess saxophones, trumpets, and French [sic] horns, which I have advocated.[6]

Sam Cope died in 1948, having fully achieved neither of his objectives. By 1960 the status of the brass band was not elevated; if anything, it was more entrenched and probably much less integrated in the musical world than Cope had hoped for and anticipated. Its musical idiom was securely fixed and that, at that time, may have been the main problem. The period 1900–60, a long era in the brass band story, was both the most musically distinctive and the least remembered because subsequent events came to obscure its major features. Yet, despite its dogged entrenchment and the isolation it had unwittingly imposed upon itself, the period produced bands and players of astonishing brilliance. What was to follow in the closing decades of the century was in many ways yet more brilliant and certainly more stylistically diverse, but it is important that the heavy conservatism that had solidified by 1960 should not obscure what 'the movement' had achieved in the most turbulent period in modern history. Apart from the consolidation of the brass band as a unique musical genre, it was the first and only time that the best bands and their finest soloists became household names across the nation. Given the social challenges that prevailed in the period, it is also likely that there was never a time when brass bands were more important to the people who played in them and the communities in which they were located. The quality of playing of the finest bands was fabulous: a claim amply evidenced by contemporary recordings. They continued to be the primary recruiting ground for bands of the military and all branches of the music profession at a time when conservatories were sometimes so bereft of brass students that they had to hire professionals for their concerts. Brass bands remained an important segment of the music industry and had a significant place in the development of recording and broadcasting. It should not be surprising that elite British bands such as Besses o' th' Barn should have made such an emphatic impact on foreign tours where they advertised this distinctively British format throughout the world (fig. 25).

Decline or survival?

Since the peak of their Victorian ascendancy, brass bands have been said to be in decline. There was arguably a numerical decline in the number of bands – but the evidence is inconclusive, and numerical decline may not be an accurate measure of their overall health. There

25. Besses o' th' Barn Band with its conductor Alexander Owen, probably 1903. The many trophies include the Thousand Guinea Trophy (partially obscured by the bass drum) which was awarded to the champion band of the Crystal Palace contest. Such postcards were produced commercially and sold at the concerts (including bandstands) where bands performed.

were probably fewer brass bands in 1960 than at the start of the century, but many new bands emerged after 1900, including some such as Grimethorpe Colliery, Foden's Motor Works and Fairey Aviation that were to be major stars. Also, any overall decline in the total number should be measured against the numerous distractions that emerged. A wave of new leisure activities in seductively colourful forms competed with banding as a pastime, but the brass band contest continued to attract audiences. Indeed, a sound argument can be made to show that the introduction of radio broadcasting increased the brass band audience significantly. The greatest challenge to all forms of British popular and light music came from America. Brass bands never attempted to compete with Duke Ellington, Glenn Miller or even John Philip Sousa; they were perfectly happy to compete against each other. Surprisingly, they survived by staying loyal to the styles, processes and audiences that were in place early in the century.

Contesting became better organised and more standardised both nationally and at local levels. The quality of adjudications seems to have gained more approval as specialists from inside the brass band movement replaced the procession of senior military bandmasters. By the first decades of the twentieth century, brass bands abandoned the practice of performing when standing in square formation with the conductor in the centre of the square (fig. 16, p. 118). This formation originated as a direct imitation of practices in military bands which, in turn, were a legacy of the requirement of military drills. It is likely that the change was evolutionary because there were always variances. For example, as early as 1860 Samuel Longbottom, conductor of the Black Dyke Band, specified to the organisers of the Crystal Palace contest that his band would form a circle rather than a square.[7]

There was also a genuine attempt to elevate both the repertoire and to broaden popular understanding of the medium. One of the more modest, but influential, band personalities in the 1920s and 1930s was Herbert Whiteley. He was the assistant to the impresario John Henry Iles and served as editor of the *British Bandsman* between 1906 and 1930. He left the magazine shortly after he persuaded Edward Elgar to write *Severn Suite*. Whiteley was a gifted musician who contributed significantly to the success of Iles's enterprises. In 1925, using the title 'Musical Adviser to the Crystal Palace Contest' (by this time Iles was immodestly styling himself 'Controlling Editor and Director General'), Whiteley wrote a letter to *The Times*, explaining the instrumentation of brass bands and the history of their original repertoire. He also revealed his ideas for adjusting the instrumental line-up by the inclusion of french horns and trumpets in D (to replace the soprano cornet), but he conceded that those ideas were unlikely to be implemented because 'daily contact with brass bands convinces me that the time is not yet ripe for change'. He ended his letter with an invitation to composers to write for brass band:

Will any composer interested in the brass band be good enough to write to me? In the interests of music and musicians in this country it is desirable that both young composers and those of acknowledged repute should not neglect the brass band.[8]

It is not certain whether Whiteley's letter had the desired effect but, while several new and successful test pieces were written, few of the period revealed striking originality. In fact, it was the repetitive use of the same styles and formats in test pieces for contests that was the main force for establishing and reinforcing performance orthodoxies. The central tenets of brass band repertoire have always been test pieces. Their number expanded to include works by a group of composers who were practised in the brass band idiom and, to a lesser extent, by composers established in the world of classical music. There was also a half-hearted attempt to attract composers who were unknowingly forming a distinctive 'school' of British light music in the period.

The interventions of major classical composers enhanced the repertoire but had only a modest effect on the brass band's musical language, which remained stoically conservative and largely formulaic. Paradoxically, the size of the dedicated audience for contests, and their national visibility in British culture, remained remarkably resilient. In 1960 the composer Herbert Howells, a distinguished professor at the Royal College of Music, was commissioned to write a new test piece for the National contest. This was *Three Figures*. A previous and successful work, *Pageantry*, was commissioned in 1934 and has been used for major contests on two subsequent occasions. Correspondence between Howells and Vaughan Morris, the organiser of the 1960 contest, survives.[9] Howells was to be one of the adjudicators and Morris was keen to explain the schedule for the day and what was expected of him. A critical issue was the period between 3.15 and 3.45 p.m., by which time contesting needed to have been completed and conclusions reached; the adjudicators would be accompanied to the Albert Hall stage and introduced to the 'mass audience', the winning band would be announced and a victory performance given. The timing was critical because, for those 30 minutes, the entire network of the BBC's main (Home) radio service would be broadcasting the event live to the nation. This was on a Saturday afternoon in the football season. Whether the movement was stronger or weaker in 1960 than it had been in 1900 is uncertain. Perhaps brass bands became numerically weaker but they continued to retain a prominent place in the public consciousness.

The start of the century was undoubtedly the high point. In 1913 the *British Bandsman* believed there to be 230 bands in Yorkshire and 90 in County Durham. This was probably an underestimation; most estimates usually were, because little account was taken of the many community bands who did not compete. If these numbers were extrapolated for the entire country, it would suggest that at that time there was a total of about 2,600 bands in England, Wales and Scotland. By 1920 the estimates for Yorkshire and Durham had dropped to 129 and 49, respectively, but even if this were accurate, the intervention of the First World War should moderate any assumption that this was a natural decline. In 1954 the estimates for Yorkshire and Durham were 110 and 40 – but another world war and multiple economic depressions provide further mitigation.[10] An alternative method of counting may give a better impression as far as the number of brass band *players* is concerned. It is certainly more positive, but it, too, uses figures largely predicated on bands that participated in contests. In the 1930s a long-lingering concern about 'borrowed players' came to a head. This was the practice of bands borrowing players who would enhance their performance in contests: it was linked to suspicions that pecuniary rewards were being used as inducements. The remedy was the creation of a registration system that aligned each player to just one band. The number of registrants by the mid-1930s had reached 90,000. Using an unrealistically simple mathematical calculation (dividing the total by 25), such a number could be sufficient for 3,600 bands. Of course, the actual number of bands was probably fewer because it is not clear whether all registrants were necessarily aligned to a band.[11] In the 1980s the conductor Peter Parkes, who was involved in the National Federation of Brass Bands, mentioned that at that time 960 bands were registered, and inferred that several weren't.[12]

The view that the brass band became a weaker feature of popular culture has been argued persuasively: the first half of the twentieth century has been characterised as the period when the brass band 'lost the powerful – in some cases central – position that it had held in popular culture' and 'by the 1950s and perhaps even earlier, the brass band had simply become yet another specialist pastime within an ever more variegated pattern of popular leisure'.[13] This is a valid summary but, as the evidence above suggests, another view should complement it. The two epic achievements of the British brass band in the period were the consolidation of its unique musical idiom through the sheer repetitiveness of its execution, and ultimately its survival in the face of unprecedented provocations. The challenges that were to confront the brass band movement in the first 60 years of the twentieth century could not have been remotely imagined at its start: two world wars, unexampled industrial depressions, and the development of new, global modes of popular music consumed through increasingly versatile media – sound recordings, film, radio and television. It was a period in which the term 'globalisation' gained its practical meaning.

Such factors may have had the counter-intuitive effect of galvanising the core audience of brass bands: they emphasised their value to the many players and their audiences by offering consistency in a changing and persistently unpredictable world. This exact set of circumstances sustained the popularity of the music of John Philip Sousa in Middle America in the same period, long after the band's high point. It could be seen as mere nostalgia for a vanishing age, but it has been more accurately termed a 'culture of reassurance': a source of nourishment through the consoling persistence of traditions and the sense of security it generates.[14]

Still male and working-class

At the start of the twentieth century, most bands were less burdened by the tastes and social codes of their original patrons and free of financial obligations incurred at the time of their formation. Relationships with commerce also changed. To various degrees, bands had become putative 'companies': practised entrepreneurs capable of raising funds for their activities. Most were in control of their own destinies, even though they routinely faced challenges. Bands with origins that attached them to a place of employment, a temperance movement or the Volunteers may have retained the titles of their original sponsors and some loyalty to them, deference even, but dependencies weakened. In most practical terms, bands formed through patronage became self-governing. Many that had not made such a transition experienced terminal decline, and there were a lot of them. Democratic procedures, often underpinned by legal or quasi-legal ordinances, were in place that ensured sound democratic governance and transparency, especially in matters of finance. The minutes of band committee meetings and similar working-class collectives, such as workmen's, mechanics' and miners' institutes, always show a punctilious regard for formalities: they survive in quantity and unfailingly demonstrate a pride in the execution of due process. Many bands were the recipients of significant benevolence from employers who valued the credit their bands brought them, but sponsors were seldom in total control. To the greatest extent, individually and collectively, brass bands were independent of everything other than their self-determined protocols, the regulations of contests and the unwritten musical and social conventions of 'the movement'.

Throughout the period, brass bands played concerts, and a specific concert repertoire developed, but contests continued to dominate the collective culture for the obvious reason that they were congregations of people who, despite rivalries, had shared musical values. They remained almost entirely working-class and almost entirely male. In 1936 British Movietone News reported that the Crystal Palace contest of that year attracted 200 competing bands made up of more than 5,000 players – only one was a woman.[15] They were resiliently loyal to the musical idiom and social rituals that had been in place by the start of the century. They were also amateur, even though some were known to provide star players with retainers. There are many examples of this. For instance, in 1938 Besses o' th' Barn Band agreed to pay the cornet player Harold Jackson a sizeable retainer for his services.[16] Jackson was one of many band players who successfully transitioned to the music profession in London.

Opportunities for social mobility in Britain in the period continued to be restricted. Relatively few people moved beyond the locality in which they were born, unless it was to fight in a war. Life expectancy increased in the twentieth century, but the conditions in which lives were led remained challenging. In the 1920s it was still routine for boys to start work the day after their 14th birthday, entering the same gruelling conditions in farms, mines and factories as adult workers. Few children from working-class homes went to university until after the middle of the century. The British National Health Service, which provided socialised universal care at the point of need, did not exist until its introduction by a Labour government in 1948. Life in factories, mills and mines was never easy. Many industrial areas in which brass bands flourished were incubators for the diseases and impediments associated with those industries, all made worse by the unhealthy circumstances in which some sectors of the population lived. The two primary diseases associated with coal mining were pneumoconiosis and silicosis, both caused by the effect of coal dust in the lungs. Both took a crippling toll on the male population who worked in mines. The first thing to go was often the teeth. In the Rhondda valleys in the 1930s, almost a quarter of coal miners had lost all their teeth by the time they were 34 years old. Malnutrition was common; even in 1939 only 2 per cent of the British school population had free school meals.[17] These factors coalesced to make life continuously challenging, but they also intensified the importance of banding in lives that were otherwise devoid of the diversion that playing in a band could provide. This factor is often overlooked. In the first half of the twentieth century, people played in bands and sang in choirs because of the feelings it stimulated. Any thoughts of self-improvement had given way to raw pleasure. After a day in a cotton mill, factory or coal mine, a group of men with brass instruments in their hands and a challenging piece of music in front of them were intellectually and emotionally liberated.

Most of the working class continued to be musically educated through informal routes. Working men's institutes were a major agency in this regard. There was a widespread intellectual curiosity and a thirst for learning and betterment. Brass bands were an important component in that process for the people who listened to them, those who directed them and their players. One survey suggested that, at the turn of the nineteenth and twentieth centuries, 'there was some kind of family musical activity in 86% of all working-class homes', a statistic that is credible if one takes account of all forms of music participation, including listening.[18] The economic depressions of the period affected bandsmen badly and caused challenges for many bands. But most found ways of coping: performances in public spaces took on a new and special importance.

Music in the open air

The first half of the twentieth century saw a major increase in brass band performances in the open air, particularly in parks. The idea that facilities should be provided for the public to gain benefit from open-air spaces had emerged as early as 1833, when a 'Select Committee for Public Walks' was instituted in the light of concerns about the negative consequences of urban growth. Its task was to 'consider the best means of securing open spaces in the immediate vicinity of populous towns, as public walks are calculated to promote the health and comfort of the inhabitants'.[19] The combination of such facilities with musical performance was introduced later. In 1856 Sir Benjamin Hall, Clerk of Works to the House of Commons, used the powers of his office to allow military bands to perform in London parks on Sundays. The facility was immediately popular and quickly replicated across the country, where it was similarly welcomed: Sunday was the only day when most of the population was not at work. But there were opposing voices. The Archbishop of Canterbury, the primate of the Anglican Church and apparently a man with plenty of time on his hands, took a different view. He summoned '550 memorials and 111,300 signatures' which he presented to Parliament as a petition for its prohibition. He also wrote to Lord Palmerston, the prime minister, with the worrying declaration that he 'could not be answerable for the religion of the Country if the Bands were not stopped'.[20] Palmerston, who favoured the concerts because they offered 'innocent recreation combined with fresh air and healthy exercise', was reluctantly obliged to accede to the demands of the established church, but it was a mistaken and short-term concession because forces that took a more positive view were quickly mobilised in greater abundance and effect. The archbishop must have been despondent at what unfolded. Three deputations representing the working classes were organised to present their petitions directly to the prime minister, and critically there was support from many upper-class dignitaries who recognised in such events the refined and improving qualities they were keen to encourage.[21] The concerts were restored. The controversy produced a result exactly opposite to that sought by the archbishop and his grudging supporters. Soon the entire country became ambitious to see these events in their localities, and it was not long before it did. But objections lingered into the following century and complaints from Sabbatarians became a seasonal feature in letters published in the *British Bandsman*, some expressed in the most alarming terms:

Dear Sir,

The devil must be defeated. As a Churchwarden I can see the playing of brass bands on a Sunday in Leeds a threat to the Holiness of the Sabbath and the awesome Wrath of God will fall on these base fellows.[22]

This part of the activity of brass bands may seem like a footnote in their history, but it isn't. The risk of stirring the 'awesome Wrath of God' was eminently worth taking when viewed from a different perspective. Concerts in parks provided bands with a welcome role in their annual cycle of activities, and they made them money. The income was important, but outdoor concerts also made their community presence more apparent, and it was a role that could be performed to good effect by bands that may have been less successful on the contest platform. While some test pieces were appropriate for parks programmes, a new repertoire emerged for bands and soloists that was targeted at entertainment. In the second half of the nineteenth century, a new facility had been introduced: permanent bandstands erected by municipal authorities. The commercial pleasure gardens of the Georgian period provided a loose precedent for the idea of the bandstand, but Victorian developments were different because many concerts were intended to be free or had a nominal admission cost, and they advanced the idea that good music in attractive open spaces could provide cultural and physical benefits for the mass of the people. The first bandstands are believed to be the two erected at the Royal Horticultural Society's gardens in London in 1861, both made of cast iron and at that time called 'band houses'.[23] By the early decades of the twentieth century, they had been built by municipal authorities across the country. At one time, it was estimated that Britain had 1,500 of them. The experience that bandstand performance provided was not just musical. It is easy to imagine how these elegant edifices, often placed as the centrepieces of beautifully landscaped spaces, provided visual as well as sonic pleasure and relaxation. It was the first time that open-air public spaces had been widely, formally and systematically developed by governing authorities for access to musical performance. Most authorities appointed officials to oversee their summer programmes in parks. This was necessary because of the sheer scale of the operation: by the late nineteenth century, seasonal open-air performances by military and brass bands had become a significant component of the country's musical life (fig. 26). In 1902 the London County Council sponsored 1,000 three-hour concerts in 40 different venues across the metropolis.[24] They were organised for a time by the composer Hubert Bath, who was Director of Music for London's parks. He was succeeded for the 1922 season by Cyril Jenkins. Both Bath and Jenkins were commissioned to write test pieces for National Brass Band Championships. Initially, the London parks used bands of the regular military, but brass bands were soon included. A programme of events was published each week in the *British Bandsman* and other periodicals. Even as late as 1962, 20 different band concerts were held in parks across the metropolis each day during the summer. Their popularity was probably greater in the provinces. In July 1893 the bandstand in South Park, Darlington, which had opened just a few weeks previously, was reportedly attended 'by an assemblage of between 2,000 to 3,000'. In Blackburn, audiences of 6,000 were regularly reported. The bandstand at the arboretum in Lincoln, which opened in 1872, could attract an audience of 10,000. Taken together, the number of people who assembled to hear brass bands play in bandstands in the summer months must have been massive – did any other form of music-making at that time gain comparable attention?[25]

26. *A band performing in the sunken bandstand at Clacton-on-Sea, early twentieth century. One of the many bandstands that drew massive audiences.*

Bands anticipated and expected their local authorities to employ them for park work. When the Gorton and Openshaw Old Band tendered the Borough of Altrincham for park work in 1947, they received a terse response:

Music in the Parks Season 1947

I thank you for your tender in connection with the above, but regret to inform you that this has not been accepted.[26]

This was inflammatory. The band immediately petitioned their Member of Parliament; he promptly petitioned a government minister, who equally promptly produced the required result and a grovelling apology from the local bureaucrat who had started it all off.

One of the main reasons for the support of these concerts was that they were educational: the programmes included arrangements of operatic and classical music, but they were also entertaining, and this is why they played an important role in the development of British seaside resorts as centres for leisure. Seaside visits, like contesting, were a leisure activity made viable by the development of railways in the nineteenth century, which made travel to coastal resorts possible at a relatively low cost. Seaside holidays became a seasonal feature of ordinary life by the early twentieth century. The idea of restful leisure that had attracted the rich to various luxurious spa resorts may have continued, but the arrival of the 'summer holiday' captured an expanding constituency from the middle and working class whose appetites favoured entertainment. Every ambitious resort had a band-stand; some had enclosed open-air seating. Other entertainments were also available: tea-dance orchestras, novelty bands, theatre bands – some northern resorts booked Welsh choirs and Scots pipers and dancers. But brass bands were particularly effective in the open air because their instruments were impervious to the vagaries of the weather, and their sound carried easily. Local bands played an important role, but major resorts organised residencies through the summer months for champion brass bands from distant locations. Northern bands did especially well. Black Dyke had regular seasons in the Channel Islands and Besses o' th' Barn under Alexander Owen seems to have been in demand every-where. Summertime was the period when bands earned most from bandstand and concert work, but much depended on whether employers would give the players time off. The management of Foden's motor works was especially generous in this respect because it viewed the band's appearances as an investment in the promotion of its brand. In May 1939 the band started a 60-day tour, usually performing at least twice a day, at 20 different British venues. The tour was due to finish on 10 September in London's Hyde Park, but it was abruptly terminated on 2 September. War with Germany was declared the following day.[27]

On the wireless

By the 1920s brass band concerts in the open air and in indoor venues, as well as contests, were the most accessible form of musical enter-tainment for a large segment of the working-class population, but this was to change as new media were introduced. The BBC started broadcasting in 1922. Sixty years later the cornet player Harry Mortimer described how, as an 18-year-old, he had anticipated it:

> At this time a new phenomenon was looming on the horizon, and the most exciting development in my career so far. Any person born since 1940 can have no idea of the importance of radio in the thirty years between 1920 and 1950. What we now take for granted, and what has since become background music to accompany the ironing or wallpapering was, then, the wonder of the age.[28]

The BBC was founded by the British state.[29] It was to be sustained by neither advertising nor any other commercial interests, but by the annual purchase of licences issued by the General Post Office to those who elected to receive radio broadcasts. Just 30,000 licences had been issued when the BBC commenced its operation. By 1939, when it was estimated that the country had just over 10.5 million homes, 9 million of them had radios. Many, probably most, of those who had no licence were unable to receive transmissions because of their mountainous or distant location.[30] The leading historian of the BBC has pointed out that in the BBC's early days 'there was much mass listening in the streets and even the villages'.[31] The first BBC radio broadcast by a British brass band is believed to have been given by the Clydebank Borough Band on 21 April 1923.[32]

The central tenet of the BBC's mission as a public-service broadcaster was 'to inform, educate and entertain'. Brass bands certainly entertained and through much of their repertoire they educated, but their most compelling fit with the BBC's mission came from their assumed popularity as entertainers of working-class audiences. By this time there were sufficient orchestras in existence for large sectors of the public to have easy access to classical music in its original form. In 1930 the Corporation formed its own BBC Symphony Orchestra under the direction of Adrian Boult. But there was always a concern at the BBC that its output would favour elite sectors of the population at the expense of the majority. In 1936 the programming of brass and military band performance, almost all of which was transmitted live, was put in the hands of Denis Wright.[33] Wright was an important figure in the brass band world at this time, but his background was not typical. The son of a surgeon, he was born in Kensington, London, and educated at the Royal College of Music. On leaving the College, he became an editor at the music publishers Chappell & Co., before working as a schoolteacher. He was neither a brass player nor at this time a brass band conductor, but in 1925 he won an open competition to write a test piece for the National Brass Band Championships: this was his tone poem *Joan of Arc*. He openly admitted that he had never purposely listened to a brass band before he wrote the piece. He was always an outsider, but his musical skills earned wide respect.

The BBC was always a deeply bureaucratic organisation, and its voluminous archive of written documents is revealing of the processes used for selecting bands for broadcasting and the challenges encountered in the early years. No matter how much the BBC tried to portray itself as a strategic organisation, its processes as a music broadcaster in its early days were largely experimental and often expedient. There had never previously been a British cultural project that aimed to reach the entire British nation in all its shapes and tastes. Administrative and diplomatic challenges accrued from contrasting attitudes in different parts of the country. The historic identities of Scotland, Wales and Northern Ireland also needed to be taken into account, as did differences between English regions. There were also other segmentations. Social class was problematic, as was the variety of musical tastes. There were also unanticipated problems. For example, the BBC's charter explicitly excluded advertising, but many of the best brass bands carried the name of a manufacturer. How could that part of the charter be upheld when a performing group was called (for example) the Munn and Felton's Footwear Band, Foden's Motor Works Band or the CWS Tobacco Factory Band? In 1932 the BBC's Midland Regional Director proposed measures for altering the names of all bands in this category, but this idea did not gain support.[34]

Brass bands were important in the general mix because, while they were perceived as a form of music that was essentially of and for the mass of the people, they could also be seen as regional. Initially, the BBC got this significantly wrong. By 1920 the most competent band in the south of England was the Callender's Cableworks Band, based in Kent. It had modest success as a contesting band (it came second in both the National and Open contests in 1927) but did not match the celebrity of northern bands. Also, while it used the standard brass band format in contests, from 1932 it often added four saxophones for concerts. Despite these issues and because of its proximity to the BBC's London studios, it was used so frequently that it was regarded by some as the BBC's resident house brass band. One of Wright's major tasks when a band section was founded was to find a practical way of getting a wider representation, but here too there were challenges. The number of good bands in each region varied significantly. The north of England, the Midlands, parts of Scotland and south Wales could provide good-quality bands, but less so in some other regions. National broadcasts came from London, while provincial stations broadcast only locally. Northern Ireland presented a particular problem. There was a long-standing row between London and Belfast, where bands were thought to be so seriously sub-standard that transmission of them was sometimes refused.

An internal memo in 1936 listed the typical 'defects' of some brass bands as broadcasting artists:

Lack of appreciation of stye of playing for best results in broadcasting
    Bands of poor technique
    Dull programmes
    Unmusical playing – in some cases uneven [even] when the programmes are good on paper[35]

To promote standards, the BBC graded bands that were potentially eligible for broadcasting (A, B, C and Z). Only bands in the highest grade would be invited to broadcast. Bands graded Z had few grounds for hope; B and C bands were monitored for improvement. A member of the BBC Music Department attended contests and surreptitiously fulfilled the role of a shadow adjudicator. He would present his adjudications to the Department in a document that was confidentially circulated. One of the obsessions in the Department was the quality of conducting; it was believed that this defect was at the heart of the musical problems that most bands exhibited:

Black Dyke Mills	Variable: inclined to be hard tonally, and unsafe technically, but still a Grade A band.
Besses o' th' Barn	A bad second-class band, under rehearsed, poor intonation at times. Not worth any more Sunday mid-day [broadcasting] periods. Only possess a handful of regular players of their own.
Bickershaw Colliery	Can do well, but at times unsafe. Programmes usually well chosen.
Brighouse & Rastrick	A noisy band, ambition seems generally low as regards programme items. Not Grade A at present.[36]

These comments, included in a sequence of documents headed 'The Brass Band Problem', were made in 1940, a year after the commencement of war, when most bands were seriously disrupted. There was no National contest that year, but there was an Open contest which Bickershaw Colliery won. In 1939 the BBC had commissioned an 'open ballot' to measure the comparative popularity of its music output. The *British Bandsman* was pleased with the results, even though there were grounds for them to have taken a different view:

Readers of the BB might be excused if a feeling came over them that dance music alone commanded a big and popular following nowadays ... brass bands are very little behind the purveyors of dance music in popular esteem ... dance music is fifth and brass bands eighth in order of popularity ... [Among] folks under 20 years of age, dance music was third and brass bands tenth. With old people over 70 brass bands are third and dance music sixteenth.[37]

In 1942 the BBC appointed Harry Mortimer as Military and Brass Bands Supervisor, a post he held until 1964. Mortimer, the most celebrated cornet player and band conductor of his generation, was also a major force for the promotion of bands, and he was able to increase the number of broadcast hours allocated to them. He joined a formidable team in the Music Department that included Adrian

Boult, Arthur Bliss and Denis Wright. One senses that Mortimer was not alone in the obligation he felt to promote the interests of brass bands; even Boult and Bliss were committed to their cause and used their considerable influence accordingly. This was an important source of support for brass bands at a time when war, economic depression and the consequent general fragmentation of society made them vulnerable. Weekly programmes such as *Listen to the Band* were widely anticipated and listened to. No other national agency of such influence cared very much for brass bands and supported their artistic welfare; one wonders what would have happened to the movement at that time without the BBC. It is touching that, according to Harry Mortimer, the 'Z' grade was mythical, because no band was ever placed in that category.[38] Bands made good money from broadcasting at times when there was little of it in circulation in local communities, and broadcasting sustained their profile.

In the war years, bands were especially important, even though many of them were disrupted. An internal document shows the pattern of broadcasting:

Monday	Brass Bandstand
Tuesday	Brass Band session (every other week)
Thursday	Music While You Work
Saturday	Brass Band session[39]

In fact, appearances were more common than this schedule suggests because of the introduction of *Music While You Work*, one of the most imaginative and successful ideas the BBC devised. This programme was transmitted live each day to factories, mills and other places of employment. It had been conceived after consultation with industry and welfare organisations and was intended to lift the spirits of the millions who contributed to the war effort by working in essential industries.

The first programme was transmitted on 20 June 1940 with the intention of lightening the monotony of workers. It was organised by the Welsh dance-band leader Wynford Reynolds, with Denis Wright overseeing the brass band contributions with advice from Harry Mortimer (Mortimer joined the BBC staff two years later). Programmes were transmitted a minimum of twice a day for half an hour. The first words spoken in each programme, always in clear and triumphant tones, were those of the title of Eric Coates's memorable introductory theme music – 'Calling All Workers'. It did not take long for everyone to realise that the programme was as important as it was popular:

It was broadcast three times a day to most factories in the country and we supplied band programmes three times a week for these sessions. This, at the time, not only filled a much-needed gap in what was often a very boring factory day, or night-shift, it was also a marvellous morale booster. Twenty-nine and a half minutes' continuous music was a hard blow [strenuous for the band players], even though some of the music was included of necessity to be of an extremely light nature, the workers being encouraged to sing to all the tunes they knew. Whether it was good for the national effort or not, it certainly built up a link between shop floor workers all over the country, and if by chance that factory also had a band of its own, so much the better.[40]

Brass bands were not the only contributors to *Music While You Work*, but they were an important component; the programme was also important for the bands. It came at a time when many of the country's best were weakened and sometimes seriously debilitated by the loss of key players to military service. The BBC co-ordinated their efforts and implicitly sustained them. The entire project also had a ring of authenticity about it; these bands were acting out a community role that had endured since the nineteenth century.

Remarkably, *Music While You Work* continued to be transmitted daily until 1967 – more than two decades after the war was won. Even in war time, the BBC's own Listener Research had shown that listening figures to the programme were 'at their highest for the night and weekend sessions, when comparatively few listeners were at work'.[41] The *Daily Mail* journalist Seton Margrave (who became better known as a writer on film) identified this as evidence of a popular preference for music that was uncluttered by highbrow values:

Here for the first time by expression of popular wish is a plan for popular music. It hits hard at more ostentatious orchestras . . . the people of Britain are looking for what is simple and honest, well known and well loved. When bands that try to be clever will try to be good they will qualify for 'MWYW', and the band that appears most often on 'MWYW' will be band of the year.[42]

He cited Victor Silvester's band, the band of the Coventry Hippodrome, and brass bands as those most likely to meet this challenge.

Gramophone recordings of brass bands were ubiquitous from the start of the recording era, largely because the sound of brass and military bands suited early recording techniques. Almost every commercial recording of a brass band, and several non-commercial recordings, made in the age of cylinder and non-microgroove disc recording (1903–60), has been identified and catalogued.[43] The list reveals an extraordinary engagement of bands with this very modern facility. It includes many recordings by star bands such as Black Dyke, which was recording from 1903, and the St Hilda Colliery Band, one of the few amateur bands to become openly professional. These wonderful recordings reveal the idiom of the brass band in the first half of the twentieth century in its considerable glory. Other bands of no great celebrity also left their mark, and it is difficult to imagine that their recordings were made for any purpose other than pride.

Contesting

The period was also marked by the consolidation of the contest, and changes to its organisation and sponsorship. There were pauses in the National contest during the war years, but the Open contests continued through both world wars. Fewer local contests were held during the war years but, throughout the period of this chapter, they continued to draw large working-class audiences. It was probably the continued alignment of brass bands with the working classes that attracted support from the tabloid press, which came to be a major patron of National contests. In 1945 a revised system of 'area' contests was introduced. The three highest-ranked winners in each area would compete for the

National championship which was sponsored by the *Daily Herald*. The sponsorship was negotiated by John Henry Iles, but the newspaper would have been alert to the benefits it presented. There were eight regional/area contests, each with four sections or leagues. It followed that 12 bands would proceed from each area to the National finals – in all, bands from 92 communities, all potential *Daily Herald* readers, and the same applied to its sister publication, *The People*, which became the sponsor in 1964 (fig. 27).

By 1945 Harry Mortimer was the leading brass band conductor and the major musical figure in the brass band world. He was part of a dynasty that included his father Fred Mortimer, the conductor of Foden's band, and his two brothers Alex and Rex. Harry conducted every winning band but two in the 12 Open and National contests held between 1944 and 1950; the two contests in which he was beaten to second place were won by bands conducted by Eric Ball. In the

27. Tullis Russell Mills Band in the finals of the 1964 National Brass Band Championships at the Royal Albert Hall, London – the last time the band played high-pitched instruments. The conductor is Drake Rimmer. The band's two youngest cornet players, John Wallace and John Miller, were to become the trumpet section of London's Philharmonia Orchestra.

history of contesting in the first half of the century, such dominance was not unusual. The rota of winners shows that certain bands had gilded periods, but there are many more where a small group of conductors dominated. There was, of course, a Victorian precedent in the successes of Gladney, Swift and Owen, but that is explained more easily by the fact that each was known for the distinctive instrumental line-ups they devised. Such variances were not present in the twentieth century. In the first decade of the twentieth century, the most successful conductor was William Rimmer, who conducted the winning bands in both major contests every year between 1905 and 1909. This was not always with the same band; in fact, in the 1906 National contest he conducted the bands that came first, second and third. Rimmer died young. His successor as the man with the winning touch was William Halliwell, who was a regular winner for decades and on five occasions conducted the top three bands in the same National or Open contests. This raises the question of what Rimmer, Halliwell, the Mortimers and the few others like them had that was so obviously absent in sufficient measure in their opponents. The most obvious answer is a talent for training amateur bands to a high standard and inspiring them to their best when it really mattered. Added to this is that this elite group was usually aligned to leading bands anyway. But it is at least equally probable that they had the firmest grasp on the central and conventional understanding of what a brass band was supposed to sound like. To put it differently, in an era (for that is what this was) when the orthodoxies and conventions of the brass band were sufficiently consolidated to be regarded as stationary, the best of them could easily, and perhaps only, be successful under a masterful leader. In 1945 the test piece for the National contest top section was Denis Wright's *Overture for an Epic Occasion*. Wright always had musical qualities high in his priorities. One writer observed that *Overture for an Epic Occasion* 'was felt not to be sufficiently difficult to "sort out" the prize winners. Some area winners would have concurred, because none appeared in the top four places.'[44] The latter point refers to the fact that Fairey Aviation Band, who won in the finals, had gained only second place in the North West area qualifying contest, and Park & Dare Band, which came third, had similarly come only second in the

South Wales area contest: evidence perhaps of the machinations that prevailed by this time in the brass bands' 'private world'.

Despite the many great performances heard in this period, it ended with the movement at the most fragile point in its history, and many were probably oblivious to what was an existential threat. The idiomatic repertoire had grown significantly, bands were regularly featured in radio and television broadcasting, and national newspapers were sponsoring major contests. The best bands produced outstanding performances and some of the best players became principals in major orchestras. Local traditions, such as the Durham Miners' Gala and the Northumberland Miners' Picnic, had lost none of their importance as annual attractions.[45] But from the perspective of hindsight, it is impossible to see it as anything other than the slow conclusion of an era. The traditional industries, which had caused so many bands to flourish, were adjusting, diminishing or vanishing. In 1960 popular culture was on the brink of its most radical and acute transformation. From almost every perspective from which brass bands could be observed, they looked old-fashioned: replete with identifiers of a distant age and devoid of the modern qualities that 1960s culture was soon to embrace. The maleness of the brass band had also become an increasingly evident symbol of its entrenchment, as was the portfolio of formulaic orthodoxies that doggedly inhibited musical development and practices. There was also the central practical factor that closeted brass bands from the rest of the musical world: in 1960 they remained tuned to a pitch standard that belonged to the Victorian period rather than to the standard that otherwise prevailed in most of the western world. Instruments were made in a pitch that was almost a semitone higher than was used elsewhere. Since 1928 high-pitched instruments were manufactured exclusively for use in brass bands, and could not be used for any other purpose without adjustment. Things had to change to prevent 'the movement' from entering what would have been a relatively brief period of terminal decline. Things did change, at remarkable speed and with equally remarkable effect.

Chapter 9

The pitch issue and
why it mattered

Life changed in Britain in the 1960s: a mood of optimism emerged as the austerity that followed the Second World War finally relented. Some have seen it as a decade marked by radical adjustments to social values; as one historian put it, 'For some it [was] a golden age, for others a time when the old secure framework of morality, authority and discipline disintegrated.'[1] Brass bands, at the most conservative and self-obsessed point of their existence, felt the consequences of those adjustments. They competed for recruitment with a new 'participatory and uninhibited popular culture, whose central component was rock music', the ease of access to which made it 'a sort of universal language'.[2] The constituency most attuned to that language was the young. It was in this period that the word 'teenager' first fell into common use: teenagers started to be perceived as a discrete and lucrative segment of the music market. The speed at which pop music grew as a participatory activity is illustrated by the sales of the instruments that were the staple components of rock groups. In 1959 the British Board of Trade relaxed restrictions on manufactured goods that had inhibited the import of American guitars into the UK. This enabled British retailers to share an expansion that was already under way in the US. In 1963 the annual outputs of the two major US guitar manufacturers, Gibson and Fender, doubled to 600,000, and within a couple of years rose to well over a million.[3] Young people who became transfixed by the charisma of rock bands could be forgiven if they regarded brass bands as a symbol of the vanishing monochrome age from which the 1960s signalled a welcome departure.

Fortunately, these developments coincided with others that were more favourable to the future of brass bands. Indeed, the greatest paradox in the brass band story occurred at this time: just as a combination of social and cultural developments were assembling to the detriment of the future of the brass band, an entirely different set of circumstances were forming that would ensure its modernisation and robust survival. Critically important was a rise in the provision of instrumental music teaching in British schools. Then came a specific event, internal to the brass band world, that portended yet another existential threat – the pitch question. The resolution of the pitch question was to be the first vital component in a process that would lead to the brass band movement reinventing itself.

The pitch question and where it came from

One of the fundamental features that had made the British brass band both distinctive and exclusive up to the 1960s was its pitch standard. 'Pitch standards' are reference points that ensure all musical instruments are in tune with each other throughout the developed world. Pitch is described using a letter and a number followed by the symbol 'Hz' (short for 'hertz') which expresses pitch by the number of vibrations or 'cycles' per second of a musical note. Before the invention of electronic devices, pitch standards were regulated by tuning forks. The tuning fork was invented in 1711 by Handel's famous trumpeter John Shore. In the modern world, the most frequently cited point of reference is the note A (the one at the midpoint of a piano keyboard), which is in perfect tune only when it is produced by a sound wave that vibrates or oscillates 440 times in each second: A440Hz.[4] A lower number, A435Hz, for example, means that the pitch of the note would be lower. In orchestral concerts, the standard is moderated by the principal oboist, who uses a tuning fork, or an analogous electronic device, to ensure the precise accuracy of a note (A), which is then sounded and to which the rest of the orchestra tunes. This pitch standard was agreed internationally in 1939 to ensure that all instruments, irrespective of where they are manufactured or used, conform to that one, common, global standard. Before the twentieth century, a variety of pitch standards was used in different regions and organisations: there was no common agreement because there were competing interests within and between different western countries. In the Victorian period the situation was especially chaotic – until the military stepped in.

In 1857 the British army, which had bands dispersed across the Empire, sought to standardise the way its band musicians were organised and trained. It was necessary, and even urgent, because each band was individually funded and effectively owned by regimental officers who, in this respect, felt little obligation to conform to any compulsions beyond those they determined. These officers seldom knew much about music, so they put their faith and money in the hands of civilian, usually foreign, bandmasters. Most, possibly all, of these bandmasters had developed unethical relationships with instrument manufacturers. These same manufacturers acted as agents for regimental officers when a new bandmaster needed to be appointed; it was a self-perpetuating cycle of corruption. A letter from Charles Boosey, principal partner in the Boosey musical instrument company, to a foreign bandmaster hopeful of an appointment to a British regimental band, explains the arrangement:

> We have one stipulation to make with you if you accept a situation through our influence. We do not ask for any remuneration, but we do expect you to support our Firm exclusively, that is to say you will send us all orders for any instruments etc. that you may require, for we need not remind you that Bandmasters have considerable influence with the officers.[5]

This was certainly true: officers were easily blinded by incomprehensible narratives about instruments and pitch and were frequently talked into buying new instruments at unnecessarily short intervals and inflated costs. There were concerns about pitch, and instabilities in its regulation, throughout Europe. In Paris in 1855 there were complaints that brass instrument makers were producing increasingly high-pitched instruments and in 1858 Berlioz accused woodwind instrument makers of 'clandestinely raising the pitch [to] give more shine to flutes, oboes and clarinets'.[6] This prompted the French government to establish a commission to determine a 'national' musical pitch. In 1859 its first national mandate for a pitch standard was declared, but it applied only to organisations that were funded or controlled by the French government.

In 1860 the British Society for the Encouragement of Arts and Manufacturing Sciences published the report of its 'Campaign for the adoption of a uniform musical pitch'. In 1859 the Society had sent letters to various organisations, societies and agencies to solicit opinions. The responses laid bare the range of contrasting positions and the strength of feelings.[7] The Church of England worried that a universal standard, if applied to church organs, could be massively expensive and probably impossible to implement; the military held to the view that a high pitch standard favoured the clarity of sound for its bands when performing in the open air; and singers, especially sopranos and tenors, felt passionately that a high pitch standard would place an untenable strain on their precious voices. The petitions of singers were especially strong and consolidated. Each of these standpoints may have been reasonable, but they were almost entirely at odds with each other. The weight of the problem became evident as the Society's inquiry took spoken evidence from major stakeholders. Some cited problems encountered by elite performers visiting from abroad who were accustomed to the alternative pitch standards used on the continent. But other, more pragmatic, obstacles to standardisation were also present, not the least of which was that thousands of instruments currently in circulation could be deemed obsolete if they conflicted with a newly imposed pitch standard: a single standard could, in the short term, act to the detriment of the entire music profession. Eventually, a consensus emerged that a national pitch standard was desirable; but there was no consensus on what that pitch should be and how it could be practically implemented. Organ builders, piano makers and the manufacturers of wind and brass instruments had good reason to support standardisation, because it would be good for business. Enthusiasm was more muted in other quarters.[8]

Of the various agencies that employed instrumentalists in Britain, including the Church, the theatres, the opera houses and their orchestras, the army was the most powerful and coherent. It occupied a massive proportion of the musical instrument market and, unlike other more fragmented sectors of musical life, it could, if it so decided, convey decisions with a single voice. Military bandsmen probably outnumbered the entirety of professional civilian instrumental musicians. The commander-in-chief was the only person with the authority and facility to enact a systematic universal shift to a common standard in the British armed forces. Despite the prevailing chauvinism at regimental level, the army was uncontroversially loyal to the Queen or, in more immediate and practical terms, to her cousin, the Duke of Cambridge, who was indeed the commander-in-chief.

Cambridge had no aesthetic interest in the pitch issue, but he recognised chaos when confronted with it. The disordered state of army music became painfully apparent in 1854 at a Grand Review in honour of the birthday of Queen Victoria at Scutari in the Crimea. Sixteen thousand men marched past a host of military leaders and foreign diplomats. It was catastrophically marred by the shambolic performance of the massed bands playing 'God Save the Queen'. When they struck up, there were as many different pitch standards as regiments, and each was playing its own arrangement of the anthem in whatever key had been settled on. The humiliation was witnessed by the General Staff of the Allied Army. This was the last straw. When Cambridge was appointed to the highest office in the British army, he enacted a scheme that would eliminate corruption, prevent further debacles of the type that had occurred at Scutari, and standardise army music for its long-term good. There were several measures in the plan, but two were fundamental. All British military bandmasters would henceforth be required to be enlisted soldiers (a measure that prompted the undignified and hasty exit of most of the foreign incumbents), and all would be trained in a new institution, initially called the 'Military Music Class', but known from 1887 as the Royal Military School of Music, at Kneller Hall in Twickenham on the outskirts of London. After prolonged and fractious negotiations with the regiments, the school opened in 1857 to train bandmasters and be the central focus for army music. As part of this process, the British military determined that it would adopt the high pitch standard irrespective of what others might decide.[9] This was done as part of a series of new measures that created auditable transparency in dealings with instrument manufacturers. Instructions were issued in April 1858:

> The General Commander-in-Chief is desirous that the instruments of the whole [army] should be of one uniform pitch and that used at the Ancient Philharmonic Concerts be selected as the standard or regulation pitch.[10]

The pitch standard for the army, wherever it was stationed, was to be A452.4Hz, almost a semitone step higher than the modern (post-1939) standard of A440Hz. This pitch was moderated by a single tuning fork retained at Kneller Hall from which copies were carefully made and distributed across the entire Empire. It became known as 'Kneller Hall pitch'. Memoranda periodically reminded commanding officers of their responsibilities regarding uniform pitch:

> uniform pitch, without which Bands cannot play together in harmony, every regiment is required to be in possession of a tuning-fork obtained from Kneller Hall, where the implements are carefully tested and attuned to the closest vibration.[11]

Regimental tuning forks were placed under the careful watch of an officer designated as Band President, 'as a security against its being tampered with and its security destroyed'.[12] It followed that all manufacturers of brass instruments for the British army had no choice but to adopt this standard and, because brass bands were supplied by the same manufacturers (brass band instruments were often advertised as 'military instruments'), it followed that they used instruments tuned to the same high pitch standard. David Blaikley, Boosey's chief acoustician, correctly observed that it was 'the first official or Government recognition or declaration of pitch in the country'.[13] The Society for the Arts had no official designated authority to decide on such matters – the British army did (fig. 28).

28. *The Kneller Hall tuning forks used to standardise the intonation for the British army, pictured here in their display case at Kneller Hall, Twickenham, prior to its closure as the Royal Army School of Music.*

Over the next three-quarters of a century, the rest of the music world veered slowly towards the lower pitch standard. While the universal standard of A440Hz was not formally agreed until 1939, it was incrementally adopted in continental Europe by the start of the twentieth century and then found favour in Britain. Throughout Europe, and despite the various conflicts of interest, there was a more modern trend towards precision and uniformity, and a consensus emerged that benefits would accrue from the setting of a single standard. The army came under considerable pressure to change but conjured up various arguments not to do so. Some were overtly political: one was that the army preferred to conform with the standard common throughout the British Empire rather than fall in with continental Europe (by inference the French). In America in 1919 some objections to the A440Hz standard were based on its origin in Germany: an 'enemy country'.[14] Other objections were more pragmatic: the minimum estimated cost to the army of such a conversion would be of the order of £36,000. But there was mounting and sustained pressure for compliance with what was evolving as a global pitch standard.

In 1928 the British military capitulated and decided to convert to the lower pitch standard (A440Hz), which was rolled out over the next two years. The reasoning that finally clinched the decision is obscure but, by that time, the interchange between military and civilian music had become more frequent and intimate, not least because the military was the almost exclusive source of recruitment for professional wind players in British civilian orchestras and bands. A model of the future was deftly provided when the BBC Military Band was formed in 1927. It was directed by Lieutenant B. W. O'Donnell, one of a family of distinguished army bandmasters, but its performers were made up entirely of London orchestral players who played low-pitch instruments. There was also a yet higher source of influence. A letter preserved in the UK National Archives, dated November 1926, suggests an intervention from the King: 'The King desires me to call your attention to . . . the pitch of military bands. This is a matter in which His Majesty has always been interested.'[15] There is scope to doubt whether musical pitch really was high in the interests of King George V, or indeed if he knew what it meant, but that is hardly the point – the letter was signed and sent.

It followed that, from 1928, only two agencies in Britain were aligned to the high pitch standard: the British brass band movement and the Salvation Army, which had also adopted that standard, perhaps because it suited outdoor performance, but more probably because it was the prevailing standard when it started manufacturing its own instruments. It was this stark reality that uncomfortably raised its head almost four decades later. Developments were prompted exclusively by commercial imperatives. In February 1964 a meeting was held between executives of the Boosey & Hawkes instrument manufacturing firm and the British Commissioner of the Salvation Army. The Salvation Army was informed that Boosey & Hawkes (which also owned the Besson brand) had decided to stop the production of all high-pitch musical instruments.

Potentially, this left the Salvation Army in the untenable position of being the world's sole producer. By the following month, the Salvation Army had reached the inevitable conclusion. It announced that the Salvation Army Supplies Department would stop producing brass instruments, and its bands would change from high to low pitch. Its instrument factory was eventually transferred to Boosey & Hawkes. The change was consolidated in 1972. One of the Salvation Army's final acts as a manufacturer was to ensure that sets of tuning slides were available to adapt existing instruments for the pitch change; the sets would be retailed at a cost of between £100 and £180. In 1964 a memorandum was issued under the heading 'Gradual Change from High Pitch Advised':

> Such a transition would take a considerable time to accomplish fully; there is no suggestion at all of a need for haste. What is accepted is that this move is desirable and to be recommended.[16]

The impact of change

The change to the pitch of brass instruments was one of the most important moments in the history of the movement, and its effects were far-reaching. Apart from the musical consequences, it had financial implications that would weigh heavily. Many bands found the move incomprehensible. A meeting of the North East Midlands Brass Band Association was typical and unanimous in concluding that:

> no useful purpose could be served in our brass band movement by this change over. The cost of alterations to existing instruments in our bands would be about £100 per band. It was felt and expressed that this cost was beyond the ability of the majority of our small self-supporting bands, whose funds are very small.[17]

These sentiments were probably stimulated by an article published in the *British Bandsman* three weeks previously under the heading 'Advantages are Incalculable'. It set out the reasons for the change and the options that were available to bands. Interestingly and unusually, the article came not from its editorial team, but from the New Zealand Salvationist Major Dean Goffin and was a reprint of the article previously published as a memorandum in the Salvation Army periodical the *Musician*. Goffin briefly laid out the historic reasons for the pitch anomaly and emphasised that 'the disadvantages' would be 'small and temporary'.[18] Such may have been the case in the Salvation Army, where bands neither competed nor carried financial burdens; for 'civilian' bands of modest means, the consequences were significant.

The views of the North East Midlands Brass Band Association were perfectly reasonable and probably widely held, but the *British Bandsman*, edited at that time by Alfred Mackler, regarded the matter less sympathetically. It summarised the issue in what it called 'plain facts': the manufacturing companies would no longer make high-pitch instruments, no one was 'trying to force bands' to make the change, and it would only cost bands £100 ('£4 for each member of a band' over a year) to make the necessary adjustment anyway:

It would be a pity if so simple a matter should become a subject for heated discussion or emotional outbursts, although we would be the last to deny any 'die-hards' their right of expression.[19]

29. *Advertisement placed in the* British Bandsman *announcing the switch to low pitch instruments by the Black Dyke Band.*

The instrument manufacturers had indeed taken their decision, and it was true that there was no viable option, but this was not the *British Bandsman* at its best. Its status in the brass band movement was central and it had a duty of care. It was one of the few occasions in the history of brass bands when the movement was powerless to influence its own circumstances. The *British Bandsman* should have recognised the importance of the moment, the inadequacy of measures in place for its mitigation, and the longer-term consequences for bands. It was addressing an entirely working-class amateur readership, among which genuine concern and even confusion had been stirred. In 1965 the manufacturers Boosey & Hawkes announced that 'the production of high-pitch instruments will be discontinued after 31st March 1965'.[20] Besson made a similar announcement three weeks later,[21] and the following October commissioned a front-page banner advertisement in the *British Bandsman* announcing the 'Big News' that Black Dyke Mills Band had purchased from them a complete set of low-pitch instruments (fig. 29).[22] Manufacturers hoped for a bonanza, anticipating that scores of bands would bolster their order books with requests for complete new sets of instruments. This didn't happen. Bands that couldn't afford new instruments were offered the much vaunted £100–£150 'conversions kits' which came as extension tubes to tuning slides and, where necessary, valve slides. This expediency was previously adopted when bands needed to play alongside orchestras or were accompanied by a properly tuned piano or organ, but it was never satisfactory and everyone with a modicum of musical intelligence knew as much. The 'kits' inevitably imposed a ruinous effect on the overall acoustical character of instruments. A length of tubing added to the tuning slide of an instrument adjusts that instrument's pitch when no valves are depressed or when a trombone slide is in its closed position, but when valves were depressed, or trombone slides extended, players were confronted with the acoustical problems that designers had battled with for most of the nineteenth century: a sequence of issues turned an instrument which was previously in tune across its range into one with chaotic intonation. Players could partially mitigate this by adjustments to the way they played. The technique known as 'lipping', which can make small adjustments to the tuning of a note, is standard, but it is not best used to mitigate the defects of an instrument;

it is used (particularly in jazz and light music) for effect. There was a further problem. One of the key features of brass instrument playing is the way performers intuitively think. Adjustment to a pitch standard is not only dependent on the instrument that is being played: an instinctive mental process on the part of the player is also at work. Even 20 years after the pitch change, some were still finding the transition difficult:

> The bands had very little choice in the matter . . . The collective brass band ear still finds it difficult to play at concert (A=440) pitch . . . One well known conductor said that it was his life's ambition to get a band to play at concert pitch, but every time fixed pitch instruments, like a piano or glockenspiel, were introduced there were problems.[23]

The first band to convert to low pitch by buying a complete new set of (British) instruments was probably the Black Dyke Band. It had tried the low-pitch kits, quickly gave up on them and returned to high pitch. Within a year the players had travelled to London to test and buy a complete set of new low-pitch Besson instruments.[24] This must have set an example that others followed, but it is impossible to calculate the number of bands that ceased to exist in the decade that followed as a direct consequence of the pitch change. Other factors were also at play to act against the survival of the weakest. Even in the 1960s changes to the economic infrastructure of the country were having an adverse effect on areas where brass bands had traditionally been strong. Coal mines along with other heavy industries and factories were closing or contracting.

Most of the pitch controversies focused on costs. The aesthetic implications were either disregarded or ignored. A representative of Reynolds of Manchester, one of the largest retailers at that time, claimed that his firm 'were doing [converting] two or three full sets a week' when the pitch change was introduced. His account of this moment in the history of brass bands reveals a man who sold brass instruments rather than played or listened to them with any discrimination:

> Conversion was really only a matter of adding length, either to the slides or the tubes. It was difficult to get some bands to accept that

they *had* to convert – others were finding that they were doing concerts with orchestras or pianists and were having problems. There were those who said it would ruin the brass band tone – take out its brightness. Bloody nonsense, but they believed it.[25]

It wasn't 'bloody nonsense' – it was patently real. Brass bands had played at high pitch for more than a hundred years. The pitch change caused a sonic transformation that was heightened significantly by another factor.

The entry of foreign instruments

In the wake of the pitch change came another adjustment that was neither anticipated nor designed. Since the early 1950s orchestral trumpet and trombone players had been buying American instruments that contrasted dramatically with those of British design. British brass instrument manufacturers such as Boosey & Hawkes and Besson had made only modest changes to their products since the beginning of the century. New models had new names, but each was closely consistent with the design that preceded it. In America it was different. Small-scale operations in the mid-nineteenth century had been superseded from the 1880s by larger firms, usually incorporating the skills of immigrant European craftsmen and designers. Also, in America there were more manufacturers with richer and more fertile ideas. The town of Elkhart, Indiana, became a major centre for wind-instrument produc-tion. The first major enterprise was that initiated by Charles Gerard Conn, an amateur cornet player with remarkable entrepreneurial talents. After the American Civil War, Conn worked variously as a grocer, baker and purveyor of doubtful quasi-medical products, including 'Konns Kurative Kream'. Within a few years of moving to Elkhart, he was the town's mayor. He then became a state senator and, from 1893, a US congressman and newspaper proprietor (he owned the *Washington Times*). Shortly after moving to Elkhart, he started making rubber-rimmed mouthpieces in partnership with the French craftsman Eugène Dupont. It started with one for Conn's personal use (to compensate for an injury to his embouchure), but the device became sufficiently famous and popular to be the basis of a large musical instrument business. From 1879 Conn became the sole proprietor of the instrument-making firm. By the late nineteenth century, the market for wind instruments in the US was massive and was to continue to grow as new forms of popular music were introduced. In 1915 Conn sold the company, but the Conn name was retained. By this time, other firms had based their manufacturing in Elkhart. The Buescher Company was followed by the Germany company Martin, and Blessing arrived in 1908. This relatively small Midwest town gained a reputation for its band instruments. So many competing companies operating in such proximity resulted in high standards of manufacture and marketing. Unlike British firms, which (leaving aside the pitch issue) produced the same instruments for whoever wanted to buy them, American operations identified larger and more distinctive markets: marching bands, orchestras and jazz bands, all of which were seen as separate segments for which distinctly tailored instruments needed to be designed. Endorsements by leading performers of the day were important (John Philip Sousa endorsed Conn instruments), but most of the US instrument designs showed a depth of thinking that had evaded British manufacturers of the same generation. New alloys were introduced: for example, in 1938 Conn developed a metal which it called 'Coprion', and which it used for the manufacture of seamless brass instrument bells. The instruments were light and had the additional merit of an attractive red-metal finish to which a transparent lacquer was applied. Perhaps the most important difference between British and American instruments was the bore size of the orchestral models. 'Bore size' refers to the width of the tubing: wider tubing produces a bigger, more mellow sound. Part of the motivation for producing wide-bore designs was the need for the instruments to be played in the increasingly large post-war concert halls that were under construction. Wider bores have an especially emphatic impact on the sound of trombones because they have fewer bends in their design – a large proportion of a slide trombone is made up of straight lengths of cylindrical tubing. The trend to produce instruments with a wider bore had started earlier in the century on both sides of the Atlantic but the changes that occurred after the war were more emphatic.

Denis Wick, principal trombone of the London Symphony Orchestra, was one of the first British performers to identify the quality of Conn instruments. He heard the New York Philharmonic Orchestra in their first post-war UK tour in 1951 and was struck by the difference between the sound of its trombone section compared to those in British orchestras of the time. By the 1960s these new wider-bore instrument sizes were being used in orchestras across Britain. The most alert British instrument retailers recognised a major opportunity. As the Manchester firm Barratt put it (fig. 30):

LOW-DOWN ON LOW PITCH
Have you realised that the most exciting advantage of the change to LOW PITCH is that you and our band can now, for the first time, enjoy the experience of playing a famous CONN instrument?

Conn instruments were beautifully made and the product of years of extensive acoustical research. They were light and visually attractive. Nothing on the market from British manufacturers compared to them. More importantly, when used with mouthpieces with deeper cups, they produced a fundamentally different sound to British instruments and were more responsive to their players than were the old, heavier, narrow-bored, high-pitched instruments they replaced.

Brass bands that were able to make the transition fully were using instruments identical to those used in symphony orchestras. These two factors – the pitch change and the increased bore size – affected the sound of the brass band significantly. The brass band instrumentation did not change, but the sound those instruments produced did, especially the trombones, which always have an important sonic influence in brass ensemble music. This provided scope for composers to deploy successively new musical languages and colours when writing for brass bands. In effect, the sequence of events neutralised the key factors that had distinguished brass band instruments from those in use elsewhere. The transformation was gradual rather than acute, but it provided a point of ignition for a wider and more complex process of modernisation that was to follow.

30. *Advertisement placed in the* British Bandsman *by Barratts of Manchester drawing attention to the attractions of low-pitch instruments made by the US manufacturer Conn.*

Chapter 10

Modernisation: Gender, education and idiom adjustments

The change to the pitch of brass band instruments in the mid-1960s could have had a catastrophic effect. In fact, despite the obvious and serious cost implications that many bands struggled to cope with, it led to what was essentially a reset, a series of events that, by the closing decades of the twentieth century, saw the consolidation of the modern brass band movement. Standard pitch and the gradual adoption of instruments of more modern design adjusted the idiom without rendering it unrecognisable or eradicating its traditions. A comparison of recordings made before the early 1960s with those issued 30 or 40 years later easily illustrates the differences in sound and style that occurred. The standard Victorian brass instrumental format remained in place, but it became routine for contesting and concert repertoire to include a wide range of tuned and untuned percussion instruments, and players developed a new inventory of techniques. All this inspired a new, entirely idiomatic and often experimental repertoire; it did not take long for the insularities and orthodoxies that afflicted much of the brass band's musical heritage to disintegrate. In many ways, it was a testing period. The 1960s and 1970s brought social and economic challenges from which bands and their players were not immune. But by the closing decades of the twentieth century, several events and trends intervened to ensure the survival of a mode of music-making that might otherwise have become moribund. The musical identity of the British brass band emerged into the twenty-first century strengthened and clarified. Here, as so often had been the case, factors internal to the band world interacted with imperatives that affected British society more generally.

Women join the movement

The most important change was the normalisation of women as members of brass bands. In the early 1960s female brass band players were rare. Even in the late 1980s there was a belief among them that they were not 'allowed' to be a member of one of the leading bands.[1] By the start of the twenty-first century, they were ubiquitous. Many became virtuosos and celebrities within and beyond the brass band world. It is impossible to ignore the reality that this process did much more than increase the recruitment pool. The fracture of what was, in any meaningful terms, a male and self-justifying monopoly had beneficial social effects on brass bands as micro-communities, but there were also positive musical consequences. Some transpired simply from the breakdown of prevailing male dogmas, but this sometimes came at a cost. The appointment of women players in some bands prompted resignations, but there has always been a total failure on the part of the few who resigned 'on principle' to explain what the principle was and why it was worth defending.[2] It is equally impossible to ignore the musical impact of female brass players, even though it is difficult to describe and more so to evidence. The trumpeter John Wallace, a product of a brass band, has spoken of the emergence of a new type of performance sensitivity that emerged at that time. It manifested itself in several ways, particularly, but not exclusively, in phrasing and an emphasis on expression, especially in quieter dynamics.[3] This claim matches other observations, but empirical proof is elusive because the style was so quickly absorbed into the wider soundscape of bands.

The normalisation of the female presence in bands turned out to be a relatively painless and entirely positive process – change owed much to the cultural influence of the feminist movement more generally – but the swiftness of its impact in the brass band world was striking. It preceded similar developments in professional music and there are grounds to suggest that transformations in the band world influenced or even caused similar developments in professional orchestras. This may seem a bold claim, but it is worth emphasising that brass instrument playing in Britain had been aligned to masculinity for generations and the (often covert) chauvinism that prevailed among male brass players was not restricted to amateurs.

Women and girls were discouraged or barred from playing brass instruments in the past for a range of reasons. All were wrong and mostly defy rational explanation in modern thought. In broad terms, the discrimination can be traced to two related factors: cultural attitudes that have been used to define differences between male and female characteristics and behaviour; and structural factors – prevailing organisational rules and conventions that implicitly or explicitly imposed impenetrable barriers that prevented women and girls from having the range of life choices that were available to men and boys. The most enduring and recurrent cultural barrier came from the belief that playing a brass instrument was an essentially masculine activity which stood in contradiction to those qualities that typified femininity. Historical evidence for this is abundant. In 1528 the Italian writer Baldassare Castiglione published his widely circulated and influential *Book of the Courtier*. It was aimed at both men and women and explained norms of behaviour that were appropriate for persons who aspired to the status of a courtier. He advised women to avoid indulgence in any 'robust and manly exertions' and offered music-making on 'strident' instruments as an example:

Imagine what an ungainly sight it would be to have a woman playing drums, fifes, trumpets or other instruments of that sort, and this is simply because their stridency buries and destroys the sweet gentleness which embellishes everything a woman does.[4]

Castiglione's utterances should, of course, be read in terms of the time in which he was writing and the social class at which they were directed, but such ideas gained wide and lasting legitimacy. Two centuries later, the English writer John Essex, in his book *The young ladies conduct, or Rules for education, under several heads; with instructions*

upon dress, both before and after marriage: and advice to young wives
(1722), emphasised that string and keyboard instruments were 'most
agreeable' for ladies, rather than wind instruments, which were
'improper' and even 'indecent'.[5]

In Paris in the 1860s, Alphonse Sax Jr (younger brother of Adolphe,
and also an inventor and maker of brass instruments) promoted an
all-female brass group, which caused a brief but open discussion of the
topic.[6] Sax advocated the idea that women could be proficient brass
players and further, that playing a brass instrument was especially beneficial to female health. In truth, his objectives were more self-interested
and commercial than ideological – he wanted to widen the market for
his instruments. His all-female brass group's inaugural concert at the
Salle Herz was well attended and a critical success, and he followed it
up by offering instruments on loan free of charge to women, along with
a course of instruction on how to play them. He compared the merits
of playing a brass instrument and its positive effect on female lungs with
the static, unnatural postures women were required to adopt when
playing string and keyboard instruments. This was at a time when the
fear of pulmonary tuberculosis, or 'consumption' as it was then called,
was rampant. He wrote open letters to newspapers and journals in
support of his ideas. Unwittingly, they showed that the prejudices he
was ostensibly contesting were as present in mid-nineteenth-century
Paris as they had been in Italy almost three hundred years earlier:

> The idea of women playing wind instruments, especially brass instru-
> ments, such as the horn, cornet and trombone, may appear bizarre
> to you at first. You will object that no lady would want to accept
> our new system of instrumental health because she would not consent
> to the temporary loss of the gracefulness of her face while she blows
> down the instrument. I do not regard this as a serious objection.
> Quite apart from the fact that it is not necessary to puff out one's
> cheeks as certain musicians do – and which is a fault resulting from
> bad teaching.[7]

There is evidence to show that women did play brass instruments
in much earlier periods of western history, but not much of it. Instances

are exceptional and sometimes difficult to explain. Representations of brass instruments in paintings, especially of trumpets being played by females (representing angels), are allegorical rather than realistic.[8] But some others, including marginal drawings and embroideries, clearly show trumpets and trombones being played by women. Whether they are to be taken literally is an open question, but the representations are often realistic. A particularly puzzling documentary example occurs in the accounts of the court of Queen Elizabeth I. Among the many documents relating to court expenditure is a list of items attributable to the Queen's Privy Purse. Privy Purse accounts were a record of the sovereign's personal expenditure and possessions. One list, in the hand of the court administrator Edmund Dowring, summarised items acquired on behalf of the Queen by John Tamworth, one of her grooms, in the years 1569–70. Most are unsurprisingly routine – clothing, bedding and other 'necessaries' – but amid them is 'One great sagbutte provided for the Queen's use [one large trombone for the Queen's use]'.[9] An obvious explanation could be that 'great sagbutte' had an alternative meaning that would negate the possibility that the Virgin Queen had a personal interest in the trombone and might even have been a player. A similar word 'sacbutt' also meant a butt of wine, but wine was not usually included in Privy Purse accounts. There is no mention of the instrument as a personal possession of the Queen in any other Elizabethan court documents.

Other early examples of women playing brass instruments are more easily explained. In Italy, nuns in convents often played instruments to accompany liturgical music, and to teach musical skills to children in their charge. However, such modest boundaries were sometimes overstepped. For example, Charles Burney, the English traveller and writer about music, heard a two-hour concert performed in his honour in Italy in 1771, in which a full range of orchestral instruments, including brass, was played by nuns.[10]

A further, and frequently exercised, misconception has been that playing a brass instrument requires a male physique. We need not go back to the sixteenth century for evidence of this species of prejudice. In 1903 an affiliation was finalised between the New York Musical Union and the American Federation of Labor. It aimed to provide a single and powerful union that would represent workers in the music profession. As regulations of the two organisations were merged, it became clear that the Musical Union would be compelled to accept women musicians, because gender equality had long been in place for members of the American Federation of Labor. This was bleak news for members of the Musical Union. Leaving aside that, for the first time, they would be forced to compete for work with a new constituency of instrumentalists, it was seen by many as a disruption to long-standing and fondly embraced notions of masculinity. Gustave Kerker, a Prussian-born composer working as musical director at the Casino Theatre, New York, and, apparently, a man of limited imagination, advocated a view he believed to be widely shared:

Nature never intended the fair sex to become cornetists, trombonists and players of wind instruments. In the first place they are not strong enough to play them as well as men, they lack the lip and the lung power to hold notes, which deficiency makes them always play out of tune. One discordant musician might not be noticed in an orchestra, but if you have several women members or a whole band composed of them, the playing verges on the excruciating.[11]

Had Kerker been more observant and less bigoted, he would have found many brilliant female brass players in and near New York City. A research project at the Smithsonian Museum in Washington, DC, in the 1980s examined early photographic and other sources that featured brass bands. It showed brass-playing girls to have been among the most prominent members of communal and domestic music-making groups in the country.[12] Had these girls wanted to become professionals in New York City before 1903, they would have been prevented by the structural barriers that organisations such as the Musical Union had applied. Structural prohibition was not new. Before the nineteenth century, brass instrument playing was confined to professionals and regulated by agencies such as the civic guilds that operated in many European countries. Irrespective of claims that their purpose was to preserve standards, it is difficult to see their primary role as anything other than protective of the dynasties in which skills and careers were passed by males across generations. This might have changed in Britian in the early nineteenth century, when the expansion of military bands paved the way for a much wider section of the population to enter the music profession, but it didn't. Women could not enlist in the British armed forces until well into the twentieth century. Neither were they involved in the formation of civilian brass bands. Leaving aside the conventions that informed the social and familial role of women in the period, it was all but impossible for most females to borrow money, and most brass bands relied on the provision of credit.

Women were always fully integrated into music-making in the Salvation Army. William Booth, the Army's founder, was insistent on it – so was his wife. In secular brass bands, the story was different. There is little evidence of overt systematic prejudice against women brass band players, because it was implicitly regarded as a male activity. When change came, it was in episodic stages rather than abruptly or as a continuous trend. Female British brass band players who emerged before the late twentieth century were exceptions and treated as such, irrespective of how proficient they were. A good example is found in the case of Gracie Cole, the first female to win the Alexander Owen scholarship, which provided three years' free tuition for a brass performer of outstanding talent. Gracie was born in County Durham. Her coal miner father taught her to play the cornet, and she was soon playing alongside him in a band. Denis Wright, a sound judge of such matters, described her as 'the outstanding lady cornetist' of her generation and 'the finest artist of the few ladies who have made a name as players of brass instruments'.[13] Wright refused a request from her father to take her as a pupil under the terms of her scholarship, but informally helped and advised her and her family. Her career trajectory illustrates the complexities faced by a brilliant woman brass player in the 1940s.

She entered the limelight playing for the Leicester Band in 1939. She was courteous, modest, and 'charmed audiences . . . by her lovely tone, her artistry and her own happy smile'. She was 15 years old. Wright reflected on her in his unpublished autobiography:

One of the few unwise moves, I consider, was her association with Besses o' th' Barn Band round about 1941–42 . . . Nearly every

weekend for some time she played as a guest artist with the band . . .
it very nearly spoilt Gracie as a player. For not only did she play
nothing but a few well-worn solos over and over again, but she got
into a bad style of playing. Gracie was a success; her youth and charm
on the stage assured that. But it looked very soon as though she would
get no further.[14]

Wright persuaded her father to take her away from Besses, 'who
were attempting to exercise proprietary rights over her'. Eventually, she
joined the Grimethorpe Colliery Band. This was short-lived because
there were 'some reactionary members who didn't hold with girls in
the Band'. She never took up the Owen scholarship. In 1941 she joined
Gloria Gaye's Ladies Band and was then permanently lost to the brass
band world. She later became a trumpeter with Ivy Benson's All Girl
Band, and after a spell with the Squadronaires, where, as the only
female, she always felt uncomfortable, she formed her own all-female
band. Her career cannot be described as unsuccessful, but it stands as
an example of the challenges a woman brass player of outstanding talent
faced at that time. She was exhibited not because she was great player,
but because she was a great player and a girl. Her talent did not shield
her from chauvinism; it probably promoted it. Her refuge was in bands
that were entirely female – a mode of entertainment that played, at
least in part, to the male gaze: as such, it conceded to the prejudices
of the time rather than opposed them (fig. 31).

The mixture of emotions that many men felt about the entry of
women into an environment that was traditionally regarded as their
own is easily read in the pages of the brass band press of the time. In
1964 the *British Bandsman* ran biographical articles on distinguished
female players under the banner headline 'The Girls at the Top'. The
first profile was of the trombonist Maisie Ringham. She was an
outstanding player; raised in Salvation Army bands, she joined the
Hallé Orchestra, becoming the first woman principal trombone in any
British orchestra. The *British Bandsman* also ran a column headed
'Band Women's Exchange', which may have had good intentions but
implicitly positioned female players as separate from the main readership. An editorial comment clumsily suggested that the column was

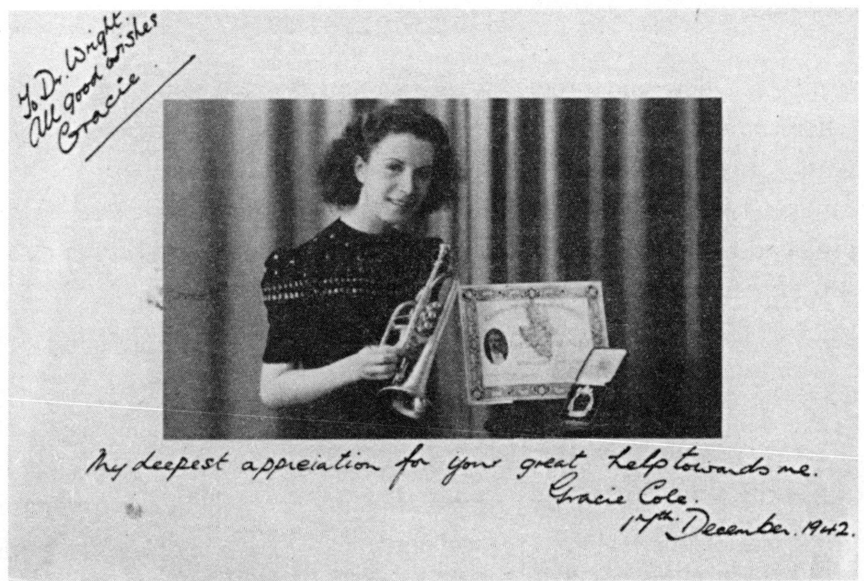

31. Postcard to Denis Wright written in the impeccable hand of Miss Gracie Cole, virtuoso cornet player.

'adding a touch of glamour' to the magazine. A starker revelation of prevailing sentiments is found in a letter to the brass band journalist Richard Arrand from the editorial team of the magazine *Brass Band Review*:

> Dear Dick,
>
> It has been suggested that we should run a women's page, not in every issue, perhaps every other issue. I am myself not certain what form such a page could take. An obvious point though would be how wives of bandsmen can help the cause.[15]

Two trends helped the normalisation of women and girls as brass band players from the 1960s. The first was an increasing, and widely acknowledged, necessity for brass bands to broaden their recruitment base. The second, and probably more important, trend came from developments in music provision in the British state education system, where boys and girls were provided with the same opportunities.

Education

In 1944 a new and progressive Education Act laid out a statutory scheme for the education of the nation's children in the post-war years.[16] In the same year, an enlightened government report on the future of teacher training emphasised the need for a curriculum that provided the widest range of skills and opportunities for learning. It was explicit when it came to music:

> The function of music teaching in school should be to provide for its continuous development as a means of expression and source of enjoyment throughout life. It should furnish all children with healthy tastes, most children with simple vocal skill and many with instrumental practice; and the exceptionally gifted should be afforded suitable facilities and teaching up to any degree of proficiency.[17]

Progress with the provision of musical instrument instruction was slow and variable because local authorities, which were responsible for enacting this provision, had so many other priorities in the long period of post-war reconstruction. By the 1960s there had been a discernible increase of instrumental tuition in state schools, and it was at this time that a new term fell into common use in Britain: 'the peripatetic teacher'. Each peripatetic teacher taught a family of instruments in a group of schools for a day or half a day each week. Most were not certificated as qualified teachers but were deemed appropriate because they were experienced players; some were retired military band musicians or semi-retired professionals. Children were taught free of charge or for a very nominal cost. By 1958 county councils employed an average of 7.6 full-time-equivalent peripatetic teachers, and there were also Saturday-morning schools where children played in orchestras and bands. By 1966, 110 of the 135 local authorities had full-time music advisers who co-ordinated these activities and there was a noticeable increase in the teaching of woodwind and brass instruments.[18] One report noted what should have been obvious to everyone: that getting young people to play a musical instrument generated more interest in music than just talking to them about it, and this approach was effective, irrespective of a child's wider attainments:

> [B]rass band work . . . has often proved more successful with pupils of quite limited general ability, and a practical approach through instruments can be much more effective than '[music] appreciation' classes.[19]

From the mid-1960s, comprehensive schools replaced the selective system that had previously distributed children at the age of 11 between academic 'grammar schools' and 'secondary modern schools' that were less academic and emphasised employment skills. The number of UK secondary schools became fewer, but the new comprehensive schools were much larger: in 1960 there were 5,801 schools for 2.7 million pupils, in 1985 the number of schools had shrunk to 4,028 but they accommodated 3.5 million pupils. Comprehensive schools could offer a wider curriculum and range of activities – that was one of the stated intentions when the idea was proposed. It is noticeable that, from the 1960s, school brass bands became more prominent in the brass band landscape, probably because of the success of the peripatetic system. Though instrumental tuition was ancillary to the main school curriculum, it was free of charge in most parts of the country and equally available to girls and boys. A 1972 survey of 800 children in Reading and Manchester showed that one-third of the boys and double that number of girls played a musical instrument.[20] A momentum had been created. By this time, there were parallel initiatives within the brass band movement, such as the National Schools Brass Band Association and the National Youth Brass Band, both formed in the 1950s: they strengthened the impetus, and a flow of brilliant young players emerged.

A further and yet more vivid indicator of the growth of brass instrument playing among the nation's young is found in the number of brass players put forward for the grade examinations of the Associated Board of the Royal Schools of Music (ABRSM). The ABRSM was formed in 1889 to provide a system of external music examinations, primarily in musical performance. Candidates were examined according to set syllabi in one of eight grades from the preliminary (Grade 1) to the advanced (Grade 8). Up to the second half of the twentieth century, the candidature was dominated by pianists, and to a lesser extent string players. For example, 69,396 pianists were examined in 1950, along with 3,612 string players. The total number of brass players examined in the same year amounted to 34. Pianists continued to be the most numerous group, but the increase in the number of brass players was striking in the following three decades. In 1950 just 20 trumpet/cornet players were examined; in 1980 the number had grown to 7,308. In 1950 there were 5 (french) horn candidates; in 1980 there were 2,008. Similarly, 9 trombone candidates in 1950 had grown to 3,113 in 30 years. Perhaps the most interesting category was the one labelled 'other brass', which could only have been made up of brass band instruments that did not fall into one of the other categories. In 1950 none were put forward for examination; in 1980 there were 7,092.[21]

Changes to the higher education system also acted in favour of brass bands. 17,337 UK students attended universities in 1950; in 1970 the number had risen to 51,189, and in 1990 it had increased further to 77,163.[22] This expansion impacted on colleges of technology and the country's polytechnics, many of which had been founded in the nineteenth century to teach courses that directly benefited industry. Some, most notably Salford College of Technology and Huddersfield College of Technology, offered diploma courses in brass band studies. In 1988 Salford became the first institution to offer a degree in Band Studies.[23] In 1997 the Labour Party, under Tony Blair, won a majority in elections for the British parliament. One of its first acts was to remove the distinction between universities and polytechnics. Overnight, the number of universities in the country more than doubled. The new universities (the former polytechnics), which had previously been overseen by a central government agency, became independent, with their own royal charters. This provided freedom to choose the subjects they taught and how they would teach them.[24] Several became more alert to the interests and demands of their localities. For the first time, institutions competed for students (rather than the reverse). This led to more opportunities for students who specialised in brass band instruments to study at undergraduate and postgraduate levels. New generations of highly talented and trained young men and women emerged to rejuvenate the brass band movement.

Interventions from modern attitudes

Before the 1960s, and leaving aside the brief appearances of established classical music composers, brass band repertoire was the product of a relatively small group of specialist composers and arrangers. The styles and formats established by the 1930s were the product of this specialised group. Among the best and most prolific was the former Salvationist Eric Ball, who wrote effectively for championship bands but was also adept at writing less demanding works for bands in the lower sections. While it is easy to recognise some fine works in this period, it is difficult to see the repertoire as it had accumulated by the early 1960s as more than formulaic and loyal to a set of musical approaches that was fundamentally conservative. The prevailing orthodoxies were enshrined in standard textbooks on the subject,[25] and those same orthodoxies defined and limited the techniques and performance conventions that brass band players deployed. This was to change fundamentally, but it did so incrementally and only after interventions from the external musical world.

From the 1960s a succession of new test pieces challenged prevailing compositional methods and performance conventions that eventually led to a fundamental adjustment to the musical language of the brass band. The process of change was not smooth, and the reactions were uneasy and complex, but it led to a fundamental modernisation of the idiom. It is important to stress that 'modernism' is not applied here in the radical sense that was witnessed in twentieth-century western music culture more generally, but it was controversial, nonetheless. The brass band world was conservative, but so was the public at large. Much of the output of modern classical composers failed to find a popular audience. Such was the case with some of the new repertoire with which bands were confronted. Banding was always a leisure activity. Players join bands to enjoy themselves as a group of like-minded people in terms they commonly understand. They have always had shared musical values, and this is where the problem resided. For any form of musical modernism to find acceptance in the brass band world, it had to have a form, a sound and a performance experience that would enhance rather than weaken the positive experience of playing.

In the 1960s and the decades that followed, these circumstances presented challenges to composers who, while staying true to their creative integrity, had no choice but to take such attitudes into account. The successful brass band composers who emerged in the later decades of the century wrote exciting original works that exhibited a deep understanding of the idiom and, critically, were a joy to play. An obligation for composers to write music that met the approval of performers was always an issue. A neat illustration of the dilemma is found in the reception of *Contest Music* by the talented Salvationist composer Wilfred Heaton, who wrote it in response to a commission for a test piece for the 1973 National contest. There was never any doubt about its originality and musical quality. The brilliant trumpeter-conductor Elgar Howarth thought it a work of genius, but it was felt that it was too modern and that it would not engage the interest of players. Eric Ball's assessment of it was pragmatic.

> Eric looked at the name on the front cover and said 'How marvellous'. He then proceeded to read the work through, slowly, turning the pages over and developing a frown. 'This is a wonderful piece, but I don't think you can use it at present, I'm a bit concerned that there isn't enough for people to do especially in the second movement'. Eric knew the problem about keeping players involved and he was so skilled at tailoring his music to the needs and abilities of players.[26]

The replacement for *Contest Music* in the 1973 contest was Hubert Bath's *Freedom*, which had made its first appearance at the National contest more than 50 years previously. In 1988, when Heaton's work was used for the purpose for which it was originally written, it provided no major challenges for audiences, and bands accepted it for what it was. By that time, there had been further incursions into the brass band world that had caused attitudes to change emphatically.

The earliest disruption came in the 1960s from the composer Gilbert Vinter. Vinter was widely admired in the music profession. When the London-based BBC Concert Orchestra was formed in 1952, Vinter was appointed as its first principal conductor. He was not a brass player, nor had he much experience of brass bands, but his compositional style, which may not seem especially radical in hindsight, was an important transformational step. His first major test piece was *Salute to Youth* (1960). Its impact was formidable because it contrasted so sharply with what bands had become used to. He confronted them and their conductors with a new set of demands and a more complex musical language. It was a relatively gentle compromise between tradition and a soft version of modernity. Its challenge to prevailing attitudes was unsettling, but it did not take long for Vinter's style to gain acceptance. Four of his compositions were subsequently used as test pieces for the finals of the National or Open contests in the 1960s.

By the 1980s the musical landscape of brass banding had changed significantly. The pitch change of the 1960s aligned brass bands with the wider musical world and in the following decades there was also a change in the demography of the brass band. A new source of recruitment from colleges and conservatoires emerged, and a new generation of composers were turning their attentions to the medium. Among the more important were Elgar Howarth, Edward Gregson, Peter Graham, Philip Sparke, Derek Bourgeois and Philip Wilby. There were also gifted arrangers such as Howard Snell and Ray Farr. Each was talented, original and intimately familiar with the idiom of the brass band, and contemporary brass playing more generally. An important new attraction was the use of percussion in contests, which provided a fundamental extension to the brass band soundscape. Percussion was first allowed in the British Open Contest in 1969 (for the performance of Gilbert Vinter's *Spectrum*). Untuned percussion had been used in a rudimentary way since the nineteenth century for marching and concerts, but its inclusion for contests was controversial, some believing that '"the drums" would cover up the faults in brass playing'. Elgar Howarth was a major advocate for the use of percussion and used it extensively in his own works:

I decided to give them [the percussionists] plenty to do with a variety of instruments, some of which were new to most brass bands. I was clear about my objectives: I wanted to stimulate an interest in bands by good young percussionists, whose talents were badly needed.[27]

Howarth's test piece *Fireworks*, written for the 1975 Open contest, was also controversial because of its rhythmic complexity: 'conductors objected to the plethora of time changes – 7/8, 5/8, 2/4 and so on'. A group of them petitioned Harry Mortimer, owner of the British Open contest, to get the work withdrawn, complaining that it was just 'mathematical rubbish'. Mortimer responded mischievously by asking, 'Are you telling me you can't conduct it?', at which point the complainants fell collectively silent.[28]

Professionals

Even in the nineteenth century, contest regulations required players to register as a member of just one band. Regulations were strengthened in the twentieth century to discourage them from moving temporarily and expediently from one band to another under an arrangement known as 'borrowed players'. It remained in force even after 1991, when it was agreed that contesting bands could include professional musicians. This provision was not as radical as it may appear because many existing band members, including those who worked as peripatetic teachers, could be regarded as professional musicians: restricting the inclusion of professionals was unsustainable because, as well as being undesirable, it was almost impossible to implement. There was never a requirement for conductors to be amateurs or for them to restrict their affiliations to one band, and it has always been common for conductors to lead several different bands at a single contest. Lower-section bands usually had their own local conductors, but some ambitious championship bands employed both a 'resident' conductor for routine weekly rehearsals and a 'professional' conductor who was drafted in for major contests, concerts or recordings.

In the second half of the twentieth century, retired military band-masters were often employed in one or other of these categories. They were usually talented, experienced, authoritative and good communic-ators. Many of the finest performances and recordings of the late twentieth century were made under the direction of former military officers, such as George Wilcocks, Peter Parks, Arthur Kenny and Denzil Stephens. In the 1970s an additional influence entered the brass band world from a group who had started as brass band players before gaining stellar status as orchestral players. Among the most influential were Elgar Howarth, James Watson, Howard Snell and Ray Farr. These players were also connected to a parallel development in professional brass playing which, in the second half of the century, had seen the rise of the modern orchestral brass ensemble.

The most important British group was the Philip Jones Brass Ensemble (PJBE) which, like many others, operated as a quintet and as a series of larger configurations, as required – ten players were usually used for PJBE tours.[29] Jones was a trumpet player at the Royal Opera House when he was inspired by a brass quartet formed from members of the Concertgebouw Orchestra of Amsterdam. His group was formed of leading orchestral players; performances started in 1951 and, by the 1970s, it had built a global reputation. Many similar groups were subsequently formed, notably the Wallace Collection under the direction of the trumpeter John Wallace. Central to the mission of both Jones and Wallace was the encouragement of a new repertoire of transcriptions and original works for brass ensemble. It followed that interest in sophisticated idiomatic writing for brass instruments in ensemble grew among a new generation of composers. These developments benefited brass bands directly because they elevated creative interest in idiomatic brass ensemble writing more generally. Interestingly, this did not weaken the distinctiveness of the traditional brass band sound – it had the opposite effect: it drew attention to its idiosyncratic qualities and musical potential. The PJBE performed its last concert in 1986. The virtuoso tuba player John Fletcher wrote a dedicatory programme note for that concert, reflecting on how the group had started and how ideas about the fundamental purpose of performance on modern brass instruments had changed in the relatively brief era of the PJBE's existence. Fletcher's comments were unintentionally prescient of musical transformations that were emerging in the brass band world:

> We all had to drastically re-think some of our most cherished notions about playing, and a good thing too. Brass players understandably are too hooked on trying to feel certain. It sets the concrete far too early in life and kills music and the joy of playing. That, dear friends, is our chief stumbling block; too much brass playing; too little conveyed pleasure. It quickly became our job to redress this balance. We did our best with the brass playing – you can't please everyone – but we worked like stink at the pleasure. At the music, the communication, the humour and, dare I say it, a higher cultural level.[30]

Elgar Howarth had been a leading member of the PJBE. He was an exceptional individual; as a student at Manchester University, he was a member of what became known as the 'Manchester School', which also included the composers Harrison Birtwistle, Peter Maxwell Davies, Alexander Goehr and the pianist John Ogdon. Howarth had a strong personality and was able to articulate ideas clearly. In 1972 he formed a relationship with the Grimethorpe Colliery Band. He made a total commitment to brass band music; in an interview in 2005 he described the change in his career to being a band composer after many years as a professional trumpeter and why he never 'felt any need to come out of that culture'.[31] His interest in contests was limited; his thoughts were centred on the development of repertoire and performance techniques. He identified three factors that needed enhancement for brass bands to survive: the commissioning of works by modernist composers; the development of the 'entertainment contest', which he believed offered the possibility of greater flexibility in repertoire within the contesting ethos; and the weakening of the isolation of brass bands from the wider musical world.[32] Each of these objectives was achieved because, by the end of the century, a new consensus emerged among brass band players about what it meant to be a brass band player.

Idiomatic changes

By the end of the twentieth century, a clear break was discernible between the formulaic approach that had typified writing for the brass band and new, more flexible and experimental approaches by composers. It was the composition of test pieces for major contests that provided the most important exemplars, but it soon spread to the wider repertoire. This new and extended idiom attracted a new generation of composers from the UK and eventually other countries to write imaginative and challenging works for brass band. Importantly, these changes were willingly embraced by the modern brass band community.

By this time, the core membership of brass bands reflected adjustments in British society. Class divisions became blurred, and access to higher education had created opportunities and the prospect of social mobility. Brass bands could no longer be described as the preserve of working-class men. Many players were educated in universities and conservatoires where they had been exposed to a wide range of performance techniques and repertoires. Brass band performance conventions became contiguous with those of orchestral players and started to reflect the way music culture was developing across the western world. The best bands abandoned lingering cautions about idiomatic expansion and conservatism was replaced by a curiosity and enthusiasm about extended playing techniques. Playing in a brass band became a more varied, challenging and rewarding experience and, while the most radical implications affected championship bands, they filtered in different degrees to the rest of the movement.

The unhindered integration of a wide range of tuned and untuned percussion instruments into the brass band was an important moment: it caused composers to think differently about the available sound palette (fig. 32). Sonorities that had been modified by the change to low pitch, and the simultaneous shift to wider-bore instruments, did not eradicate the distinctiveness of the traditional sound because the standard brass instrumentation remained intact. But there were other important sonic adjustments. Perhaps the most obvious concerned vibrato. Vibrato is caused by minute and continuous undulations in pitch that affect the timbre of a sounding note. It is deployed in many

32. The Cory Band under Philip Harper showing one of the conventional modern seating arrangements and the range of tuned and untuned percussion.

forms of instrumental and vocal music. For example, the left hands of violinists and cellists often remain in continuous motion when playing a sustained note: this is how they create vibrato. Before the 1960s most brass band players used vibrato continuously. Early recordings suggest that the practice was already in place at the start of the twentieth century. In modern brass bands, it is used more discriminatingly in the service of lyrical expression, particularly in solo passages. It is usually less discernible in accompanying parts. There was also a minor revolution in the way instruments were used. Composers turned to the creation of new sound colours by abandoning previous conventions in favour of variety, and by featuring more adventurous combinations of instruments; and instruments such as the tenor horn, flugelhorn, baritone, and the bass instruments which had previously been limited to roles that supported harmonies and textures, were foregrounded to reveal their own distinctive voices. Mutes, which were seldom used in brass bands, became standard for all instruments and were used extensively. Musical languages that had been developed in classical music, such as asymmetrical rhythmic writing, less predictable harmonies, and advanced performance techniques of the type that had been developed in the classical avant-garde and jazz, were deployed freely. Some composers – and bands themselves – also experimented with the spatial placements of performers. Some composers also incorporated electronic sounds.

Appendix 2 provides links to sound recordings that are illustrative of compositional styles, works and performance techniques described in this book.

Chapter 11

Internationalisation and its impact

The British model of the brass band was adopted by countries outside the UK in different ways, at different times and for a variety of reasons. None closely mirrored the circumstances and events that underpinned its creation in Britain in the mid-nineteenth century, but British-style bands, wherever they emerged, were almost always amateur. Most in the southern hemisphere and Asia were a product of colonisation, but in Europe and North America it was different. Even by the mid-nineteenth century, most European countries and North America had their own histories of amateur bands which, like the British, interrupted the rarefied professional traditions of brass playing that had previously prevailed. The British model was attractive outside the UK in the mid-twentieth century because it was so highly developed and suitable for amateurs, not least because a substantial and appropriate printed repertoire was readily available. But evidence suggests that it was the unique sound of the British brass band that was its compelling feature. Many, but not all, foreign British-style brass bands were developments of existing bands that had a different format in which brass instruments were prominent, but many were formed ab initio as a direct imitation of the British model. In general, and leaving aside developments in former colonies, there were usually two contextual features in places where British-style brass bands were formed. Firstly, there existed some form of amateur community instrumental music-making tradition that was indebted to an earlier

263

influence of military bands; and secondly, there was an effective commercial infrastructure in place for the production and supply of brass instruments – this, too, was usually part of a military legacy. A further influence, common but not universal, were Salvation Army bands which were present in many countries before the end of the nineteenth century.

Throughout this chapter, I use the adjective 'European' to describe bands of continental Europe in the modern era. This may be appropriate as a generalisation, but a more detailed study would take greater account of developments in individual countries and of the individuals (there were many of them) who had championed the British model when such developments were nascent. Those developments started in earnest in the mid-twentieth century and, by the close of the century, the best European bands were sufficiently advanced to equal the best in the UK and exert an important new influence on the repertoire and idiom of the brass band movement more generally. In this respect, the more recent internationalisation of the British brass band model should be regarded as an important stage of its modernisation. For example, while it is common for European bands to perform works from the traditional brass band repertoire, they have always shown a marked interest in new works. In 1982 the British band conductor Howard Snell, who had visited Germany with the Desford Colliery Band, commented that:

> People abroad come to brass bands with a totally unprejudiced view – they don't have the English clichés written into their minds ... I had a lot of people quizzing me afterwards – they couldn't quite see why all these people in coloured jackets were playing such inconsequential music to such a high standard.[1]

This probably captures an essential element of the modernising culture of European bands, even though it was largely implicit: while they copied the format and the idiom, they were relatively unburdened by its less appealing traditions and prejudices. Snell also identified a broader international trend:

If America and Japan and . . . European countries really catch on to the idea of British style brass bands and banding, then watch out. There'll be a world cup twenty years from now and it'll be quite an achievement if British bands even qualify for the final.[2]

He was wrong about the world cup but otherwise correct. It took little more than two decades for many European bands to reach the standard of the best in Britain. In so doing, they also established a coherent network and a clarity of purpose. In 2025 around half of the 20 most successful bands in the world were based in countries outside the UK.[3] Each stage of this development enhanced the British brass band movement and hastened its departure from the conservatism and insularity under which it had once laboured.

Colonialism and neo-colonialism

The earliest phase of the British brass band diaspora was its export with British emigrants to the Victorian colonies. The first civilian bands were small and expediently formed, but they developed as quickly as did the settlements they inhabited, and it took relatively little time for efficient bands to be established in Australia and New Zealand. In 1924 the Newcastle Steelworks Band from Western Australia, formed just eight years previously, toured Britain and surprised everyone by winning the British Open Contest. It was the start of a permanent and mutually beneficial relationship between the British movement and its equivalents in the Antipodes. Even by the start of the twentieth century, brass bands were seen as quintessentially British, and this suited the colonisation project, which always carried the tacit assumption that one of its purposes was to transplant British culture to foreign lands. Other forms of British music-making were similarly exported, but brass bands in military and civilian settings appear to have been the earliest forms of instrumental music-making to have been coherent and well organised. The first sounds of western instrumental music in places where it had not been previously heard came from bands attached to colonising military forces. They did their usual work of emphasising the status of colonising governments through the soft-power rituals of ceremony. Civilian bands may also have contributed to this on a smaller scale and in more local circumstances, but their role as entertainers was equally valued. It followed that bands were enrolled in the service of official and quasi-official agencies such as police forces and other uniformed groups set up by civic authorities. As early as 1832 a Sydney newspaper reported that the town had an infantry band that was a 'brass band' constituted of 30 players.[4] In the same year and the same town, a band calling itself 'Mr Harper's Professional Brass Band' was advertising its services, and this was probably one of the first of Australia's entertainment and dance bands.[5] By the 1850s reports of brass band performance, both military and civilian, proliferated in the newspapers of most larger settlements across the country.

An interesting subtext to the story of early colonial bands, particularly those stationed in Asia and the southern hemisphere, concerns the subsequent appropriation and use of discarded military band instruments by indigenous communities. This topic has been the subject of extensive study by anthropologists and ethnomusicologists and has revealed rich forms of hybrid western and local ethnic musical languages that have thrived to modern times.[6] Fieldworkers have written of the multi-coloured soundscapes produced by such bands. Some, such as the Indian wedding bands which operate from shopfronts across the country, have developed lasting and distinctive traditions.[7]

Religious organisations of various denominations used brass bands. The Salvation Army was operational in Australia from 1879 and active in 59 other countries by 1916. By 1941 its mission had spread to 97 countries worldwide. There is little doubt that its influence on the musical life of foreign countries was emphatic, if unintentionally so. Irrespective of their location, a feature of all Salvationist units was a common and clearly understood organisational structure. From its earliest days, the Army prioritised connectiveness between its branches and its central command to ensure that its mission would not be compromised through geographical expansion. Salvationists abroad were not left alone; they were provided with supplies and support, and this came to include brass musical instruments. In 1882, less than four years after its formation, services in Adelaide were 'enlivened by the Salvation Army Brass Band', and similar reports came from New Zealand.[8]

It is important to stress that, while modern postcolonial narratives could easily counter such a proposition, the Salvation Army was not (at least formally) a colonising agency. Salvationists were Christian missionaries: they were not restricted to parts of the world colonised by Britain or any other country. It was certainly not limited to the boundaries of the British Empire – much of its work was in European countries. Its diaspora touched more regions of the world than any other globalising agency, apart perhaps from the Catholic Church. For example, it was active in countries such as Japan and China, which were never formally colonised by Britain. Salvationist musicians were required to be registered as such; in 1940, the Army had a total of 50,514 musicians in its bands.[9] The international congresses held in London in the first decade of the twentieth century, with their hundreds of foreign bandsmen, provided stark evidence of that growth even much earlier in the century.

British brass bands were transported to colonised countries by people who carried the instruments, skills and knowledge of the British model and style. The standard instrumentation is unlikely to have been commonly used until the early twentieth century. Bands were particularly strong in the mining areas of New South Wales and in South Australia's 'Little Cornwall'. Alignments to the British model were promoted by visiting British bands, conductors and adjudicators. Such was the case in the Antipodes in the early twentieth century. A good living could be made at the various festivals, contests and other cultural events organised in the larger towns. Cyril Jenkins, the composer of *Life Divine* and *Coriolanus*, regularly adjudicated at Australian *eisteddfodau* and anywhere else for which a good fee was on offer. James Ord Hume, a Scottish former military bandmaster, is regarded as a major influence; he visited Australia and New Zealand in 1903 and 1924. There were also visits by British bands. Besses o' th' Barn Band, under Alexander Owen, included Australia in its world tour of 1907 and returned there in 1910. One writer has suggested that 'the heyday' of brass banding in Australia and New Zealand was probably in the 1920s and 1930s.[10] This may be true but, as was the case in Britain, the calculation was probably based on quantitative rather than qualitative factors.

Links between colonised countries and British instrument makers and retailers were also strong. Order books of British brass instrument makers in the late nineteenth century show the issue of many invoices to foreign bands and commercial intermediaries. Their business was not restricted to the countries of the formal Empire: it extended to territories that were under some form of protectorate or diplomatic arrangement that stopped short of colonisation but had a similar cultural effect. China can be regarded in these terms, as can Egypt following its brief period as a British protectorate.[11] The introduction of western brass instruments to China is most frequently attributed to the efforts of Sir Robert Hart, the most important and celebrated British civil servant based there in the closing decades of the nineteenth century. He formed a band constituted mainly of brass instruments. Many western bands and orchestras were formed in China, but there is little evidence of the formation of British-style bands on a scale that matches the size and population of the country.[12] In Japan the earliest recorded use of brass instruments followed their import in 1841 by the Dutch East India Company. In the decades that followed, brass instrument playing gained popularity, and most Japanese military bands were formed using European instruments. Community and other amateur bands and school brass bands emerged from the 1890s. The Salvation Army appears to have been particularly influential in the country. One of the 11 elite staff bands of the Salvation Army was formed in Tokyo. It has been suggested that, 'in the modern era half a million Japanese regularly play on brass instruments in amateur wind bands, orchestras and brass bands'.[13] The dominant format in Japan became the wind band, but bands using the British format, such as the Nexus Brass Band formed in 1995, were also influential. A further and major driving force for western music in Japan was the presence in the country from 1967 of Yamaha Instruments, which became one of the world's largest manufacturers of musical instruments.[14]

Amateur brass histories in Europe and America

Neither of the two most conspicuous factors that gave rise to the British brass band movement in the Victorian period were exclusively British. The development of new sophisticated forms of military music in the first half of the nineteenth century had an emphatic impact on British musical life, but it was a Europe-wide phenomenon. Prussia and other German-speaking countries, along with Belgium and France, were especially prominent, but most continental countries experienced similar developments concurrently. The other critical factor was the development of modern species of chromatic brass instruments. This, too, was not an exclusively British feature. The most important improvements originated in continental Europe: mid-Victorian, British-made instruments were variants of continental ideas. The only mechanical brass instrument for which a claim might be made that it was 'invented' in Britain is the keyed bugle, but even that instrument may have been indebted to models that were in circulation in Europe almost a decade earlier. All the valve instruments that formed the brass band were based on continental inventions, and the best calculation of the origin of the trombone is that it was first made in Germany (probably Nuremberg) early in the second half of the fifteenth century.

European countries have their own distinctive histories of amateur brass playing, most of which emerged in the mid-nineteenth century. They ran in parallel with the British brass band movement but were not aligned to it. A ubiquitous and significant form in northern and central Europe were bands attached to volunteer fire brigades. In some countries, these civic units were sufficiently similar and common in purpose to have a printed repertoire. The most organised and connected groups were in Nordic countries, particularly Finland, where several emerged in the 1870s,[15] but there were similar formations in central European countries, particularly Poland, where volunteer fire-brigade bands were required to operate within a national regulatory framework. From 1921 a 'Main Association of Fire Brigades' included in its remit a requirement to educate and inspect its bands, and according to its periodical, *Przegląd Pożarniczy*, it also organised band contests. In 1931 the Association's president, Stanisław Twardo, claimed that over 900 such bands were active across the country.[16] Central Europe was also an important design and manufacturing centre for brass instruments. The Červený company was founded in Bohemia in the mid-1840s. By around 1880 it was employing 100 workers and producing 3,000 brass instruments a year. In 1895 it supplied 6,000 brass instruments for the Russian army.[17]

Bands in Nordic countries were always distinctive because of their instrumentation and repertoire, but also because instruments designed and manufactured there had characteristics that distinguished them from those produced elsewhere. For example, the Swedish *kornett*, which was based on earlier Prussian models, was different in shape and sound to cornets of the same range made in France and Britain. This difference was regularly a matter of comment, especially from German observers:

The tone colour of their instruments is softer than that of our cavalry bands, more like that of light infantry. There are fewer trumpets, also they use a lighter articulation – in this way a milder, soft tone is obtained.[18]

33. The Lijan Sextet, c.1896–1906. The instruments with their distinctive conical bells are a legacy of earlier Prussian designs.

Swedish brass sextets were usually formed of three *kornetts* and instruments that equate to the tenor horn and baritone with trombone or tuba (fig. 33). The Finnish version, known as *torisveitsikko*, were usually septets with percussion and gained a sufficiently settled idiom to attract a dedicated repertoire, to which Jean Sibelius famously contributed.[19] *Torisveitsikko* probably owes its origins to Finnish military band formations but, from the later nineteenth century, it was a consistently amateur tradition. From 1842 Danish army bands (other than the wind band of the Royal Guard) were constituted by formal decree entirely of brass instruments with percussion. They were relatively small – usually about 17 players – but this military form and the standards it inspired cast an important influence on the development of amateur brass music. By the 1880s amateur brass bands were also formed in Iceland.[20]

In Hispanic countries the presence of all-brass bands was less prominent in the nineteenth century and has largely remained so. There was a strong and lasting preference for mixed wind and brass bands, and concert bands have remained popular in Spain, Portugal and South America. Italian civic bands have similarly been inclined to use mixed instrumentation but there has been an unbroken tradition of civic and other town bands in Italy since the Renaissance. In 2025 an Italian band using the British format competed in the European championship.

The word *fanfare* is used to describe a specific formation that has been and remains popular in western Europe. It originated in France and developed as an amateur format from the late nineteenth century. In its modern manifestation the *fanfare* is made up mainly of brass instruments, and a full set of percussion. Saxophones are introduced in some of the larger bands. The format is popular in several countries including Belgium, Switzerland, the Netherlands and Luxembourg and has attracted an original repertoire. Some *fanfare* bands have transitioned to the British model. The modern form is believed to be indebted to proposals made to the French government by Adolphe Sax in 1845 as part of the reorganisation of French military music. Sax offered ideas for the instrumentation of different types of military regiment. He suggested that a combination of natural trumpets and horns with modern brass instruments of his own design, along with saxophones, would be appropriate for cavalry regiments. A consensus approximating to a standard instrumentation for *fanfares* emerged by about 1870 and it was probably from this that the amateur tradition came.[21] The growth of amateur brass playing in France benefited from the *orphéoniste* movement: a post-Revolution attempt to promote music-making in the population. It was initially directed at choral singing but extended to instrumental music in the second half of the nineteenth century. One writer has estimated that between 1860 and 1908 the number of amateur brass and wind bands attached to the movement in France increased twentyfold from 400 to 8,000.[22] There is insufficient evidence about the make-up and musical practices of these bands to draw many general conclusions about them. One of the *orphéonique* authorities established a commission in 1857 which led to the publication of quasi-mandatory instrumental groupings for brass bands and wind bands of various sizes, but the practical impediments for unifying such a vast scheme, in the terms put forward, were formidable, and this suggests it is unlikely that the initiative had the desired effect.[23]

German-speaking countries were at the forefront of military music in the nineteenth century and had a prominent and important brass-instrument manufacturing industry, as did Austria which was one of the few countries in which the trombone continued to flourish in the eighteenth century when it was obsolete in most other places. Among the amateur formations that originated in the nineteenth century and continued in a modified form is the *Posaunenchor*. The name suggests a trombone group, but this is one of many misnomers that have arisen from faulty translations of biblical texts. It originated in the early 1840s and has always been formed of a mixture of brass instruments. The association of *Posaunenchöre* with Lutheran churches gave cause for them to be referred to as *evangelische Posaunenchöre*. They pre-date the wide availability of valved brass instruments but, from the twentieth century, and because their primary function has been to accompany hymn and psalm singing, there has been a tendency to favour instruments that produce a mellow sonority (such as those that equate to flugelhorns, tenor horns and euphoniums).

An earlier practice with origins in Bohemia, Moravia and Poland provided what was probably the first and most sustained tradition of amateur brass playing anywhere. It was part of the musical development of the Church of the Moravian Brethren. The Moravian Church has its origins in Bohemia in the fifteenth century under the leadership of Jan Hus, who was executed for heresy in 1415. His supporters formed the clandestine Protestant group known as the *Unitas fratrum* (Unity of the brethren). In 1722 it underwent a renewal under the leadership of Count Nikolaus Ludwig von Zinzendorf. It was in the Protestant community formed on the estate of von Zinzendorf at Herrnhut in modern Saxony that the Moravian use of brass instruments originated: they were used to accompany the singing of chorales and fulfil other ritualistic roles. By the mid-eighteenth century there had been a global diaspora of Moravian brethren. Settlements in the Netherlands had trombone ensembles by 1746, and by 1790 there were 16 brass ensembles in Germany. Congregations also settled in territories that were to be part of the United States. Sources on the musical activities of the Moravian Church survive in quantity and have been the subject of several specialist studies. The Moravian community at Bethlehem, Pennsylvania, was using trombones, trumpets and horns by 1745 and acquired a new set of instruments in 1754. This was unambiguously an amateur music tradition which has survived to modern times as an important component of Moravian life and of the history of music in America.[24]

Bands were formed for military units in pre-revolutionary America,[25] but it was not until the early nineteenth century that secular civilian bands appeared. In New York City the band formed by Allen Dodworth, one of an influential musical family that emigrated from Yorkshire, switched to an entirely brass formation by 1835.[26] Several all-brass bands followed, the most celebrated being that formed in Boston by Edward Kendall in 1838. In 1856 the Boston music critic J. S. Dwight wrote that 'brass bands' were 'virtually everywhere' but was equivocal about their merit:

All brass bands sound alike [with the] same essential quality of tone, the same family type through its seeming variations; the same aggravating increase of force, without increase of meaning.[27]

This may have been true at the time of writing, but things changed when bands that incorporated woodwind instruments gained commercial success and artistic approval; however, these were fully professional groups. American and British bands of the second half of the nineteenth century cannot be meaningfully compared because of the very different sizes of the two countries, and the absence in America of contesting at a scale that would have moderated the remoteness of their bands, elevated standards and increased the idiomatic repertoire. Most amateur American bands were formed in small-town communities and had a limited set of roles. Some repertoire collections from the period survive. They include an 1849 manuscript collection of 40 compositions made for the Manchester (New Hampshire) Band, which comprised 14 brass instruments and percussion,[28] and a more interesting collection made for bands associated with Benjamin H. Grierson. Grierson was a gifted musician but gained more celebrity as a cavalry officer in the American Civil War. Many bandsmen, and sometimes complete bands on both the Confederate and Unionist sides, enrolled in the army at the start of the war. The Grierson collection contains music from before and after the war, including works copied between 1846 and 1849 for the band at Youngstown, Ohio, where Grierson lived as a boy, and other sets arranged much later in his career. As is the case with the Manchester books, the greatest number are settings of dance tunes, marches and other light pieces, such as medleys and song tunes.[29]

The outstanding feature of amateur banding in the US has been its scale and variety. A large part of the massification of brass instrument playing originated in the ubiquitous college and high-school marching wind band tradition, which was promoted relentlessly by instrument manufacturers from the start of the twentieth century. The C. G. Conn company, for example, targeted it as its primary market and enlisted the services of John Philip Sousa for its endorsement.[30] The British model is just one of many forms that have clusters of intertest groups. The North American Brass Band Association (NABBA), which was formed in 1983, is the co-ordinating body for all-brass bands, and its alignment to the history and features of the British model is unambiguous.[31] Several local contests have been held, with its main annual national contest event having a championship section, three lower sections and a youth section. The set test pieces for national contests are usually works written for that purpose in Europe. For example, the advertised 2026 Championship test piece, as this book was being written, is *The Lost Circle* by Jan van der Roost, which was used for the 2024 British Open Contest. The first section test piece is Eric Ball's *Journey into Freedom*, written for the British National Contest in 1967. A good proportion of the NABBA adjudication panel is made up of British musicians. The most impressive feature in the United States has been the willingness of players to subscribe to the UK format when so many other options are available to them. Yet more surprising is their success in attracting audiences. Much of this speaks of the traditional role of brass bands in communities and the dedicated audiences that have gathered round them.

European integrations

Some European bands became interested in the British model from the 1950s, but substantial alignment did not gather pace until the 1970s. Within three decades, the best European bands easily matched their UK equivalents. The speed, enthusiasm and volume of European engagement was remarkable. By the opening years of the twenty-first century, the adoption of the British model in Europe was so developed that many continental bands were differentiated from the British only by their geography and the national affiliations to which they were aligned: otherwise, they shared an idiom, a repertoire, standards and common ambitions. The process that led to this conclusion started in the immediate post-war years, when a path of influence and expertise ran in one direction: British bands and several of their major person-alities were frequent visitors to European countries where the British model was exhibited and taught.

The model will also have been known through earlier radio broad-casting and gramophone recordings. In the war years, BBC broadcasting became a tool for propaganda that was often directed at foreign audi-ences through its Empire Entertainments Unit – later known as the Overseas Entertainment Unit. People in European countries became avid listeners. This was at a time when brass band music was broadcast almost daily on the BBC. Gramophone records of British brass bands were probably less accessible in Europe until the early 1950s, following the first release of 33rpm discs in 1948. There were tours of the Netherlands and Belgium by elite British bands such as Foden's and Munn and Felton's in the 1950s and later by Black Dyke and other major contest winners. They attracted large audiences and made an important impression. Denis Wright visited the Netherlands several times from 1951 as a band conductor and trainer. He was probably an important influence: he was a sound musician, a competent trainer and a systematic strategist. It took him little time to identify problems that could be rectified by more direct alignments to the British style. In his autobiography he reflected on the band at Groningen in the Netherlands and their 'tonal weakness', which he believed was caused by the 'two saxophones' which were 'musical interlopers'.[32] The advice was taken and replicated across the country. A year later, a letter appeared in the *British Bandsman* from a member of the Leeuwarden Band, predicting that 'in the not-too-distant future, brass band playing – as you know it – will cease to be a purely British affair'.[33] Wright was also to have a major influence on the development of the British model in Denmark, Sweden and Switzerland. After his retirement from the BBC in 1955, he applied himself to this activity full-time and with the zeal of a missionary: he forged links that developed into friendships and spent weeks at a time introducing bands to the British style. Developments in the Netherlands quickly yielded results. An international contest was held in Kerkrade in 1951 with the ambitious title 'The World Music Festival'. It attracted bands from other European countries and some from further afield. In 1953 and 1970 the contest was won by the National Band of New Zealand. The GUS (Footwear) Band (formerly Munn and Felton's), then at the height of its most successful period, won in 1966.

Visits to European countries by British brass bands and major personalities associated with them became more frequent from the 1960s. By this time, many European bands were imitating the British model. Visiting UK bands made a striking impression, as did the individual players, conductors and trainers who regularly travelled to Europe, effectively as musical consultants. The major attraction of the British instrumental format was always its unique sound, but a more obvious reason was that there was no tenable alternative for amateur bands of the size. It is easy to overlook the simple fact that, by the mid-twentieth century, the British brass band model had become established as the only distinctive, well-developed, standard form of large brass ensemble that was possessed of a large, varied and complex repertoire. The European *fanfare* and *harmonie* bands could have been judged alternatives but they were less standardised and held fewer attractions. Other recognisable combinations were either much smaller, aimed at professional players or, despite their appropriation of the title 'brass band', had a much more serendipitous and mixed format which did not rival the distinctive sound of the British model. Also, by this time, the British brass band system, with its 'sections' distinguished by technical competence, had generated a massive bespoke repertoire for bands of different technical abilities.

In 1973 the United Kingdom joined the European Economic Community (known also at that time as the Common Market). One of its provisions was that citizens of its member countries were allowed free and unhindered passage across all borders of the Community. The extent to which this hastened the adoption of the British format is difficult to assess, but it must have made integration easier and faster. This certainly happened in the music profession, where international collaborations, especially in the field of period performance, can be seen as exemplars of Europeanism as a cultural rather than a merely political and economic phenomenon. The subsequent growth of British-style banding was a European movement, but its formative stages occurred distinctively within individual countries, often led by enthusiastic personalities or groups. An interesting feature that soon became obvious was the apparently unquestioned adoption of contesting. The model could have been adopted without it, but it wasn't: contesting was always perceived as a component that could not be disaggregated from the totality of the British model. It followed that contesting had the same developmental impact on European banding as it did in the formative years of brass bands in Victorian Britain: it strengthened connections, raised standards, contributed decisively to the consolidation of musical idioms and provided the entire project with popular exposure and momentum.

The first contest for bands of the Netherlands was held in Utrecht in 1971. It became the Dutch National Contest a decade later, by which time there were sufficient bands for them to be distributed by ability into two sections. An open contest was also established, which attracted bands from other continental countries. The first Swiss brass band contest was held in Lausanne in 1972, and a Swiss Brass Band Federation was formed in 1978. A Belgian confederation had been formed a year earlier. In Denmark, contests were held for wind bands of any combination. By 1970, 18 of the 21 bands that competed were all-brass bands, and the UK model was consolidated in 1976. The first Norwegian Band Championship was held over three days in 1966, but of the 1,300 bands that subscribed to the Norwegian Bands Federation at that time, only 60 to 70 were all-brass and not all subscribed fully to the UK instrumental format, though it did not take long for there to be a gradual drift towards the model – Norway was to become one of the major centres for brass bands, where they receive significant support. The British model was also adopted in France, Germany and Sweden.[34] As this book was being written, 26 bands from ten countries, other than those of the UK, were listed in the top 50 ranked bands in the world.[35] Perhaps the most important development was the emergence of a group of elite European bands in different continental countries that were being regarded as mentors.

The differences between contesting regulations in Europe and Britain were relatively minor. A comparison between the main British contest and the European Championship provides an illustration of their proximity. Each requires players to be registered exclusively to the band with which she or he competes. Both the UK National and British Open contests require the performance of a set test piece which is usually commissioned for that purpose. The European Championship is the same, but bands must additionally compete, playing a work of their own choice of up to 20 minutes' duration, under the same conductor. The winner is the band with the highest consolidated score; a draw is avoided by prioritising the winner of the set test piece contest. Equally interesting is a difference concerning the permitted instrumental format. In each contest, the test pieces are written for the standard British brass band instrumentation. Regulations for the British National Contest state:

> The Contest is open to brass bands only, consisting of a maximum of 25 brass players plus percussionists, as required by the band. Brass instrumentation will be from the following list: Eb Soprano Cornet, Bb Cornet, Bb Flugel Horn, Eb Tenor Horn, Bb Baritone, Bb Euphonium, Slide Trombones, Eb and EEb Bass, Bb and BBb Bass. A brass player may only play ONE brass instrument, unless required [otherwise] by the score.[36]

The equivalent European Championship regulation is more compact but also more flexible:

> The Championship is open to brass bands only consisting of a maximum of 35 players including percussionists who should perform in dress of a uniform nature.[37]

In practice, the differences are slighter than might appear. There are usually five percussionists. So, a maximum of five additional brass players can be accommodated in the European contest. European bands usually add an additional cornet, and double any other part that is judged appropriate, but the scoring of the works performed remains that of the standard British format.

Europe and the band story: Past and future

The success of European bands, and the stimulus it has provided for brass bands everywhere, prompt thoughts about the brass band story more generally, especially the trajectory of its history and perhaps even its future. Irrespective of later twentieth-century developments identified elsewhere in this book, it is easy to identify fundamental continuities. The mid-Victorian origins of the British brass band provided a shape and momentum that remain largely intact. Those groups of relatively poor, working-class men unwittingly created a powerful tradition, of which bands throughout the world are modern-day beneficiaries. Three fundamental continuities are most conspicuous. The first and most important is the brass band sound and idiom, the roots of which were formed by about 1880. It has been refined through the creation of, and adjustments to, idiomatic repertoire and an incremental elevation of standards, but its fundamental components are easily distinguishable as a Victorian inheritance. The few historical and period-instrument performances of early repertoire that have been recorded, along with the musical evidence upon which those recordings have been based, support this idea.[38] There may have been subsequent refinements, but it all points to the British brass band's sound world being essentially a product of the nineteenth century.

The second critical continuity has been contesting and its persistent cultural centrality. Contesting has sometimes been a target of criticism within the brass band world, especially in the final quarter of the twentieth century when other aspects of modernisation were developing; but the contest ethos was resilient – its importance has never weakened. It is doubtful whether any other form of sophisticated instrumental music-making has been attached so strongly to contesting, and this too is an unambiguously Victorian product. It is easy to explain its histor-ical attraction, but the rationale for its endurance is both more challenging and more interesting. Contest successes are deployed by bands throughout the world as verifications of their worth, but their importance is greater than what winners take from them. Their essen-tial value touches all bands, even the perennial losers. It was contests that made the brass band story a national and international phenomenon and provided the structure that has sustained it. For the first century of their existence, band contests were one of the most popular forms of mass musical entertainment, but they also brought congregations of players together from far and wide, to listen to each other and feel part of a network – or a 'movement', as they preferred to call it. Those congregations have always been united by a commonly understood musical idiom. Contests were adopted outside Britain probably for similar reasons. Arguments about their aesthetic justification are rendered meaningless in all practical terms, because contests can't be disaggregated from the brass band story: they are one of its vital components and they function – as do all major cultural products – to bind people and things together into discernible and coherent shapes. They determine the events and episodes that make annual calendars, create connections and provide the spaces for common emotions. They also provide the stage for great performances which nourish the movement and keep it alive. The indebtedness to this part of the Victorian inheritance should also be a cause of pride rather than embarrassment, and European and American alignments should be celebrated as a continuation of this same story rather than a departure from it.

The third continuity is less easy to explain and impossible to quantify. It concerns amateurism in its most positive sense and the strength that practitioners gain from each other and their collective endeavour. This has probably always been the case, but it has become more overt and visible since the 1960s when the heavy masculinity of the brass band gave way to a more natural form and character. I have witnessed the approving glances that pass across bands amid performances and the congratulatory hugs (a female introduction) that often mark their conclusion. Playing in a brass band is a hobby, but few hobbies place such responsibilities on their participants, cause such bonds to form and promote such emotional well-being.

Internationalisation has become a key component of the enrichment of the brass band in the modern world. Globalisation is often overstated. It has an important place in any historical narrative, but globalisation did not neutralise national and local characteristics; in many ways, it made them more apparent. The performances of the best European and US bands easily match those of the British, but an attentive listener will discern differences at the most subtle levels. The generations of European conductors and composers, who have turned their talents to the genre, come with a separate set of experiences and cultural backgrounds. This has long been evidenced as a musical phenomenon in conservatories where students are encouraged to spend time at European or US institutions (and vice versa) because they are culturally different and need to be understood as part of a rounded education. So, while the growth of European bands can properly be seen as an export of a Victorian model, the force of influence is no longer in one direction, and this too must be seen as a positive development.

Positive developments are always to be welcomed because one of the perennial features that the British brass band story has revealed is a tendency for it to view itself in negative terms. Since the late nineteenth century, bands have been reported to be on the brink of extinction. This has never happened. Even in the 1960s, when a litany of events and trends seemed to give credibility to the voices of doom, the brass band story did not end: it changed and became enlightened.

As this book was being written, I read that 54 bands had entered the Yorkshire area contests; this is just one of the eight regional contests. The most viewed website for the brass band movement advertises a range of concerts, contests and other events.[39] In May 2025, the European Open Championship was held over four days in Stavanger, Norway. All tickets for each day were sold within 15 minutes of their availability. I noticed that 26 of Britain's universities were represented at a recent universities' band contest. I wish I had heard them, but I went to an 'entertainment contest' instead and heard 15 bands, each playing 25-minute programmes. One was my local band, which runs five separate bands – a championship-section band and four others, including a community band for all-comers. Its band room is active seven days a week. In the Buckinghamshire town of Amersham, a new purpose-built band centre accommodates the activities of its eight bands.[40] These stories are not exceptional. Such is also the case in European countries, where bands have become deeply woven into their communities.

One of the most interesting bands is Brass Band Treize Étoiles (fig. 34) of the canton of Valais in southern Switzerland. Formed in 1973, it has an A Band and a B Band. The A Band is the elite contesting group; the B Band competes in the first section and has an average age of 18. The name Treize Étoiles (thirteen stars) is derived from the thirteen stars that form the flag of Valais. The players who make up Brass Band Treize Étoiles are the best players drawn from the best village bands of Valais. Its success in contests has been remarkable, but it regularly performs in the towns of Valais and other Swiss cantons. This idea – that an elite band is drawn from a much wider constituency of playing activity – is not unique and is a commendable trend throughout Europe. Not just because it provides a sound local recruitment base for

34. Members of Brass Bund Treize Étoiles with the British Open trophy at the Symphony Hall, Birmingham, following the band's victory in 2024.

the best bands, but because of the significant contribution it makes to local musical life.

In October 2024 the British Open Brass Band Contest was held at the Symphony Hall in Birmingham. Eighteen bands competed, playing *The Lost Circle*, a new work by the Belgian composer Jan van der Roost. In all, including the percussionists and the conductors, 558 musicians took part. All but a couple of hundred seats had been sold in advance – the ticket-office supervisor said, 'It's always like this for the band contest.' The media company *Wobplay* (owned by the Salvation Army) streamed the event to audiences in Europe, America, Oceania, Asia and Africa. There were some terrific performances – the adjudicators must have been adjusting their winning order continuously. The band drawn number 15 seemed very young. All the solo cornet players were young women. I noticed that during the perform-ance the players were exchanging encouraging glances, and at the conclusion several embraced each other. Like most of the other bands, their techniques were easily up to the formidable challenges posed by *The Lost Circle*, but they had something extra: technically perfect, balanced and finely nuanced. The audience, attentive and learned, rose in acclamation. Everyone knew they were the winners. It was indeed Brass Band Treize Étoiles. It is difficult to see this as anything other than positive evidence of a continuation of the brass band story.

Glossary

The words and terms provided here are restricted to those used in the book. I have indicated in relevant endnotes where more detailed information can be found. The most succinct and accurate source is usually *The Cambridge Encyclopaedia of Brass Instruments*.

Advanced techniques	Term used to describe modernist performance techniques. They include lip glissandos, multiphonics (more than one note sounding simultaneously), growls and flutter-tonguing. Many of these effects originated in jazz or one of its precursors such as circus music.
Arrangement	Adaption of an existing piece of music for a different set of instruments or voices. 'Transcription' has a similar meaning.
Bell	The terminal (horn-shaped) flare of a brass instrument.
Bombardon	Valved bass instrument of the tuba type; the word fell out of use in the twentieth century. In the brass band world, the terms 'E-flat bass' and 'B-flat bass' are used rather than 'tuba', which is more commonly used for the orchestral instrument.
Bore	The bore of a brass instrument is the width of its tubing measured at any point by its diameter. The general descriptors most often used are: narrow bore, medium bore and wide bore. The wider the bore, the more mellow the sound. Another general determinant relating to bore is the proportion of conical and cylindrical tubing that is incorporated in any given instrument.

Brass instrument family
One of the two main families of wind instruments. The other is the woodwind family. The term can cause confusion because a 'brass instrument' is one in which notes are generated by the vibration of the player's lips. So, a saxophone (for example), though usually made of brass, is not a member of the 'brass instrument family' because the notes are produced by the vibration of a reed. Some lip-vibrated (brass) instruments are not made of brass or any other metal.

Chromatic trumpet
A trumpet used in England in the first half of the nineteenth century. It incorporated a short slide with a return spring operated by the player's left hand which gave access to notes outside a single harmonic series – thus, it was a *chromatic* trumpet.

Chromatic(ism)
A chromatic scale is one in which every successive semitone step is sounded. A chromatic brass instrument is one that can sound every semitone step between what is recognised as the lowest note in its range and the highest. On some instruments, low 'pedal' notes can be obtained that are below the chromatic range.

Clarino
Normally used to describe the very high register on a 'natural' trumpet (the clarino range). It is also used as an adjective for the playing of those notes (clarino playing). Being high in the harmonic series, the range contains notes that are adjacent in pitch.

Clef
Notation symbols placed at the start of each set of stave lines to define the name and sound of notes that are placed on or between them. Brass band music is unusual in that the parts of all valve instruments are written in the treble clef. This Victorian convention was intended to help groups of band players learn to play from written music.

Cornet
A valved brass instrument designed to play in the treble range. There are nine B flat cornets in a standard brass band and one soprano cornet (in E flat).

Cornett
Also called *cornetto* in Italian and *Zink* in German. A lip-vibrated treble instrument with finger holes similar to those on a recorder. It was made of wood and bound in leather, but sound was produced by players' lips vibrating in a mouthpiece. It flourished in the sixteenth and seventeenth centuries.

Cornopean
A three-valve treble brass instrument similar to the cornet. It is often used as a synonym for the early cornet or *cornet à pistons*, but it was an independent development, with distinct features. It may have been introduced by the London maker Charles Pace.

GLOSSARY

Dynamics
: In music, the word refers to variations in volume or loudness.

Embouchure
: The part of the lips on which the mouthpiece rests and through which air passes, causing the lips to vibrate to produce musical notes.

Entertainment contest
: A type of contest in which works, chosen by a band, are played within a set time – usually around 20 minutes. Bands often assemble programmes around an extramusical theme and incorporate audiovisual elements and spoken texts.

Flugelhorn
: The valved equivalent of the keyed bugle. It has the same range as the B flat cornet, but its wider tubing and bell produce a more mellow sound. Just one flugelhorn is included in the standard brass band.

French horn
: The type of horn used in orchestras. They are not included in British-format brass bands (the term is properly written as 'french horn' rather than 'French horn').

Full score
: The music used by a conductor. It lays out every part independently on successive horizontal staves.

Glissando
: An effect produced on the trombone by moving the slide in either direction when playing a sustained note. The effect can be imitated on valve instruments using the embouchure.

Harmonic series
: In the context of brass instruments, it refers to the series of notes that can be played on an instrument without adjustment to its tube length.

Harmonie
: In the eighteenth century, this term described a small band of mixed wind that performed *Harmoniemusik* in aristocratic settings. It has also been used loosely in subsequent periods to mean a wind band of the military type.

Hertz (Hz)
: The internationally recognised unit of measurement for pitch. It expresses pitch as the frequency of vibrations in a second. In modern standard tuning, the note A vibrates at 440 cycles a second (A440Hz).

Keyed bugle
: A treble instrument with keys. Patented by Joseph Haliday in 1810. It fell into obsolescence by the late 1870s. The flugelhorn is a valve version of the keyed bugle.

Mouthpiece
: The detachable part of a brass instrument that rests on a player's embouchure. They come in various designs but always serve the same purpose.

Mute — Device placed in the bell of a brass instrument to change the character (timbre) of its sound. There are many different designs that generate different timbres and effects. There is evidence of brass instrument muting from the sixteenth century. Many modern mute designs were introduced for jazz effects.

Natural instrument — A modern term for historic brass instruments that had no mechanisms such as valves, keys or slides to change the pitch of notes.

Nominal pitch — The pitch of a brass instrument as defined by the harmonic series that can be sounded without the use of valves or the extension of the slide of a trombone. So, for example, an E flat tenor horn can sound the E flat harmonic series without depressing valves.

Ophicleide — A baritone/bass keyed instrument: the bass equivalent of the keyed bugle. It was invented by Halary and patented by him in 1821. It fell into obsolescence in the late 1870s, but it is played well by some modern period-instrument performers.

Part-book — A manuscript book in which the parts for an individual band member were copied, usually by hand – the part-book for the first trombone, second horn, etc.

Pedal note — The lowest note of a harmonic series – also referred to as the 'fundamental'. Pedal notes are usually regarded as lying outside the normal tessitura of an instrument but are often used for effects. Exceptions to this generalisation are the serpent and ophicleide, which have such notes in their range.

Percussion — Instruments that are sounded by one part striking another. Untuned percussion instruments (such as a side drum) have no discernible pitch. Tuned percussion such as xylophones can be played melodically.

Period performance — Also called historically informed performance (HIP). It refers to performances in which the circumstances that prevailed in the period when the music was first heard (original instruments, performance conventions, etc.) are imitated.

Pitch — A term applied in several ways and contexts, but it primarily refers to the frequency of vibrations of musical notes. See also 'Pitch standard' and 'Nominal pitch'. The pitch of a note is usually signified by a letter and a number followed by Hz – such as A440Hz. Purist acousticians maintain that frequency is a measurable physical phenomenon while pitch is a perception: the two are closely related but not identical.

GLOSSARY

Pitch standard — A method for ensuring that instruments are in tune with each other. The modern global standard is A440Hz, meaning that the note A is in tune when it registers a frequency of 440 vibrations or oscillations a second.

Range — The range is the (chromatic) pitch compass defined by the distance between the lowest and highest notes usually written for an instrument or voice.

Repiano cornet — Name given to a brass band part played by one of the B flat cornets. The part usually supports (or 'doubles') one of the other parts as required. 'Repiano' probably derives from the Italian word meaning 'filling' – the parts *fill in* or support other musical lines.

Sackbut — Also given in other spellings (sacbut, sagbutt, etc.), the word used in Britain before the nineteenth century for trombone.

Saxhorn — The name given to a family of valve instruments invented by Adophe Sax. Individual instruments in the family eventually acquired different names.

Score — The music from which a conductor conducts (see also 'Short score' and 'Full score').

Serpent — The baritone/bass version of the cornett; the name derives from the instrument's shape.

Short score — An abbreviated score. In a brass band, it usually takes the form of a solo cornet part with printed subscript annotations.

Slide — A slide trombone has a 'U'-shaped cylindrical slide that allows its player to adjust the length of tubing of the instrument when playing. Slides are also fitted to valve instruments so that they can be finely tuned – a tuning slide adjusts the overall pitch, a valve slide adjusts the tuning of a valve: in both cases the adjustments are small.

Soprano cornet — A valved brass instrument pitched in E flat: higher than the other cornets – just one is included in a standard brass band.

Standard brass band instrumentation — The instrumental format for which brass band music has been scored since the start of the twentieth century. It is made up of soprano cornet in E flat, 9 Cornets in B flat, flugelhorn, three tenor Horns in E flat, two euphoniums, two baritones, two tenor trombones, one bass trombone, two tubas in E flat, two tubas in B flat. Percussion instruments (tuned and untuned) as required.

GLOSSARY

Tessitura	The most used part of the range of an instrument or voice. For example, a bass trombone is usually played using the lower notes of its range, even though it has other higher notes in its compass.
Test piece	A work written for, or used in, brass band contests.
Timbre	The distinctive aural quality of a musical sound. The same note, at the same pitch and volume, played on a euphonium and a trombone, differs only in timbre.
Valves	Mechanical devices incorporated into brass instruments which allow the player to instantly alter the length of tubing through which vibrating air is travelling. In a brass band, most valve instruments require three valves (operated with the right hand) to be chromatic. Some modern instruments have four valves.

Appendix 1

Instruments and people of the first generation of brass bands

There was never a formal announcement about the standard instrumental format of the British brass band, but a consensus seems to have formed by the late 1870s, largely based on the formations used by the most successful band trainers/conductors of the time.

Before the twentieth century, most bands were formed expediently, often using the instruments sold by manufacturers as starter sets. These were frequently supplemented by other instruments if players were available locally, and might have included keyed bugles, ophicleides and even clarinets. Irrespective of such improvisations, there is plenty of evidence to show that Victorian bandmasters/trainers made careful and intelligent musical judgements. The application forms that bands had to complete to enter contests allow us to identify the instrumentations used at the first Crystal Palace contests in the early 1860s. They also indicate the music each band played but, frustratingly, the actual arrangements are mostly lost. A rare exception is the repertoire of the Cyfarthfa Band from south Wales which flourished between about 1846 and 1878 and for which complete sets of parts survive. Otherwise, the best available sources for widely used repertoire are brass band 'journals': sets of printed music supplied monthly for an annual subscription fee. Journal music survives in many archives, libraries and private collections. In the first decades of the brass band, these journals, or locally adapted versions of them, were probably the most performed brass band music. They were intentionally written to be adaptable for the instruments at hand. The music was not demanding but it was intended to be enjoyable for performers and entertaining for listeners. The arrangements were most often the work of military bandmasters and almost all pieces contained were arrangements of existing works.

Another set of information provides an impression of the musical shape of the first generation of contesting brass bands; it is drawn from surviving entry forms of bands that entered the four contests held at London's Crystal Palace between 1860 and 1863. The extracts given here are also no more than a sample intended to provide a general impression.

Brass band journal music

The four instrumentations given below show different early stages in the development of printed music for bands. The earliest is the journal published by Wessel & Co. It adds cornet parts to parts for established brass instruments such as trumpets, french horns, the keyed bugle and ophicleide. Later journals show a clear transition to the new generation of brass band (cornets and saxhorn instruments). It is important to stress that this music was almost always adapted for the instruments at hand.

1844	*Wessell's Brass Band Journal*	Solo Cornet-à-Pistons, first and second Cornet-à-Pistons, two Horns, three Trombones, and Ophicleide with *ad libitum* parts for D flat Cornet-à-Pistons, [keyed] Bugle, two Horns, three Trumpets and Kettle Drums.
1860	*Davidson's Journal*	1st, 2nd and 3rd Cornet in B flat, Repiano Cornet in B flat, Soprano Cornet in E flat, 1st and 2nd Horn in E flat, 1st and 2nd Baritone in B flat, Tenor Trombone, Euphonium in E flat, Percussion.
1860	*Chappell's Journal*	1st Solo Piston, 2nd Solo Piston, 1st Piston or Flugel Horn in B flat, 2nd Piston or Solo Horn in B flat, Piccolo Piston in E flat or E flat clarinet, Alt horn in B flat, 2 Trumpets in E flat ad lib, 2 Corni [french horns] in E flat ad lib, 2 Sax horns in F, Euphonium, 1st and 2nd Trombone, 3rd Trombone, Basso.
1869	*Distin's Brass Band Journal* (published by Boosey)	For a band of ten: 1st Cornet in B flat, 2nd ditto; 1st Cornet in E flat; 1st and 2nd Tenors in E flat; Euphonion; Bombardon; Side and Bass drum. Extra parts may be had for: Repiano Cornet in B flat, Cornets 3rd and 4th in B flat; Solo Tenor in E flat, 2nd Baritone in B flat, 1st and 2nd Trombone in B flat, Bass Trombone and Contra Bass in B flat.

Persons and their occupations in Crystal Palace entry forms[1]

The contests were organised by Enderby Jackson in association with the Crystal Palace Company and various railway companies. All bands were required to submit an entry form. Each player was named, along with his occupation and the instrument he played, and the title of the music the band would perform was also provided (in fact, some submitted two works, while some left this section blank). Players' occupations were needed to verify their amateur status. A reproduction of an original entry form is given as fig. 11, p. 74.

Not all entry forms survive, and the selection is not fully representative of those that do. For example, most of the bands came from northern counties of England.

I have included information about bands from the Midlands and the south because it provides interesting information but it is not an accurate representation of the proportion of southern bands that entered. Only one band from Wales competed (Cyfarthfa) but its entry form is lost. It appears that there were none from Scotland or Ireland.

No interventions have been made to correct the original sources other than a few explanatory annotations inserted in square brackets. I have added the year of the contests where this has been available. Some forms were not fully completed. Variances in the names of instruments ('euphonium' and 'euphonion', for example) reflect the transitionary stage of those relatively new words. Spelling errors sometimes reflect the same thing, but more frequently they show that the contest forms were often completed by men who had had very little schooling and probably read and wrote music better than they did words.

Brighouse Band Yorkshire and Huddersfield (1860) Grand Selection from Lucrecia Borgia Donezetti	Stalybridge Old Band (1860) Overture, William Tell, Rossini	Netherton, East Worcestershire, near Dudley (1860) Overture in Handel
Nm George [?] Occ [?] Inst Soperano D flat	Lead John Reece Mst James A. Shelling	Nm John Wooldridge Occ Spade Finisher Inst Cornet a piston Ab
Nm Wm ? Occ Cotton twister Inst Soperano 2nd Bb	Nm James A. Shelling Occ Professor Inst Cornet Bb	Nm George Talbot Occ Clerk Inst Soprano Db
Nm Abraham Thornton Occ Stone Pitcher Inst Solo Cornett in Ab	Nm John Reece (Leader) Occ Roller Coverer Inst Soprano Eb	Nm Benjamin Connop [?] Occ Farmer Inst Cornet a piston Ab
Nm John [?] Occ Dyer Inst Cornett 2nd in Ab	Nm William Schofield Occ Iron Molder Inst Soprano Eb	Nm John Craig Occ Cordwainer Inst Cornet a piston Ab
Nm Benjamin Tifany Occ Wire Drawer Inst Cornett 3rd in Ab	Nm William Hilton Occ School Master Inst Cornett Bb	Nm Thomas Woodhouse Occ Wood Turner Inst Cornet a piston Ab
Nm Joseph Biatey Occ Dyer Inst Cornett 3rd in Ab	Nm Columbus Sykes Occ Cotton Spinner Inst Cornett Bb	Nm James Westwood Occ Forgeman Inst Cornet a piston Ab
Nm Edward Roberts Occ Cotton Twister Inst Tenor Sax in Eb	Nm David Mellor Occ Overlooker Inst Cornett Bb	Nm John Perry Occ Horsenail Maker Inst Tenor Sax Db
Nm Joseph Jackman Occ Stone Mason Inst Tenor Sax in Db	Nm Samuel Reece Occ Joiner Inst Cornett Bb	Nm John Raybould Occ Spade Finisher Inst Tenor Sax Eb

Brighouse Band Yorkshire and Huddersfield (1860) Grand Selection from Lucrecia Borgia Donezetti	Stalybridge Old Band (1860) Overture, William Tell, Rossini	Netherton, East Worcestershire, near Dudley (1860) Overture in Handel
Nm James Shaw Occ Stone Pitcher Inst Trombone 1st in G [?]	Nm Joseph Hinchliffe Occ Calico Weaver Inst Flugal Horn Bb	Nm Thomas Simmins Occ Blacksmith Inst Tenor Sax Db
Nm Syrius Broomhead Occ Stone Pitcher Inst Trombone 2nd in G [?]	Nm Samuel Tootill Occ Calico Weaver Inst Althorn Cb	Nm Joseph Granger Occ Moulder Inst Baritone Bb
Nm Joseph Sutcliffe Occ [?] Inst Trombone Bass in G	Nm Samuel Stubbs Occ Calico Weaver Inst Althorn Cb	Nm Dudley Hill Occ Horsenailmaker Inst Baritone Bb
Nm Dyson Waikes Occ Stone Pitcher Inst Sax Horn Bass in Ab	Nm Seth Gill Occ Joiner Inst Baritone	Nm John Wilson Occ Moulder Inst Euphonia Bass Bb
Nm David Womersly Occ Wire Drawer Inst Ophecliede 1st [?] in C	Nm James Willerton Occ Skip Maker Inst Alto Trombone F	Nm Samuel Danlo [?] Occ Miner Inst Euphonia Bass Ab
Nm John Schofield Occ Dyer Inst Ophecliede 2nd in C?	Nm Hiram Schofield Occ Painter Inst Tenor Trombone C	Nm William Westwood Occ Forgeman Inst Euphonia Bass Ab
Nm George Green Occ Wire Drawer Inst Ophecliede 2nd in C	Nm Joe Green Occ Calico Weaver Inst Bass Trombone G	Nm Edwin Wooldridge Occ Spade Finisher Inst Ophecleide C
Nm Thos Shaw Occ Wever Inst Ophecliede Bass in C	Nm John Mac[?] Occ Labourer Inst Ophecliede C	Nm William Bashford Occ Horsenailmaker Inst Bombardon Eb
Nm Samuel Hirst Occ Carrier [?] Inst Contra Bass in Eb	Nm Francis Walsh Occ Calico Weaver Inst Ophecliede C	Nm Joseph Pearson Occ Horsenailmaker Inst Bombardon Eb
Nm Charles Sheard Occ Wever Inst Contra Bass in Eb	Nm Thomas Cunliffe Occ Overlooker Inst Bombardone Cb	Nm John Scott Occ Miner Inst Bass Drum
	Nm Edward Cooper Occ Calico Weaver Inst Contra Bombardone Cb	

Mossley Amateur Brass Band, Lancashire, near Staley Bridge (1860) Grand Selection 'Sonambula', Bellini Chors 'Worthy is the Lamb and Amen', Handel	Allendale Town Sax Horn Band (1860) Selection from Attila, Verdi Selection from Ernani, Verdi	16 Kent Rifle Volunteers, Sittingbourne (1860) [?]
Nm William Taylor Occ Cotton Operative Inst Soprano Sax Horn E♭ and D♭	Nm James Holmes (Leader) Occ Lead Ore Smelter Inst Sax Soprano D♭	Nm George Young Occ Naturalist Inst Soprano Cornet
Nm Roger Fawcit Occ Labourer Inst Solo Cornet E♭ and B♭	Nm Christy Holmes Occ Engineer Inst Solo cornet A♭	Nm William Harris Occ Confectioner Inst 1st Cornet
Nm Edward Robinson Occ Joiner Inst 2nd Cornet A♭ and B♭	Nm John Clemitson Occ Lead Ore Smelter Inst Cornet A♭	Nm Andrew Goodhew Occ Boot maker Inst Solo Cornet
Nm James E. Robinson Occ Cotton Operative Inst 3rd Cornet A♭ and B♭	Nm Thomas Harrison Occ Lead Ore Miner Inst Cornet A♭	Nm Henry [Harry?] Renshaw Occ Plumber Inst 2nd Cornet
Nm James Brooks Occ Cotton Operative Inst 3rd Cornet A♭ and B♭	Nm John Barrow Occ Lead Ore Smelter Inst Cornet A♭	Nm Henry G. Pilcher Occ Clerk Inst 2nd Cornet
Nm Joseph M. Robinson Occ Joiner Inst Flugel Horn A♭ and B♭	Nm William [?] Clemitson Occ Lead Ore Smelter Inst Cornet A♭	Nm Freairic [?] Harry [?] Occ Confectioner Inst Alto Sax Horn
Nm Thomas Broadbent Occ Cotton Operative Inst Sax Tuba A♭ and B♭	Nm Joseph Barrow Occ Lead Ore Smelter Inst Sax Alto A♭	Nm Richard Rossiter Occ Upholster Inst 1st Tenor
Nm Charles J. Robinson Occ Grocer Inst Tenor Sax Tuba 1st E♭	Nm Thomas Fairlamb Occ Joiner Inst Sax Alto A♭	Nm Daniel Barns Occ Grocer Inst 2nd Tenor
Nm John Greaves Occ Woollen Operative Inst Tenor Sax Tuba 2nd E♭	Nm William Fairlamb Occ Joiner Inst Sax Tenor D♭	Nm James Jay Occ Tailor Inst Baritone

Mossley Amateur Brass Band, Lancashire, near Staley Bridge (1860) Grand Selection *'Sonambula'*, Bellini Chors 'Worthy is the Lamb and Amen', Handel	Allendale Town Sax Horn Band (1860) Selection from Attila, Verdi Selection from Ernani, Verdi	16 Kent Rifle Volunteers, Sittingbourne (1860) [?]
Nm William Byrom Occ Cotton Operative Inst Tenor Sax Tuba 3rd Eb	Nm Jacob Clemitson Occ Joiner Inst Sax Tenor Db	Nm James Jackson Occ Bookmaker Inst Euophonium
Nm James Rhodes Occ Cotton Operative Inst Baritone Bb	Nm John Dickinson Occ Labourer Inst Sax Barytone Db	Nm Charles Smith Occ Upholster Inst Bombardon
Nm Samuel Taylor Occ Woollen Operative Inst Euphonion Bb	Nm William Russell Occ Shoemaker Inst Tenor Trombone C	Nm Charles Spin Occ Tailor Inst Side Drum
Nm Edward Greaves Occ Cotton Operative Inst Bass Bb	Nm Thomas Russell Occ Tailor Inst Bass Trombone G	Nm John Cook Occ Tailor Inst Bass Drum
Nm John Sykes Occ Cotton Operative Inst Tenor Trombone C	Nm Roger Routledge Occ Shoemaker Inst Ophecleide C	
Nm Robert Schofield Occ Cotton Operative Inst Bass Trombone G	Nm Joseph Coulson Occ Mason Inst Sax Solo Bass Ab	
Nm James Sykes Occ Cotton Operative Inst Contre Bass Eb	Nm John Robinson Occ Labourer Inst Sax Bass Bb	
Nm Abel Heys Occ Woollen Operative Inst Contre Bass Eb	Nm Thomas Dickinson Occ Lead Ore Miner Inst Contra Bass Db	
Nm William Howard Occ Cotton Operative Inst Contra Bass Eb	Nm George Russell Occ Labourer Inst Contra Bass Double Bb	

Liverpool Alliance (1860)	Second Shropshire Rifle Volunteer Corps (1861)	Sherwood Brass Band, Sutton in Ashfield (1862)
Overture, Temptation by T. Morris Waltzes, Whisper of Love by S. Richardson	**Cavatina 'Giovani d'Arco', Verdi**	**Grand Selection Bianca, Balfe. Selection Ruy Blas, Howard Glover**
Nm I. G. Rungden Occ Bandmaster Inst Soprano E♭	Nm John Moore Occ Actuary of Savings Bank Inst Cornetto E♭	Nm Amos Caunt Occ Stocking Weaver Inst Cornet E♭
Nm I. Sullivan Occ Shipwright Inst Cornet B♭	Nm William Ralphs Occ Joiner Inst 1st Cornet B♭	Nm John Naylor Occ Stocking Weaver Inst Cornet E♭
Nm I. Downey Occ Man Chemist Inst Cornet B♭	Nm William Marsh Occ Engine Fitter Inst Repiano Cornet B♭	Nm Redfern Scott Occ Stocking Weaver Inst Cornet B♭
Nm P. Tracey Occ White Smith Inst Cornet B♭	Nm James Ralphs Occ Bricklayer Inst 2nd Cornet B♭	Nm John Ellis Occ Stocking Weaver Inst Cornet B♭
Nm G. Rungden Occ Clerk Inst Cornet B♭	Nm Thomas Cotterill Occ Joiner Inst 3rd Cornet B♭	Nm Joseph Learson Occ Stocking Weaver Inst Cornet B♭
Nm T. Fagan Occ Joiner Inst Cornet B♭	Nm Edward Wynn Occ Brazier Inst 1st Horn E♭	Nm Benjamin Pitt Occ Stocking Weaver Inst Alto Horn or flugel B♭
Nm S. Berry Occ Porter Inst Sax Horn E♭	Nm Thomas Lutner Occ Moulder Inst 2nd Horn E♭	Nm Samuel Oldham Occ Stocking Weaver Inst Alt Horn E♭
Nm W. Spence Occ Watchmaker Inst Sax Horn E♭	Nm Henry Bilston Occ Engine Fitter Inst 1st Tenor Saxhorn E♭	Nm Henry Ascroft Occ Stocking Weaver Inst Alt Horn E♭
Nm I. Dugdale Occ Flagger Inst Barytone B♭	Nm Thomas Wycherley Occ Gardener Inst 2nd Tenor Saxhorn E♭	Nm John Elliott Occ Fitter Inst Tenor Horn E♭

Liverpool Alliance (1860)	Second Shropshire Rifle Volunteer Corps (1861)	Sherwood Brass Band, Sutton in Ashfield (1862)
Overture, Temptation by T. Morris **Waltzes, Whisper of Love by S. Richardson**	**Cavatina 'Giovani d'Arco', Verdi**	**Grand Selection Bianca, Balfe. Selection Ruy Blas, Howard Glover**
Nm I. Musker Occ Sampler Inst Barytone B♭	Nm Jack Harrison Occ Cooper Inst 3rd Tenor Saxhorn E♭	Nm John Dennis Occ Stocking Weaver Inst Bariton B♭
Nm W. Doyle Occ Joiner Inst Sax Bass B♭	Nm Thomas Hubball Occ Joiner Inst 1st Baryton Saxhorn B♭	Nm Samuel Hall Occ Stocking Weaver Inst Trombone Tenor C
Nm I. Kilroy Occ Smith Inst Sax Bass B♭	Nm Joseph Ralphs Occ Bricklayer Inst 2nd Baryton Saxhorn B♭	Nm James Handley Occ Stocking Weaver Inst Trombone Tenor C
Nm I. Killen Occ Porter Inst Contre Bass E♭	Nm Thomas Wynn Occ Sawyer Inst Euphonion C	Nm Joseph Scott Occ Stocking Weaver Inst Trombone Bass G
Nm I. Jones Occ Clerk Inst Tenor Trombone C	Nm John Lewis Occ Photographic Artist Inst Ophicleide C	Nm Edward Handley Occ Stocking Weaver Inst Trombone Bass G
Nm W. Hill Occ P.C. Letter Carrier Inst Cymbals	Nm Thomas Banks Occ Stone Mason Inst Bombardon E♭	Nm Edward Linhe Occ Stocking Weaver Inst Ophicliede Solo C
Nm W. Jones Occ Stoker Inst Bass Drum	Nm Samuel Jones Occ Joiner Inst Bass Drum	Nm Samuel Cauldwell Occ Stocking Weaver Inst Uphonian Bass B♭
Nm G. Williams Occ French Polisher Inst Side Drum		Nm William Green Occ Stocking Weaver Inst Bombardon E♭
Nm I. Fletcher Occ Cabinet Maker Inst Side Drum		Nm Charles Learson Occ Stocking Weaver Inst Bombardon E♭
		Nm John Scott Occ Stocking Weaver Inst Drum

Doncaster Volunteer Rifle Corps (1860) Grand Selection Opera *Martha*, Flotow		Mossley Amateur Brass Band, near Staley Bridge (1861) Grand Selection '*Lucrezia Borgia*', Donizetti Grand Scena, 'The Execution', *Il Travatore*, Verdi		Melbourne [Derbyshire] (1862) Selection from D[onizetti's] *Lucrezia Borgia*	
Nm	G.F. Birkinshaw	Nm	William Taylor	Lead	Leonard Warren
Occ	Professor of Music	Occ	Operative		
Inst	Soprano Sax Db	Inst	Soprano Sax Db		
Nm	Boy J. Hyde	Nm	James Brooks	Nm	Henry Newbold
Occ	At School	Occ	Operative	Occ	Warp Hand
Inst	Soprano Sax Db	Inst	Soprano Sax Db	Inst	Soprano Sax Db
Nm	B. Hyde	Nm	Roger Fawcett	Nm	Henry Warren
Occ	Fitter	Occ	Operative	Occ	Gardener
Inst	Solo Cornet Ab	Inst	1st Cornet Ab	Inst	Soprano Sax Db
Nm	J. Green	Nm	Tenas [?] Buckley	Nm	Samuel Moore
Occ	Fitter	Occ	Operative	Occ	Engineer
Inst	Cornet 1st Ab	Inst	Ripiena Cornet Ab	Inst	Soprano Sax Db
Nm	Wm Parsons	Nm	James E. Robinson	Nm	Leonard Warren
Occ	Fitter	Occ	Operative	Occ	Grocer etc [?]
Inst	Cornet 2nd Ab	Inst	2nd Cornet Ab	Inst	Cornopean Ab
Nm	J. Crawshaw	Nm	Thomas Broadbent	Nm	Newton Hibbert
Occ	Apprentice to a Stone Mason	Occ	Mechanic	Occ	Warp Hand
Inst	Cornet 2nd Ab	Inst	3rd Cornet Ab	Inst	Cornopean Ab
Nm	R. Crawshaw	Nm	James Howard	Nm	Robert Parker
Occ	Iron and Brass Turner	Occ	Operative	Occ	Saddler
Inst	Cornet 3rd Ab	Inst	4th Cornet Ab	Inst	Cornopean Ab
Nm	John Ward	Nm	Edward Robinson	Nm	John Tivey
Occ	Apprentice to the China and Glass Trade	Occ	Carpenter	Occ	Gardener
Inst	Cornet 3rd Ab	Inst	Tenor Primo Eb	Inst	Cornopean Ab
Nm	T. Green	Nm	Thomas Sykes	Nm	William Cook
Occ	Apprentice to be a Gas Fitter	Occ	Operative	Occ	Warp Hand
Inst	Althorn 1st Eb and Db	Inst	Tenor 2nd Eb	Inst	Cornopean Ab
Nm	John Hewitt	Nm	William Sidebottom	Nm	George Watham
Occ	Fitter	Occ	Operative	Occ	Warp hand
Inst	Althorn 2nd Eb and Db	Inst	Tenor 3rd Eb	Inst	Tenor Sax Db

Doncaster Volunteer Rifle Corps (1860) Grand Selection Opera *Martha*, Flotow	Mossley Amateur Brass Band, near Staley Bridge (1861) Grand Selection '*Lucrezia Borgia*', Donizetti Grand Scena, 'The Execution', *Il Travatore*, Verdi	Melbourne [Derbyshire] (1862) Selection from D[onizetti's] *Lucrezia Borgia*
Nm Wm Allen Occ Carriage Body Maker Inst Baritone B♭ and A♭	Nm Joseph Sidebottom Occ Operative Inst Baritone B♭	Nm Maxwilliam Sylvester Occ Warp Hand Inst Tenor Sax D♭
Nm James Butler Occ Fitter Inst Tenor Trombone C	Nm Samuel Taylor Occ Bobbin Turner Inst Solo Bass B♭	Nm Joseph Bowley Occ Mechanic Inst B♭ Bass Sax
Nm Wm Morcomb Occ Carriage Painter Inst Bass Trombone G	Nm Edward Greves Occ Operative Inst Bass Sax B♭	Nm Isaac Harvey Occ Pot Maker Inst B♭ Barytone
Nm J. Hardwick Occ Brass Turner Inst Solo Ophecliede C	Nm James Sykes (first public player on a 4 keyed . . . [?] Occ Operative Inst Bombardon E♭	Nm James Salsbury Occ Warp Hand Inst Trombone C
Nm H. Parkin Occ Joiner Inst Bass B♭	Nm Robert Schofield Occ Operative Inst Bombarton E♭	Nm Thomas Tivey Occ Wheelwright Inst Ophicleide C
Nm T. Hedge Occ Carriage Body Maker Inst Bombardone E♭	Nm Abel Heys [?] Occ Woollen Manufacturer Inst Bombardon E♭	Nm Edward Dunnicliff Occ Book Maker Inst Bombardon E♭
Nm C. Hardwick Occ Fitter Inst Bombardone E♭	Nm John Sykes Occ Operative Inst Tenor Trombone C	Nm William Vincey Occ Coal Dealer Inst Drum
Nm S. Salmon Occ Fitter Inst Bombardone E♭	Nm Charles J. Robinson Occ Grocer Inst Bass Trombone G	
	Nm Thomas Haigh Occ Carpenter Inst Drummer and book carrier	

(John Foster & Son) Black Dike Mills, Queenshead, near Halifax (1860)	W. L. Marriner Band, also the Band of the 35th West York Rifle Volunteer Corps, Keighley (1861)	Dodsworth's Bradford Brass Band (1862)
Selection, La Sonnambula, Bellini	**Selection from 'Attila', Verdi Mus2 Overture to 'Zampa', Herold**	**Ernani, Verdi, Maritana, Wallace**
Nm Galloway Frank Occ Warehouseman Inst Soprano Cornet E♭	Nm Joseph Turner Occ Wool Sorter Inst Cornet A♭	Nm I.W. Dodsworth Occ Band Master Inst Soprano Cornet E♭
Nm Jonas Jagger Occ Warp Dresser Inst Brass Clarionet E♭	Nm David Mitchell Occ Blacksmith Inst Soprano D♭	Nm A. Horner Occ Overlooker Inst 2nd Cornet E♭
Nm William Rushworth Occ Wool Sorter Inst Solo Cornet B♭	Nm John Crossley Occ Wool Sorter Inst Soprano D♭	Nm J. Bakes Occ Warp Dresser Inst Solo Cornet B♭
Nm Jubal Rothera [?] Occ Wool Sorter Inst Re-piano Cornet B♭	Nm Henry Whitaker Occ Wool Sorter Inst Cornet A♭	Nm A. Oddy Occ Mechanic Inst Repiano Cornet B♭
Nm John Rushworth Occ Machine Wool Comber Inst Second Cornet B♭	Nm Cyrus Haggas Occ Pupil Teacher Inst Cornet A♭	Nm [?] Bentley Occ Cabinet Maker Inst 2nd Cornet B♭
Nm Joe [?]son Occ Warp Twister Inst Second Cornet B♭	Nm James Ambler Occ Paper Manufacturer Inst Horn E♭	Nm W. Burnley Occ Clerk Inst Flugel Horn B♭
Nm Robert Rushworth Occ Warp Dresser Inst Alto Sax B♭	Nm William Midgley Occ Shop Assistant Inst Horn E♭	Nm S. Wheelhouse Occ Weaver Inst Valve Trombone B♭
Nm Jonas Fawcett Occ Wheelwright Inst French Horn B♭	Nm Joseph Wood Occ Wool Sorter Inst Alt Horn D♭	Nm J. Dodsworth Occ Office Boy Inst Euphonium B♭
Nm Abram Halliday Occ Cordwainer Inst Tenor Sax B♭	Nm William Clapham Occ Iron Founder Inst Baritone A♭	Nm [?] Wheelhouse Occ Overlooker Inst Bombardon E♭
Nm John Smith Occ Wool Sorter Inst Fugle Horn B♭	Nm Robert Gladstone Occ Wool Sorter Inst Bass D♭	Nm Thos. Leach Occ Baildon Inst Bombardon E♭

(John Foster & Son) Black Dike Mills, Queenshead, near Halifax (1860)	W. L. Marriner Band, also the Band of the 35th West York Rifle Volunteer Corps, Keighley (1861)	Dodsworth's Bradford Brass Band (1862)
Selection, La Sonnambula, Bellini	Selection from 'Attila', Verdi Mus2 Overture to 'Zampa', Herold	Ernani, Verdi, Maritana, Wallace
Nm Greenwood Firth Occ Warp Dresser Inst Tenor Trombone C	Nm Holmes Smith Occ Warp Dresser Inst Tenor Trombone B♭	Nm D. Bailey Occ Furnace Man Inst Bombardon E♭
Nm Abram Oldfield Occ Machine Wool Comber Inst Bass Trombone C	Nm William Ackroyd Occ Wool Sorter Inst Tenor Trombone B♭	Nm W. Graham Occ Warp Dresser Inst Trombone G
Nm William Firth Occ Wool Washer Inst Bombardon E♭	Nm Robert Greenwood Occ Wool Sorter Inst Bass Trombone G	Nm Scarbro Pickard Occ Stone Mason Inst Trombone G
Nm Samuel Halliday Occ Cordwainer Inst Bombardon E♭	Nm Joseph Clapham Occ Mechanic Inst Bass D♭	Nm I. Robinson Occ Stone Mason Inst Tenor Trombone B♭
Nm John Taylor Occ Warp Dresser Inst Euphonium B♭	Nm John Ogden Occ Overlooker Inst Bombardon E♭	Nm W. Burley Occ Brass Moulder Inst Tenor Sax E♭
Nm John Aldroyd Occ Wool Sorter Inst Baritone B♭	Nm John Banks Occ Gardener Inst Bombardon E♭	Nm J. Firth Occ Warp Dresser Inst Tenor Sax E♭
Nm James Greenwood Occ Warehouseman Inst Ophecleide C	Nm John Midgley Occ Music Seller Inst Double Slide Contra Bass Trombone bb	Nm F. Bakes Occ French Polisher Inst Tenor Sax E♭
Nm Samuel Longbottom Occ Manufacturer Inst Conductor	Nm John Sugden Occ Joiner Inst Conductor (not Leader)	

Messrs Bagnal's Gold's [Hill] Sax Horn Band, near Birmingham (1860) Scene, Aria, Opera, Miro by Verdi Scene, Placco by W. Perry	The Portsmouth Sax Horn Band	Cestrian Amateur Band [Chester]
Nm W. Blandford Occ Musician Inst Bandmaster / Cornet Bb	Nm Wm Besant Occ Professional Inst 1st Cornet Bb	Nm Charles Hull Occ Bandmaster Inst Ab Cornet
Nm George Rogers Occ Pattern Maker Inst Cornet Bb	Nm Chas Caswell Occ Wheelwright Inst 1st Cornet Bb	Nm Thomas Daires Occ Newspaper Clerk Inst Ab Cornet
Nm William Maybury Occ Shingler Inst Cornet Bb	Nm Henry Lee Occ Baker Inst Cornet	Nm Charles Long Occ Fitter Inst Ab Cornet
Nm John Radford Occ Sawyer Inst Cornet Bb	Nm James Hatchard Occ Painter Inst Eb Soprano	Nm David Roberts Occ Book-keeper Inst Db Cornet
Nm William Stevenson Occ Machine Tender Inst Cornet Bb	Nm Henry Reed Occ Joiner Inst Bb Alt Horn	Nm Henry Hiatt Occ Printer Inst Db Cornet
Nm Isaac Smith Occ Roller Inst Cornet Bb	Nm Chas Lee Occ Blacksmith Inst Bb Baritone	Nm John R. Ellis Occ Hair Dresser Inst Ab Cornet
Nm John Kilsley Occ Puddler Inst Cornet Bb	Nm Chas Barron Occ Tailor Inst Bb Baritone	Nm George Harrison Occ Hour Agent's Clerk Inst Ab Cornet
Nm Ian Duffield Occ Roller Inst Sax Tenor Eb	Nm Samuel Pearce Occ Tailor Inst Bb Euphonium	Nm James Prince Occ [?] Inst Ab Cornet
Nm John Coley Occ Mine Burner Inst Sax Tenor Db	Nm John Keelling Occ Blacksmith Inst Bb Euphonium	Nm Bennett B. Foulkes Occ Publican Inst Db Alto Horn
Nm Richard Thomas Occ Puddler Inst Barytone Bb	Nm Chas Croutcher Occ Tailor Inst Bombardon	Nm Edward Lancaster Occ Photographist Inst Db Sax Horn
Nm William Thomas Occ Roller Inst Solo Bass Bb	Nm Geo Guy Occ Painter Inst Bombardon	Nm Thomas B. Foulkes Occ Ironmongers Assistant Inst Db Sax Horn

Messrs Bagnal's Gold's [Hill] Sax Horn Band, near Birmingham (1860) Scene, Aria, Opera, Miro by Verdi Scene, Placco by W. Perry	The Portsmouth Sax Horn Band	Cestrian Amateur Band [Chester]
Nm Joseph Fletcher Occ Roller Inst Solo Bass B♭	Nm John Lancombe Occ Tailor Inst E♭ Alt Horn	Nm William Turnbull Occ Upholsterer Inst D♭ Sax Horn
Nm Hugh McAdam Occ Machine Tender Inst Contra Bass E♭	Nm Henry Simmons Occ Coppersmith Inst E♭ Alt Horn	Nm James Kelly Occ Solicitors Clerk Inst A♭ Euphonium
Nm Daniel Tilley Occ Back Furnace Man Inst Contra Bass E♭	Nm Alfred Reaves Occ Caulker Inst Bass Drum	Nm Richard Davies Occ Printer Inst A♭ Sax Horn
Nm Isaiah Lowe Occ Screw Turner Inst Soprano D♭		Nm William Jones Occ Shoemaker Inst C♭ Bombardon
Nm Paul Smith Occ Roller Inst Side Drum		Nm Richard Weatherall Occ Waggon Inspector Inst C♭ Bombardon
Nm Thomas Pailow Occ Sawyer Inst Bass Drum		Nm Michael Gibson Occ Reporter Inst Ophecleide
		Nm John Harrison Occ Painter Inst Ophecleide

Repertoire and recordings: A guide to listening

This appendix supplements parts of the book where repertoire and performance are discussed. It is a selective guide to recordings of British-model brass bands which can be accessed through commercial or (more often) open-content sources. The recordings may exist in one or more of three formats: CDs, including remastering of earlier formats; paywall online resources, such as commercial streaming and download services; and open-access materials. Included in the latter category are the collections of public agencies such as universities and copyright libraries, online private collections and the digitised heritage collections created by individual bands. Many of the recordings in the list can be identified using key words (titles of works, or composer names) in the most popular search engines. Searches may also yield videos of live performances.

The most important and reliable source for scholarly information on early brass band recordings is Frank Andrews's *Brass Band Cylinder and Non-microgroove Disc Recordings, 1903–1960*, which lists all known recordings of British brass bands made prior to the introduction of the 33rpm disc.[1] Other sources and recordings are also worthy of exploration.

University of California Santa Barbara Cylinder Audio Archive

This is the world's largest open-access cylinder recording collection. It contains some of the earliest recordings ever made. It includes recordings of Jules Levy and other early virtuoso brass soloists, as well as recordings by major US bands, including the band of J. P. Sousa. UCSB Cyclinder Audio Archives: https://cylinders.library.ucsb.edu/ (accessed 21 July 2025)

Foden's Band Heritage Site

This includes an impressive and searchable collection of digitised recordings from between 1914 and 1943. It provides a profile of the band's musical history in that period. The site also contains modern re-recordings: https://www.

fodensbandheritage.co.uk/ (accessed 22 July 2025). The original recordings are lodged at the British Library as the 'Alan Littlemore Collection'. It is worth noting that all the recordings in this collection were made prior to the change to a low pitch (A440Hz) standard.

Cyfarthfa Band recordings

The earliest surviving, and largely complete, handwritten brass band repertoire is that of the Cyfarthfa Band of Merthyr Tydfil, south Wales. A 1995 BBC documentary programme of the Wallace Collection's reconstruction of that repertoire on period instruments is available as part of the Open University's Open Learn series. *The Celebrated Cyfarthfa Band*: https://www.open.edu/openlearn/history-the-arts/history/welsh-history-and-its-sources/content-section-4.3 (accessed 19 July 2025).

Internet Archive

A massive open-access multi-media collection which includes audio recordings. It is best searched by band name. Audio files can be downloaded free of change when an account is registered (also free). Some of the recordings are only available as samples: https://archive.org/ (accessed 23 July 2025).

YouTube

YouTube is famously the world's largest video-sharing platform and, at the time of writing, is owned by Google. It includes what is probably the most extensive and accessible collection of sound and video recordings of brass bands. The search facility is exceptional. Recordings can be found quickly using any relevant key words. Most of the recordings cited below are available in full, or in part, on YouTube.

A selective list of recordings

It is important to stress that this is a selective and representative list of brass band repertoire. It does not indicate a canon so it is not an indicator of 'the best' works written for bands – it would be an entirely different list if such were the intention.[2] It is separated into three groups: works composed for, or used as, test pieces for British National and Open Championships and the European Championship; arrangements of existing works that served the same purpose (all by date of performance); and a small collection of miscellaneous popular concert works, including solos. The latter group is short and restricted, but internet searches using titles as key words may lead to a wider and later range of works.

A comprehensive and searchable list of the 600 works published in the Salvation Army's Festival series between 1923 and 2005 is available at Festival Series Brass Pieces: Salvation Army Music Index: https://samusicindex.com/brass?series=Festival+Series (accessed 22 July 2025).

Contest test pieces: original works

Composer	Work	Date[3]
Fletcher, Percy	*Labour and Love*	1913
Jenkins, Cyril	*Life Divine*	1921
Bath, Hubert	*Freedom*	1922
Geehl, Henry	*Oliver Cromwell*	1923
Wright, Denis	*Joan of Arc*	1925
Keighley, Thomas	*A Midsummer Night's Dream*	1926
Holst, Gustav	*A Moorside Suite*	1928
Bantock, Granville	*Oriental Rhapsody*	1930
Elgar, Edward	*Severn Suite*	1930
Ireland, John	*A Downland Suite*	1932
Keighley, Thomas	*A Northern Rhapsody*	1935
Wright, Kenneth	*Pride of Race*	1935
Bliss, Arthur	*Kenilworth*	1936
Howells, Herbert	*Pageantry*	1937
Wright, Denis	*Overture for an Epic Occasion*	1945
Ball, Eric	*Resurgam*	1950
Leidzén, Erik	*Sinfonietta for Brass Band*	1955
Perkin, Helen	*Carnival*	1957
Rubbra, Edmund	*Variations on 'The Shining River'*	1958
Vinter, Gilbert	*Salute to Youth*	1962
Vinter, Gilbert	*Spectrum*	1969
Arnold, Malcolm	*Fantasy for Brass Band*	1974
Howarth, Elgar	*Fireworks*	1975
Gregson, Edward	*Connotations for Brass Band*	1977
Simpson, Robert	*Volcano*	1979
Gregson, Edward	*Dances and Arias*	1984
Bourgeois, Derek	*Diversions*	1986
Sparke, Philip	*Harmony Music*	1987
Heaton, Wilfred	*Contest Music*	1988
Butterworth, Arthur	*Odin*	1989
Lloyd, George	*English Heritage*	1990
McCabe, John	*Cloudcatcher Fells*	1992
Wilby, Philip	*Masquerade*	1993

Composer	Work	Date
Graham, Peter	*On Alderley Edge*	1997
Graham, Peter	*Harrison's Dream*	2000
Gregson, Edward	*Rococo Variations*	2008
Graham, Peter	*On the Shoulders of Giants*	2010
Deleruyelle, Thierry	*Fraternity*	2017
Van der Roost, Jan	*The Lost Circle*	2024
Roberts, Stephen	*Star Crossed Lovers*	2025

Arrangements used as test pieces

Composer and arranger	Work	Date
Rossini, arr. W. Rimmer	*Overture William Tell*	1912
Verdi, arr. C. G. Godfrey	*Selection from works of Verdi*	1916
Wagner, arr. M. Johnstone	*Lohengrin*	1922
Brahms, arr. D. Wright	*Academic Festival Overture*	1937
Berlioz, arr. F. Wright	*Les Francs Juges*	1961
Verdi, arr. F. Wright	*The Force of Destiny*	1962
Elgar, arr. E. Ball	*Froissart*	1981
Liszt, arr. B. Gray	*Les Préludes*	2001
Holst, arr. S. Roberts	*The Planets Suite (Venus and Jupiter)*	2003

Concert works

Composer/arranger	Work[4]	Date
Arban, Jean-Baptiste	*Carnival of Venice* Cornet solo	c.1859
Binge, Ronald	*Cornet Carillon*	1954
Copland, Aaron., arr. Howard Snell	*Hoe Down*	1983
Hartmann, John	*Facilita* Cornet solo	1877
Hartmann, John	*Carnival of Venice* Cornet solo	1882
Howarth, Elgar	*In Memoriam RK*	1976
Levy, Jules	*Whirlwind Polka*	1862
Moss, Katie, arr. Derek Broadbent	*The Floral Dance*	1977
Mussorgsky, Modest arr. Elgar Howarth	*Pictures at an Exhibition*	1977
Parker, Handel	*Deep Harmony*	1854

Composer/arranger	Work	Date
Pryor, Arthur	*Variations on the Bluebells of Scotland* Trombone solo	c.1895
Ravel, Maurice arr. Howard Snell	*Daphnis et Chloé*	c.1984
Trad., arr. Howard Snell	*Greensleeves*	c.1983
Williams, John, arr. Farr, Ray	*Indiana Jones*	1984
Williams, John, arr. Farr, Ray	*Superman*	1978
Wright, Denis	*Concerto for Cornet*	1941

Notes

ABBREVIATIONS

CEBI	*The Cambridge Encyclopaedia of Brass Instruments*, ed. Herbert et al. (2019)
GDMI2	*The Grove Dictionary of Musical Instruments*, ed. Libin (2014)
GDMM	*Grove's Dictionary of Music and Musicians* (1st edn)
HML	Horniman Museum Library, London
HUBBA	Huddersfield University Brass Band Archive
LBL	British Library, London
NG2	*The New Grove Dictionary of Music and Musicians, Second Edition*, ed. Sadie et al. (2000)
ODNB	*Oxford Dictionary of National Biography*
OED	*Oxford English Dictionary*
RCM	Library of the Royal College of Music
RSMA	Royal Society of Musicians Archive, London
SAIHC	Salvation Army International Heritage Centre, London
SCA	Shropshire County Archives, Shrewsbury
SURNC	Salford University, Roy Newsome Collection
UKNA	National Archives of the United Kingdom

PROLOGUE

1. The band became known as the Treorchy Secondary Schools Band and in 1962 was the first youth band to reach the finals of the Championship Section of the National Brass Band Contest at the Royal Albert Hall, London.

INTRODUCTION

1. The commercial was for Hovis bread. It was directed by Ridley Scott and shot in the Dorset town of Shaftesbury.
2. The statement is believed to have been made first in 1904 and the idea was formed into a book published a decade later: Schmitz (1914).
3. *Daily Telegraph*, 4 September 1882.
4. *Census Report* (1881), Vol. IV, 32.
5. The configuration of french horns, which are not constituents of British-type brass bands, is such that the valves are manipulated by the player's left hand. But the same general principle applies. Some brass band instruments such as euphoniums have fourth valves that refine the instrument's intonation or give access to additional, lower notes. These are depressed using the left hand.
6. The name 'British Open' was adopted later. It is the oldest annual contest and has been held each year since 1853, apart from 1859 when there was no contest and 2020 and 2021 when it was cancelled because of the Covid pandemic. The Belle Vue Gardens closed in 1981; the contest then moved to a different venue in Manchester, and to Birmingham in 1997.
7. The standard source for this data is 4barsrest: https://4barsrest.com (accessed 24 March 2025).
8. *War Cry*, January 1881.

CHAPTER 1

1. See, for example, Thomson (1991), 56.
2. Slater (1908), 114.
3. A few engravings from the second half of the fifteenth century appear to show trumpeters reading music, but these probably depict players of the slide trumpet – a precursor of the trombone.
4. See Tarr and Dickey (2007) and Brown (1976). Both provide excellent overviews and illustrations of how music was embellished by wind players in the period.
5. See for example Herbert (2006), 84.
6. *CEBI*, 130.
7. MacDermott (1948), 30.
8. Burney (1785), 7. The 'spacious buildings' were Westminster Abbey and the Pantheon Theatre in London's Oxford Street. Trombone parts were included in two of Handel's oratorios: *Israel in Egypt* and *Saul*. Both had their first performances in London in 1739. It is believed that visiting German musicians played the trombone parts. See Herbert (2006), 121–3.
9. From the sixteenth century, the word 'orchestra' was used to mean the part of a performance space where instrumentalists played. It is also used in some nineteenth-century sources to mean a platform erected for the accommodation of instrumentalists. See *OED*: 'orchestra' 2b.
10. For conventions regarding marching at this time, see Herbert and Barlow (2013), 20–4.
11. Gervase Markham, *Souldiers Grammar* (1626), quoted in Grose (1786), 318.
12. *Morning Chronicle*, 8 July 1795.
13. Binns (1959), 9.
14. National Library of Ireland, MS13,527, 'J K Mackenzie letters'.

15. Shropshire County Archives, Shrewsbury. 190/286. These sources are partly summarised in Herbert and Barlow (2013), Ch. 5.
16. RSMA, filed under 'Booth, Robert Handel', 7 August 1887. Other biographical information is from relevant decennial census returns.
17. McGuffie (1966b), 13.
18. For a more detailed description of dress and mannerisms associated with the British army in the period, see Myerly (1996).
19. The entry on 'Wind Bands' in the first edition of *Grove's Dictionary of Music and Musicians*: written by the military bandmaster J. A. Kappey, it provides a list of optional sizes for military bands suitable for regiments of various countries. *GDMM*, Vol. 4, 463–73.
20. *Queens Regulations and Orders for the Army* had several revisions in the nineteenth century. The units excluded from forming bands were those that were deemed to have no public-facing role, such as supply depots.
21. The title 'Royal Military School of Music' was conferred by Queen Victoria in 1887. The title of the institution at the time of its opening in 1857 was 'The Military Music Class'.
22. War Office General Order 27/550, a supplement to the Recruiting Regulations of 1903. Kneller Hall 103/586, dated April 1892, provides similar information. For an overview of the training of musicians in children's homes, see Herbert and Barlow (2013), Ch. 6.
23. War Office, General Order 27/550 (1903), 1.
24. This topic is covered in greater detail in Herbert and Barlow (2013), 137–46.
25. *GDMM*, Vol. IV, 472. The volumes were published sequentially; Vol. IV was published in 1889.
26. For more information on both these reports, see Herbert and Barlow (2013), 146–53.
27. Newsome (2005), 15.
28. Banfield (2018), 64–5.
29. Millington (1884), 102–3. Millington contradicts this, claiming that the band was a wind band with a serpent and horns and that a yeomanry band was formed in 1854, but there is no reason to give priority to this version of events.
30. Jackson (1896), n.p.
31. Lancashire County Records Office, CCC1 1187/18 (Clifton of Lytham Muniments).
32. For more information on the royal bands, especially the Duke of Cumberland's Band, see Herbert and Barlow (2013), App. 3. The surviving repertoire of this band now forms part of the Hanover Royal Music Archive, at the Beinecke Rare Book and Manuscript Library, Yale University: OBS MSS 146, Series III, 'Duke of Cumberland Band Archive'.
33. Gammon (1985), 127.
34. *West Sussex Journal*, 7 January 1879.
35. Gammon (2000), 140.
36. Millington (1884), 103.
37. Brownlow (1996), 233. Brownlow provides a good overview of professional trumpet playing in the period.
38. This information is obtained from the sequence catalogued as 'Bradford Brass Band account book 1854–1858': West Yorkshire Archive Service, Bradford

(DB 16/C31). A contemporaneous note at the start of the book states that the band was formed in 1845 and reformed in 1852.

39. For an overview and catalogue of sources relating to the Distin family, see Farr (2013), *passim.*
40. Whitehead (2017).
41. See Trevett (2025).
42. For further information on the Cyfarthfa Band, see Herbert and Myers (1988). Herbert (1990a) and Herbert (1991a).
43. 'Music in Humble Life', *Household Words*, Vol. 1 (1850), 161.

CHAPTER 2

1. *Cork Examiner*, 16 September 1844. The letter appears to have been quoted in full, but the recipient is not named.
2. Marriner Account book (1861), n.p. See also Gammon (2000), 140.
3. For example, British patent No. 2661, Oct 311860.
4. Humphries (2000), 20.
5. See also Humphries (2016/17).
6. This view is based on scrutiny of various sources at the William J. Hogan Archive at Tulane University, Louisiana.
7. Herbert (2006), 267–71. Trombone glissando occurs when a player moves the slide in either direction while holding a sustained note. As the slide passes through various pitches, it produces a distinctive effect. Early 'tailgate' jazz players, who often called the effect a 'smear', used it liberally. Tailgate is so called because early jazz bands often played on open carts or trucks, placing the trombonist at the rear, over the tailgate, so that their slide movements were unhindered.
8. See *CEBI* for more detailed explanations of these instruments, and terms associated with their performance.
9. For fuller explanations of what follows, see relevant entries in *CEBI* and Campbell, Myers and Gilbert (2025), *passim.*
10. Herbert (2006), 60–1.
11. Bullard (1993).
12. See *CEBI*, 234–7. It is possible that the instrument originated in a separate, earlier development.
13. Denis Wright was a strong advocate for having two flugelhorns in brass bands.
14. A smaller number of models operate by diverting the airway to make it shorter and consequently elevate the pitch. Examples of ascending valves include the double horn where the fourth valve raises the basic pitch from F to B flat and some trombones for children with short slides which have a valve raising the pitch from B flat to C.
15. *CEBI*, 430–7. This article, by Sabine Klaus, provides the best succinct and illustrated history of the various versions of the valve.
16. 'Music in Humble Life' (see Ch. 1, n. 43). The author is unnamed, but it is known to have been written by Dickens's father-in-law, George Hogarth.
17. *Halifax Courier and Guardian*, 15 September 1855. Dyke was often rendered 'Dike' in the nineteenth century, and the place in which the mill is located (Queensbury) was called Queenshead until the middle of the century.

18. Myers (2018).
19. Rose (1895).
20. Waterhouse (1993), 165.
21. Ehrlich (1985), Ch. V.
22. Professor Arnold Myers created a detailed (unpublished) handlist of this collection. The Horniman Museum subsequently added its own numbering system to it. A similar collection of materials relevant to US makers is held at the National Music Museum at the University of South Dakota.
23. The company was originally founded in collaboration with Eugène Dupont, who was previously an employee of Distin. The partnership lasted only until 1879 when Conn became the sole proprietor.

CHAPTER 3

1. *Musical Herald*, 4 July 1846.
2. Alice King, 'Village Bands', *Girl's Own Paper*, 8 November 1884.
3. The population figures are drawn from Mitchell and Deane (1962). It should be stressed that the 1841 census is generally regarded as 'the first modern census'. For an explanation and evaluation of the British census, see Higgs (2005).
4. Thompson (1972), 445.
5. This information is taken from the surviving contest forms which now form part of the archive of the Royal Conservatoire of Scotland. I am grateful to Arnold Myers for giving me sight of them and the database he constructed from them.
6. See for example Ehrlich (1990) and Di Martino, Popp and Scott (2017), Ch. 5.
7. Ingle (2004), 147–8. The date of the formation of this band is given as 1845 rather than 1844 in an annotation in its account book.
8. It is not entirely clear why this word was adopted. 'Caminando' is a Spanish word literally meaning 'walking' or 'marching'.
9. For example, the monthly and annual account books of Rudall Carte & Co. include agenda items on 'loans' and 'settlements of loans to employees' as a recurrent item. HML, Rudall Carte Account Books.
10. Herbert and Myers (1988), 65.
11. Irwell Springs (1914).
12. *Llanelly and County Guardian*, 28 October 1886. Additional sources kindly provided by Dr David Evans of Bangor University.
13. Morcambe Library, Lancashire: 'Treasurers Book for Members of the St George's Works Brass Band'.
14. HML, Besson Directors Minute Books, 12 May 1896 [n.p.].
15. Gammage (1969), 184–5.
16. BBC Archive: Northumberland Miners' Picnic 1961: https://bedlington.uk/forums/topic/9523-bbc-archive-northumberland-miners-picnic-1961/ (accessed 15 May 2025).
17. *Western Flying Post*, 25 October 1863.
18. Banfield (2018), 119.
19. Rose (1895), 303.

20. The printed edition of the *British Bandsman* ended in 2022. It continued nominally as a website.
21. Odello (2014), 436.
22. The magazine was originally called *Mainzer's Musical Times and Singing Circular*. Mainzer's name was dropped from the title when it was taken over by Novello. It was called the *Musical Times* from 1904.
23. Clefs are signs placed at the start of each line of music to define the pitch of each written note. For example, piano music usually has the left-hand part (low notes) written in the bass clef, and the right-hand part (higher notes) in the treble clef. All valve instruments in the brass band are written in the treble clef, irrespective of their pitch. This Victorian learning aid also meant that players could easily shift from one instrument to another, if needed, without the notated music providing an additional challenge. The bass trombone has the only part written in the bass clef.
24. For example, a selection from Donizetti's *Figlia di Regimento* (1855) is scored for 24 parts (including percussion) and is one of several published in the format. I am grateful to Ray Farr for giving me sight of this score.
25. *Distin's Journal*, Boosey (1869).
26. The arrangement, which survives in private ownership, was by James Smyth, director of the band and orchestra of the Royal Artillery.
27. Taylor (1979), 72. Taylor was quoting a letter from Gladney published in *Brass Band World* in 1901. For the photograph, see the website of Meltham & Meltham Mills Band: https://staging.melthamband.co.uk/ (accessed 2 January 2025).
28. See, for example, the *Brass Band Annual* for 1895, 26.
29. Respectively, *Wright and Round's Amateur Band Teacher's Guide* (1889) and the same publisher's *Brass Band News* (November 1889).
30. Rose (1895), 125.
31. *An Act to consolidate and amend Laws relating to the Militia in England* (1852).
32. Montefiore (1908), 403.
33. Attributed to a speech at Merchant Taylors' Hall in 1858, the phrase was quoted three times in the *Hansard* report of a debate at the House of Commons, 25 June 1868: https://hansard.parliament.uk/Commons/1868-06-25/debates/b79cad5f-ecda-498b-a58a-9ba346e45302/MrDisraeliSSpeech AtMerchantTaylorsHall%E2%80%94Question (accessed 4 November 2015).
34. *Hansard* report of a debate at the House of Commons, 25 June 1868.
35. Rose (1959), 97.
36. *Annual Returns of the Volunteer Force*, quoted in Beckett (1982), 104.
37. Rose (1959), 108.
38. *The Times*, 25 June 1860.
39. This was one of the outcomes of the 1887 Volunteer Capitation Inquiry. It did not find its way into the regulations of Volunteer forces until 1895.
40. *The Times*, 22 August 1860.
41. 'Rule book for the Preston Volunteer Corps': LBL, current MS number unconfirmed because of a data breach.
42. Myers (2018), 162. The document is shown in facsimile in the article.
43. Herbert and Barlow (2013), 171.
44. Herbert and Barlow (2013), 171.

45. Herbert and Barlow (2013), 171.
46. *Hansard*, 22 March 1886, Col. 1511: https://hansard.parliament.uk/
    Commons/1886-03-22/debates/73c494ce-1efa-4c4b-bde0-3da6a1d5a750/
    Army(AuxiliaryForces)%E2%80%94TheVolunteerCapitationGrant (accessed
    1 July 2025).
47. *Volunteer Service Gazette*, 25 July 1868.
48. Livings (1975), 12–15.
49. Herbert and Barlow (2013), 166.
50. This calculation is based on the prices advertised by Boosey, trading as Distin
    & Co., c.1873 (price lists compiled by Arnold Myers in Herbert (2000), 308–9).
51. *Report of the Bury Departmental Committee*, 2213.
52. *The Times*, 28 August 1860. There was an unconvincing rebuttal of these figures
    in a letter to the paper on 31 August 1860. The London Rifle Brigade was the
    representative unit of the Corporation of London. Its president was the Lord
    Mayor and its Honorary Colonel was the Duke of Cambridge. Its stellar funding
    came from public subscription, which was listed in *The Times*, 22 March 1860.
    See also Beckett (1982), 178.
53. Harfield (1967).

CHAPTER 4

1. Hampson (1892–3), 70. An open-source edition is available at: https://besses.
   co.uk/book/1818-1892-Besses-Hampson-Biography.pdf (accessed 2 August
   2025).
2. *All the Year Round*, 12 November 1859, 65.
3. Timothy Power, 'Musical Competition in Ancient Greece and Rome', paper
   given to the *Competition(s) in Music: Interdisciplinary Research Perspectives*
   symposium at the University of the Arts, Berlin, 2 September 2025. This
   international symposium was part of a project leading to the *Oxford Handbook
   on Musical Competitions*, planned for publication in 2027. https://www.udk-
   berlin.de/en/university/college-of-music/institutes/department-of-musicology-
   music-theory-composition-and-sound-engineering/musicology/veranstaltungen/
   live-talk-musik-konkurrenz-music-competition-1/ (accessed 7 September 2025).
4. Matthias Heyman, '"A Sense of Togetherness": Socialisation and Sociability in
   Two Belgian Jazz Competitions', paper given to the *Competition(s) in Music:
   Interdisciplinary Research Perspectives* symposium (see n. 3 above).
5. For the history of *eisteddfodau*, see Herbert, Clarke and Barlow (2023),
   Ch. 5.
6. *Concours* were not entirely free of controversy of the type that sometimes
   concluded band contests. The announcement by Gabriel Fauré (the director of
   the Conservatoire) of the winner of the 1906 trombone *concours* caused mass
   booing in the audience.
7. Howarth regarded the entertainment contest as the 'brainchild' of the former
   cornet player Bram Gay. Howarth and Howarth (1988), 154. The most high-
   profile entertainment contest is the annual Brass in Concert Championship.
8. Russell and Elliot (1936), 79–81.
9. Jackson (1896), *passim*.
10. *British Bandsman*, 24 December 1904.

11. The Vienna conference was one of the first international congresses on musical pitch. More on this subject is given in Ch. 9.
12. Quoted in SURNC RNA F/2/6. Jackson autobiography, n.p.
13. Quoted in SURNC RNA F/2/6. Jackson autobiography, n.p.
14. Quoted in Russell and Elliot (1936), 172.
15. *Leeds Mercury*, 17 September 1853.
16. *Leeds Mercury*, 17 September 1853.
17. The contest was not held in 1859. It has been held every other year, with the exception of 2020 and 2021 when it was cancelled because of the Covid pandemic.
18. Hoppen (1998), 289, based on data from Mitchell (1988).
19. SURNC RNA F/2/6. Jackson autobiography, n.p.
20. *Morning Chronicle*, 11 July 1860.
21. See Boardman (2022).
22. Musgrave (1995), 194–8.
23. The data here are taken from *Life in London and Sporting Chronicle*, 8 July 1860. They show lower numbers than those in daily newspapers which repeated Jackson's inflated figures and did not take account of bands that didn't show up.
24. *Daily Telegraph*, 11 July 1860. Other sources quoted above in this section are, respectively, *The Times*, 11 July 1860; *Era*, 15 July 1860; and *Leeds Mercury*, 12 July 1860.
25. See Boardman (2022) for information about the financing of the Crystal Palace event.
26. Boardman (2022), 585, for attendance figures for each the event.
27. Boardman (2022), 592.
28. See, for example, Boardman (2022).
29. *Brass Band Annual* (1895), Introduction.
30. The full text of 'The Absent-minded Beggar' is published on the website of the Kipling Society: https://www.kiplingsociety.co.uk/poem/poems_beggar.htm (accessed 17 September 2024).
31. *Morning Post*, 22 January 1900.
32. *Leeds Mercury*, 23 July 1900.
33. Hailstone (1987), 19.
34. Hailstone (1987),, 18.
35. *Brass Band News*, March 1882.
36. The bass trombone pitched in G became obsolete when modern designs were introduced from the US in the 1960s. The G trombone was almost exclusively restricted to Britain and its colonies before that time.
37. Berlioz (1844 and 1856). The Berlioz treatise is cited twice in the bibliography of this book: both the original French (1844) edition and the popular Novello translation of 1856.
38. *Brass Band News*, February and March 1882.
39. The most accurate summaries of the careers of Gladney, Owen and Swift is found in their respective entries in the *ODNB*.
40. Bands received an annotated short score. This meant that the melodic (and by implication harmonic) content was determined by one of the Godfreys. The arrangements were the work of each bandmaster.
41. *Brass Band News*, 12 September 1885.

42. *British Bandsman*, 22 September 1913.
43. SURNC, Wright autobiography. n.p.
44. Mandel (1860).
45. Maund (1997), 50.
46. SURNC, Wright autobiography. n.p.

CHAPTER 5

1. Quoted in Wollenberg and McVeigh (2004), 2.
2. Gronow (1865), 267. The event is not dated in the source, but it refers to the recent war and mentions Cramer, Lindley and Dragonetti, all of which helps date it.
3. Quoted in Hoppen (1998), 373.
4. Ehrlich (1985), 236.
5. *General Report of the 1881 Census of England and Wales*, Vol. IV, 35.
6. For an explanation of the development of tonic sol-fa and other forms of notation for singing, see Rainbow (1967).
7. Joseph Bennett 'A Mainzer Class', *Musical Times and Singing Class Circular*, July 1898.
8. Mainzer sold the magazine to the publisher Alfred Novello two years after it was founded. It was then retitled the *Musical Times and Singing Class Circular* before adopting the *Musical Times* title in 1904. The final issue of the *Musical Times* was released in December 2024.
9. Quoted in *NG2*, Vol. 18, 890.
10. *Birmingham Journal*, 11 June 1831.
11. Weber (1975), 159–68 (various tables relating to the social make-up of the Society).
12. Weber (1975), 65.
13. See Ehrlich (1995), *passim*.
14. Briggs (1968), 174.
15. *Musical World*, 28 May 1853. The article 'A Sketch of the Life of Jullien' was serialised in the May, June and July issues of that year. The massacre of the Louvre undoubtedly refers to events at the Tuileries Palace in 1792.
16. Carse (1951), Ch. 2.
17. *Illustrated London News*, 23 November 1850.
18. *Illustrated London News*, 24 November 1849.
19. *Bradford Observer*, 22 February 1855.
20. Russell (1997), 78.
21. The cornet player Dufresne was one of the first soloists to be featured in Musard's concerts, and a discrete class for the cornet had been instigated at the Paris Conservatoire in 1833. It was taught by Pierre-Joseph Meifred as part of the horn class.
22. For more detailed descriptions of the cornet and the cornopean see, respectively, *CEBI*, 123 and 132.
23. Brownlow (1996), App. B. Brownlow names each trumpeter who appears in an English musical directory of the period.
24. The one trumpeter not also registered as a cornetist was William Wyatt, who is mentioned in Ch. 2 as the last devotee of the chromatic trumpet.

25. Morrow (1895), 139.
26. *NG2*, see 'Arban'.
27. Mathez (1977), 18. This is a free translation. Mathez gives a literal translation along with a facsimile of the letter.
28. The first edition was published in Paris by Escudier but is undated; it was probably published in 1859 or perhaps a little earlier.
29. Arban makes the claim in a footnote to the preface of his *Method* crediting Boehm's writing for the flute.
30. Levine (1988), 104.
31. New York Public Library Archives, MssCol 315.
32. *The Standard*, 5 October 1901.
33. The inclusion of a harp was not unusual. Many bands of the regular army included harps for concerts.
34. Bierley (2006), 166–7.
35. Bierley (2006), 101. I record my gratitude to the Headquarters of the US Marine Band (The President's Own) for access to its archives and sight of these documents.
36. *Shrewsbury Chronicle*, 3 March 1901.
37. *Manchester Guardian*, 1 March 1905.
38. Schwartz (1975), 111.
39. Levine (1988) *passim*.
40. Levine (1988), 107.
41. Levine (1988), 105.
42. Levine (1988), 165.
43. For a helpful overview of 'middlebrow', see McKibbin (1998), 386–418.

CHAPTER 6

1. *Salvation Army Yearbook* (2003).
2. *ODNB*, see 'Booth, William'.
3. *ODNB*, 'Booth, William'.
4. *Christian Mission Magazine* (n.d.), quoted in Holz (2006), 69.
5. Herbert (2000), 191.
6. SAIHC, *War Cry* (1883), 60–1.
7. SAIHC, *War Cry*, 24 February 1881.
8. SAIHC, *War Cry*, 27 May 1885. The first bands were intended to be a set of nine brass instruments and percussion, but it is doubtful whether this format was routinely used.
9. SAIHC, *War Cry*, 13 October 1895.
10. For a detailed overview of Salvation Army brass instrument production, see Myers (2020).
11. BBCWA R27/28/1, Internal memo to Denis Wright, 11 August 1936. The matter was referred for expert judgement. The resolution, and the identity of 'D.E.S', have not been identified – the abbreviation probably stands for an office (such as Director of Entertainment Services).
12. Interview with William Booth, March 1900, quoted in Holz (2006), 63.
13. *Musical Salvationist* (May 1897), 68–9.
14. See Cox (2011), *passim*, and Wiggins (1945). Cox provides the definitive work on Slater.

15. SAIHC, Booth correspondence. Letter from Booth to his daughter, 21 June 1881.
16. Slater (1908), 80.
17. Commissioner George Railton, quoted in Cox (2011), 85.
18. Cox (2011), 85. Quoted from Richard Slater's diary, 31 July 1908.
19. For a more extended description of the association of the Salvation Army with the Crystal Palace, see Musgrave (1995), 204–11.
20. Cox (2011), 84.
21. *British Bandsman*, 9 July 1904.
22. SAIHC, SEC/3/0/1–SEC/3/0/6. This set of documents gives the terms of the commission, its outcomes and minutes of the interviews that provided the evidence for its conclusions.
23. SAIHC, SEC/3/0/1, 5.
24. SAIHC, SEC/3/0/1, 5.
25. For a distillation of the outcome of the inquiry, see Holz (2006), 115–17.
26. A complete list of the 600 works published in the Festival series up to 2005 is given at Festival Series Brass Pieces: Salvation Army Music Index: https://samusicindex.com/brass?series=Festival+Series (accessed 25 July 2025).
27. Quoted in Holz (2006), 37.
28. Holz (2006), 131.
29. Holz (2006), 132.
30. For an analysis that offers a version of events that is defensive of Bramwell Booth, see Smith (1929).
31. This is a very general outline that should not obscure the extent to which local corps simplified or combined different forms of service to meet prevailing needs and preferences. The same proviso applies to the deployment of the various musical genres performed by bands.
32. Slater (1908), 2–3.
33. Slater (1908), see 'Household Troops Band'.
34. *War Cry*, 12 March 1887.
35. Boon (1978), 27.
36. Boon (1978), 28.
37. Myers (2020), 32.
38. Myers (2020), 37. See also Herbert (2000) for year-on-year numbers of band players globally.
39. It is often stated that Besson was taken over by Boosey & Hawkes in 1948. In fact, the consolidation of a takeover was not completed until the late 1960s. In the interim, Besson manufacture shared the same premises as Boosey & Hawkes, and the Besson brand continued to trade independently. See Howell (2016), 118.
40. SAIHC, File 5. Press release dated 22 January 1992.
41. Cobb (2006), n.p.
42. See Salvationinst Publishing & Supplies: https://www.sps-shop.com/ (accessed 10 April 2025).

CHAPTER 7

1. Finnegan (1989), 53.
2. Each example is taken from the collection of entry forms for the Enderby Jackson Crystal Palace contests.

3. Quoted in Bythell (1991), 6–7.
4. For a discussion of 'The invention of traditions', see Hobsbawm and Ranger (1983).
5. Cobbett (1830), 242.
6. For an outline of such bands in the south of England in the late eighteenth and early nineteenth centuries, see Lomas (1992).
7. Temperley (1979), 197–8.
8. Temperley (1979), 198. Temperley's source was the work of the Anglian parson K. H. MacDermott.
9. Barrel organs were introduced into Anglican churches, but Gammon points out that in most cases they were put in churches where there had previously been little or no instrumental music. Gammon (1985), 46.
10. The county of Sussex has attracted particular interest. Much of this is due to the pioneering work of K. H. MacDermott, who published his *Sussex Church Music in the Past* in 1923. His later (1948) publication deals with a broader expanse of the subject.
11. Quoted in Gammon (1985), 30.
12. MacDermott (1948), 32–3. The date given by MacDermott is approximate.
13. For a 'Nominal List' of volunteer corps and their locations, see Beckett (1982), App. VII.
14. Beckett (1982), 260.
15. Burstow (1912), 50.
16. Quoted in Gammon (1985), 130.
17. Alice King, 'Village Bands', *Girl's Own Paper*, 8 November 1884.
18. Rose (1895), 302.
19. *Musical World*, 4 April 1885.
20. Gammon (1985), 122.
21. Quoted in Lomas (1990), Vol. 2, 49.
22. Ord Hume (1900), 11.
23. *Western Times*, 10 August 1861.
24. Manchester Library M463/3.
25. Manchester Library M196.
26. Bevan (2013), 527.
27. *British Bandsman*, December 1896.
28. A Church Girls Brigade with the same broad intentions to the Church Lads Brigade was founded in 1901. The two organisations amalgamated in 1978.
29. *British Musician*, June 1893.
30. Mayhew (1851).
31. *British Musician*, December 1896.
32. *British Musician*, August 1896.
33. 'Brass Band Contests: History & Background': https://www.masterflex-hose.co.uk/brass-band-contests (accessed 13 March 2025).
34. *Guardian*, 2 June 2015.
35. The film is freely available on Youtube: '1960: The Delight of the Miners' Brass Band Picnic': https://youtu.be/Jgek8ZE32PI (accessed 29 April 2025).
36. 'Durham Miners' Gala': https://www.bbe.org.uk/BBEPortal/BBEPortal/News/Archive-blog/Brass-Bands-Archive-blog-collieries.aspx (accessed 11 March 2025).

37. Durham Record Office, 'Coal Mining and Durham Collieries': https:// durhamrecordoffice.org.uk/our-records/coal-mining-and-durham-collieries/ (accessed 11 March 2025).
38. Former Sacristan miner Dave Wray, quoted in Gildea (2024), 361.
39. Prominent Features, Channel Four Films and Miramax Films, UK release date 1 November 1996.
40. The documents and much of the book collections of Miners' Institutes are assembled as a discrete research collection at Swansea University: https://www. swansea.ac.uk/library/south-wales-miners-library/collections-resources/ (accessed 26 July 2025).
41. Bailey (1978), 107.
42. Quoted in Rose (2010), 249.
43. *British Bandsman*, 4 October 1913.
44. Phillip McCann, 'Black Dyke Band': https://www.blackdykeband.co.uk/ profiles/phillip-mccann-principal-cornet-1973-1988/ (accessed 13 March 2025). I am grateful to Mr McCann for allowing me to include this transcript of his interview.

CHAPTER 8

1. Finnegan (1989), 47 and Ch. 5, *passim*.
2. Finnegan made the point that, by the 1980s, the presence of females in bands was increasingly common and attributed it to changes in the UK education system.
3. Quoted in Russell (2000), 84.
4. Rose (2010), 197.
5. Golby (1986), 230.
6. *British Bandsman*, 26 February 1903.
7. The reference to Black Dyke comes from the band's contest application form for the Crystal Palace contest of 1860. The Newcastle Steel Works Band of Australia is reported to have sat in contest formation at the 1924 British Open Contest; whether this was genuinely innovative is uncertain. Bythell (1994), 148–9.
8. *The Times*, 7 February 1925.
9. RCM, Add Ms 12422–12434.
10. Russell (2000), 70–1.
11. SURNC, Wright autobiography, n.p.. The calculation is unrealistic because it is a simple division of the total number of players by 25.
12. Howarth and Howarth (1988), 190.
13. Russell (2000), 68.
14. Harris (1983), 11.
15. British Movietone News, 'Brass Band Festival', 28 September 1936: https:// www.youtube.com/watch?v=7oEQALz9gtI (accessed 9 January 2026).
16. Copy of the contract in the author's possession.
17. Smith (1988), 11.
18. Rose (2010), 197.
19. 'Public Parks: Conclusions and Recommendations': https://publications. parliament.uk/pa/cm201617/cmselect/cmcomloc/45/4510.htm (accessed 18 April 2025).

20. Quoted in Binns (1959), 108.
21. House of Commons Parliamentary Papers 1856 (281) and 1856 (251).
22. Quoted in Hailstone (1987), 76.
23. Rabbitts (2018), 39–41.
24. McVeigh (2024), 273.
25. 'The History of the Bandstand': https://www.pavilionsformusic.co.uk (accessed 21 January 2025).
26. HUBBA, Letter to A. Thompson Esq. from the Borough of Altrincham, 14 May 1947.
27. Littlemore (2000), 76.
28. Mortimer (1981), 65.
29. The BBC started broadcasting as the British Broadcasting Company on 18 October 1922. Its name was changed to the British Broadcasting Corporation on 1 January 1927.
30. Science Museum: '2LO Calling: The Birth of British Public Radio': https://www.sciencemuseum.org.uk/objects-and-stories/2lo-calling-birth-british-public-radio (accessed 12 August 2024). Population figures taken from 1931 census data and quoted in Mitchell (1962), 239.
31. Briggs (1986), 76.
32. Gavin Holman, 'Broadcasting Brass Bands: The Early Years' (2017): https://www.researchgate.net/publication/320084817_Broadcasting_Brass_Bands_the_early_years (accessed 7 July 2024).
33. Kenneth Wright (no relation to Denis) had been at the BBC as its Station Director at Manchester. He was an important influence on the creation of a 'Band Section' which was formed in 1936 under Walter O'Donnell, the conductor of the BBC Wireless Military Band. Denis Wright was responsible for brass bands under O'Donnell's supervision. See also Newsome (1995), 76–7.
34. BBCWA R27/28/2, internal memoranda, 16 and 18 April 1932.
35. BBCWA R27/28/3, internal memorandum, 5 August 1936.
36. BBCWA R27/28/3, internal memorandum from Denis Wright, headed 'Regional Bands', 9 January 1940.
37. *British Bandsman*, 18 March 1939.
38. Mortimer (1981), 123.
39. BBCWA R27/28/4, internal memorandum, 'Proposed brass band output', n.d.
40. Mortimer (1981), 129. Earlier reference in unnumbered papers in the BBC Written Archives.
41. BBCWA, quoted in Baade (2012), 79.
42. Baade (2012), 80.
43. Andrews (1997).
44. Newsome (2006), 91.
45. See, for example, the BBC Television Documentary *Monitor* programme, available on YouTube: '1960: The Delight of the Miners' Brass Band Picnic': https://youtu.be/Jgek8ZE32PI (accessed 19 April 2025).

CHAPTER 9

1. Marwick (1998), 3.
2. Marwick (1998), 19.

3. Atkinson (2021), 134.
4. Hertz or Hz is the standard measure of pitch by oscillations per second.
5. Binns (1959), 26.
6. Gribenski (2023), 9.
7. Correspondence relating to the campaign for a standard pitch is retained in the archives of what is now the Royal Society of the Arts: RSA/PR/GE/121/10/5. Several related documents are also retained in its collections.
8. For an overview of the pitch debate, see Gillin and Gribenski (2021), also available at: https://doi.org/10.1093/pastj/gtaa007 (accessed 28 January 2025).
9. For an explanation of pitch standards and their history as it has affected brass instruments, see *CEBI*, 322–5.
10. Binns (1959), 64.
11. Miller (1912).
12. Miller (1912).
13. Herbert and Barlow (2013), 210.
14. Gribenski (2023), 119.
15. UKNA, WO32 3914 113275, General (Code 62(A)): Pitch of Military Band instruments: change to the standard pitch. Letter, Buckingham Palace, 7 November 1926.
16. [Salvation Army] *Musician*, 21 March 1964.
17. *British Bandsman*, 25 April 1964.
18. *British Bandsman*, 4 April 1964.
19. *British Bandsman*, 30 May 1954.
20. *British Bandsman*, 6 February 1965.
21. *British Bandsman*, 27 February 1965. The Besson company became closely aligned to Boosey & Hawkes in 1948, but the process was not concluded until 1968 (Howell 2016, 118). In the meantime, Besson operated as an independent brand.
22. *British Bandsman*, 16 October 1965.
23. Taylor (1973), 185.
24. Newsome (2005), 133–4.
25. Taylor (1983), 190.

CHAPTER 10

1. See Howarth and Howarth (1988), 108, 201–2 and 212.
2. According to Roy Newsome, a one-time resident conductor of the Black Dyke Band and its biographer, the appointment of female players 'caused quite a reaction, even to the point of one or two band members resigning': Newsome (2005), 200.
3. Personal communication.
4. Bull (1967), 215.
5. Essex (1722), 84.
6. Ellis (1999).
7. Letter from Sax to *Le courrier médical*, 11(xxxvi) (6 September 1862), 314, translated and quoted in Ellis (1999), 236.
8. For a detailed discussion of the allegorical and symbolic treatment of trumpets and other musical instruments in the visual arts, see Winternitz (1979), *passim*.

9. LBL, Harl Roll AA23. Quoted with a facsimile of the manuscript in Herbert (2006), 79–80.
10. For more examples, see Herbert (2006), 79–80.
11. Neuls-Bates (1996), 202–3.
12. Hazen and Hazen (1987).
13. SURNC, Wright autobiography, n.p.
14. SURNC, Wright autobiography, n.p.
15. SURNC, Dick Arrand papers. Letter dated 4 October 1974 from *Brass Band Review* to Arrand.
16. *An Act to reform the law relating to education in England and Wales*, 1944 (also known as the Butler Act).
17. *Report of the Committee appointed by the President of the Board of Education to consider the Supply, Recruitment and Training of Teachers and Youth Leaders*, 1944 (also known as the McNair Report), 155
18. Purvis (2017), 69.
19. Quoted in Purvis (2017), 83–4.
20. Thackray (1972).
21. Wright (2013), 149.
22. 'Education: Historical Statistics': House of Commons Library Paper, SN/SG/4252, 27 November 2012. Other data on educational statistics in this section of the chapter is taken from this source. All provisos relating to the data are explained in the same source: https://commonslibrary.parliament. uk/research-briefings/sn04252/ (accessed 16 October 2024).
23. For an overview of informal secondary education, see Newsome (2006), Ch. 9 and particularly the section on higher-education band curricula in which Newsome was personally involved.
24. Polytechnics were founded to serve the needs of industries, especially those centred on science and engineering. Until the passing of the 1992 Further and Higher Education Act, oversight of the polytechnic sector was the responsibility of the Council for National Academic Awards.
25. See, for example, Wright (1935).
26. Interview with Peter Wilson, quoted in Hindmarsh (2025), 141. For a detailed account of the reception of *Contest Music*, see Hindmarsh (2025), 132–8.
27. Howarth and Howarth (1988), 150.
28. Howarth and Howarth (1988), 150.
29. For a detailed overview and analysis of these developments, see Miller (2022).
30. Miller (2022), 102.
31. Interview available at: https://www.youtube.com/watch?v=KpRP_c_1wJw (accessed 6 August 2025).
32. Howarth and Howarth (1988), 149.

CHAPTER 11

1. Taylor (1983), 247.
2. Taylor (1983), 262.
3. 'World Rankings': https://www.4barsrest.com/rankings/ (accessed 13 July 2025).
4. *Sydney Gazette and New South Wales Advertiser*, 25 August 1832.
5. *Sydney Monitor*, 25 August 1832.

6. See, for example, Booth (2017) on Indian wedding bands and Boonzajer Flaes (1999) on bands of the southern hemisphere, and, more generally on brass bands in colonies, Herbert and Sarkissian (1997).

7. See Booth (2017), *passim*.

8. *Express and Telegraph* (Adelaide), 7 March 1882.

9. These figures are taken from various editions of the *Salvation Army Yearbook* and include junior and senior 'bandsmen'. A composite of the statistics from 1878 to 1998 is given in Herbert (2000), 312–15.

10. Bythell (2000) 231.

11. Egypt was a British protectorate only between 1914 and 1922, but there were extensive British interests in the country before and after that period.

12. For an overview, see *CEBI*, 98–103.

13. *CEBI*, 227.

14. For a detailed overview, see *CEBI*, 226–8.

15. Karjalainen (1997), 88.

16. Kierzkowski (2023), 118–19.

17. Waterhouse (1993), 60–1.

18. *Badische Landespost*, 29 August 1882. Quoted in Nillson (2001), 176: 'Die Tonfärbung der Instrumente ist weicher als die unserer Kavalleriemusiken, mehr denen der Jäger ähnlich, die Trompeten sind schwächer besetzt,..dazu guter leichter Ansatz, so erzielt sich denn aus dem Ganzen ein milderer gedämpfter Ton' (free translation in the chapter).

19. These include *Andantino and Minuet* (JS 45, 1890–1), *Förspel* (JS 83, 1891) and *Tiera* for band and percussion (JS 200, 1899).

20. For a detailed overview of bands in Nordic countries, see *CEBI*, 297–301.

21. *CEBI*, 107.

22. Leterrier (2018), 9.

23. Rauline (2004), *passim*.

24. For an overview of brass instruments in Moravian communities, see Carter (2006).

25. See Camus (1976), *passim*.

26. Hazen and Hazen (1987), 297–306.

27. Hazen and Hazen (1987), 104.

28. Hamm (1983), 279.

29. Wagner (1998) provides transcriptions of several scores, an historical introduction and critical commentary. For an outline of early published music for brass in the US, see Shive (1993).

30. US National Music Museum, Conn Papers. Salesman's Handbook, c.1910.

31. North American Brass Band Association (NABBA): https://nabba.org (accessed 17 July 2025).

32. Quoted in Newsome (1995), 183.

33. *British Bandsman*, 26 July 1952, quoted in Newsome (1995), 184.

34. Much of this information is taken from Newsome (2006), 306–21, which provides additional detail.

35. 4barsrest.com. The data changes regularly.

36. National Brass Band Championships of Great Britain, '2025 National Rules': https://www.regional-contest.org.uk/lsc/wp-content/uploads/2024/12/Nationals-Rulebook-2025-Master.pdf (accessed 17 July 2025).

37. European Brass Band Championships, 'Rules and Regulations': https://ebba.eu.com/wp-content/uploads/2024/11/EBBA-Rules-and-regulations-EBBC-2025.pdf (accessed 17 July 2025).
38. For example, *The Origin of the Species: Virtuoso Victorian Brass Music from Cyfarthfa Castle, Wales*. Nimbus Records NI5470 (1996): a period-instrument reconstruction of part of the repertoire of the Cyfarthfa Band, c.1847–78.
39. 4barsrest.com.
40. Amersham Band: https://amershamband.com (accessed 19 July 2025).

APPENDIX 1

1. The entrance application forms from which these data are drawn are now in the archives of the Royal Conservatoire of Scotland. Other parts of the surviving set may be distributed in other collections, private and public.

APPENDIX 2

1. Andrews (1997).
2. A much longer list of 'Principal Works' for brass band is given in Newsome (2006), App. G.
3. The date is that of the contest at which the work was first performed. Some works were adopted for that purpose but written earlier.
4. Cornet solos, often using the *air varié* format, are often performed on other valved instruments.

Bibliography and sources

The bibliography contains details of all published books, book chapters and articles in academic journals I have quoted or referred to. Other publications I have consulted are also included. It is arranged as a single alphabetical sequence by author and date. If an item has no named author, it is placed in the alphabetic sequence by its title and date, for example *Queen's Regulations and Orders for the Army* (1868). London: Her Majesty's Stationery Office.

References to newspapers and magazines are cited in endnotes at the point they occur, as are references to other materials, published or unpublished, that have been accessed in archives. Material accessed online is cited by URL and the date of access in endnotes. Other less orthodox source categories, such as personal communications, are also explained in relevant endnotes.

Titles of some frequently cited reference works are abbreviated in endnotes and given in their full form in the bibliography. Entries in dictionaries and encyclopaedias, with very few exceptions, are cited by volume and page number rather than by their header/title. The names of frequently cited archives and libraries are also abbreviated – the key to these abbreviations is given on the first page of the Notes (see p. 310). Other archives are cited in full in endnotes.

Several published and unpublished primary source materials are in university and public archives which have often been catalogued as large groups of documents related by period or topic. I have used the collection description they have been given, but in some cases documents can be identified only as part of a cognate group rather than individually. When this book was being written, special circumstances prevailed at the British Library and at the Lancashire Records Office, Bradford. The former was affected by a serious data breach and the latter was amid major building work which caused part of its collections to be temporarily inaccessible. The staff of both institutions were unfailingly helpful in challenging circumstances, but there remained a small number of sources for which I could not check references as closely as I would have liked. Instances that were so affected are signified in endnotes at the point they occur.

BIBLIOGRAPHY AND SOURCES

Other sources of information for readers

Brass band enthusiasts, several of whom are experts, have contributed to a large corpus of open-access research materials that can be found using the major search engines. These include the 'history' or 'heritage' pages of many individual brass bands. The following brief list is indicative of a route to a much larger body of material that is freely available:

4barsrest

The main website for information about brass bands in the modern world, it also contains archive information and is the most extensive collection of data on brass band contests: https://www.4barsrest.com/news/latest (accessed 20 August 2025)

Salford University, Roy Newsome Collection

Based on the personal collection of Roy Newsome, it includes digitalised copies of all editions of the brass band magazine *Brass Band World*: https://www.salford.ac.uk/library/archives-and-special-collections/salford-digital-archives/about-brass-band-news-and-posters (accessed 20 August 2025)

IBEW: Brass Bands Historical Resources

A vast collection of articles, images and bibliographical information, expertly curated by Gavin Holman: http://www.ibew.org.uk/ (accessed 20 August 2025)

Brass Band England

The website of the largest British brass band association: https://www.bbe.org.uk/what-we-do/the-brass-bands-archive (accessed 20 August 2025)

European Brass Band Association

The co-ordinating body for European brass bands, including the European Brass Band Championships: https://ebba.eu.com/about/ (accessed 20 August 2025)

North American Brass Band Association

The body that co-ordinates brass bands in North America: https://nabba.org/ (accessed 20 August 2025)

Historic Brass Society Journal

The primary academic journal for all aspects of the history of brass musical instruments; Vol. 1 was issued in 1989. All volumes are made available as open-access copies two years after their publication: https://www.historicbrass.org/publications/hbs-journal (accessed 20 August 2025)

Andrews, F. (1997). *Brass Band Cylinder and Non-microgroove Disc Recordings, 1903–1960*. Winchester: Piccolo.

Armsby, H. (2023). 'The Role of Gender in the British Brass Band'. PhD, The Open University.

Atkinson, P. (2021). *Amplified: A Design History of the Electric Guitar*. London: Reaktion Books.

Baade, C. L. (2012). *Victory through Harmony: The BBC and Popular Music in World War II*. Oxford and New York: Oxford University Press.

Bailey, P. (1978). *Leisure and Class in Victorian England: Rational Recreation and the Contest for Control 1830–1885*. London: Routledge & Keegan Paul.

Banfield, S. (2018). *Music in the West Country: Social and Cultural History across an English Region*. Woodbridge: Boydell and Brewer.

Banton, M. (2008). *Administering the Empire, 1801–1968: A Guide to the Records of the Colonial Office in the National Archives of the UK*. London: University of London, Institute of Historical Research.

Batten, J. (1956). *Joe Batten's Book: The Story of Sound Recording*. London: Rockliff.

Beckett, I. F. W. (1982). *Riflemen Form: A Study of the Rifle Volunteer Movement 1859–1908*. Aldershot: Ogilby Trusts.

Berlioz, H. (1844 and 1856). *Grand traité d'instrumentation et d'orchestration modernes* [1843]. Paris: Schonenberger. English translation [1856]. (See also Macdonald (2009))

Bevan, C. (2013). *Encyclopaedia of British Amateur Bands . . . 1790–1914 with Addendum 1914–1919*. Winchester: Piccolo Press.

Bierley, P. E. (1973). *John Philip Sousa: American Phenomenon*. New York: Prentice Hall.

Bierley, P. E. (1984). *The Works of John Philip Sousa*. Columbus, OH: Integrity Press.

Bierley, P. E. (2006). *The Incredible Band of John Philip Sousa*. Urbana, IL: University of Illinois Press.

Binns, P. L. (1959). *A Hundred Years of Military Music: Being the Story of the Royal Military School of Music, Kneller Hall*. Gillingham: Blackmore Press.

Boardman, P. (2022). 'From Extraordinary Success to No Considerable Results: Victorian Music Entrepreneurialism and the Crystal Palace Brass Band Competition 1860–1863'. *Nineteenth-Century Music Review* 19(3): 575–98.

Boon, B. (1978). *Play the Music, Play! The Story of Salvation Army Bands*. London: Salvationist Publishing & Supplies.

Boon, B. (1985). *The Story of the International Staff Band*. St Albans: Record Greetings, Ltd.

Boonzajer Flaes, R. M. (1999). *Brass Unbound: Secret Children of the Colonial Brass Band*. Amsterdam: Royal Tropical Institute.

Booth, G. D. (2017). *Brass Baja: Stories from the World of Indian Wedding Bands*. New Delhi: Oxford University Press.

Brand, V. and Brand, G. (1979). *Brass Bands in the 20th Century*. Letchworth: Egon.

Brand, V. and Brand, G. (1986). *The World of Brass Bands*. Baldock: Egon.

BIBLIOGRAPHY AND SOURCES

Briggs, A. (1968). *Victorian Cities*. Harmondsworth: Penguin Books.

Briggs, A. (1986). *The BBC: The First Fifty Years*. Oxford: Oxford University Press.

Brown, H. M. (1976). *Embellishing Sixteenth-century Music*. Oxford: Oxford University Press.

Brownlow, J. A. (1996). *The Last Trumpet: A History of the English Slide Trumpet*. Stuyvesant, NY: Pendragon Press.

Bull, G. (ed. and trans.) (1967). Castiglione, Baldassare: *The Book of the Courtier*. Harmondsworth: Penguin.

Bullard, B. (ed. and trans.) (1993). *Musica getutscht: A Treatise on Musical Instruments by Sebastian Virdung*. Cambridge: Cambridge University Press.

Burney, C. (1785). *An account of the musical performances in Westminster Abbey and the Pantheon . . . in commemoration of Handel*. London: T. Payne and Son (facsimile ed. New York: Da Capo Press).

Burstow, H. (1912). *Reminiscences of Horsham*. Horsham: The Christian Church Book Society.

Bythell, D. (1991). *Water: A Village Band 1866–1991*. Rossendale: Water Band.

Bythell, D. (1994). 'Class, Community, and Culture: The Case of the Brass Band in Newcastle'. *Labour History* 67: 144–55.

Bythell, D. (1997). 'Provinces versus Metropolis in the British Brass Band Movement in the Early Twentieth Century: The Case of William Rimmer and his Music'. *Popular Music* 16(2): 151–63.

Bythell, D. (2000). 'The British Brass Band in the Antipodes: The Transplantation of British Popular Culture'. In Herbert, T. (ed.), *The British Brass Band: A Musical and Social History*. Oxford and New York: Oxford University Press: 217–44.

Campbell, M., Myers, A. and Gilbert, J. (2025). *Sounding Brass: Brasswind Instruments and How They Work*. Cham, Switzerland: Springer Nature Link.

Camus, R. F. (1976). *Military Music of the American Revolution*. Chapel Hill, NC: University of North Carolina Press.

Canin, X. (2025). *Jean-Baptiste Arban 1825–1889*. Noisy-le-Sec: Petit Page.

Carnelley, J. (2015). *George Smart and Nineteenth-century London Concert Life*. Woodbridge: Boydell Press.

Carse, A. (1951). *The Life of Jullien: Adventurer, Showman-conductor and Establisher of the Promenade Concerts in England, Together with a History of Those Concerts up to 1895*. Cambridge: Heffer.

Carter, S. (2006). 'Trombone Ensembles of the Moravian Brethren in America'. In Carter. S. (ed.), *Brass Scholarship in Review*. Hillsdale, NY: Pendragon: 77–110.

Census Report (1881) [UK]. Parliamentary Papers 1883, LXXXX [c.3797].

Cipolla, F. and Hunsberger, D. (eds) (1994). *The Wind Ensemble and its Repertoire: Essays on the Fortieth Anniversary of the Eastman Wind Ensemble*. Rochester, NY: University of Rochester Press.

Clayton, M., Herbert, T. and Middleton, R. (eds) (2002). *The Cultural Study of Music: A Critical Introduction* (2nd edition). New York and London: Routledge.

Cobb, S. (2006). *Performance based portfolio encapsulating the performance profile of the international staff band of the Salvation Army*. DMA, University of Salford.

Cobbett, W. (1830). *Rural rides in the counties of Surrey, Kent, Sussex . . . with economical and political observations relative to matters applicable to, and illustrated by, the state of those counties respectively*. London: W. Cobbett.

Copeland, P. (1991). *Sound Recordings*. London: British Library.

Coutts, F. L. (1973). *The Better Fight, 1914–1946*. London: Hodder and Stoughton.

Cox, G. (2011). *The Musical Salvationist: The World of Richard Slater (1854–1939), 'Father of Salvation Army Music'*. Woodbridge, Suffolk and Rochester, NY: Boydell Press.

Day, T. (2000). *A Century of Recorded Music: Listening to Music History*. New Haven, CT: Yale University Press.

De Keyser, Ignace (2003). 'The Paradigm of Industrial Thinking in Brass Instrument Making during the 19th Century'. *Historic Brass Society Journal* 15: 233–58.

DeNora, T. (2000). *Music in Everyday Life*. Cambridge: Cambridge University Press.

Di Martino, P., Popp, A. and Scott, P. (eds) (2017). *People, Places and Business Cultures: Essays in Honour of Francesca Carnevali*. Woodbridge: Boydell.

Doctor, J. R. (1999). *The BBC and Ultra-modern Music, 1922–1936: Shaping a Nation's Tastes*. Cambridge: Cambridge University Press.

Doubleday, V. (2008). 'Sounds of Power: An Overview of Musical Instruments and Gender'. *Ethnomusicology Forum* 17(1): 3–39.

Duffy, C. (1987). *The Military Experience in the Age of Reason*. London: Routledge Keegan and Paul.

Dumoulin, G. (2006). 'The Cornet and Other Brass Instruments in French Patents of the First Half of the Nineteenth Century'. *Galpin Society Journal* 59: 77–100.

Ehrlich, C. (1985). *The Music Profession in Britain since the Eighteenth Century: A Social History*. Oxford and New York: Clarendon Press.

Ehrlich, C. (1989). *Harmonious Alliance: A History of the Performing Right Society*. Oxford and New York: Oxford University Press.

Ehrlich, C. (1990). *The Piano: A History*. Oxford and New York: Clarendon Press.

Ehrlich, C. (1995). *First Philharmonic: A History of the Royal Philharmonic Society*. Oxford and New York: Oxford University Press.

Ellis, K. (1999). 'The Fair Sax: Women, Brass-Playing and the Instrument Trade in 1860s Paris'. *Journal of the Royal Musical Association* 124(2): 221–54.

Essex, J. (1722). *The young ladies conduct, or Rules for education, under several heads with instructions upon dress, both before and after marriage: and advice to young wives*. London: J. Brotherton at the Bible in Cornhill.

Farr, R. (2013). *The Distin Legacy: The Rise of the Brass Band in 19th-century Britain*. Newcastle upon Tyne: Cambridge Scholars Publishing.

Finn, M. C. (2003). *The Character of Credit: Personal Debt in English Culture, 1740–1914*. Cambridge and New York: Cambridge University Press.

Finnegan, R. H. (1989). *The Hidden Musicians: Music-making in an English Town*. Cambridge: Cambridge University Press.

Fulcher, J. (1979). 'The Orphéon Societies: "Music for the Workers" in Second-Empire France'. *International Review of the Aesthetics and Sociology of Music* 10(1): 47–56.

Gammage, R. G. (1969). *History of the Chartist Movement, 1837–1854*. London: Merlin Press.

Gammon, V. A. F. (1985). 'Popular Music in Rural Society: Sussex 1815–1914'. PhD, University of Sussex.

Gammon, V. and S. (2000). 'The Musical Revolution of the Mid-Nineteenth Century: From "Repeat and Twiddle" to "Precision and Snap"'. In Herbert, T. (ed.), *The British Bass Band: A Musical and Social History*. Oxford and New York: Oxford University Press: 122–54.

Gehrhardt, M. (2024). '"By the Army, for the Army": The Salvation Army's Early Retail Activities, Criticisms and Responses in the Late 19th and Early 20th Centuries'. In Gosling, G. C., Green, A. R. and Millar, G. (eds), *Retail and Community*. Bristol: Bristol University Press: 72–88.

Gildea, R. (2024). *Backbone of the Nation: Mining Communities and the Great Strike of 1984–85*. New Haven, CT, and London: Yale University Press.

Gillin, E. and Gribenski, F. (2021). 'The Politics of Musical Standardization in Nineteenth-Century France and Britain'. *Past & Present* 251(1): 153–87.

Golby, J. M. (ed.) (1986). *Culture and Society in Britain 1850–1890: A Source Book of Contemporary Writings*. Oxford: Oxford University Press.

Gribenski, F. (2023). *Tuning the World: The Rise of 440 Hertz in Music, Science, & Politics, 1859–1955*. Chicago, IL, and London: University of Chicago Press.

Griffin, E. (2002). 'Popular Culture in Industrializing England'. *Historical Journal* 45(3): 619–35.

Gronow, R. H. (1865). *Celebrities of London and Paris: being a third series of reminiscences and anecdotes of the camp, the court, and the clubs; containing a correct account of the Coup d'état*. London: Smith, Elder.

Grose, F. (1786). *Military antiquities respecting a history of the English army: from the Conquest to the present time . . . By Francis Grose*. London: printed for S. Hooper.

Grove, G. (ed.) (1879–89). *A Dictionary of Music and Musicians (A.D. 1450–1880)*. London: MacMillan and Co.

Hailstone, A. (1987). *The British Bandsman Centenary Book: A Social History of Brass Bands*. Baldock: Egon.

Haine, M. (1980). *Adolphe Sax: 1814–1894: sa vie, son œuvre et ses instruments de musique*. Brussels: Éditions de l'Université de Bruxelles.

Hamm, C. (1983). *Music in the New World*. New York and London: Norton.

Hammond, D. (2017). 'British Army Music in the Interwar Years: Culture, Performance and Influence'. PhD, The Open University.

Hampson, J. N. (1892–3). *Origin, History and Achievements of the Besses-o' th'-Barn Band*. Northampton: Jos. Rogers.

Harfield, A. G. (1967). 'The Great Volunteer Review at Salsbury on 29th May, 1867'. *Journal of the Society for Army Historical Research* 45: 149–68.

Harper, T. (1837). *Instructions for the Trumpet with the Chromatic Slide, the Russian Valve Trumpet, the Cornet à Pistons or Small Stop Trumpet and the Keyed Bugle* (2nd edition). London: Published by the author.

Harris, N. (1983). 'John Philip Sousa and the Culture of Reassurance'. In Newsom, J. (ed.), *Perspectives of John Philip Sousa*. Washington, DC: Library of Congress: 11–42.

Hattersley, R. (1999). *Blood & Fire: The Story of William and Catherine Booth and their Salvation Army*. London: Little, Brown.

Hazen, M. H. and Hazen, R. M. (1987). *The Music Men: An Illustrated History of Brass Bands in America, 1800–1920*. Washington, DC: Smithsonian Institution Press.

Herbert, T. (1990a). 'The Repertory of a Victorian Provincial Brass Band'. *Popular Music* 9(1): 117–32.

Herbert, T. (1990b). 'The Sackbut in England in the 17th and 18th Centuries'. *Early Music* 18(4): 609–16.

Herbert, T. (1991a). 'A Lament for Sam Hughes: The Last Great Ophicleidist'. *Planet: The Welsh Internationalist* 87: 66–75.

Herbert, T. (ed.) (1991b). *Bands: The Brass Band Movement in the 19th and 20th Centuries*. Milton Keynes: Open University Press.

Herbert, T. (ed.) (2000). *The British Brass Band: A Musical and Social History*. Oxford and New York: Oxford University Press.

Herbert, T. (2006). *The Trombone*. New Haven, CT, and London: Yale University Press.

Herbert, T. (2010). 'Trombone Glissando: A Case Study in Brass Instrument Performance Idioms'. *Historic Brass Society Journal* 22: 1–18.

Herbert, T. (2011). '". . . men of great perfection in their science": The Trumpeter as Musician and Diplomat in England in the Later Fifteenth and Sixteenth Centuries'. *Historic Brass Society Journal* 23: 1–23.

Herbert, T. and Barlow, H. (2013). *Music and the British Military in the Long Nineteenth Century*. Oxford and New York: Oxford University Press.

Herbert, T., Clarke, M. and Barlow H. (eds) (2023). *A History of Welsh Music*. Cambridge: Cambridge University Press.

Herbert, T. and Myers, A. (1988). 'Instruments of the Cyfarthfa Band'. *Galpin Society Journal* 41: 2–10.

Herbert, T. and Myers, A. (2010). 'Music for the Multitude: Accounts of Brass Bands Entering Enderby Jackson's Crystal Palace Contests in the 1860s'. *Early Music* 38(4): 571–84.

Herbert, T., Myers A. and Wallace, J. (eds) (2019). *The Cambridge Encyclopaedia of Brass Instruments*. Cambridge: Cambridge University Press.

Herbert, T. and Sarkissian, M. (1997). 'Victorian Bands and their Dissemination in the Colonies'. *Popular Music* 16(2): 165–79.

Herbert, T. and Wallace, J. (eds) (1997). *The Cambridge Companion to Brass Instruments*. Cambridge and New York: Cambridge University Press.

Higgs, E., (2005). *Making Sense of the Census Revisited: Census Records for England and Wales 1801–1901, A Handbook for Historical Researchers*. London: Institute of Historical Research and the National Archives of the UK.

Hind, H. C. (1934). *The Brass Band*. London: Hawkes & Son.

Hindmarsh, P. (2000). 'Building a Repertoire: Original Compositions for the Brass Band, 1913–1998'. In Herbert, T. (ed.), *The British Brass Band: A Musical and Social History*. Oxford and New York: Oxford University Press: 245–77.

Hindmarsh, P. (2025). *Wilfred Heaton: Composer-Conductor-Craftsman, his Life and Music*. Poynton, Cheshire: PHM Publishing.

Hobsbawm, E. J and Ranger, T. O. (1983). *The Invention of Tradition*. Cambridge: Cambridge University Press.

Hollinshead, K. (1994). *The Major and His Band: The Story of Abram/Bickershaw Colliery Band*. Bradford: Kirklees Music.

Holz, R. W. (2006). *Brass Bands of the Salvation Army: Their Mission and Music*, Vol. 1. Hitchin: Streets.

Hoppen, K. T. (1998). *The Mid-Victorian Generation, 1846–1886*. Oxford and New York: Clarendon Press.

Horwood, W. (1992). *Adolphe Sax, 1814–1894: His Life and Legacy*. Baldock: Egon Publishers.

Houghton, W. E. (1985). *The Victorian Frame of Mind 1830–1870*. New Haven, CT: published for Wellesley College by Yale University Press.

Howarth, E. and Howarth, P. (1988). *What a Performance! The Brass Band Plays*. London: Robson.

Howell, J. (2016). 'Boosey & Hawkes: The Rise and Fall of a Wind Instrument Manufacturing Empire'. PhD: City University of London.

Howell, J. and Myers, A. (2015). 'Hawkes & Son, Instrument Makers'. *Galpin Society Journal* 68: 121–49.

Humphries, J. (2000). *Childhood and Child Labour in the British Industrial Revolution*. Cambridge: Cambridge University Press.

Humphries, J. (2016/17). 'François Brémond and Paul Dukas's Villanelle'. *The Horn Player: The Magazine of the British Horn Society* 14(1): 33–4.

Ingle, G. (2004). *Marriner's Yarns: The Story of Keighley Knitting Wool Spinners*. Lancaster: Carnegie.

Jackson, E. (1896). 'The Origin and Importance of Brass Band Contests'. *Music Trade Review* (serialised).

Irwell Springs (1914.) *Irwell Springs (Bacup) Band*. Bacup: Bacup Times.

Karjalainen, K. (1997). 'The Brass Band Tradition in Finland'. *Journal of the Historic Brass Society* 9: 83–96.

Kierzkowski, M. A. (2023). 'Wind Bands in Poland c.1800–1939'. PhD: The Open University.

Leterrier, S-A. (2018). 'Choral Societies and Nationalist Mobilization in Nineteenth Century France'. In Lajosi, K. and Stynen, A. (eds), *Choral Societies and Nationalism in Europe*. Leiden and Boston, MA: Brill: 33–52.

Levine, L. W. (1988). *Highbrow/Lowbrow: The Emergence of Cultural Hierarchy in America*. Cambridge, MA, and London: Harvard University Press.

Libin, L. (ed.) (2014). *The Grove Dictionary of Musical Instruments, Second Edition* (5 vols). New York and Oxford: Oxford University Press.

Littlemore, A. (2000). *Foden's Band: One Hundred Years of Musical Excellence*. Chapel-en-le-Frith: Caron Publications.

Livings, H. (1975). *That the Medals and the Baton Be Put on View: The Story of a Village Band, 1875–1975*. Newton Abbot: David & Charles.

Lodge, E. A. (1895). *The brass band at a glance, a chart showing pitch, compass and capabilities of all instruments*. Huddersfield: E. A. Lodge.

Lomas, M. J. (1990). 'Amateur Brass and Wind Bands in Southern England between the Late Eighteenth Century and circa 1900' (2 vols). PhD: The Open University.

Lomas, M. J. (1992). 'Secular Civilian Amateur Wind Bands in Southern England in the Late Eighteenth and Early Nineteenth Centuries'. *Galpin Society Journal* 45: 78–98.

MacDermott, K. H. (1923). *Sussex Church Music in the Past: An Account of the Old Singers and Minstrels, the Bands, Psalmodies and Hymn-books of Sussex Churches from the End of the 17th Century to the Latter Half of the 19th Century*. Chichester: Moore & Wingham.

MacDermott, K. H. (1948). *The Old Church Gallery Minstrels: An Account of the Church Bands and Singers in England from about 1660 to 1860*. London: S.P.C.K.

Macdonald, H. (2009). *Berlioz's Orchestral Treaties: A Translation and Commentary*. Cambridge: Cambridge University Press.

McGuffie, T. H. (1966a). 'The Lord Bradford Militia Documents in Shirehall, Shrewsbury, Salop'. *Journal of the Society for Army Historical Research* 44: 135–46.

McGuffie, T. H. (1966b). *Rank and File: The Common Soldier at Peace and War, 1642–1914*. New York: St. Martin's Press.

McGuire, C. E. (2009). *Music and Victorian Philanthropy: The Tonic Sol-fa Movement*. Cambridge: Cambridge University Press.

McKibbin, R. (1998). *Classes and Cultures: England, 1918–1951*. Oxford: Oxford University Press.

McVeigh, S. (2024). *Music in Edwardian London*. Woodbridge: Boydell & Brewer.

Mainzer, J. (1841). *Singing for the million: a practical course of musical instruction*. London: n.p.

Mandel, C. F. (1860). *A treatise on the instrumentation of military bands: describing the character and proper employment of every musical instrument used in reed bands*. London: Boosey & Sons.

Marwick, A. (1998). *The Sixties: Social and Cultural Transformation in Britain, France, Italy and the United States, 1958–74*. Oxford: Oxford University Press.

Mathez, J.-P. (1974–6). 'J.B. Arban. Biography'. *Brass Bulletin* (serialised): 9(3) (1974), 11–14; 10(1) (1975), 9–16; 11(2) (1975), 9–25; 12(3) (1975), 8–18; 13(1) (1976), 4–14; 14(2) (1976), 3–7; 15(3) (1976), 15–22.

Mathez, J.-P. (1977). *Joseph Jean-Baptiste Laurent Arban, 1825–1889: portrait d'un musicien français du XIXe siècle*. Moudon: Éditions Bim.

Maund, B. (1997). 'Elgar's "Brass Band Thing"'. *Elgar Society Journal* 10: 46–60.

Mayhew, H. (ed. Day, R. and Day, D.) (1851). *London Labour and London Poor*. Ware: Wordsworth Classics of World Literature.

Miller, G. (1912). *The Military Band*. London: Novello.

Miller, J. (2022). *The Modern Brass Ensemble in Twentieth-century Britain*. Woodbridge: Boydell & Brewer.

Millington, W. M. (1884). *Sketches of Local Musicians and Music Societies*. Pendlebury: Pendlebury Journal.

Mitchell, B. R. (1988). *British Historical Statistics*. Cambridge: Cambridge University Press.

Mitchell, B. R. and Deane, P. (1962). *Abstract of British Historical Statistics*. Cambridge: Cambridge University Press.

Mitroulia, E., Dumoulin, G. and Eldredge, N. (2008). 'On the Early History of the Périnet Valve'. *Galpin Society Journal* 61: 217–55.

Mitroulia, E. and Livings, A. (2011). 'The Distin Family as Instrument Makers and Dealers 1845–1874'. *Scottish Music Review* 2: 1–11.

Montefiore, C. S. (1908). *A history of the volunteer forces from the earliest times to the year 1860, being a recital of the citizen duty*. London: A. Constable & Co., Ltd.

Morrow, W. (1895). 'The Trumpet as an Orchestral Instrument'. *Proceedings of the Musical Association* 21: 133–47.

Mortimer, H. with Lynton, A. (1981). *Harry Mortimer on Brass: An Autobiography*. Sherborne: Alpha Books.

Musgrave, M. (1995). *The Musical Life of the Crystal Palace*. Cambridge: Cambridge University Press.

Myerly, S. H. (1996). *British Military Spectacle from the Napoleonic Wars through the Crimea*. Cambridge, MA: Harvard University Press.

Myers, A. (1985). *The Glen Account Book, 1838–1853*. Edinburgh: Edinburgh University Collection of Historic Musical Instruments.

Myers, A. (2000). 'Instruments and Instrumentation of British Brass Bands'. In Herbert, T. (ed.), *The British Brass Band: A Musical and Social History*. Oxford and New York: Oxford University Press: 155–86.

Myers, A. (2018). 'Made in Manchester: Instruments of the Higham Firm'. *Galpin Society Journal* 71: 161–78.

Myers, A. (2020). 'Instrument Making of the Salvation Army'. *Galpin Society Journal* 73: 30–58.

Myers, A. (ed.) (2025). *Historic Musical Instruments in the Royal Conservatoire of Scotland*. Glasgow: The Royal Conservatoire of Scotland.

Myers, A. and Eldredge, N. (2006). 'The Brasswind Production of Marthe Besson's London Factory'. *Galpin Society Journal* 59: 43–74.

Neuls-Bates, C. (1996). *Women in Music: An Anthology of Source Readings from the Middle Ages to the Present*. Boston, MA: Northeastern University Press.

Newsom, J. (ed.) (1983). *Perspectives on John Philip Sousa*. Washington, DC: Library of Congress.

Newsome, R. (1995). *Doctor Denis: The Life & Times of Dr. Denis Wright*. Baldock: Egon.

Newsome, R. (1998). *Brass Roots: A Hundred Years of Brass Bands and Their Music, 1836–1936*. Aldershot and Brookfield, VT: Ashgate.

Newsome, R. (2005). *150 Golden Years: The History of the Black Dyke Band*. London: World of Brass Publications.

Newsome, R. (2006). *The Modern Brass Band: From the 1930s to the New Millennium*. Aldershot and Burlington, VT: Ashgate.

Nex, J. (2015). '18th- and 19th-century Musical Instrument Makers in the Archives: A Personal View'. *Fontes Artis Musicae* 62(3): 238–53.

Nilsson, A.-M. (2001). 'Brass Instruments in Small Swedish Wind Ensembles during the Late Nineteenth Century'. *Historic Brass Society Journal* 13: 176–209.

Nilsson, A.-M. (2017). *Musik till vatten och punsch: Kring svenska blåsoktetter vid brunnar, bad och beväringsmöten*. Stockholm: Gidlunds Förlag.

Odello, D. (2014). 'British Brass Band Periodicals and the Construction of a Movement'. *Victorian Periodicals Review* 47(3): 432–53.

Ord Hume, J. (1900). *Chats on Amateur Bands*. London: Richard Smith & Co.

Philip, R. (2004). *Performing Music in the Age of Recording*. New Haven, CT: Yale University Press.

Purvis, R. (2017). 'Young People's Access to Local Authority Instrumental Music Tuition in England: A Historical and Contemporary Study'. PhD: University of London.

Queen's Regulations and Orders for the Army (1844). London: Parker, Furnivall and Parker.

Queen's Regulations and Orders for the Army (1868). London: Her Majesty's Stationery Office.

Rabbitts, P. A. (2018). *Bandstand: Pavilions for Music, Leisure and Entertainment*. Swindon: Historic England.

Rainbow, B. (1967). *The Land without Music: Musical Education in England 1800–1860 and its Continental Antecedents*. London: Novello.

Rauline, J.-Y. (2004). '19th-Century Amateur Music Societies in France and the Changes of Instrument Construction: Their Evolution Caught between Passivity and Progress'. *Galpin Society Journal* 57: 236–45.

Reid, C. (1984). *The Music Monster: A Biography of James William Davison, Music Critic of The Times of London, 1846–78: With Excerpts from his Critical Writings*. London, Melbourne and New York: Quartet Books.

Reily, S. A. and Brucher, K. (eds) (2013). *Brass Bands of the World: Militarism, Colonial Legacies, and Local Music Making*. Farnham and Burlington, VT: Ashgate.

Reily, S. A. and Brucher, K. (eds) (2018). *The Routledge Companion to the Study of Local Musicking*. New York and London: Routledge.

Rorive, J.-P. (2004). *Adolphe Sax, 1814–1894: inventeur de génie*. Brussels: Racine.

Rose, A. S. (1895). *Talks with Bandsmen: A Popular Handbook for Brass Instrumentalists*. London: W. Rider and Son, Ltd. Facsimile edition with introduction by Arnold Myers [1995]. London: Tony Bingham.

Rose, B. (1959). 'The Volunteers of 1859'. *Journal of the Society for Army Historical Research* 37(151): 97–110.

Rose, J. (2010). *The Intellectual Life of the British Working Classes*. New Haven, CT, and London: Yale University Press.

Russell, D. (1997). *Popular Music in England, 1840–1914: A Social History*. Manchester: Manchester University Press.

Russell, D. (2000). '"What's Wrong with Brass Bands?": Cultural Change in the Brass Band Movement'. In Herbert, T. (ed.), *The British Brass Band: A Musical and Social History*. Oxford and New York: Oxford University Press: 68–121.

Russell, J. F. and Elliot, J. H. (1936). *The Brass Band Movement*. London: Dent.

Sadie, S. and Tyrrell, J. (eds) (2001). *The New Grove Dictionary of Music and Musicians, Second Edition*. New York: Grove.

Salvation Army (1883). *The Salvation War*. London: Salvation Army.

Salvation Army (1925). *Orders and Regulations for Corps Officers*. London: SP&S.

Salvation Army (1927). *Orders and Regulations for Soldiers*. London: SP&S.

Salvation Army (1928). *Outlines of Salvation Army History*. London: SP&S.

Sandall, R., Wiggins, A. R. and Coutts, F. L. (1979). *The History of the Salvation Army*. New York: Salvation Army.

Schmitz, O. A. H. (1914). *Das Land ohne Musik: englische Gesellschaftsprobleme*. Munich: G. Muller.

Schwartz, H. W. (1975). *Bands of America*. New York: Da Capo Press.

Scott, J. L. (1970). 'The Evolution of the Brass Band and its Repertoire in Northern England' (2 vols). PhD, University of Sheffield.

Shive, C. S. (1993). 'The First Music for Brass Published in America'. *Historic Brass Society Journal* 5: 203–12.

Slater, R. (1908). *The Salvation Army Dictionary of Music*. London: Salvation Army Book Dept.

Small, C. (1998). *Musicking: The Meanings of Performing and Listening*. Hanover, NH, and London: University Press of New England.

Smith, D. (1988). '"Wales between the Wars"'. In Herbert, T. and Jones, G. E. (eds), *Wales between the Wars*. Cardiff: University of Wales Press: 1–12.

Smith, F. (1929). *The betrayal of Bramwell Booth: the truth about the Salvation Army revolt and a defence of General Bramwell Booth against the unwarrantable and un-Christian attack made upon him by the 'High Council' of the Salvation Army*. London: Jarrolds.

Tarr, E. H. (2003). *East Meets West: The Russian Trumpet Tradition from the Time of Peter the Great to the October Revolution, with a Lexicon of Trumpeters Active in Russia from the Seventeenth Century to the Twentieth*. Hillsdale, NY: Pendragon Press.

Tarr, E. H. and Dickey, B. (2007). *Bläserartikulation in der alten Musik: eine kommentierte Quellensammlung / Articulation in Early Wind Music: A Source Book with Commentary*. Winterthur: Amadeus.

Taylor, A. R. (1979). *Brass Bands*. London: Granada.

Taylor, A. R. (1983). *Labour and Love: An Oral History of the Brass Band Movement*. London: Elm Tree.

Taylor, D. (2013). *English Brass Bands and their Music, 1860–1930*. Newcastle upon Tyne: Cambridge Scholars Publishing.

Temperley, N. (1979). *The Music of the English Parish Church, Vol. 1*. Cambridge: Cambridge University Press.

Temperley, N. and Banfield, S. (2010). *Music and the Wesleys*. Urbana, IL: University of Illinois Press.

Thackray, R. (1972). 'Attitudes to Music in Schools'. *Education for Teaching*, April 1972: 53–69.

Thompson, E. P. (1972). *The Making of the English Working Class*. Harmondsworth: Penguin.

Thomson, J. M. (1991). *The Oxford History of New Zealand Music*. Aukland: Oxford University Press.

Tomlinson, J. (2021). 'Deindustrialisation and "Thatcherism": Moral Economy and Unintended Consequences'. *Contemporary British History* 35(4): 620–42.

Trevett, C. (ed.) (2025). *Cyfarthfa Castle and Park 1825–2025: A People's History*. Merthyr Tydfil: Merthyr and District Historical Society.

Van Dulken, S. (1999). *British Patents of Invention, 1617–1977: A Guide for Researchers*. London: British Library.

Vincent, C. (1908). *The Brass Band and How to Write for It*. London: Vincent Music Company.

Vincent, D. (1989). *Literacy and Popular Culture: England 1750–1914*. Cambridge: Cambridge University Press.

Von Steiger, A. (2016). 'Sax Figures: Can We Deduce Details of Adolphe Sax's Instrument Production from the Sources?'. *Revue belge de Musicologie / Belgisch Tijdschrift voor Muziekwetenschap* 70: 129–48.

Wagner, L. J. (ed.) (1998). *Band Music from the Benjamin H. Grierson Collection*. Madison, WI: A-R Editions.

Walker, P. J. (2000). '"A Carnival of Equality": The Salvation Army and the Politics of Religion in Working-Class Communities'. *Journal of Victorian Culture* 5(1): 60–82.

Walton, J. K. and Walvin, J. (eds) (1983). *Leisure in Britain 1780–1939*. Manchester: Manchester University Press.

Waterhouse, W. (1993). *The New Langwill Index: A Dictionary of Musical Wind-instrument Makers and Inventors*. London: Tony Bingham.

Weber, E. (1976). *From Peasants into Frenchmen: The Modernization of Rural France 1870–1914*. Stanford, CA: Stanford University Press.

Weber, W. (1975). *Music and the Middle Class: The Social Structure of Concert Life in London, Paris and Vienna*. New York: Holmes & Meier.

White, K. J. and Myers, A. (2004). 'Woodwind Instruments of Boosey & Company'. *Galpin Society* Journal 57: 62–214.

Whitehead, L. (2017). 'The House Bands of the Marquises of Breadalbane c.1804–60'. *Galpin Society Journal* 70: 179–97.

Wiggins, A. R. (1945). *Father of Salvation Army Music*. London: SP&S.

Winternitz, E. (1979). *Musical Instruments and their Symbolism in Western Art*. New Haven, CT, and London: Yale University Press.

Wollenberg, S. and McVeigh, S. (2004). *Concert Life in Eighteenth-century Britain*. Aldershot and Burlington, VT: Ashgate.

Wright, D. (1935). *Scoring for Brass Band*. Colne, Lancashire: J. Duckworth, Ltd.

Wright, D. (1967). *Scoring for Brass Band*. London: Baker.

Wright, D. C. H. (2013). *The Associated Board of the Royal Schools of Music: A Social and Cultural History*. Woodbridge: Boydell Press.

Wright, D. C. H. (2020). *The Royal College of Music and its Contexts: An Artistic and Social History*. Cambridge: Cambridge University Press.

Wright, F. (ed.) (1957). *Brass Today*. London: Besson & Co.

Yeo, E. and Yeo, S. (1981). *Popular Culture and Class Conflict 1590–1914: Explorations in the History of Labour and Leisure*. Brighton: Harvester.

Zealley, A. E., Ord Hume, J. and Somerville, J. A. C. U. (1926). *Famous Bands of the British Empire: Brief Historical Records of the Recognised Leading Military Bands and Brass Bands in the Empire*. London: J. P. Hull.

Index